Lecture Notes in Computer Science 14704

Founding Editors

Gerhard Goos
Juris Hartmanis

The series Lecture Notes in Computer Science (LNCS), including its subseries Lecture Notes in Artificial Intelligence (LNAI) and Lecture Notes in Bioinformatics (LNBI), has established itself as a medium for the publication of new developments in computer science and information technology research, teaching, and education.

LNCS enjoys close cooperation with the computer science R & D community, the series counts many renowned academics among its volume editors and paper authors, and collaborates with prestigious societies. Its mission is to serve this international community by providing an invaluable service, mainly focused on the publication of conference and workshop proceedings and postproceedings. LNCS commenced publication in 1973.

Adela Coman · Simona Vasilache
Editors

Social Computing and Social Media

16th International Conference, SCSM 2024
Held as Part of the 26th HCI International Conference, HCII 2024
Washington, DC, USA, June 29 – July 4, 2024
Proceedings, Part II

Editors
Adela Coman
University of Bucharest
Bucharest, Romania

Simona Vasilache
University of Tsukuba
Tsukuba, Japan

ISSN 0302-9743   ISSN 1611-3349 (electronic)
Lecture Notes in Computer Science
ISBN 978-3-031-61304-3   ISBN 978-3-031-61305-0 (eBook)
https://doi.org/10.1007/978-3-031-61305-0

Foreword

This year we celebrate 40 years since the establishment of the HCI International (HCII) Conference, which has been a hub for presenting groundbreaking research and novel ideas and collaboration for people from all over the world.

The HCII conference was founded in 1984 by Prof. Gavriel Salvendy (Purdue University, USA, Tsinghua University, P.R. China, and University of Central Florida, USA) and the first event of the series, "1st USA-Japan Conference on Human-Computer Interaction", was held in Honolulu, Hawaii, USA, 18–20 August. Since then, HCI International is held jointly with several Thematic Areas and Affiliated Conferences, with each one under the auspices of a distinguished international Program Board and under one management and one registration. Twenty-six HCI International Conferences have been organized so far (every two years until 2013, and annually thereafter).

Over the years, this conference has served as a platform for scholars, researchers, industry experts and students to exchange ideas, connect, and address challenges in the ever-evolving HCI field. Throughout these 40 years, the conference has evolved itself, adapting to new technologies and emerging trends, while staying committed to its core mission of advancing knowledge and driving change.

As we celebrate this milestone anniversary, we reflect on the contributions of its founding members and appreciate the commitment of its current and past Affiliated Conference Program Board Chairs and members. We are also thankful to all past conference attendees who have shaped this community into what it is today.

The 26th International Conference on Human-Computer Interaction, HCI International 2024 (HCII 2024), was held as a 'hybrid' event at the Washington Hilton Hotel, Washington, DC, USA, during 29 June – 4 July 2024. It incorporated the 21 thematic areas and affiliated conferences listed below.

A total of 5108 individuals from academia, research institutes, industry, and government agencies from 85 countries submitted contributions, and 1271 papers and 309 posters were included in the volumes of the proceedings that were published just before the start of the conference, these are listed below. The contributions thoroughly cover the entire field of human-computer interaction, addressing major advances in knowledge and effective use of computers in a variety of application areas. These papers provide academics, researchers, engineers, scientists, practitioners and students with state-of-the-art information on the most recent advances in HCI.

The HCI International (HCII) conference also offers the option of presenting 'Late Breaking Work', and this applies both for papers and posters, with corresponding volumes of proceedings that will be published after the conference. Full papers will be included in the 'HCII 2024 - Late Breaking Papers' volumes of the proceedings to be published in the Springer LNCS series, while 'Poster Extended Abstracts' will be included as short research papers in the 'HCII 2024 - Late Breaking Posters' volumes to be published in the Springer CCIS series.

I would like to thank the Program Board Chairs and the members of the Program Boards of all thematic areas and affiliated conferences for their contribution towards the high scientific quality and overall success of the HCI International 2024 conference. Their manifold support in terms of paper reviewing (single-blind review process, with a minimum of two reviews per submission), session organization and their willingness to act as goodwill ambassadors for the conference is most highly appreciated.

This conference would not have been possible without the continuous and unwavering support and advice of Gavriel Salvendy, founder, General Chair Emeritus, and Scientific Advisor. For his outstanding efforts, I would like to express my sincere appreciation to Abbas Moallem, Communications Chair and Editor of HCI International News.

July 2024   Constantine Stephanidis

HCI International 2024 Thematic Areas
and Affiliated Conferences

- HCI: Human-Computer Interaction Thematic Area
- HIMI: Human Interface and the Management of Information Thematic Area
- EPCE: 21st International Conference on Engineering Psychology and Cognitive Ergonomics
- AC: 18th International Conference on Augmented Cognition
- UAHCI: 18th International Conference on Universal Access in Human-Computer Interaction
- CCD: 16th International Conference on Cross-Cultural Design
- SCSM: 16th International Conference on Social Computing and Social Media
- VAMR: 16th International Conference on Virtual, Augmented and Mixed Reality
- DHM: 15th International Conference on Digital Human Modeling & Applications in Health, Safety, Ergonomics & Risk Management
- DUXU: 13th International Conference on Design, User Experience and Usability
- C&C: 12th International Conference on Culture and Computing
- DAPI: 12th International Conference on Distributed, Ambient and Pervasive Interactions
- HCIBGO: 11th International Conference on HCI in Business, Government and Organizations
- LCT: 11th International Conference on Learning and Collaboration Technologies
- ITAP: 10th International Conference on Human Aspects of IT for the Aged Population
- AIS: 6th International Conference on Adaptive Instructional Systems
- HCI-CPT: 6th International Conference on HCI for Cybersecurity, Privacy and Trust
- HCI-Games: 6th International Conference on HCI in Games
- MobiTAS: 6th International Conference on HCI in Mobility, Transport and Automotive Systems
- AI-HCI: 5th International Conference on Artificial Intelligence in HCI
- MOBILE: 5th International Conference on Human-Centered Design, Operation and Evaluation of Mobile Communications

List of Conference Proceedings Volumes Appearing Before the Conference

1. LNCS 14684, Human-Computer Interaction: Part I, edited by Masaaki Kurosu and Ayako Hashizume
2. LNCS 14685, Human-Computer Interaction: Part II, edited by Masaaki Kurosu and Ayako Hashizume
3. LNCS 14686, Human-Computer Interaction: Part III, edited by Masaaki Kurosu and Ayako Hashizume
4. LNCS 14687, Human-Computer Interaction: Part IV, edited by Masaaki Kurosu and Ayako Hashizume
5. LNCS 14688, Human-Computer Interaction: Part V, edited by Masaaki Kurosu and Ayako Hashizume
6. LNCS 14689, Human Interface and the Management of Information: Part I, edited by Hirohiko Mori and Yumi Asahi
7. LNCS 14690, Human Interface and the Management of Information: Part II, edited by Hirohiko Mori and Yumi Asahi
8. LNCS 14691, Human Interface and the Management of Information: Part III, edited by Hirohiko Mori and Yumi Asahi
9. LNAI 14692, Engineering Psychology and Cognitive Ergonomics: Part I, edited by Don Harris and Wen-Chin Li
10. LNAI 14693, Engineering Psychology and Cognitive Ergonomics: Part II, edited by Don Harris and Wen-Chin Li
11. LNAI 14694, Augmented Cognition, Part I, edited by Dylan D. Schmorrow and Cali M. Fidopiastis
12. LNAI 14695, Augmented Cognition, Part II, edited by Dylan D. Schmorrow and Cali M. Fidopiastis
13. LNCS 14696, Universal Access in Human-Computer Interaction: Part I, edited by Margherita Antona and Constantine Stephanidis
14. LNCS 14697, Universal Access in Human-Computer Interaction: Part II, edited by Margherita Antona and Constantine Stephanidis
15. LNCS 14698, Universal Access in Human-Computer Interaction: Part III, edited by Margherita Antona and Constantine Stephanidis
16. LNCS 14699, Cross-Cultural Design: Part I, edited by Pei-Luen Patrick Rau
17. LNCS 14700, Cross-Cultural Design: Part II, edited by Pei-Luen Patrick Rau
18. LNCS 14701, Cross-Cultural Design: Part III, edited by Pei-Luen Patrick Rau
19. LNCS 14702, Cross-Cultural Design: Part IV, edited by Pei-Luen Patrick Rau
20. LNCS 14703, Social Computing and Social Media: Part I, edited by Adela Coman and Simona Vasilache
21. LNCS 14704, Social Computing and Social Media: Part II, edited by Adela Coman and Simona Vasilache
22. LNCS 14705, Social Computing and Social Media: Part III, edited by Adela Coman and Simona Vasilache

https://2024.hci.international/proceedings

Preface

The 16th International Conference on Social Computing and Social Media (SCSM 2024) was an affiliated conference of the HCI International (HCII) conference. The conference provided an established international forum for the exchange and dissemination of scientific information related to social computing and social media, addressing a broad spectrum of issues expanding our understanding of current and future issues in these areas. The conference welcomed qualitative and quantitative research papers on a diverse range of topics related to the design, development, assessment, use, and impact of social media.

A considerable number of papers this year focused on research on the design, development, and evaluation of social media, exploring topics such as opinion data crawling, crowdsourcing, and recommendation systems, and delving into aspects related to user experience and user behavior. The undeniable influence of Artificial Intelligence on the technological landscape has prompted numerous works focused on the use of AI and Language Models in social media, investigating their multifaceted impact in the field, such as for the identification of malicious accounts and deepfakes, the improvement of search capabilities, the recognition of emotions and detection of human values, as well as the development of improved recommendation systems. The power of social media and its positive impact across various application domains inspired contributions regarding education and learning, culture, business, eCommerce, as well as computer-mediated communication. In the context of learning, the topics explored include academic writing, learning experience, ethics in education, specialized social networks for researchers, platforms for students with disabilities, and the impact of AI in education-related social media and platforms. In business and eCommerce, papers delve into aspects related to branding, consumer behavior, as well as customer experience and engagement. Finally, appraising the role of social media in fostering communication, strengthening social ties, and supporting democracy, contributions explored novel interpersonal communication approaches, hybrid working environments, opinion analysis, media memory shaping, disaster management, social learning, and online citizen interaction. As editors of these SCSM proceedings volumes, we are pleased to present this unique and diverse compilation of topics offering valuable insights and advancing our understanding of the current and future issues in the field.

Three volumes of the HCII 2024 proceedings are dedicated to this year's edition of the SCSM conference. The first focuses on topics related to Designing, Developing and Evaluating Social Media, User Experience and User Behavior in Social Media, and AI and Language Models in Social Media. The second focuses on topics related to Social Media in Learning, Education and Culture, and Social Media in Business and eCommerce. Finally, the third focuses on topics related to Computer-Mediated Communication, and Social Media for Community, Society and Democracy.

The papers in these volumes were accepted for publication after a minimum of two single-blind reviews from the members of the SCSM Program Board or, in some cases, from members of the Program Boards of other affiliated conferences. We would like to thank all of them for their invaluable contribution, support, and efforts.

July 2024   Adela Coman
Simona Vasilache

16th International Conference on Social Computing and Social Media (SCSM 2024)

Program Board Chairs: **Adela Coman**, University of Bucharest, Romania, and **Simona Vasilache**, University of Tsukuba, Japan

- Francisco Javier Alvarez-Rodriguez, *Universidad Autónoma de Aguascalientes, Mexico*
- Andria Andriuzzi, *Université Jean Monnet Saint-Etienne, Coactis, France*
- Karine Berthelot-Guiet, *Sorbonne University, France*
- James Braman, *Community College of Baltimore County, USA*
- Magdalena Brzezinska, *WSB Merito University, Poland*
- Adheesh Budree, *University of Cape Town, South Africa*
- Hung-Hsuan Huang, *University of Fukuchiyama, Japan*
- Ajrina Hysaj, *University of Wollongong in Dubai, UAE*
- Ayaka Ito, *Reitaku University, Japan*
- Carsten Kleiner, *University of Applied Sciences & Arts Hannover, Germany*
- Jeannie S. Lee, *Singapore Institute of Technology (SIT), Singapore*
- Kun Chang Lee, *Sungkyunkwan University (SKKU), Korea*
- Margarida Romero, *Université Côte d'Azur, France*
- Gabriele Meiselwitz, *Towson University, USA*
- Ana Isabel Molina Diaz, *University of Castilla-La Mancha, Spain*
- Takashi Namatame, *Chuo University, Japan*
- Hoang D. Nguyen, *UCC, Ireland*
- Kohei Otake, *Sophia University, Japan*
- Daniela Quinones, *Pontificia Universidad Católica de Valparaíso, Chile*
- Virginica Rusu, *Universidad de Playa Ancha, Chile*
- Cristian Rusu, *Pontificia Universidad Católica de Valparaíso, Chile*
- Tomislav Stipancic, *University of Zagreb, Croatia*
- Yuanqiong Wang, *Towson University, USA*

The full list with the Program Board Chairs and the members of the Program Boards of all thematic areas and affiliated conferences of HCII 2024 is available online at:

http://www.hci.international/board-members-2024.php

HCI International 2025 Conference

The 27th International Conference on Human-Computer Interaction, HCI International 2025, will be held jointly with the affiliated conferences at the Swedish Exhibition & Congress Centre and Gothia Towers Hotel, Gothenburg, Sweden, June 22–27, 2025. It will cover a broad spectrum of themes related to Human-Computer Interaction, including theoretical issues, methods, tools, processes, and case studies in HCI design, as well as novel interaction techniques, interfaces, and applications. The proceedings will be published by Springer. More information will become available on the conference website: https://2025.hci.international/.

General Chair
Prof. Constantine Stephanidis
University of Crete and ICS-FORTH
Heraklion, Crete, Greece
Email: general_chair@2025.hci.international

https://2025.hci.international/

Contents – Part II

Social Media in Business and eCommerce

Social Media in Learning, Education and Culture

Improving the Learning Experience in Ethics Education with Groupware: A Case Study

Claudio Álvarez[1]($\boxtimes$) ⓘ, Gustavo Zurita[2] ⓘ, and Luis A. Rojas[3] ⓘ

[1] Facultad de Ingeniería y Ciencias Aplicadas, Universidad de los Andes, Santiago, Chile
`calvarez@uandes.cl`

[2] Departamento de Control de Gestión y Sistemas de Información, Universidad de Chile, Santiago, Chile
`gzurita@fen.uchile.cl`

[3] Facultad de Ingeniería, Arquitectura y Diseño, Universidad San Sebastián, Santiago, Chile
`lrojasp1@docente.uss.cl`

Abstract. Incorporating ethics into engineering education is crucial to address the intricate challenges of societal technologization, artificial intelligence, and automation. A cross-disciplinary and ongoing ethical education, engaging students with practical scenarios relevant to their field, has been identified as a superior approach for ethical training of engineers. Realizing this advanced ethical training necessitates dedicated support for both instructors and students. This paper introduces a major enhanced version 2.0 of EthicApp, a case-based collaborative learning platform that facilitates ethical education. The platform enables individual and collective examination of ethical cases across various disciplines. EthicApp 2.0 promotes analysis and collaborative decision-making in ethical contexts. A formative study of EthicApp 2.0 was conducted with software engineering students at a South American university (N = 109). The study utilized tasks involving semantic differential scales and the ranking of case stakeholders. Students performed these tasks on personal computers and smartphones, with random assignment. The study confirmed that EthicApp 2.0 could be used for various task types without prior training. Instructors can repurpose learning designs and monitor activities in real-time effectively. However, it was observed that the mobile interface posed usability challenges, and responses submitted via smartphones tended to be shorter. Despite these limitations, EthicApp 2.0 shows promise for scalability to larger samples and integration into diverse courses, aiding in developing ethical competencies as a cross-disciplinary skill.

Keywords: Students' Experience · Ethics · Software Engineering Education

1 Introduction

Teaching ethics in engineering is clearly a necessity, considering the increasing complexity of work and our societies. This complexity largely arises from the pervasive technologization of society and, currently, the emergence of new technological challenges stemming from the development of the fourth industrial revolution [1], artificial

© The Author(s), under exclusive license to Springer Nature Switzerland AG 2024
A. Coman and S. Vasilache (Eds.): HCII 2024, LNCS 14704, pp. 3–22, 2024.
https://doi.org/10.1007/978-3-031-61305-0_1

intelligence [2], and work automation [3]. Equipping decision-makers in industry and politics becomes critical to combat corruption and foster corporate and state governments that operate justly and in solidarity with the pursuit of the common good for society.

Ethics education in engineering has grown due to the push from accreditation agencies and publicized unethical behaviors in various sectors [4, 5]. Ethics courses are often standalone or discipline-specific [5], with the former being more prevalent in South America. Typically, these courses are taught by philosophers or ethicists rather than scientists or engineers, making applied ethics education in fields like artificial intelligence or logistics rare. Many engineering students see traditional, theory-heavy ethics courses as a mere graduation requisite [6]. When these courses focus only on memorizing professional codes, students miss out on a deeper understanding of ethical implications in diverse situations [7].

The authors advocate for ethics in engineering to be taught as a continuous, cross-disciplinary skill, emphasizing the importance of awareness and decision-making at both individual and societal levels [8]. Students should regularly encounter and analyze ethical situations tied to their specific engineering disciplines. While case-based learning can be effective [9], adopting this cross-cutting approach comes with curriculum design, content development, and teaching methodology challenges. Designing these cases necessitates collaboration between engineering and ethics experts, and instructors need training in effective teaching strategies. These complexities can act as barriers to implementing this holistic approach to ethics education in engineering.

The present authors have developed EthicApp [10, 11], a Computer-Supported Collaborative Learning learning design platform to support case-based ethics teaching in higher education. EthicApp allows students to analyze an ethical case and answer questions individually and as a group. Group discussions can be anonymous, and group formations can be based on heterogeneity criteria (bringing together students with different views), homogeneity, or at random. The instructor can monitor all the work students are doing in real-time and use the content generated by the students for discussions.

In this study, we report on the first trials of a new 2.0 major version of EthicApp (hereinafter referred to as EthicApp 2.0), which incorporates enhancements to the user interface to improve the overall user experience. Furthermore, the trials documented here detail the execution of ethical case analysis activities for the first time with students from a software engineering curriculum in Mobile Applications Development and Operating Systems and Networks courses. During the trials, we engaged students with two types of analyses: evaluations based on semantic differential items and appraisals based on ranking case stakeholders according to virtue-based ethics criteria. We gauged the students' perceptions of the tool's usability for both types of analysis using the SUS scale [12], complemented by open-ended items to gather students' perspectives on their experience, including the most positive aspects and areas requiring enhancement. The following sections describe the background of the current research, the EthicApp 2.0 tool, the pilot activities conducted, the analysis of their outcomes, a discussion of the findings, and finally, conclusions and future work.

2   Research Background

2.1   Ethics Education in Engineering

While ethics education is recognized as crucial in engineering curricula, students often regard it as a peripheral requirement [6] and tend to view ethics in terms of rules to be memorized rather than complex moral principles [7]. The increasing importance of ethics across professions, such as information systems, auditing, marketing, and taxes, necessitates the development of professionals capable of navigating ethical dilemmas [13]. This aligns with 21st-century skill frameworks that stress the importance of preparing individuals for morally complex scenarios [14]. Professional bodies and accreditation agencies have also echoed the need for ethical instruction in the field [4].

Traditionally, ethics education in STEM and business disciplines has followed a rationalist approach focused on applying codes, leading to less in-depth analysis of ethical situations [7]. [6] note that this approach aligns with engineers' tendency toward tangible and measurable facts but warns that it risks simplifying ethical reasoning into rule application without deep understanding or consideration of consequences. Such an approach can also leave students ill-equipped to discern between competing ethical standards [15].

The need for ethical decision-making in engineering is well-documented, yet schools often adopt a reactive approach centered on compliance with legal and regulatory standards [16]. Advancing ethical and socially responsible decision-making requires proactive pedagogical innovation in ethics education, preparing students to apply ethical principles in professional contexts and to prevent corporate misconduct [17].

2.2   Case-Based Learning

Case-Based Learning (CBL) is a methodology that utilizes real or hypothetical cases to promote problem-solving and decision-making. By presenting students with simulated or actual situations and encouraging them to analyze, discuss, and apply prior knowledge, CBL aims to equip students with practical skills and knowledge for real-life scenarios [18]. CBL also supports social constructivism and active learning by stimulating critical thinking and problem-solving. Empirical studies have shown that CBL is effective in various fields, including ethics [19]. CBL can also be carried out online using web technologies and CSCL. However, there are limited CBL experiences supported by CSCL. Thus, more research is needed to understand both social and individual behavior in these contexts and to understand better how to design effective teaching and learning processes at the intersection of CSCL and ethics education, which can elicit social interactions and meaningful learning.

3   EthicApp 2.0

3.1   Project Background and Goals

EthicApp 2.0 was conceived as part of a research project carried out by researchers from the University of Chile, forming a part of a suite of tools designed to enhance the development of 21st-century skills in higher education students [20], including communication skills, critical thinking, and ethical discernment. In the realm of these competencies, EthicApp 2.0 emerged as a tool focused on facilitating ethical reflection and the exercise of ethical discernment for educators based on the case method approach [10]. In its most fundamental definition, EthicApp 2.0 is a web-based software tool that enables students to analyze an ethical case through various phases or sub-activities, which incorporate questions about the case defined by the teacher. These questions can be answered individually or discussed in small groups. The educator, in turn, can monitor the activity by accessing the responses written by the students and groups, providing feedback, and discussing with the students the potential solutions to the case being analyzed.

Initially, the software was developed as a prototype and used in numerous pilot activities, with cases in the areas of business ethics, academic ethics, leadership ethics, and research ethics. Given the highly experimental nature of the tool in its early stages, the developers designed a teacher interface with a high degree of configurability to allow flexibility during the activities. For instance, it allowed educators to create new activity phases by specifying several parameters in real-time (i.e., interaction mode, use of anonymity, use of chat rooms, configuration of groups, question text and format, etc.), as opposed to executing a completely pre-designed activity from the start. The developers valued this flexibility because it would enable the improvisation of activities, questions, and conditions for collaborative work in class at the teacher's or researchers' discretion, according to the students' responses to the activities at the time. However, the wide variety of configuration options in the user interface resulted in a poor user experience for the educators due to confusion and a lack of confidence in the tool. A second usability and user experience issue related to the design of the educator interface, which did not offer intuitive and user-friendly navigation.

Due to the aforementioned usability and user experience issues, very few educators were willing to use the tool independently. Typically, the authors of this paper had to assist the educators during the pilots, which became less scalable as the adoption of the tool reached new countries and institutions.

Since 2022, the authors of the present work have spearheaded the development of EthicApp 2.0. This new tool version has been developed as an open-source project under the MIT license [21]. The open-source project's roadmap proposes three strategic objectives for the long-term development and sustainability of EthicApp 2.0:

- **Make life easier for educators**: Recognizing educators as gatekeepers of educational technology innovations—that is, those who ultimately decide whether or not to use the tool as intended by its designers and institutional leadership—we aim to simplify the EthicApp 2.0 interface to make it attractive, intuitive, and easy for educators to use. This includes designing features that make sense to them and better align with their pedagogy, as well as planning processes and habits. With this goal, we seek to enable educators to carry out ethical case analysis activities with their students conveniently without it becoming a burden regarding time dedication.
- **Make life easier for developers**: The first version of EthicApp 2.0 was developed as a prototypical research software by a single software developer, with the maintainability and extensibility of the software not being the focus. In developing EthicApp 2.0, the authors have made a considerable effort to reduce the complexity of the

software through refactoring, removing unused code, and adopting consistent programming styles and patterns focused on good maintainability practices. Tools such as linters, scripts to automate the development environment setup process, and Docker have been adopted to facilitate deployment in development, staging, and production environments.

- **Adopt an open-source software development process for project sustainability**: A governance model and organizational design for the project have been defined, processes to maintain the roadmap, backlog, and issues (defects, feature requests, improvement suggestions), and practices to facilitate the incorporation of new contributors to the project.

3.2 Features

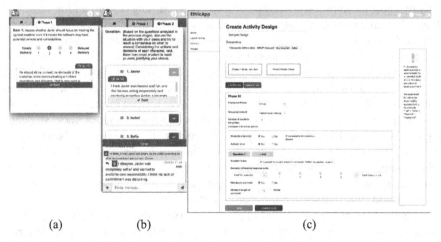

(a)　　　　(b)　　　　　　　(c)

Fig. 1. (a) Semantic differential task in a mobile device, (b) ranking task in a mobile device, (c) teacher's learning design authoring tool.

Teacher's Features: EthicApp 2.0 allows educators to create learning designs, which are structured activities for the analysis of ethical cases that may consist of one or more phases. Each phase allows for an array of configuration options as described below:

- **Set of questions**: Within a learning design phase, students can be presented with one or several questions. It is possible to define questions based on semantic differential scales or the ranking of a list of options (see Fig. 1 (a)-(b)). Questions can also require a written justification or be posed as open-ended queries.
- **Interaction mode**: The initial phase in a learning design is always individual. From the second stage onward, subsequent phases can be either individual or group-based.
- **Grouping mode**: For phases defined as group-based, it is possible to determine the group size and the algorithm used to compose the groups. There is a basic algorithm for random group composition, as well as algorithms that allow for the formation of heterogeneous groups with a diversity of perspectives or homogeneous groups.

- **Displaying responses from previous phases**: It is possible to define whether, in a group phase, students should see their own responses and those of their peers from earlier phases of the learning design. It can also be specified from which previous phases to show responses.
- **Chat**: In the group phases, a text-based chat room can be provided to participants, similar to applications like WhatsApp or Telegram.
- **Anonymity**: In group phases, the option for anonymity can be chosen so that peers communicating in a group do not appear to others in the chat or in their responses from previous phases identified by their names, but rather by a letter randomly assigned by the tool.

To create learning designs, EthicApp 2.0 offers an authoring tool (see Fig. 1(c)), allowing educators to edit an instructional design as a sequence of stages, with the flexibility to adjust the abovementioned parameters. The learning designs within EthicApp 2.0 are shareable among educators, meaning they can be made publicly accessible by other teachers and tailored and adapted to meet their specific needs. Learning designs are searchable by keywords that match their title and/or description. Educators generate their activities by instantiating (launching) these learning designs, indicating that they are designed for reuse. Teachers can access their ongoing and completed activities through searchable listings directly from the home screen. Upon initiating an activity by launching a learning design, teachers are provided with a dashboard that tracks students' progress through each learning design phase. Moreover, the dashboard enables teachers to manage the execution of the activity, allowing students access to the subsequent phase of the learning design or the conclusion of the activity. The dashboard generates a code that teachers can distribute to students to join the activity and allows educators to review individual student responses and the chat logs of groups.

To facilitate teacher's access to the features described above, EthicApp 2.0 provides a home screen with shortcut buttons that lead to common tasks, such as launching a new activity, seeing activity dashboards, and creating a new learning design. These functions are accessible from a consistent top-level navigation area, which contrasts with the approach of the original EthicApp 2.0, where the focus was on the improvisation of learning activities and on-the-fly configuration for this intent.

Students' Features. The student interface is structured to allow access to an existing activity by entering the code provided by the teacher, or to directly access an activity they have previously joined without needing a code by finding the activity listed. Upon entering an activity, the student views the content of the active phase. This content includes the questions and responses from peers in previous phases, as defined by the learning design. If the current phase allows for interaction with group members, the student can access a chat room to meet and communicate with them. Once the students have answered the questions of the current phase, they await the teacher's advancement to the subsequent phase.

4 Pilot Study

4.1 Goals

The overarching goal of the current study is to conduct a formative evaluation [22] of the EthicApp 2.0 software, deploying it for the first time in an educational setting comprised of cohorts of software engineering students. This evaluation encompasses aspects from the perspectives of both educators and students.

From the educators' viewpoint, the primary objective is to evaluate the interface and functionality to verify and validate that the new features, such as authoring learning design, launching activities based on learning designs, and monitoring activities through dashboards, operate correctly and consistently with the tool's design.

From the students' perspective, the main goal is to assess the tool's usability using a standardized instrument SUS [12], and to capture their subjective valuations of their experience with the tool through open-ended items in a survey process. Based on these measurements, we are interested in comparing the usability of EthicApp 2.0 in relation to two types of tasks, namely, answering semantic differential questions and ranking options. Furthermore, we aim to compare these tasks on smartphones and laptops. In addition to usability measured with the SUS, we are interested in determining whether the distributions of the length of students's written responses vary with different devices. Thus, a specific objective is defined to determine if there is a difference in the perception of usability, user experience, and length of response, considering the type of task and device.

4.2 Hypotheses

Based on the goals presented previously, the pilot study conducted intends to contrast the following hypotheses:

- H_1: There is no difference in the perceived usability of EthicApp 2.0 (i.e., as per SUS scale scores) for semantic differential activities between smartphone users versus PC/laptop users.
- H_2: There is no difference in the perceived usability of EthicApp 2.0 for ranking activities between smartphone users versus PC/laptop users.
- H_3: There is no difference in the perceived usability of EthicApp 2.0 between semantic differential activity and ranking activity for smartphone users.
- H_4: There is no difference in the perceived usability of EthicApp 2.0 between semantic differential activity and ranking activity for PC/laptop users.
- H_5: There are no differences in the length of text responses generated by students considering different types of devices per each type of activity.

4.3 Educational Context and Samples

In the pilot study presented here, the participant student samples are from the software engineering curriculum ("Civil Engineering Degree in Computer Science") at Universidad de los Andes, Chile, in the courses of Operating Systems and Networks (sixth-semester course, $N = 52$), and Mobile Application Development (eighth-semester course, $N = 57$). The teacher in all activities is the first author of this study.

4.4   Ethical Cases and Learning Designs

Case Texts: For this study, two versions of a case in software engineering were developed by the present authors (see Fig. 2). This is because EthicApp 2.0 is intended to be tested with students performing two different types of tasks, namely, answering semantic differential questions, which feature two opposite terms on a four-point scale, and on the other hand, ranking-based questions, in which elements of the case (e.g., its actors) must be ordered considering some ethical criterion. In both versions, a team of software developers is presented as facing a series of tensions within their organization from which different ethical conflicts emerge.

Case for Analysis based on Semantic Differentials

In the city of Comala, a financial hub whose night lights shimmer like fireflies against the dark expanse, stands the Majestic Bank of Universal Prosperity (MBUP), a renowned financial institution. Here, the brightest minds in software engineering are deeply engaged in creating revolutionary software that promises to change the financial world.

Javier Morales, a software engineer with eyes weary yet full of dreams and aspirations, leads this monumental project. His mind, a hotbed of codes and algorithms, is constantly refining the lines of code that will breathe life into the groundbreaking banking software.

Sofía Robles, the meticulous and determined Project Manager, always keeps one eye on the clock and the other on the calendar, hopeful to see the project completed within the stipulated timeframe, to the delight of the client, the relentless and demanding Adrián Luna, representative of the Bank. His steps echo with authority through the corridors, and his voice resonates with the firm expectation of perfection.

Amidst lines of code and cups of coffee, Isabel Ríos, the astute Quality Analyst, scrutinizes each line of code for imperfections. Her fingers fly over the keyboard, noting every anomaly and vulnerability found, aware that a single error could cost someone their life's savings.

Time, that inexorable tyrant, marches on, and with it, the tension in the air thickens. Javier, whose mind is torn between quality and promptness, feels the weight of responsibility on his shoulders. Days turn into nights, and nights into days, as Javier's hands dance frantically over the keyboard, striving to shape flawless software before time runs out.

Adrián, oblivious to the sacrifices and tensions of the development team, only sees the clock ticking and the deadline approaching, and his patience starts to wane. He demands perfection and speed, a combination that, for Javier, seems more and more like an unattainable mirage.

Isabel, with the diligence and precision of a surgeon, points out every defect and vulnerability, aware that each is a potential disaster waiting to happen. Javier, feeling the breath of time on his neck, struggles between correcting every imperfection or delivering on time a software with possible hidden faults.

Sofía, the mediator between quality and timeliness, attempts to weave a delicate balance between Adrián's expectations and the realities of development. Her mind, a strategic chessboard, looks for moves that satisfy all but do not compromise the integrity of the project.

Each character in this technological dance carries on their shoulders the weight of decisions that could alter the financial destiny of thousands. Javier, at the eye of the storm, wonders if it is possible to serve two masters: uncompromising quality and demanding speed. As he develops the project, unbeknownst to anyone, he is involved in several selection processes at other companies. He thinks he can escape the situation and evade his responsibility in the project by switching to another job.

Case for Analysis based on Rankings

The Majestic Bank of Universal Prosperity (MBUP) in Comala found itself in a whirlwind of expectations and pressures as it attempted to launch an innovative financial software to the world. Javier Morales, the mastermind behind the software, stood at a crossroads of ambition and responsibility, aspiring to new professional horizons while simultaneously addressing the demand for a flawless and timely work.

One afternoon, Sofía Robles, whose eyes missed no detail, accidentally discovered that Javier was being courted by other companies and that, discreetly, he had decided not to share this detail with the team. She confronts him and, to Javier's surprise, she suggests that if he is to accept a new offer, he should do so in a way that does not harm the ongoing project. Sofía, a lover of order and compliance, has a plan B: to involve Marta, an external software engineer with whom she has previously worked, and who could be an excellent substitute if Javier decides to leave.

Isabel Ríos, while committed to quality, also sees a personal advancement opportunity in the imminent software launch, considering the possibility of using her position and knowledge to start her own technological initiative. Meanwhile, she observes that the code Javier produces, although robust, contains omissions that she, in an act of protection towards her own future interests, decides not to highlight in her reports.

Adrián Luna, the demanding client, receives a tip from a friend about Javier's potential departure and, instead of confronting the situation, sees an opportunity to negotiate down the project's cost in exchange for his silence, taking advantage of his knowledge of the team's weaknesses.

The network of decisions and secrets silently intertwines in the corridors of the BMPU, where each actor, trying to safeguard their interests, operates from a place where professional and personal ethics are tested under the bright lights of Comala.

Fig. 2. Cases used in semantic differential (above) and ranking (below) activities.

Semantic Differentials Learning Design. In the semantic differentials activity (see Table 1), there is an initial phase of preparations (phase 0), where students are given instructions to create their user account on EthicApp 2.0 and join the activity. This is followed by the case reading and then three phases of individual responses with questions about different aspects of the case. After this, there is a group discussion phase in which the students must discuss the three previous questions and negotiate consensus responses. Finally, the educator leads a discussion analyzing the case and the discussed questions, citing examples of responses developed by the students and groups.

Table 1. Learning design for the semantic differentials activity.

Phase	Indications, Question & Response Format	Time
0	Session Initiation	10 m
1	Case Reading (see Fig. 2)	8 m
2	**Interaction mode:** Individual **Question:** Put yourself in Javier's shoes for a moment. Reflect on whether Javier should fully inform the client about the identified problems and risks or whether he should resolve them internally without communicating them **SD Scale (4 points):** Total Transparency (1) – Total Concealment (4) **Written Justification:** Required, 10 words minimum	5 m
3	**Interaction mode:** Individual **Question:** Assess whether Javier should focus on meeting the agreed deadline, even if it means the software may have potential defects and vulnerabilities **SD Scale (4 points):** Timely Delivery (1) – Delayed Delivery (4) **Written Justification:** Required, 10 words minimum	5 m
4	**Interaction mode:** Individual **Question:** Consider how much Javier should try to satisfy the client's expectations and needs in relation to maintaining the integrity and quality of the software **SD Scale (4 points):** High Commitment to the Client (1) – Low Commitment to the Client (4) **Written Justification:** Required, 10 words minimum	5 m
5	**Interaction mode:** Groups of three, heterogeneously composed, with chat, anonymous **Question:** Based on the questions analyzed in the previous stages, discuss the situation with your peers and try to reach an agreement on how to respond to each of the following questions (the same as in previous phases) **SD Scale (4 points):** Total Transparency (1) – Total Concealment (4) Timely Delivery (1) – Delayed Delivery (4) High Commitment to the Client (1) – Low Commitment to the Client (4) **Written Justification:** Required, 10 words minimum	20 m
6	**Debriefing (teacher-mediated analysis and discussion)**	10 m

Ranking Learning Design. In the ranking activity (see Table 1), as with the semantic differentials, there is an initial phase of preparations. Afterward, students read the case and then proceed to two ranking activities of case actors according to different value criteria. Subsequently, groups of three students are formed, and they carry out two phases where they repeat the questions they had answered earlier individually. Finally, the educator concludes the activity by analyzing the questions and referencing various responses to exemplify positions regarding the valuation tasks of the case actors.

4.5 Measures

The student's perception of the usability of EthicApp 2.0 was measured using the ten-item System Usability Scale (SUS) questionnaire, with its items translated into Spanish. At the end of the instrument, a five-level Likert item (same format as the other SUS items) was added with the statement "I would like to use this application again in a software engineering course" and two open-ended items to capture the students' perceptions of the most favorable aspects of their experience, and what should be improved. The students' responses in the activities were processed to obtain their original word length without the removal of stop words or other elements (Table 2).

Table 2. Learning design for the ranking activity.

Phase	Indications, Question & Response Format	Time
0	Session Initiation	10 m
1	Case Reading (see Fig. 2)	8 m
2	**Interaction mode:** Individual **Question:** Considering the actions and decisions of each character (Javier, Sofía, Isabel, and Adrián), rank them from most prudent to least prudent, justifying your choice **Written Justification:** Required, per each ranking position, 10 words minimum	5 m
3	**Interaction mode:** Individual **Question:** Based on the information provided and the actions of the characters (Javier, Sofía, Isabel, and Adrián), rank them from the most just to the least just actor, and explain why **Written Justification:** Required, per each ranking position, 10 words minimum	5 m
4	**Interaction mode:** Groups of three, heterogeneously composed, with chat, anonymous **Question:** [Based on the questions analyzed in the previous stages, discuss the situation with your peers and try to reach a consensus on what to answer] Considering the actions and decisions of each character (Javier, Sofía, Isabel, and Adrián), rank them from most prudent to least prudent, justifying your choice **Written Justification:** Required, per each ranking position, 10 words minimum	10 m
5	**Interaction mode:** Groups of three, heterogeneously composed, with chat, anonymous **Question:** [Based on the questions analyzed in the previous stages, discuss the situation with your peers and try to reach a consensus on what to answer] Based on the information provided and the actions of the characters (Javier, Sofía, Isabel, and Adrián), rank them from the most just to the least just actor, and explain why **Written Justification:** Required, per each ranking position, 10 words minimum	10 m
6	**Debriefing (teacher-mediated analysis and discussion)**	10 m

4.6 Procedure

In both courses where this study was conducted, student participation was voluntary, with the incentive of bonus points on evaluations in their respective courses and under-informed consent given by the students to the researchers through an online Google form. The activities were carried out outside of class hours via Zoom in the months of September and October 2023. In the Operating Systems and Networks course, only the ranking activity was conducted, while in the Mobile Applications course, both designed activities, semantic differentials, and ranking, were carried out.

Hours before each activity with EthicApp 2.0, the researchers reviewed the list of students who had consented. They performed a random assignment for each student who was obligated to use a PC/laptop or smartphone. This random assignment was carried out in a Google Sheet with the list of enrolled students, using the random function that generates values between 0 and 1, and decision logic to assign each type of device randomly with a 0.5 probability. The list with the device assignments was then informed to the students one to two hours before each activity.

4.7 Analyses

This study defines the perception of the usability of EthicApp 2.0 by students, expressed as an SUS scale score, as a dependent variable of interest. This variable is subject to two independent variables: the type of task and the type of device. Initially, the data are checked for normality (Shapiro-Wilk test) and homogeneity of variances (Levene's test). Depending on whether these conditions are met or not, parametric or non-parametric tests are applied. Additionally, the length of the response message is another dependent variable influenced by the type of device and the type of task, with the data subjected to the same type of analysis.

All analyses in this study were performed using R version 4.3 and several packages, including dplyr, tidyr, psych, and ggplot2.

5 Results

5.1 Student Participation

The number of participants was satisfactory because student participation in the pilot activities was voluntary and rewarded with bonus points on certain course assessments (See Table 3). In the first pilot, 31 students (54.4%) filled out the consent form, and 27 (47.4%) participated in the EthicApp 2.0 trial and provided a complete response to the usability and experience evaluation questionnaire. In the second pilot, nearly half of the class (42.3%) completed the consent form, and 24 students (46.1%) participated in the EthicApp 2.0 pilot. In the third pilot, participation declined. Of the 22 students who filled out the consent form (42.3%), only 17 (32.7%) participated in the pilot, and it coincided that those who were absent were supposed to use smartphones, which reduced the participation of these devices in this last session of pilots.

Table 3. Students' participation in the pilot study.

Cohort	Activity	Consent Forms	EthicApp 2.0 w/PC	EthicApp 2.0 w/Smartphone	SUS Responses
Mobile Applications	Ranking	31	14	13	27
Operating Systems and Networks	Ranking	25	11	13	23
Mobile Applications	Semantic Differentials	22	11	6	16

5.2 Questionnaire

Students' responses to the usability and user experience questionnaire (see Table 4) yielded data with non-normal distributions. For the sake of comparison, Wilcoxon's signed rank test was conducted for each item among the distributions with the highest and lowest mean values (i.e., M_{max} and M_{min}, respectively). A Kruskal-Wallis test was also conducted per each item considering the four conditions under study; however, these tests resulted in significant differences in none of the cases.

Regarding the first item (i01), students tend to view EthicApp 2.0 as a tool they would not frequently use in their curricular subjects. This is understandable due to the academic culture prevalent in engineering schools, where conducting ethical case analysis activities in software engineering courses is uncommon. Arguably, students perceive such ethical case analysis activities as an exceptional and sporadic matter rather than an activity they regularly engage in. Regarding the complexity of the tool (i02), there are no statistically significant differences between the conditions; the greatest difference is just 0.44 points. It can be established that the responses are, on average, close to the midpoint of the scale. As for ease of use (i03), significant differences are observed, close to one point, between semantic differentials on a PC, and ranking on a smartphone. Concerning the need for assistance to use the tool (i04), the mean response is slightly above the midpoint across all conditions, indicating that students feel they require help using EthicApp 2.0. This could be explained by the fact that the students did not receive any training on the tool before participating in each of the study conditions. During the pilots, the instructor in charge resolved their queries. Regarding integrating the tool's functions (i05), we observe a significant difference close to one point between semantic differentials on a PC and ranking on a smartphone. Students generally respond around the midpoint concerning their perceptions of the interface's inconsistency (i06). While there are no significant differences between the conditions, there is a half-point difference between semantic differentials on a PC and ranking on a smartphone. Students consider the application to be learnable (i07), with responses tending to exceed the scale's midpoint and without significant differences between conditions. As for the difficulty of use (i08), the responses were between 3.08 (semantic differential on a smartphone) and 3.67 (ranking on a smartphone). Although the differences between conditions are not

Table 4. Questionnaire results comprising SUS and experience-related items.

	PC				Smartphone						
	Semantic Differential (N=11)		Ranking (N=24)		Semantic Differential (N=6)		Ranking (N=24)				
Item Text	*M*	*SD*	*M*	*SD*	*M*	*SD*	*M*	*SD*	Δ*M*	*W*	*p*-value
i01 I think I would use EthicApp 2.0 frequently.	1.64	0.92	1.79	0.93	1.50	0.84	1.29	1.08	0.50	-	*n.s.*
i02 I find EthicApp 2.0 unnecessarily complex.	3.27	0.47	3.21	1.06	3.00	0.89	2.83	1.20	0.44	-	*n.s.*
i03 I think EthicApp 2.0 was easy to use.	3.55	0.52	3.00	1.10	3.17	0.41	2.58	1.28	0.96	193.5	<0.05
i04 I think I would need the help of a technically knowledgeable person to use EthicApp 2.0.	3.46	0.82	3.13	1.08	3.50	0.55	3.21	1.18	0.38	-	*n.s.*
i05 The functions in EthicApp. 2.0 are well integrated.	3.27	0.47	3.00	0.72	2.33	0.82	2.67	1.17	0.94	54	<0.05
i06 I think EthicApp 2.0 is very inconsistent.	3.55	0.52	3.04	0.96	2.83	1.17	3.13	1.04	0.71	-	*n.s.*
i07 I imagine that most people would learn to use EthicApp 2.0 very quickly.	3.46	0.52	3.29	1.04	3.33	1.03	3.00	0.98	0.46	-	*n.s.*
i08 I find EthicApp 2.0 very difficult to use.	3.46	0.93	3.46	0.72	3.67	0.52	3.08	1.21	0.58	-	*n.s.*
i09 I feel confident using EthicApp 2.0.	3.09	1.04	2.92	0.88	3.33	0.82	3.13	0.68	0.42	-	*n.s.*
i10 I needed to learn many things before I could use EthicApp 2.0.	3.64	0.51	3.54	0.59	4.00	0.00	3.58	0.72	0.46	102	*0.06*
SUS Score	80.9	9.70	75.9	15.7	76.7	11.1	71.3	18.5	9.66		n.s.
i11 I would like to use EthicApp 2.0 again in some course of my career.	3.18	1.17	3.29	1.16	3.00	1.41	3.33	1.20	0.33	-	*n.s.*

Δ*M*=|*M*$_{max}$ - *M*$_{min}$| *W*=Wilcoxon test statistic

statistically significant, there appears to be a trend that the user interface for the ranking activity on a smartphone is more difficult to use than in other conditions. Users rate, on average, the midpoint of the scale in terms of feeling confident using EthicApp 2.0 (i09) and tend to affirm that they had to learn many things before using the tool (i10), though they learned as they used the tool, with the help of the instructor.

Regarding total SUS scores, the highest average score of 80.9 was obtained for semantic differentials on a PC, while the lowest score was reached for ranking on a smartphone (Fig. 3). This is consistent with the previously analyzed user evaluations. However, the SUS score gap between the different conditions was not statistically significant as per Wilcoxon's signed rank test, given that data was found non-normal. Thus, considering student participation and the conditions under which this pilot study was conducted, there is no conclusive evidence to reject hypotheses H_1 to H_4.

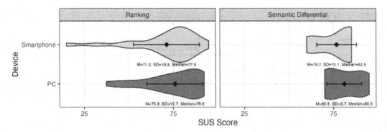

Fig. 3. SUS scale score distributions per task type and device.

5.3 Students' Experience

Regarding the overall valuation of the experience by the students, the average rating tends to be positioned slightly above the midpoint; however, there is significant variability in the ratings (see Fig. 4). There are students for whom the experience was more relevant and meaningful, and to a lesser extent, those who consider that they would not participate in an EthicApp 2.0 activity in a software engineering course.

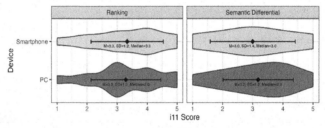

Fig. 4. Distribution of questionnaire item 11 (i.e., "I would like to use this application again in a software engineering course") responses.

Figure 5 displays the frequency with which themes emerged in the student's responses to the open-ended item i12, which asked respondents to identify positive aspects of EthicApp 2.0. Most themes were mentioned by respondents who used both PC and smartphones. The most common themes included the opportunity to understand different viewpoints from other individuals ("Different viewpoints"), as well as the chance to engage in discussions with others ("Discussion") and to do so anonymously ("Anonymity"). In line with the results obtained from the SUS questionnaire items, PC users particularly emphasized ease of use compared to smartphone users. Conversely, a larger proportion of the theme "Design" was noted among smartphone users than PC users. The item "Design" related to the design of the activity process, meaning that it was composed of phases that allowed the analysis and discussion of the case in a structured and transparent manner for the students due to the transitions between phases being controlled by the teacher and the system itself. The themes "Analysis," "Thinking," and "Reflection" also frequently appeared in the responses, indicating that students view them as positives in their experience with EthicApp 2.0. The theme "Authenticity" was also recurrent, referring to the possibility of anonymous discussion that allowed students to express their stances more authentically.

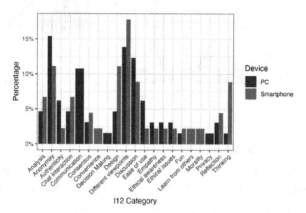

Fig. 5. Presence of topics in students' responses to item 12 (i.e., about positive aspects of EthicApp 2.0) in the questionnaire.

In Fig. 6, it is possible to observe the themes that emerged in relation to item 13 of the questionnaire, which pertains to aspects of EthicApp 2.0 that should be improved. In this case, we observe greater differences among users participating in different activities. Users who took part in the ranking activity emphasized that the interface layout should be refined ("UI Layout" theme). This is because, on the one hand, reorganizing the list's elements to be ranked is not intuitive, and on the limited screen space of a phone, it becomes somewhat uncomfortable. On the other hand, writing justifications for ranking decisions requires activating the space to write by pressing a button on the rankable element, which is not explicit in the interface and must be discovered by the user. Moreover, the text area for writing the justification is small ("Sizing of elements" theme). Another issue with the interface is the deployment of the chat interface. The interface appears on the lower half of the phone's screen, leaving little space above to review the responses written by other students.

Another recurring critique from students was related to the aesthetics of the interface, including the iconography and fonts used. This critique was present in both the ranking activity and the semantic differentials.

Some students expressed the need for clearer instructions on the task at hand, even calling for more explicit directions about the entire process of the activity being undertaken. Finally, a non-negligible aspect is the fact that students must read the ethical case in a relatively short amount of time, and then, when making decisions, they must recall the actors, their roles in the case, decisions, etc., which requires them to be constantly moving between the case document and the response interface. Some students reported discomfort related to having to switch back and forth between these parts of the interface and, ultimately, depending on their working memory to remember case details to respond within the interface.

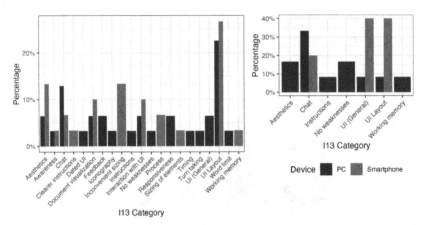

Fig. 6. Presence of topics in students' responses to item 13 (i.e., about aspects needing improvement) regarding the rankings activity (left) and the semantic differentials activity (right).

5.4 Response Length

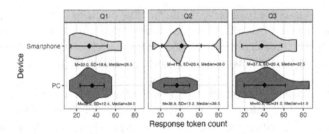

Fig. 7. Response length per device type and question in the semantic differential activity.

In the semantic differential activity, we did not observe significant differences in the lengths of students' text responses when comparing PC versus smartphone (see Fig. 7), according to Wilcoxon's signed rank test comparing the distributions of response lengths under these conditions. This can be considered a positive outcome, meaning that students do not exhibit a systematic tendency to write more or less content in their justifications when using a mobile device versus a PC, despite expressing discomfort with the UI layout, especially in the case of smartphones.

Regarding the ranking activity (see Fig. 8), only in phase 1 is there a significant difference ($W = 490.5$; $p < 0.05$) between the conditions, with the total word count written on PC averaging 32.4% higher per student on PC than with a smartphone. In phase 2, a difference in means of 27% is also observed; however, it was not found to be statistically significant. Consequently, the results indicate that writing on a smartphone does tend to be shorter than on a PC when students work on the ranking activity. Considering the results, no systematic evidence exists to reject H5 conclusively.

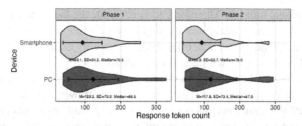

Fig. 8. Total response length per device and phase in the ranking's activity.

5.5 Teacher's Experience

For the execution of the pilots, the instructor was able to pre-create the two contemplated instructional designs based on tasks involving semantic differential and ranking questions, respectively, before the sessions with the students. Then, in each session with the students, he launched an activity based on the corresponding design. He could launch an activity based on the semantic differentials design and use the ranking design twice, launching a separate activity for each cohort.

The new learning design creation interface functioned as intended. However, the activity monitoring through dashboards still suffers from certain functional defects, particularly related to the automated and transparent updating of student statuses. At times, updates do not occur consistently, and it is necessary to refresh the page in the web browser manually. Nevertheless, unlike the previous version of EthicApp 2.0, where it was necessary to configure each phase of the activity at run time, the instructor did not have to attend to these aspects once the activity was launched and could focus on giving instructions to the students on how to proceed in each phase of the activity and review various responses from the students and groups as the activity progressed.

6 Discussion

Ethical education in engineering is gaining relevance in the present time due to societal transformations brought about by technological advancements. Now more than ever, engineers need an understanding of their role in society, the impact of technical decisions on other stakeholders, and the reality that working within complex organizations requires navigating the intricacies of ethical conflicts across interpersonal dynamics, power relations, and the ethical use of technology, information, and automation.

The present authors propose EthicApp 2.0 as a pedagogical tool to facilitate the analysis of ethical situations in higher education. Institutions are compelled by societal needs and formal accreditation requirements to offer ethical education that prepares professionals to make and face ethical decisions. There is a debate over whether ethical training should be confined to ethics courses or integrated into disciplinary courses. An exclusive focus on ethics courses risks disconnecting ethical teaching from the professional realm of disciplines, becoming overly theoretical and philosophical. Conversely, teaching ethics solely within curricular courses, such as engineering, as in this study, risks trivializing or relativizing ethical analyses by leaving the teaching to engineers without philosophical training. Therefore, adequate ethical education must reconcile the teaching of philosophical foundations and objective judgment elements to address ethical situations and, on the other hand, offer students learning experiences consistent with the professional practice they will face upon graduation.

EthicApp 2.0 is a tool that could be incorporated into ethics courses and professionalizing subjects. It brings significant benefits, such as allowing equal participation of all students in ethical case analysis activities, enabling students to understand others' viewpoints without fear of criticism or judgment, thanks to anonymity, and thus allowing them to authentically express their ethical judgments and decisions. Instructors can create and share reusable learning designs, saving time in activity preparation. During execution, instructors benefit from analyzing and evaluating students' responses in real-time, providing quality formative feedback. After activities conclude, instructors and researchers can review how students reason and what ethical principles and concepts they can apply to the situations analyzed.

For the success of the above, the authors recognize the priority of EthicApp 2.0 being useful, easy to use, and providing an optimal user experience for various instructors. From the students' perspective, it is crucial that they can use EthicApp 2.0 very intuitively without requiring time-consuming training by the instructor. It is also essential for instructors to find EthicApp 2.0 easy for conducting activities tailored to their needs, providing cases and learning designs relevant to their teaching area.

This study verified that the functions allowing instructors to create, reuse, and monitor the execution of learning designs are sufficient and suitable for scaling and validating the tool with a larger sample of instructors. It was determined that while there was no statistically significant difference regarding EthicApp 2.0's usability and user experience with different devices and task formats, there are conditions under which EthicApp 2.0 appears to be less favorably rated by users, particularly when students perform ranking tasks on smartphones. The ranking task is notably more challenging for students than marking values on a semantic differential scale. Additionally, while valued and deemed helpful by students, the chat interface requires a redesign to better accommodate screen space constraints. Improvements in mobile usability are a priority, as in face-to-face classroom settings, this is how students interact with EthicApp 2.0, whereas in remote settings, students use PCs more commonly.

The findings reported in this study, particularly those comparing the user experience and usability of the semantic differential interface on PC vs. smartphone and also comparing this activity with ranking, should be treated with caution due to the small sample size that performed the semantic differential activity, especially those who used smartphones for this task.

7   Conclusions and Future Work

In this study, we present an evaluation of the usability and user experience of EthicApp 2.0, an educational technology tool designed to facilitate the teaching of professional ethics across a range of disciplines through case-based learning methodology. The assessment was conducted with students in the sixth and eighth semesters of two software engineering courses at a private Chilean university.

The study determined that the type of device used in the activities (i.e., PC or smartphone) can influence student satisfaction with the tool and that the tool presents some usability issues related to the specific type of task performed. In particular, the tool requires integrating multiple functions for document viewing, chatting, and response editing, which on a mobile device presents significant challenges for design and achieving optimal usability. Despite this, students could use the tool in the pilot activities without any prior training, simply following the instructions given by the instructor during the pilots. Furthermore, the functions for creating and executing learning designs allow instructors considerable time savings in preparing activities, as the learning designs are fully reusable. Additionally, during the execution of the activities, instructors can focus their attention on reviewing student responses to provide feedback rather than focusing on configuration aspects as was necessary in the previous version of EthicApp.

In the future, we will scale EthicApp 2.0 to a more significant number of educational contexts and student cohorts in ethics courses and disciplinary courses, which will allow the authors to validate the improvements that will be incorporated into the tool because of this study and to continue the usability and user experience evaluation with these cohorts. The focus of the usability improvements will be on enhancing ease of use on mobile devices. Additionally, aspects of user experience related to the aesthetics of the interface will be improved, as well as the timely delivery of instructions and on-demand help to the user.

Acknowledgments. We thank EthicApp 2.0 maintainers Ignacio Garcés and Miguel Angel Barraza and developers and research assistants Matías Rivera, Javier Soto, Joaquin Gracia, and Vicente Gana for contributing to the EthicApp software.

References

1. Rymarczyk, J.: Technologies, opportunities and challenges of the industrial revolution 4.0: theoretical considerations. Entrep. Bus. Econ. Rev. **8**(1), 185–198 (2020)
2. Huang, C., et al.: An overview of artificial intelligence ethics. IEEE Trans. Artif. Intell. (2022)
3. Acemoglu, D., Restrepo, P.: The race between man and machine: implications of technology for growth, factor shares, and employment. Am. Econ. Rev. **108**(6), 1488–1542 (2018)
4. ABET. Criteria for accrediting computing programs (2017). https://www.abet.org/%20accreditation/accreditation-criteria/%20criteria-for-accrediting-computing-programs-2018-2019/
5. Hess, J.L., Fore, G.: A systematic literature review of US engineering ethics interventions. Sci. Eng. Ethics **24**, 551–583 (2018)
6. Génova, G., González, M.R.: Teaching ethics to engineers: a socratic experience (2016)
7. Sunderland, M.E.: Using student engagement to relocate ethics to the core of the engineering curriculum. Sci. Eng. Ethics **25**, 1771–1788 (2019)
8. Schwartz, M.S.: Ethical decision-making theory: an integrated approach. J. Bus. Ethics **139**, 755–776 (2016)
9. Mulhearn, T.J., et al.: Review of instructional approaches in ethics education. Sci. Eng. Ethics **23**, 883–912 (2017)
10. Álvarez, C., et al.: Scaffolding of intuitionist ethical reasoning with groupware: do students' stances change in different countries? In: Wong, LH., Hayashi, Y., Collazos, C.A., Alvarez, C., Zurita, G., Baloian, N. (eds.) Collaboration Technologies and Social Computing. CollabTech 2022. LNCS, vol. 13632, pp. 261–278. Springer, Cham (2022). https://doi.org/10.1007/978-3-031-20218-6_18

11. Álvarez, C., Zurita, G., Carvallo, A.: Analyzing peer influence in ethical judgment: collaborative ranking in a case-based scenario. In: Takada, H., Marutschke, D.M., Alvarez, C., Inoue, T., Hayashi, Y., Hernandez-Leo, D. (eds.) Collaboration Technologies and Social Computing. CollabTech 2023. LNCS, vol. 14199, pp. 19–35. Springer, Cham (2023). https://doi.org/10.1007/978-3-031-42141-9_2

12. Bangor, A., Kortum, P., Miller, J.: Determining what individual SUS scores mean: adding an adjective rating scale. J. Usability Stud. **4**(3), 114–123 (2009)

13. Roybark, H.M.: Educational interventions for teaching the new auditor independence rules. J. Account. Educ. **26**(1), 1–29 (2008)

14. Dede, C.: Comparing frameworks for 21st century skills. 21st Century Skills Rethink. How Stud. Learn. **20**(2010), 51–76 (2010)

15. Holsapple, M.A., et al.: Framing faculty and student discrepancies in engineering ethics education delivery. J. Eng. Educ. **101**(2), 169–186 (2012)

16. Cornelius, N., Wallace, J., Tassabehji, R.: An analysis of corporate social responsibility, corporate identity and ethics teaching in business schools. J. Bus. Ethics **76**, 117–135 (2007)

17. Mintz, S., Morris, R.E.: Ethical Obligations and Decision Making in Accounting. McGraw-Hill US Higher Ed USE, New York (2022)

18. Kolodner, J.L., Owensby, J.N., Guzdial, M.: Case-Based Learning Aids. In: Handbook of Research on Educational Communications and Technology, pp. 820–852. Routledge, Abingdon-on-Thames (2013)

19. Choi, I., Lee, K.: Designing and implementing a case-based learning environment for enhancing ill-structured problem solving: classroom management problems for prospective teachers. Educ. Technol. Res. Dev. **57**, 99–129 (2009)

20. Griffin, P., Care, E.: Assessment and Teaching of 21st Century Skills: Methods and Approach. Springer, Cham (2014). https://doi.org/10.1007/978-3-319-65368-6

21. EthicApp_Development. GitHub. n.d. https://github.com/EthicApp-Development/

22. Rodríguez, P., Nussbaum, M., Dombrovskaia, L.: Evolutionary development: a model for the design, implementation, and evaluation of ICT for education programmes. J. Comput. Assist. Learn. **28**(2), 81–98 (2012)

The Appeal, Efficacy, and Ethics of Using Text- and Video-Generating AI in the Learning Process of College Students: Predictive Insights and Student Perceptions

Magdalena Brzezinska(⊠) (iD)

WSB Merito University, Poznan, Poland
`magdalena.brzezinska@wsb.poznan.pl`

Abstract. This article explores the subjective appeal and effectiveness of three selected instances of generative artificial intelligence (generative AI) in the perception of sophomore undergraduate students at WSB Merito University in Poznan, Poland. Thoughtful introduction of AI tools to instruction is discussed, with the underlying goal of preparing college students for life during the 5th industrial revolution and providing them with skills needed for the evolving job market. The author presents a case study involving a curriculum-related group assignment designed to implement text- and video-generating AI in a Culture and History of English-language college course, while student autonomy, creativity, engagement, and deep thinking are highlighted. The task execution phase is followed by a qualitative and quantitative survey-based analysis conducted to evaluate the attractiveness and efficacy of AI in the learning process as viewed by the students. Additionally, the ethical aspect of (mis)using artificial intelligence is addressed. The findings contribute to the ongoing discourse on the integration of AI in tertiary education and shed light on the potential advantages and hazards of incorporating AI tools into a humanities class.

Keywords: Generative AI · Text- and Video-generating AI · College Education

1 Introduction

The article focuses on the subjective appeal and efficacy of three selected tools of generative artificial intelligence (generative AI, as defined by Lv (2023, 208), Nah et al. (2023), or Cao & Dede (2023)) tested by sophomore undergraduate English Philology students of the WSB Merito University in Poznan, Poland.

Akin to numerous relatively recent and rapidly spreading phenomena and dynamic processes, the examination of generative artificial intelligence and its potential applicability to and impact on education is ongoing, and the findings are anything but conclusive. Even consistently obtained results are likely to describe short-term rather than long-term effects, the latter of which may become evident only within several years.

A. Coman and S. Vasilache (Eds.): HCII 2024, LNCS 14704, pp. 23–42, 2024.
https://doi.org/10.1007/978-3-031-61305-0_2

In fact, the paramount aspect yet to be determined is how any type of AI should be treated in education: as a mere tool or, indeed, a prosthetic. Tse, Esposito, and Goh notice that we are experiencing an unprecedented ambiguity between humans and machines (2019, 11) and the ongoing, fifth industrial revolution, growing at an increasingly rapid pace and challenging widely accepted notions about the progression of technology, may alter human values and even our **purpose as humans** to a significantly higher degree than the previous industrial revolutions (ibidem, 69; emphasis of this author). Consequently, AI may not be disregarded either in education or in everyday life, for it has become an inevitable element of the contemporary landscape. "The roles of AI in education must be carefully evaluated for its strengths and potential contribution, and ultimately considered as part of a learning programme which builds foundational skills and then emphasizes their use for advanced problem solving in context," postulates UNESCO in its analytical report (2023, 27).

It remains challenging to conclusively ascertain through scientific means how widespread the use of AI in education is, but a recent Forbes article (Hamilton, 2023) cites its survey from October 2023, claiming that 60% of educators use AI in their classrooms and the figures are increasing. In Poland, within two months of introducing ChatGPT, 51% of teachers reported that they used that generative technology and 40% of them utilized it at least once a week (Polska Agencja Rozwoju Przedsiębiorczości [Polish Agency for Enterprise Development], 2023: 10). In personal communication, 100% of the author's students declared their use of AI, in particular generative one, for academic or professional purposes. As regards AI in tertiary education, a study commissioned by Microsoft and conducted by International Data Corporation (2020), which involved 509 higher education institutions in the United States, indicated that nearly all respondents, specifically 99.4 percent, anticipate that AI will be pivotal in improving their institution's competitiveness within the next three years.

1.1 The Rationale for a Methodologically Justified Introduction of AI in Education

In their recent report, Cao and Dede (2023) conclude that it is critical for educators to understand the nature of generative AI to "navigate the evolving landscape of education" and to ensure that it remains a transformative, process-focused human experience rather than a product-oriented transaction. At the same time, Tse, Esposito & Goh (2019, 199) postulate that "it is necessary to disrupt the current education model to better prepare future generations to enter the workforce," at the same time observing that 50% of what is taught in bachelor's courses may become obsolete within half a decade, and it is virtually impossible to predict the direction in which the job market will be developing or what new, yet nonexistent, jobs might appear. (ibidem, 193–195; see also Cao & Dede, 2023, and Anderson, 2023) Thus, to anticipate the unforeseeable, and prepare students for the world of AI, speculate the authors, it might be beneficial to retool education and focus on inherently human skills (ibidem, 204–230; see also Krueger, 2023). This might empower students by giving them the ability to articulate themselves more effectively, process information with greater ease, and gain a confident understanding of the interaction between humans and machines.

Simultaneously, the Future of Jobs Report 2023 reveals that more than 85% of surveyed organizations recognize that the primary factor propelling transformation within their structures is the heightened adoption of new and cutting-edge technologies along with the expansion of digital accessibility. Schroeder (2023), in turn, cites Resume Builder's report on a survey conducted among 1,187 business leaders in which it was established that 91% of those who are presently seeking to fill positions are looking for employees with ChatGPT experience. He thus underscores the necessity for higher education to instantly respond to employers' expectations in that respect.

2 A Case Study: Introducing Generative AI to a Sophomore College Class

Following the above suggestions (see also Krueger, 2023), the author of this article undertook to adapt her educational practices by implementing text- and video-generating AI to equip her students with relevant tools and useful strategies to be employed in class and in the future workplace. She followed Schroeder's (2023) recommendation to incorporate modern technologies into the standard course content and supplement the assignments that already existed in the syllabus and were crucial for the anticipated learning outcomes. Students were provided with an insight into various AI generators and given an opportunity to craft effective prompts, related to the field of study or their potential employment, and to create follow-up prompts to refine AI's responses. The instructor hoped for possible disruptions in the existing patterns of students' thinking to jumpstart creativity (Karout & Harouni, 2023; Krueger, 2023; Kącki, 2021), in accord with Cao's postulate (2022, in Cao and Dede (2023)) that "educators' role is not to funnel students' voices towards a pre-determined solution, but to create favorable conditions for collective interaction and shape the dialogic space as the discussion unfolds to support students to improve their ideas together."

When discussing momentous events in British history within the course of Culture and History of English-speaking countries, the instructor demonstrated the use of AI by simulating an interview between a 21st-century college student and William the Conqueror using ChatGPT and a self-designed prompt. She acted following Schroeder's (2023) recommendations related to the process of reshaping college classes by complementing materials with AI rather than replacing them. The aim was to augment student intelligence (Anderson, 2023), enhance the learning experience, and improve learning outcomes, instead of limiting the role of a human teacher (Liu, Demszky, & Hill, 2023) or making students indolent, unmotivated, or uninspired (Krueger, 2023). Transparency and accountability in the use of AI were also stressed (Greene, 2023).

Additionally, the instructor sensitized her students to the possible ChatGPT fallacies, such as lacking consciousness, self-awareness, high-order thinking, and metacognition (Cao & Dede, 2023; Kocoń et al., 2023); giving false or conflicting information (Cao & Dede, 2023; Anderson, 2023; Keeler, 2023; Jimenez, 2023; Kocoń et al., 2023; OpenAI Help Center); or perpetuating biases (Tse, Esposito & Goh, 2019, 95–98 and 223; Greene-Harper, 2023; Chauhan, 2023; Hough, 2023), which may adversely impact learning outcomes. To avoid potential issues, she asked her students to double-check the facts, dates, and figures supplied by generative AI.

As recommended by Cao & Dede (op. cit.; see also Geryk, 2023), AI was, almost literally, used as a dialog partner rather than an omniscient guru. Students were sensitized to the fact that generative AI is incapable of feeling, metacognition, or higher-order thinking, albeit characterized by such undeniable advantages as accessibility, flexibility, "infinite patience," and mostly non-judgmental nature (inasmuch as possible regarding the input on which it was trained.) When inquired, AI itself stressed that "while ChatGPT aims to mimic human interactions, it is a machine learning model and does not possess true understanding or consciousness. It generates responses based on patterns learned from vast amounts of text data but lacks genuine comprehension or awareness." (personal communication, 11/21/2023), which is precisely what makes students indispensable agents of creative, critical, and meaningful interactions.

Furthermore, the instructor emphasized the process and transformative experience rather than the product, thus promoting engagement and deep thinking, as suggested by Cao & Dede (op. cit.), and the task was formulated as a mini project, as recommended by Bates (2022), Brzezinska (2022), or Piki & Brzezinska (2023). Students were to obtain and manipulate adequate data and use them critically and creatively to receive a desired product, thus becoming the inevitable and irreplaceable human factor capable of understanding the purpose of complicated activities performed by generative AI. Hence, AI was not excluded, rejected, or perceived as a threat to achieving educational outcomes but rather, it was incorporated into the didactic process.

Additional potential implicit benefits included increasing student interest and motivation by using 21st-century generative tools, bringing history to life, and making the past relevant for sophomore students.

2.1 The Process: Introduction

Initially, during an in-person Culture and History of English-speaking Countries class, the instructor demonstrated the use of three selected tools (ChatGPT, Fliki (Brzezinska, 2024), and inVideo (Brzezinska, 2023)) creating an interview between a historical figure (William the Conqueror) and a 21st-century college student and then transforming the interview into two videos. During script creation, she used the self-formulated prompt: "Create an interview between a 21st-century college student and William the Conqueror about the conquest of England. Adopt appropriate styles of speech and mention important dates related to the conquest."

Discussing the 1066 conquest was part of the class curriculum, while the adoption of appropriate language was related to the learning outcome of improving the linguistic skills of the sophomore students – non-native English speakers – and making the learners aware of style and historical changes in the English language.

The acquired knowledge of the three tools and the skills necessary to use them effectively could then be employed by the instructor's students to formulate prompts for generative AI to create an interview with the late Queen Elizabeth II about British colonialism and decolonization (both also being elements of the course curriculum). There was also an option to transform the created interviews into videos.

Two AI-powered text-to-speech and text-to-video generators, Fliki and inVideo, were selected for their relatively different characteristics and functionalities. Among others, Fliki allowed for the choice of a persona's voice and the selection/creation of a persona's image (although the AI-generated image in the instructor's video had a pixelated, blurred eye); on the other hand, in the free version of the generator, a 2-min video exhausted the monthly credits for video-creation, which was only revealed when the instructor finished creating another video and was unable to save it. Certain other disadvantages were automated free-of-charge voices, which had no natural melody, and the fact that all the elements (text fragments, etc.) had to be uploaded gradually rather than at once.

As for inVideo, some advantages were the ability to select the audience, the "look and feel," and the platform for which the video was to be created (e.g., YouTube, Facebook, etc.), as well as the fact that the whole script could be uploaded at once, and the generator created the whole video from scratch. Also, the website claimed to provide assistance if the created video was flagged for copyright reasons. On the other hand, the disadvantages included huge watermarks and branding in the free version; the inability to select images, characters, or voices; and the fact that playback was unsupported for Firefox (yet, the instructor was able to view the video once it was downloaded).

2.2   The Process - Execution

During the stage of interview creation, the instructor explained that the students might use/adapt the general prompt crafted by her, i.e., "Create an interview between a 21st-century college student and (**name**) about the (**historical fact**). Adopt appropriate styles of speech and mention important dates related to the (**fact**)." However, she also strongly encouraged students to use their own prompts and ideas, thus promoting autonomy and creativity.

The interview creation stage was preceded by discussing articles related to British colonialism and the ensuing lack of redress of colonial sins by the royal family of Great Britain. After the discussion, the students were grouped in threes or fours to use the acquired information to produce interviews with the late Queen Elizabeth II regarding the controversial issues.

The obligatory elements of the assignment were: including facts from the articles, creating an interview, and checking the accuracy of ChatGPT or another selected AI-powered text generator – if it was used. The utilization of generative AI was optional but encouraged.

It turned out that no group decided to complete the assignment on their own, and each one decided to employ ChatGPT for the purpose. The approach was not criticized by the instructor, who was willing to accomplish two goals: to promote the creative and critical use of AI in the classroom and to avoid creating a culture of shame and fear (France, 2020: 151–156). In contrast, none of the groups created a video in class. Instead, they undertook to present the interview in the form of a role-play.

Two examples of student-created interviews are included in Appendixes 3 and 4.

After class, two surveys, a qualitative one [Appendix 1] and a quantitative one [Appendix 2], were conducted to investigate students' opinions on the value of employing generative AI for interview and video creation and to examine the undergraduates' app-roach to (un)ethical use of artificial intelligence. In the qualitative analysis, the research sample was 29 sophomore English Philology students: non-native English speakers, 25 of whom were female and 4 were male. For the quantitative analysis, the sample was 25 students, with 21 female students and 4 male ones. Both the qualitative and the quantitative surveys were conducted during in-person classes, and they were anonymous to ensure the impartiality and objectivity of the results. The quantitative survey was conducted two weeks after the qualitative one.

Prior to the study, ChatGPT was asked for a prediction regarding its outcomes. The author undertook to examine whether any of AI's predictions were accurate, and if so, which ones.

3 Predictions of Generative AI

When inquired: "How do you predict college students' opinions regarding the use of ChatGPT and AI in their college education? What advantages and disadvantages might they mention?", ChatGPT came up with the following response:

"While I can't predict individual opinions, I can provide some general insights into potential advantages and disadvantages that college students might mention regarding the use of ChatGPT and AI in their education.

Advantages

- 24/7 Availability:

  – ChatGPT can provide instant assistance at any time, allowing students to seek help with their studies or assignments outside of regular office hours.

- Personalized Learning:

  – AI can adapt to individual learning styles and pace, offering a personalized learning experience that caters to the needs and pences of each student.

- Quick Answers and Clarifications:

  – Students may appreciate the ability to quickly get answers to specific questions or clarifications on course materials, helping them stay on track with their studies.

- Assistance with Homework and Projects:

  – ChatGPT can aid students in brainstorming ideas, refining arguments, or providing guidance on various aspects of their assignments.

- Language Practice:

  – ChatGPT can be used as a tool for language practice, helping students improve their writing and communication skills.

Disadvantages.

- Lack of Human Interaction:

  - Some students may miss the interpersonal aspect of learning and the nuanced feedback that a human instructor or peer can provide.

- Limited Understanding of Context:

  - AI may struggle to grasp the specific context of a student's question, leading to potential misunderstandings or incorrect guidance.

- Overreliance and Reduced Critical Thinking:

  - Depending too heavily on AI for answers might discourage students from developing critical thinking skills and the ability to independently analyze and solve problems.

- Ethical Concerns:

  - Students may express concerns about the ethical implications of AI in education, including issues related to data privacy, bias in algorithms, and the responsible use of technology.

- Technical Issues:

  - Reliance on technology introduces the possibility of technical glitches or system failures, disrupting the learning process and causing frustration.

- Depersonalization of Education:

  - The use of AI might contribute to a sense of depersonalization in education, with students feeling like they are interacting with a machine rather than engaging in a meaningful educational relationship.

It's essential to note that opinions can vary widely among college students, and factors such as individual preferences, technological literacy, and the specific use cases of AI in education can significantly influence their perspectives. The successful integration of AI into education will likely require a balanced approach that combines the strengths of AI with the invaluable aspects of human interaction and teaching." (personal communication, 11/23/2023).

4   Student Perceptions Regarding the Appeal and Efficacy of Text- and Video-Generating AI in the Learning Process – A Qualitative Analysis

An anonymous Google survey, which consisted of 10 questions cited in Appendix 1, was conducted among the instructor's whole class of 2025 of the WSB Merito University in Poznan, Poland.

4.1   Fliki and InVideo – Qualitative Research Results

As regards the subjectively perceived attractiveness of the AI video-generating apps, addressed by question 1, inVideo was preferred by 17 students while Fliki was favored by 12 students (Fig. 1).

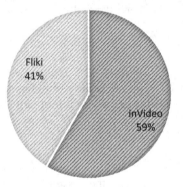

Fig. 1. AI video-generating apps - subjective attractiveness

In the open-ended question 2, asking for arguments in favor of the selected choice, students who preferred inVideo claimed that it was more engaging (68.42%) since more numerous and varied pictures were used, and the interview consisted of video clips rather than still frames. The students also appreciated subtle background music and claimed that the final product looked "more natural." They appreciated the "accurate" voice and the aesthetic. However, the respondents complained that the generator's free version, with only one voice for both the interviewer and the interviewee, made it difficult to identify who was speaking at a given time.

Interestingly, the students in favor of the other generator, Fliki, even though not a majority, gave more detailed answers, stating, e.g., that the interlocutors' voices seemed less robotic, making it easier for the viewers to concentrate, follow the content, and identify which of the two speakers was talking (66.667%). They also appreciated the fact that the image of each interlocutor was paired with one of the two pre-selected voices, and therefore, the "pictures/characters matched the dialog." As opposed to inVideo, which used too much visual information, "the video was more interesting than the content," and there was an inconsistent, unrelated, constantly changing background, commented the respondents.

4.2   ChatGPT – Qualitative Research Results

100% of the surveyed students used ChatGPT for the creation of the interview. None of the groups decided to draft the conversation without the help of generative AI.

In question 4, the respondents were asked to "check all that apply." Thus, several students selected both ["I used ChatGPT"] "to create the whole interview" and "to create parts of the interview," therefore, the results do not add up to 100%. However, most answers (68.97%) indicated that ChatGPT was used to create the whole interview, while 41.38% of students claimed that they utilized the generator to create parts of the interview. 17.24% employed the chatbot to check the grammatical accuracy of the interview, and 24.14% generated ideas with its help.

In response to question 5, 62.07% of the respondents stated that they did not write any part of the interview on their own. 24.14% of the students created their own interview questions, 1 student modified the questions asked by ChatGPT, 2 students prompted ChatGPT to mention specific facts, situations, and people, and 3 students corrected erroneous facts.

It may be concluded that while more students chose ChatGPT to do most of the assignment, around one-fifth of the respondents used it to boost their critical thinking and creativity through brainstorming ideas, and the same proportion undertook to formulate interview questions on their own. A particularly interesting and ingenious answer providing insight into the process was supplied by the only student who checked the "other" box. The student explained: "First, I pasted both articles. Then I told [ChatGPT] to summarize each article. Then I told [it] to create an interview based on what I had sent [it]. I combined my ideas with the [interview] that [it] created."

Of the respondents who claimed to have written some parts of the interview on their own, 6.9% used Google Translate to check grammatical accuracy, and 3.45% "asked AI if it could add anything that could be crucial or make my questions more interesting." The overwhelming majority didn't use ChatGPT, Google Translate, or any other AI to work on the interviews further. A cautious conclusion might thus be drawn that the students who worked on certain sections of the interviews on their own may have exhibited more autonomy and self-reliance.

Even though most respondents relied on generative AI to create the whole interview, interestingly, in response to question 7, only 55.17% expressed their full satisfaction with the product created. Nearly a half – as many as 44.82% – liked "some parts." (Fig. 2).

When asked to specify what they liked about the (parts of the) interview generated by AI, the respondents provided valuable detailed feedback. They appreciated the unique opportunity to create such an interview, claiming that "it was like going back in time," and they enjoyed the way ChatGPT "made the Queen talk," "as if she wrote [the interview] herself." They also commented that "AI really got into the role of Queen Elizabeth (used the royal language, etc.)." The way in which the generator delivered information was liked, the data provided were deemed relevant, and the interviews were seen as "well organized, written nicely and accurately."

The most valued aspects were the language (31.034%) and the information provided (27.59%). Some of the comments related to those characteristics were: "the language was appropriate," "the language and complexity of answers," "the language was advanced/

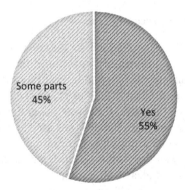

Fig. 2. Students' responses to the question of whether they liked the (parts of the) interview created by ChatGPT

far better than the one I'd use on my own," "interesting, relevant, coherent, accurate and well-structured answers."

Remarkably, the shortcomings mentioned in point 9, where students were asked to specify what they disliked about the AI-generated text, also focused mostly on the language. Nearly one-fourth (24.14%) complained that the language was "monotonous," "not "real" enough," "not natural," or "a bit artificial." The same percentage of respondents stated that the generator was "too general at times" or "it writes too much." One respondent phrased it as: "sometimes [AI] doesn't give facts; it just uses words to create a very long sentence," while two others commented: "too much unessential information, and it was difficult to understand the key point," and also: "some answers were like beating about the bush." One-fifth (20.26%) saw ChatGPT as repetitive ("many similar sentences," "repetitions"), which seems to stand in contradiction to Kocoń et al. (2023, 14). Some students also perceived the sentences created as "too complicated," or "too long." An insightful respondent replied: "AI doesn't understand certain words the way a real person does. Therefore, at times, it seemed a bit harsh/too straightforward." Finally, inaccuracies and factual errors were mentioned by 3 respondents.

Aware of the fact that 100% of her students employed AI to perform the task and as many as 62.07% did not personally author any section of the assigned interview, the instructor was curious about the students' ideas on how to ensure that AI such as ChatGPT is used ethically. Perhaps unsurprisingly, some responses focused on restrictions, such as identifying unoriginality ("check the assignment for emotions," "check if students know certain words or structures that appear in the work they submitted"), banning AI use ("use another AI tool within ChatGPT that would ban unethical users from entering the app," "no access to AI during tests or examinations") or penalization ("make sure that students understand the consequences of using AI; punish them if they use AI unethically"). One of the respondents came to the sad conclusion that "students will always find their way to cheat, either with ChatGPT or another alternative."

Yet, proactivity on the part of an instructor was also strongly stressed ("Just teach them how to do it. There is no way to ensure it is used 100% ethically, but we can convince them, show [them] ways to use it as an "addition," not as something that does everything for you," "teach students how to use it, e.g., as an inspiration, for idea generation, to check grammar or vocabulary," "tell students they can use it partly; [do] not be strict about not using it at all," "ask students to rewrite AI-generated parts on their own").

5   Student Perceptions Regarding the Appeal and Efficacy of Text- and Video-Generating AI in the Learning Process – A Quantitative Analysis

To gather quantitative data, 9 Likert-scale questions, 3 per each AI-powered generator, were asked to measure students' attitudes and perceptions.

25 respondents, 21 females and 4 males, indicated their level of agreement by selecting one of 5 options.

The survey was conducted two weeks after the qualitative analysis (Table 1).

Table 1. Student satisfaction related to the use of ChatGPT, Fliki, and inVideo.

ChatGPT								
Question	Response					Median	Mean	Standard Deviation
	1 (very dissatisfied)	2 (dissatisfied)	3 (neutral)	4 (satisfied)	5 (very satisfied)			
Q1	0	0	6 (24%)	15 (60%)	4 (16%)	4	3.92	0.64
	1 (not at all)	2 (slightly)	3 (moderately)	4 (very)	5 (extremely)			
Q2	0	7 (28%)	8 (32%)	10 (40%)	0	3	3.12	0.83
	1 (not at all likely)	2 (slightly likely)	3 (moderately likely)	4 (very likely)	5 (extremely likely)			
Q3	0	3 (12%)	9 (36%)	8 (32%)	5 (20%)	4	3.60	0.96
Fliki								
Question	**Response**					**Median**	**Mean**	**Standard Deviation**
	1 (very dissatisfied)	2 (dissatisfied)	3 (neutral)	4 (satisfied)	5 (very satisfied)			
Q4	0	0	16 (64%)	9 (35%)	0	3	3.36	0.49
	1 (not at all)	2 (slightly)	3 (moderately)	4 (very)	5 (extremely)			
Q5	1 (4%)	3 (12%)	11 (44%)	10 (40%)	0	3	3.20	0.82

(*continued*)

Table 1. (*continued*)

ChatGPT

Question	Response					Median	Mean	Standard Deviation
	1 (not at all likely)	**2** (slightly likely)	**3** (moderately likely)	**4** (very likely)	**5** (extremely likely)			
Q6	1 (4%)	8 (32%)	12 (48%)	4 (16%)	0	3	2.76	0.78

inVideo

Question	Response					Median	Mean	Standard Deviation
	1 (very dissatisfied)	**2** (dissatisfied)	**3** (neutral)	**4** (satisfied)	**5** (very satisfied)			
Q7	0	0	13 (52%)	12 (48%)	0	3	3.48	0.51
	1 (not at all)	**2** (slightly)	**3** (moderately)	**4** (very)	**5** (extremely)			
Q8	0	5 (20%)	10 (40%)	8 (32%)	2 (8%)	3	3.28	0.89
	1 (not at all likely)	**2** (slightly likely)	**3** (moderately likely)	**4** (very likely)	**5** (extremely likely)			
Q9	2 (8%)	5 (20%)	14 (56%)	2 (8%)	2 (8%)	3	2.88	0.97

The questions asked:

Q1: How satisfied are you with ChatGPT in assisting you with your academic assignments?

Q2: To what extent has ChatGPT improved your learning experience and understanding of course materials?

Q3: How likely are you to recommend the use of ChatGPT to your peers for academic purposes?

Q4: How satisfied are you with the functionalities of Fliki for potentially creating video content for your academic projects?

Q5: To what extent can Fliki contribute to the improvement of your multimedia presentations and assignments?

Q6: How likely are you to use Fliki for future academic multimedia projects?

Q7: How satisfied are you with the functionalities of inVideo for potentially creating video content for your academic projects?

Q8: To what extent can inVideo contribute to the improvement of your multimedia presentations and assignments?

Q9: How likely are you to use inVideo for future academic multimedia projects?

5.1 Analysis of the Obtained Results

With regard to ChatGPT, no respondents expressed a lack or an extreme lack of satisfaction when using the generator for academic assignments, with 60% choosing the "satisfied" option. Overall, the level of satisfaction seemed high. Curiously, however, even though all the respondents were likely to recommend ChatGPT for academic purposes, with 52% very or extremely likely, that did not seem to translate into a subjective perception of an improvement in the learning experience or understanding of course materials, with 68% of respondents having selected "slight" or "moderate" enhancement. It was also notable that the question regarding the chatbot's recommendation had the second-highest standard deviation of 0.96. A tentative conclusion may therefore be drawn that the students effectively used their critical thinking skills in distinguishing between the efficiency of the tool and its potential capacity to augment their learning experience or to facilitate course content comprehension.

As regards video-generating AI, a significant number of respondents (64%) expressed a neutral sentiment towards Fliki. Even though the subjective satisfaction with its functionalities was perceived as neutral to satisfactory, it seemed rather unlikely that the respondents would use Fliki for their future multimedia projects. Only 4% were in favor of the perspective. Curiously, the anonymous respondent who stated that the generator could not contribute to the improvement of their presentations and/or assignments selected the "slightly likely" option when answering the next question ("How likely are you to use Fliki for future academic multimedia projects?"). In turn, the person who was "not at all likely" to use the tool for enhancing their future presentations was also "moderately" satisfied with the functionalities of the text-to-video converter.

The students seemed to slightly prefer inVideo for creating video content, with 52% being neutral and 48% satisfied with the functionalities of the generator. A large percentage of the respondents (80%, varying from "moderately" to "extremely") seemed to perceive the tool as conducive to the improvement of their assignments. Nevertheless, a perhaps surprising finding was that even though, overall, 40% of students believed that both generators were "very" or "extremely effective" when employed for the purpose, only 16% of the respondents were "very" or "extremely likely" to actually use the tools, while the standard deviation seems to indicate that the respondents were more unanimous with regard to Fliki (0.78) rather than inVideo (0.97).

In summary, all three AI-powered text and text-to-video generators were liked by the students, with no "dissatisfied" or "very dissatisfied" responses selected. While ChatGPT was largely seen as useful and worthy of recommendation, the undergraduates did not seem to be convinced that it could optimize their educational experience and comprehension of course content. In turn, Fliki and inVideo received a less univocal response, and there was a discrepancy between their perceived appeal and the likelihood of their being used.

6   Conclusion

The qualitative and quantitative analyses regarding AI- powered text and video generators (ChatGPT, Fliki and inVideo), shed light on the nuanced preferences and perceptions of sophomore English Philology students of the WSB Merito University and brought certain thought-provoking findings.

The opinion of Tse, Esposito & Goh (2019, 223) that "communication skills – the ability to express ideas as words – are humanity's purview. To the extent that machines can communicate well, it's only due to the person behind it programming the scripts" is undoubtedly valid. However, text-generating AI does seem quite effective when mimicking human interactions, which was confirmed by the author's research.

The qualitative examination of ChatGPT usage showed the students' significant reliance on the chatbot, with the majority of respondents employing it to create entire interviews. Felicitously, several students utilized ChatGPT creatively and/or critically, for idea generation, error correction, or improvement of self-created content.

Despite the widespread reliance on ChatGPT, a significant proportion of students was satisfied with only some parts of the AI-generated interviews. Intriguingly, both the appreciation and the concerns were largely related to language. The respondents highlighted the generator's language proficiency, sense of style, and some ability to mimic historical usage of English; however, they also commented on repetitive language, excessive information, and occasional misunderstanding of their intentions.

As for qualitative insights, there was a preference for inVideo, based on its perceived engagement, aesthetic qualities, and the use of moving rather than still images. The respondents who valued Fliki appreciated the more human-like voices and the structure that was easy to follow.

Quantitative analysis showed that the students were highly satisfied with ChatGPT and likely to recommend its use for academic purposes. This, however, did not necessarily correlate with the students' perceived enhancement in the learning experience or better understanding of course content. Curiously, Fliki and inVideo, while generally liked and seen as potentially improving the quality of assignments, were not very likely to be used for future tasks.

When assessing (un)ethical use of artificial intelligence, the students suggested a balance of proactive teaching on ethical practices and some restrictive measures. They were also aware that attempts to misuse AI tools may be inevitable.

The predictions of ChatGPT, significantly more general in their nature, were confirmed as regards implicit appreciation of quick answers and assistance with homework and projects. However, the students focused on the more practical aspects of the tools at hand, so, e.g., 24/7 availability or personalized learning was not mentioned in the surveys. Also, contrary to the instructor's expectations, the designed task did not prove explicitly conducive to language practice; however, the students appreciated the linguistic aptitude of the text generator.

Regarding the potential disadvantages anticipated by ChatGPT, lack of interpersonal human interaction or human instructor feedback was neither observed by the students nor discussed in the questionnaires, most possibly due to the fact that the instructor prevented both by designing the assignment as group work and provided her students with real-time, just-in-time, formative critique. Yet, the students did comment on the

AI generator's limited understanding of context. In turn, even though the assignment was not graded, the instructor noticed beyond a doubt the students' overreliance on AI. Nonetheless, that did not result in curbing the students' critical thinking skills, which may have been partly owed to the instructor's heightening the sensitivity of her students to potential fallacies of generative AI.

Even though her study encompassed a whole sophomore class, the author is aware that the cohort was not numerous. Therefore, the research will be continued and expanded to compare the findings with those yet to be obtained.

Disclosure of Interests. The author has no competing interests to declare that are relevant to the content of this article.

Appendix 1

Qualitative Survey Questionnaire

1. Which of the AI created videos did you like more: Fliki or inVideo? Mark only one oval (Fliki, inVideo)
2. **Why** did you like it more? (an open-ended question)
3. Have you used ChatGPT to create your interview with Queen Elizabeth? Mark only one oval (yes, no)
4. If you used ChatGPT, how did you use it? Check all that apply.

   - To create the whole interview
   - To create parts of the interview
   - To check the grammatical accuracy of your interview
   - To generate ideas for the interview
   - Other (if so, explain)

5. Did you write any part of the interview **on your own**? Which ones? (an open-ended question)
6. If you wrote any parts **on your own**, did you use ChatGPT, Google Translate, or any other AI to work on them further? How? (an open-ended question)
7. Did you like the (parts of the) interview generated by ChatGPT? Mark only one oval.

   - Yes
   - No
   - Some parts
   - Other: ....

8. What did you **like** about the (parts of the) interview generated by ChatGPT? (an open-ended question)
9. What, if anything, **didn't** you like about the (parts of the) interview generated by ChatGPT? (an open-ended question)
10. Your ideas on how to ensure that students use **AI** (such as ChatGPT) ethically: .... (an open-ended question)

Appendix 2

Quantitative Survey Questionnaire
1. ChatGPT:

a. **How satisfied are you with ChatGPT in assisting you with your academic assignments?**
    1 (Very Dissatisfied) - 2 (Dissatisfied) - 3 (Neutral) - 4 (Satisfied) - 5 (Very Satisfied).

b. **To what extent has ChatGPT improved your learning experience and understanding of course materials?**
    1 (Not at all) - 2 (Slightly) - 3 (Moderately) - 4 (Very) - 5 (Extremely).

c. **How likely are you to recommend the use of ChatGPT to your peers for academic purposes?**
    1 (Not likely at all) - 2 (Slightly likely) - 3 (Moderately likely) - 4 (Very likely) - 5 (Extremely likely).

2. Fliki:

a. **How satisfied are you with the functionalities of Fliki for potentially creating video content for your academic projects?**
    1 (Very Dissatisfied) - 2 (Dissatisfied) - 3 (Neutral) - 4 (Satisfied) - 5 (Very Satisfied).

b. **To what extent can Fliki contribute to the improvement of your multimedia presentations and assignments?**
    1 (Not at all) - 2 (Slightly) - 3 (Moderately) - 4 (Very) - 5 (Extremely).

c. **How likely are you to use Fliki for future academic multimedia projects?**
    1 (Not likely at all) - 2 (Slightly likely) - 3 (Moderately likely) - 4 (Very likely) - 5 (Extremely likely).

3. inVideo:

a. **How satisfied are you with the functionalities of inVideo for potentially creating video content for your academic projects?**
    1 (Very Dissatisfied) - 2 (Dissatisfied) - 3 (Neutral) - 4 (Satisfied) - 5 (Very Satisfied).

b. **To what extent can inVideo contribute to the improvement of your multimedia presentations and assignments?**
    1 (Not at all) - 2 (Slightly) - 3 (Moderately) - 4 (Very) - 5 (Extremely).

c. **How likely are you to use inVideo for future academic multimedia projects?**
    1 (Not likely at all) - 2 (Slightly likely) - 3 (Moderately likely) - 4 (Very likely) - 5 (Extremely likely).

Appendix 3

An Example of an AI-Assisted Student-Created Interview

Interviewer: Your Majesty, as a student of English philology, I'm eager to explore sensitive historical topics.

1. How do you reflect on the British Empire's colonial history during your reign, and what lessons can be learned?

    Queen Elizabeth II: The British Empire's history is complex; we must acknowledge achievements and shortcomings, learning for a world where nations coexist with respect.
2. Considering Britain's role in the transatlantic slave trade, how should the legacy of slavery be addressed today?

    Queen Elizabeth II: Reconciliation requires acknowledging the pain caused by slavery. Education, dialogue, and addressing systemic inequalities are crucial for a just and inclusive society.
3. On the Kohinoor diamond controversy, how do you view its ownership and the responsibility to address historical artifacts?

    Queen Elizabeth II: The Kohinoor's complex history necessitates discussions involving all relevant parties to find a fair resolution respecting history and heritage.
4. Reflecting on Mahatma Gandhi's Salt March, how do you perceive the impact of nonviolent movements on history?

    Queen Elizabeth II: Nonviolent movements, like the Salt March, highlight the strength of peaceful activism in challenging oppressive systems, emphasizing the enduring power of collective action.
5. Regarding the symbolic moment holding hands with a young Black child, how do you view the importance of such gestures in fostering unity and understanding in discussions on racial equality?

    Queen Elizabeth II: Moments like holding hands symbolize human connection and compassion, stressing the importance of breaking down barriers for shared humanity. Fostering unity requires genuine engagement, listening, and dismantling divisive prejudices.

Appendix 4

A Sample of an AI-Assisted Student-Created Interview

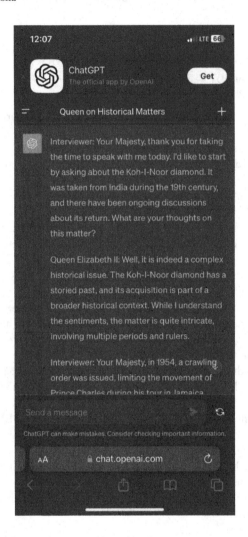

References

Anderson, J.: Educating in a world of artificial intelligence. Harvard Graduate School of Education, 9 February 2023. https://www.gse.harvard.edu/ideas/edcast/23/02/educating-world-artificial-intelligence

Bates, A.: Teaching in a Digital Age: General Guidelines for Designing, Teaching and Learning. Pressbooks, Montreal, 18 August 2022. https://pressbooks.bccampus.ca/teachinginadigitalage v3m/

Brzezinska, M.: Global skills in the global pandemic: how to create an effective bichronous learning experience during an emergency shift to remote instruction. In: Auer, M.E., Pester, A., May, D. (eds.) Learning with Technologies and Technologies in Learning. LNNS, vol. 456, pp. 679–706. Springer, Cham (2022). https://doi.org/10.1007/978-3-031-04286-7_32

Brzezinska, M.: Conversations with Conquerors: William the Conqueror [Video]. YouTube, 20 November 2023. https://www.youtube.com/watch?v=79EbAsqVc7U

Brzezinska, M.: Interviews with Conquerors: William the Conqueror [Video]. YouTube, 6 January 2024. https://www.youtube.com/watch?v=J7ntiB8oB7I

Piki, A., Brzezinska, M.: Teaching and learning in the new normal: responding to students' and academics' multifaceted needs. In: Coman, A., Vasilache, S. (eds.) Social Computing and Social Media. HCII 2023. LNCS, vol. 14026, pp. 116–136. Springer, Cham (2023). https://doi.org/10.1007/978-3-031-35927-9_9

Cao, L. Y.: Developing Teachers' Contingent Responsiveness in Dialogic Science Teaching via Mixed-reality Simulations: A Design-based Study [Apollo - University of Cambridge Repository] (2022). https://www.repository.cam.ac.uk/handle/1810/343119

Cao, L., Dede, C.: Navigating a world of generative AI: suggestions for educators. Harvard Graduate School of Education. Next Level Lab, 28 July 2023. https://nextlevellab.gse.harvard.edu/2023/07/28/navigating-a-world-of-generative-ai-suggestions-for-educators/

Chauhan, N.S.: Reinforcement Learning from Human Feedback (RLHF). The AI Dream, 19 August 2023. https://www.theaidream.com/post/reinforcement-learning-from-human-feedback

Does ChatGPT tell the truth? | OpenAI Help Center. (n.d.-b). https://help.openai.com/en/articles/8313428-does-chatgpt-tell-the-truth

France, P.E.: Reclaiming Personalized Learning: A Pedagogy for Restoring Equity and Humanity in Our Classrooms. Corwin Press, Thousand Oaks (2020)

Geryk, M.: Artificial intelligence in higher education industry. Just a brief introduction to complexity of an issue of future challenges. Zeszyty Naukowe, **2023**(172) (2023). https://doi.org/10.29119/1641-3466.2023.172.13

Greene, R.T.: The pros and cons of using AI in learning: is ChatGPT helping or hindering learning outcomes? eLearning Industry, 24 April 2023. https://elearningindustry.com/pros-and-cons-of-using-ai-in-learning-chatgpt-helping-or-hindering-learning-outcomes

Hamilton, I.: Artificial intelligence in Education: Teachers' opinions on AI in the classroom. Forbes Advisor, 6 December 2023. https://www.forbes.com/advisor/education/artificial-intelligence-in-school/

International Data Corporation: Future-Ready Institutions: Assessing U.S. Higher Education's Sector's AI Adoption and Capabilities (2020). https://edudownloads.azureedge.net/msdownloads/FutureReadyBusiness_HigherEducation_AI_US_Design_final_2.pdf

Hough, L.: Students: AI is Part of Your World. Harvard Graduate School of Education, 24 May 2023. https://www.gse.harvard.edu/ideas/ed-magazine/23/05/students-ai-part-your-world

Jimenez, R.: In the Age of AI ChatGPT, Do Learners Still Solely Rely on Human Mentors? - Stories, Scenarios, Microlearning and Workflow Learning Platform. Stories, Scenarios, Microlearning and Workflow Learning Platform, 29 June 2023. https://vignetteslearning.blog/2023/06/in-the-age-of-a-i-chatgpt-do-learners-still-solely-rely-on-human-mentors/?mc_cid=6b906f03aa&mc_eid=5f38e8a88c

Karout, D., Harouni, H.: ChatGPT is unoriginal—and exactly what humans need. WIRED, 14 June 2023. https://www.wired.com/story/chatgpt-education-originality/

Kącki, E.: Creative artistic activity of robots. Wydawnictwo Poligraf. (2021)

Keeler, A.: Um no ChatGPT – you are NOT thinking. Teacher Tech With Alice Keeler, 25 August 2023. https://alicekeeler.com/2023/08/25/um-no-chatgpt-you-are-not-thinking/

Kocoń, J., et al.: ChatGPT: jack of all trades, master of none. Inf. Fusion, 99, 101861 (2023). https://doi.org/10.1016/j.inffus.2023.101861

Krueger, N.: What educators — and students — can learn from ChatGPT. ISTE, 14 May 2023. https://iste.org/blog/what-educators-and-students-can-learn-from-chatgpt

Liu, J., Demszky, D., Hill, C.H.: AI can make education more personal (Yes, really) (Opinion). Education Week, 28 August 2023. https://www.edweek.org/leadership/opinion-ai-can-make-education-more-personal-yes-really/2023/08

Lv, Z.: Generative artificial intelligence in the metaverse era. Cogn. Robot. **3**, 208–217 (2023). https://doi.org/10.1016/j.cogr.2023.06.001

Nah, F.F., Zheng, R., Cai, J., Siau, K., Chen, L.: Generative AI and ChatGPT: applications, challenges, and AI-human collaboration. J. Inf. Technol. Case Appl. Res. **25**(3), 277–304 (2023). https://doi.org/10.1080/15228053.2023.2233814

Polska Agencja Rozwoju Przedsiębiorczości [Polish Agency for Enterprise Development]: Wykorzystanie sztucznej inteligencji w edukacji Dodatek specjalny do miesięcznika „Rynek pracy, edukacja, kompetencje. Aktualne trendy i wyniki badań" (październik 2023) [The use of artificial intelligence in education. Special supplement to the monthly magazine "Labor Market, Education, Competencies. Current trends and research results"], October 2023. https://www.parp.gov.pl/index.php/component/publications/publication/2015 (2023, October)

Schroeder, R.: Productively and painlessly integrating AI into classes. Inside Higher Ed I Higher Education News, Events and Jobs. https://www.insidehighered.com/opinion/blogs/online-trending-now/2023/07/19/productively-and-painlessly-integrating-ai-classes. Accessed 19 July 2023

The Future of Jobs Report 2023. World Economic Forum, 30 April 2023. https://www.weforum.org/publications/the-future-of-jobs-report-2023/digest/. Accessed 31 Dec 2023

Tse, T.C.M., Esposito, M., Goh, D.: The AI Republic: Building the Nexus Between Humans and Intelligent Automation. Lioncrest Publishing, Austin (2019)

UNESCO United Nations Educational, Scientific and Cultural Organization, Miao, F., Shiohira, K., Wally, Z., & Holmes, W.: International forum on AI and education: steering AI to empower teachers and transform teaching, 5–6 December 2022; analytical report. United Nations Educational, Scientific and Cultural Organization (2023). https://unesdoc.unesco.org/ark:/48223/pf0000386162?locale=en

A Tale of Academic Writing Using AI Tools: Lessons Learned from Multicultural Undergraduate Students

Ajrina Hysaj[1]([✉]) [iD], Georgina Farouqa[2] [iD], Sara Azeem Khan[1] [iD], and Laith Hiasat[3] [iD]

[1] University of Wollongong in Dubai, Dubai, United Arab Emirates
ajrinahysaj@uowdubai.ac.ae
[2] CEHE – Dubai, Dubai, United Arab Emirates
dr.georginafarouqa@cehe.ae
[3] Rochester Institute of Technology, Dubai, United Arab Emirates

Abstract. The aim of the current study was to explore the perceptions of undergraduate students of usefulness of using AI tools to write academically. For this study, we utilized a mixed method approach using a structured questionnaire to collect data relevant to the frequency of plagiarism that students commit while completing different kinds of assessments in universities. The sample group consisted of university students and participants were selected through purposeful random sampling. The selection of participants was based on the inclusion criteria that helped in understanding the problem. The questionnaire was made available to participants in an online format and sent by (SNS) or/ and email. The questionnaire was created using Qualtrics. It consisted of 12 questions aimed at understanding students' act of plagiarism while completing assessment as well as the use of AI to complete academic work. The questionnaire emphasized the identification plagiarism frequency and use of AI to complete tasks. Participants were provided with a selection of two to five pre-determined response options and one open-ended response option. In total, 53 questionnaires were completed. Responses were thematically analysed using QDA Miner Lite 2.0.7, qualitative, and mixed method analysis software. Finally, recommendations for further research were presented.

Keywords: Academic Writing · AI tools · Plagiarism

1 Introduction

The variety of education systems worldwide for approximately two decades, has been trying to introduce different technological advances to schools and universities worldwide aiming the facilitation of teaching process and improved students' academic satisfaction [1, 26, 29, 60]. Understandably, the management and policy makers have been supporting these efforts and are very optimistic about the use and the benefits of these advances in education [2, 26, 27, 30, 67]. Furthermore, the continuous utilisation of AI tools by learners in all levels of the education system and particularly in higher education has been encountered with a variety of challenges, starting with the lack of desire of teachers to accept the use of such tools, to the array of difficulties that are related to the purpose, benefits and drawbacks of using AI tools [3, 19, 33, 49].

For the last twenty years or so, an extensive body of research has been trying to understand students' perceptions about the utilization of the AI tools [37, 44]. While the concepts of teaching and learning evolve continuously, it is important to consider the use of AI tools as a reality that we as educators cannot, and should not ignore or even worse try to ban or stop it [4, 5, 17, 33, 34, 37, 44]. The ways that students study vary, and are constantly changing alongside with the number and functions of AI tools, therefore, it is valuable to not only understand the AI tools but more importantly understand the perceptions of our students about the use of these tools [6, 17, 18, 31, 44]. In that way the use of AI tools may support teaching and learning process rather hinder it. The difficulties that students face when studying in higher education are of academic and personal nature and although it is somehow a considerable effort to get to know most of the struggles that students go through, it is nevertheless crucial to explore their purposes in using AI tools [7, 37].

Education is a very innovative and adaptable field in relation to the material development and curriculum alignment [23, 24, 28, 29, 40, 54]. For example, educators worldwide are pioneer of the opinion that students' learning needs to be facilitated through a variety of means, and that the feedback provided by students in regard to the learning and teaching processes should be taken into consideration [8, 25]. Nevertheless, when it comes to the implementation of new technological advances in education and especially AI tools the focus of the educators becomes the shift of power and the enchanted territories offered by the use of technology and AI [9, 29, 30]. Technology and AI become a rather unwanted friend and, in many cases, a non-proclaimed enemy that in most instances provides unwanted or unappreciated challenges and struggles. Furthermore, many educators view AI as a threat to the education system or as an unwanted gift that hinders students' knowledge acquision [10, 33]. COVID- 19 pandemic created favorable conditions for the utilization of AI tools in higher education in a variety of ways prior known or unknown.

The extend of the utilization of technological or AI tools depends on many societal, economic and political factors; nevertheless, the use of AI tools impacts us all in one way or the other. Technological advances are most of the times seen as a progressive force that not only creates new frontiers of research but most importantly it empowers people with tools that facilitate development and growth [45, 65, 66]. Prior to COVID-19, the use of technology in higher education was seen with scepticism for a variety of reasons starting from the inability to fully comprehend its usage to lack of understanding of its benefits [11, 37, 39–41]. Nevertheless, now technology has become synonymous with higher education in the form of whiteboard or smarts boards, smart projectors, conference call applications like WebEx, Zoom and Teams, as well as in the form of LMS like Edmodo, Moodle, Blackboard, Canvas and most recently the extensive use of AI tools. The aim of this article was to explore the perceptions of the usefulness of AI tools by multicultural students in higher education when writing academically.

2   Literature Review

2.1   Exploring the Perceptions of Students and Teachers on the Utilization of AI Tools in Higher Education

Now more than ever before in the history of higher education students are utilising the AI tools to complete assignments or attempt exams. The extent by which AI tools are utilised in higher education by students of all majors has necessitated the need to explore the ways and forms that these tools are being utilised and the frequency of their use [12, 13, 45, 65, 66]. While the levels and reasons for utilisation of AI tools by students in higher education may vary based on students' unique circumstances, and their individual needs or it is worth exploring the use of AI in higher education so we as educators can facilitate teaching while allowing the use of AI tools [5, 14]. Furthermore, the process of utilising the AI tools requires a careful consideration of all parties involved in higher education, therefore, it is worth analysing the use of these tools by students, so we as educators can amend the ways we teach, and share generic or discipline related knowledge [5, 45]. Understanding the use of AI tools in generic or discipline related subjects not only supports our understanding of our students needs when using the tools but also it empowers us with the functions these AI tools may have and more specifically, it educates us about ways these tools are used by our students [15, 42].

As the process of teaching and learning is interconnected with the needs of students and teachers alike, the necessity of understanding the AI tools is interconnected with the successful and ethical use of these tools. Students' viewpoints on the use of technology and AI tools are different and are connected with factors that have intellectual, personal and societal value [57, 65]. The exciting and cautious types of uses of AI tools may differ from student to student based on their specific needs and reasons [3, 6, 16, 17, 57]. For instance, students who may find grammar concepts difficult may utilise the AI tools to write with a more sophisticated language. On the other hand, students who lack an extensive vocabulary may consider the academic texts, randomly used to write a literature review, as very challenging and may use a variety of AI tools to paraphrase and summarise these texts to the extent of understanding them better or even changing them completely [9, 18].

Other common uses of AI tools by students are related to generating ideas about unknown concepts or notions [8, 9, 19]. For instance, some students may have acquired a considerable amount of general knowledge prior to attending university, while others lack general knowledge on specific topics and may use the AI tools to empower themselves with such information. Moreover, it is understood that the abrupt and widespread use of AI tools in educational institutions places the less technology savvy educators of students at a disadvantage and imposes an additional burden to the curriculum adaptation. In the higher education sector, one group of people who tend to embrace the use of technology faster and at a larger scale compared to others are the faculty members of engineering and computer sciences faculties [8, 20, 59]. Commonly, these educators take a leading role in conducting the much-needed training sessions for other faculty members, and serve as the avant-garde force of the application of AI in universities. In academic study skills classes, the implementation of AI tools is associated with consecutive adaptations of methods of delivery, classroom or online activities and assessment tasks and their submission form [21, 36]. Adaptations of the material and assessment tasks that occur due to the implementation and use of technology should be reflected in the alignment of subject outcomes, classroom activities and assessment tasks [13, 22]. Education and progression are considered to be equally important, and in the perspective of implementation of the use of technological tools like the AI tools they are required to provide a certain level of conformity to each other to ensure successful co-existence for the benefit of students, educators and the higher education system as large [11, 13, 23, 24, 32].

3 Exploration of Utilization of AI Tools in Academic Study Skills Classes

AI tools are now utilized in teaching and learning environments in all four corners of the globe [25, 40, 42]. Levels of utilization of AI tools vary and are connected with individual preferences of teachers and students, as well as with institutional preferences [11, 13, 26]. Understandably, the levels of positivity and excitement for the prospect of using AI tools by some educators for reasons that may or may not be justifiable to all people. Similarly, the levels of enthusiasm deriving by the prospect of utilizing AI tools in learning process, reasonably, vary in students too [27, 49, 50]. Undoubtedly, individual preferences of reluctance to utilise AI tools in teaching and learning processes are overshadowed by those of institutions that tend to be backed up by research that emphasizes the positive aspects of using technology and its specific user-friendly tools.

The rapid advances of AI tools and their subsequent extensive spread throughout the globe, have created the necessity to explore and understand their use, their benefits and their drawbacks [7, 21–23, 28, 34, 35, 37]. Understanding the nature of AI tools and their utilization in academic study skills settings, as well as the level of adaptations needed for the content to be delivered appropriately, is the main concern of management and policy makers in higher education and as such is transferred to the educators involved in teaching study skills classes, to be acted upon [29, 58]. Teachers and instructors of academic study skills are required to understand the application of their content when using AI tools to facilitate learning [30, 58]. In other words, they are required to exit their comfort zone and experiment with technology and AI tools [32, 33, 58, 64]. Justifiably, the understanding of the utilization of technological tools in academic study skills classes takes time to be comprehended and embraced [28–31, 66]. Like all changes, the variations imposed by the use of the unknown AI tools create anxiety, fear and confusion in academic study skills teachers to say the least. Furthermore, teachers as well-grounded professionals, reasonably require in-depth understanding of the benefit and use of any tools that they are required to be used in their classrooms or in the online platform [21, 24, 26, 32, 34, 67].

Understanding the use of AI tools in the process of teaching and learning is a requirement imposed to academic study skills teachers by their profession [4, 24, 25, 35, 64]. In other words, it is necessity that teachers are well-informed about the AI tools and their application to enhance learning process of their students well before the practical applications of the same in classrooms or in the online platform [37, 53, 65]. Increased teacher awareness about the uses and benefits of the AI tools can result in enjoyable teaching experience for teachers [36, 39, 40, 62, 68]. Moreover, awareness about AI tools can lead the way to a successful learning experience for students and has the potential to minimize the undue stress for teachers. Hindrance of the adequate use of AI tools can potentially slow down the process of learning and create in students an increased level of disinterest to complete tasks or submit work in an audio, video or written format [41, 51, 53, 63].

4 Academic Writing Using AI Tools and Plagiarism

The extent by which AI use has spread throughout the world in one way or the other affects us all. So much so that we are all involved in our daily lives with many gadgets and tools that use some sort of AI functions and in many instances, and we depend so heavily on these tools, that their existence is dearer to us than values that we grow up believing in and have been nurturing throughout our lives [10, 42, 63]. Although the creation process of AI tools and continuous development are no doubt the expertise and contribution of coders and programmers, the utilization of AI tools is benefiting us all and a lot of it is even offered for free like is the case of Automatic Article Generator (AAG) or AI Text Generator. From the viewpoint of students or people who generally find academic writing as complex, dry and abstract, these tools could be seen as lifesavers since they provide them with the much needed "support" to produce the kind of work needed to pass subjects or even achieve a decent GPA [23, 29, 43, 44]. Nevertheless, in the lenses of us educators these tools, if used to deceive the whole system of higher education, are morally and academically inappropriate and deceitful [46, 47]. The algorithm writing that AI is capable of producing was first thought to be at an infant stage from a Scopus, grammatical, content and academically appropriate structure.

Nevertheless, according to the article by Motlagh et al. [48] these tools have evolved during the last two years, in a rapid and steady upward fashion, positioning us the educators a fragile and awkward situation. As people who are directly involved with curriculum design and method of delivery of our respective subjects, we expect a minimum involvement of our students with the matter taught during our sessions [40, 42, 47]. Traditionally this has been the case for decades, however, as AI gets extensively involved in designing of AAG or Text-processing tools this resembles an unspoken battle between humanity and AI [15, 44, 49]. According to Motlagh et al. [48], AI in the shape of programs like Text-processing gives us an alternative equal if not superior to human capacity in terms of intelligence and material production. Rationale behind this statement is supported by the studies by Kaplan and Haenlein, [39], Thacker [56], and Kumar et al. [43]. The value of algorithm has long been recognized in all mathematical sciences, mainly due to the constant progression of computational and computability usage in different fields. The basic usage of Turing machine paradigm in contemporary computing which started in 1936 [60], has now evolved to the theory that AI is a newly born intellectual non-living machine. This newly created concept on the nature of AI creates the environment for its recognition and makes it worthy to be explored and understood from a variety of angles such as the actual scope and usage in producing academic writing as well as for the limits and dangers associated with it [14, 50, 51]. According to Sudlow [54], such endeavour is required to be undertaken by coders and programmers while taking into consideration the repercussions that these AI tools have on the psychological, linguistic, relational, policy and ethical basis. Nevertheless, according to Humble and Mozelius [22] and Hancock, Naaman and Levy [23] coders and programmers are not necessarily considering the linguistic and social aspects of these technologies, in contrary they are more focused on their intellectual capacities as these tools are competing with human brain and are a display of Turing's definition on intellect and the knowledge accumulated through years and experience [12, 66].

5 Methodology

For this study, we utilized a mixed method approach using a structured questionnaire to collect data relevant to the frequency of plagiarism that students commit while completing different kinds of assessments at four-year universities in UAE. The sample group consisted of university graduate and undergraduate students. Participants were selected through purposeful random sampling. The selection of participants was based on the inclusion criteria that helped in understanding the problem. The questionnaire was aimed at providing insight from undergraduate student perspectives. The questionnaire was made available to participants in an online format and sent by (SNS) or/ and email. The questionnaire was created using Qualtrics. It consisted of 12 questions aimed at understanding students' act of plagiarism while completing assessment as well as the use of AI to complete academic work. The questionnaire was part of a PhD thesis by one of the authors of this articles and the questionnaire aimed at identifying plagiarism frequency and use of AI to complete tasks. Participants were provided with a selection of two to five pre-determined response options and one open-ended response option. In total, 53 questionnaires were completed. Responses were thematically analysed using QDA Miner Lite 2.0.7, qualitative, and mixed method analysis software.

6 Results

The first objective of the study was to better understand how frequent do students plagiarise while completing different kinds of assessments like exams, research papers and projects. The results are displayed in Table 1, 2, and 3. The second objective of the study was to get a clear insight into the use of AI tools in academic writing. The results are displayed in Table 4, 5 and 6.

Approximately (41%) of participants plagiarised more than twice during an exam, using their own notes or the notes of others. Other (13%) plagiarised twice and similarly (11%) copied only once. These findings indicate that more than 50% of students plagiarised at least twice during exams. According to data collected through the questionnaire (33.3%) of participants stated that they never cheated during an exam. The frequency of plagiarism while writing a research paper is presented in Table 2.

Table 2 shows that half of participants did not plagiarise while completing a research paper. Around quarter of participants (24.1%) copied more than twice. Few (9.3%) plagiarised only once while (14.8) copied twice. One participant commented "I don't remember if I did so". The analysed data indicates that the frequency of plagiarism while writing a research paper decreased when compared to cheating during exams. It

Table 1. Exams

Cover and included terms	Occurrence Frequency	Percentage comments
1. Frequency		
1.1 Once	6	11.1%
1.2 Twice	7	13%
1.3 More than twice	22	40.7%
1.4 Never	18	33.3%
1.5 Do not remember	1	1.9%

Table 2. Research Paper

Cover and included terms	Occurrence Frequency	Percentage comments
1. Frequency		
1.1 Once	5	9.3%
1.2 Twice	8	14.8%
1.3 More than twice	13	24.1%
1.4 Never	27	50%
1.5 Others	1	1.9%

Table 3. Projects

Cover and included terms	Occurrence Frequency	Percentage comments
1. Frequency		
1.1 Once	6	11.1%
1.2 Twice	4	7.4%
1.3 More than twice	12	22.2%
1.4 Never	32	59.3%

was important to further explore plagiarism during projects as another way of assessing students. Results are shown in Table 3.

As indicated in Table 3. More than two thirds of participants never copied assignments while completing a project. Approximately (30%) plagiarised their work on projects. These results provide further evidence that the percentage of plagiarism drops when the level of student engagement increases and students' need to cheat becomes less. In this study it was also important to further understand whether students use AI to complete assignments and which specific tool they use. Results are shown in Table 4.

Table 4. AI for Academic Work

Cover and included terms	Occurrence Frequency	Percentage comments
1. Usage		
1.1 Yes	27	52.8%
1.2 No	7	13.2%
1.3 Sometimes	18	34%
2. Software		
2.1 Chat GPT	44	83%
2.2 Others	9	17%

Table 4 illustrates that most students (86%) use AI to complete their academic assignments. Few (13.2%) participants reported that they never used AI for their work. A similar percentage was of (83%) used Chat GPT as an AI software. It is probable that these findings were related to easiness or comfort using these tools. The analysed data shown in Table 5 presents evidence that shows the level of comfort and easiness experienced by students while using AI.

Table 5. AI Usage for Academic Writing

Cover and included terms	Occurrence Frequency	Percentage comments
1. Comfort		
1.1 Very comfortable	13	24.5%
1.2 Comfortable	17	32.1%
1.3 Somehow comfortable	11	20.8%
1.4 Uncomfortable	10	20.8%
1.5 Others	2	1.8%
2. Easiness		
2.1 Easy	42	79.2%
2.2 Not easy	8	15.1%
2.3 Somehow easy	2	3.8%
2.4 Others	1	1.9%

As shown in Table 5, more than half of participants felt comfortable using AI. (20.8%) felt somehow uncomfortable. Similarly, the same number of participants felt uncomfortable using AI. Data also shows that most participants (80%) found that it was easy to use these tolls to complete their academic writing tasks. It was important for this study to understand whether students try to mask their AI written assignments to make them similar to those written by humans. Results are shown in Table 6.

Table 6. Humanizing AI Text

Cover and included terms	Occurrence Frequency	Percentage comments
1. Online tools		
1.1 Yes	20	37.7%
1.2 No	33	62.3
2. Online tools		
1.1 Yes	14	26.4%
1.2 No	39	73.6%

More than third of participants use online tools to humanize their AI written work. Similarly, more than quarter of participants intentionally make errors in their assignments to show that they were written by themselves. Many participants did not write any errors in their assignments, nor did they use online tools for their work.

7 Discussion

This study revealed the use AI tools is viewed in a variety of ways from students and teachers alike. Furthermore, this study highlighted the need that students have is using AI tools when completing academic writing tasks like essay, reports or case studies [20, 52, 53]. Specific measures and procedures that involve the use of AI tools are required to be taken into consideration when analysing the needs that students have when completing academic writing tasks [5, 18, 46, 54, 55]. The aim of utilizing the AI tools when teaching academic writing should be implemented while maintaining high levels of academic integrity [37]. In other words, although educators should not tend to stop the use of AI tools by students, at the same time they need to equip students with the ability of understanding the ethical use of such tools to facilitate a successful experience in higher education [42, 56]. Furthermore, as the use of AI tools may became a necessity of any work environment, equipping students with this type of knowledge not only serves to the benefit of students when in university, but also it paves the way to their subsequent success in their professional life [17, 57]. Moreover, the study highlighted the requirement that AI tools may be used by teachers to design curriculum or provide formative feedback while allowing teachers to focus on their teaching performance and classroom management. The creation of a communicative and supportive environment in academic classes while allowing students to use AI tools may not only support the knowledge acquisition but also educate students about the ethical implications of AI tools [29, 37, 58].

8 Conclusion and Recommendations

No one can deny that academic writing skills play a vital role in students' successful experience in higher education [24, 25, 59, 62]. Students need to develop their vocabulary and grammar skills to cope with their studies in general [19, 61]. Furthermore, the completion of academic assessment tasks in many instances involves the use of AI tools [16]. This study found that students used AI tools for a variety of purposes and these purposes are of individual and academic nature. Moreover, this study found that it is important for educators to get involved in the process of the use of AI tools by students as active participants rather than passive and distant spectators. Also, the study found the need to consider plagiarism when academic integrity when considering the use of AI tools when writing academically. The findings of the current study indicate that aspects of academic writing can be supported by the use of AI tools if used efficiently and ethically. However, as pointed out by Hysaj and Suleymanova [24] as well as Hamam and Hysaj [19], it is the responsibility of academic writing teachers to make pragmatic decisions as to how much to encourage the use of AI tools, so they can shape students' discourse abilities and facilitate their learning and triumphant entrance to the broader academic community. These decisions may include choices to use the specific features of AI tools for pedagogical and andragogical purposes to ease the undue amount of stress experienced due to the lack of adequate knowledge when writing academically in a variety of general of discipline related topics.

References

1. Abd-Elaal, E.S., Gamage, S.H., Mills, J.E.: Artificial intelligence is a tool for cheating academic integrity. In: 30th Annual Conference for the Australasian Association for Engineering Education (AAEE 2019): Educators Becoming Agents of Change: Innovate, Integrate, Motivate, pp. 397–403 (2019)
2. Abdulghani, H.M., Sattar, K., Ahmad, T., Akram, A.: Association of COVID-19 pandemic with undergraduate medical students' perceived stress and coping. Psychol. Res. Behav. Manag. 871–881 (2020)
3. Adarkwah, M.A.: I'm not against online teaching, but what about us?: ICT in Ghana post COVID-19. Educ. Inf. Technol. 26(2), 1665–1685 (2021)
4. Akhmedov, B., Shuhkrat, K.: Cluster methods of learning English using information technology. Sci. Prog. 1(2), 40–43 (2020)
5. Alotaibi, N.S., Alshehri, A.H.: Prospers and obstacles in using artificial intelligence in Saudi Arabia higher education institutions—the potential of AI-based learning outcomes. Sustainability 15(13), 10723 (2023)
6. Aizenberg, E., Van Den Hoven, J.: Designing for human rights in AI. Big Data Soc. 7(2), 2053951720949566 (2020)
7. Barron, L.: AI and Literature. In: AI and Popular Culture, pp. 47–87. Emerald Publishing Limited, Bingley (2023)
8. Bissessar, C.: To use or not to use ChatGPT and assistive artificial intelligence tools in higher education institutions? The modern-day conundrum–students' and faculty's perspectives. Equity Educ. Soc. 27526461231215083 (2023)
9. Burkhard, M.: Student perceptions of AI-powered writing tools: towards individualized teaching strategies. Int. Assoc. Dev. Inf. Soc. (2022)
10. Chatterjee, S., Bhattacharjee, K.K.: Adoption of artificial intelligence in higher education: a quantitative analysis using structural equation modelling. Educ. Inf. Technol. 25, 3443–3463 (2020)
11. Coelho, H., Primo, T.T.: Exploratory apprenticeship in the digital age with AI tools. Prog. Artif. Intell. 6, 17–25 (2017)

12. Copeland, B.J., Sylvan, R.: Beyond the universal turing machine. Australas. J. Philos. **77**(1), 46–66 (1999)
13. Delgado, H.O.K., de Azevedo Fay, A., Sebastiany, M.J., Silva, A.D.C.: Artificial intelligence adaptive learning tools: the teaching of English in focus. BELT-Braz. Engl. Lang. Teach. J. **11**(2), e38749–e38749 (2020)
14. Dobrev, D.: A definition of artificial intelligence. arXiv preprint arXiv:1210.1568 (2012)
15. Eaton, S.E.: Plagiarism in higher education, 2021
16. Gayed, J.M., Carlon, M.K.J., Oriola, A.M., Cross, J.S.: Exploring an AI-based writing assistant's impact on English language learners. Comput. Educ. Artif. Intell. **3**, 100055 (2022)
17. Farouqa, G., Hysaj, A.: Exploring faculty members perception of utilizing technology to enhance student engagement in the United Arab Emirates: technology and the ICAP modes of engagement. In: Meiselwitz, G. (eds.) Social Computing and Social Media: Applications in Education and Commerce. HCII 2022. LNCS, vol. 13316, pp. 67–76. Springer, Cham (2022). https://doi.org/10.1007/978-3-031-05064-0_5
18. Fitria, T.N.: Artificial intelligence (AI) technology in OpenAI ChatGPT application: a review of ChatGPT in writing English essay. ELT Forum J. Engl. Lang. Teach. **12**(1), 44–58 (2023)
19. Hamam, D., Hysaj, A.: Technological pedagogical and content knowledge (TPACK): higher education teachers' perspectives on the use of TPACK in online academic writing classes. In: Stephanidis, C., Antona, M., Ntoa, S. (eds.) HCI International 2021 - Posters. HCII 2021. CCIS, vol. 1421, pp. 51–58. Springer, Cham (2021). https://doi.org/10.1007/978-3-030-786 45-8_7
20. Hamam, D., Hysaj, A.: The aftermath of COVID 19: future insights for teachers' professional development in higher education. J. Asia TEFL **19**(1), 303 (2022)
21. Hancock, J.T., Naaman, M., Levy, K.: AI-mediated communication: definition, research agenda, and ethical considerations. J. Comput.-Mediat. Commun. **25**(1), 89–100 (2020)
22. Humble, N., Mozelius, P.: Artificial intelligence in education—a promise, a threat or a hype. In: Proceedings of the European Conference on the Impact of Artificial Intelligence and Robotics, pp. 149–156, October 2019
23. Hysaj, A., Elkhouly, A.: Why do students plagiarize? The case of multicultural students in an Australian university in the United Arab Emirates. Integrity in Education for Future Happiness, pp.64–77 (2020)
24. Hysaj, A., Suleymanova, S.: The analysis of developing the application of critical thinking in oral and written discussions: the case of Emirati students in the United Arab Emirates. In: 2020 IEEE International Conference on Teaching, Assessment, and Learning for Engineering (TALE), pp. 819–824. IEEE, December 2020
25. Hysaj, A., Suleymanova, S.: Safeguarding academic integrity in crisis induced environment: a case study of Emirati engineering and IT students in a private university in the UAE. In: Meiselwitz, G. (eds.) Social Computing and Social Media: Applications in Marketing, Learning, and Health. HCII 2021. LNCS, vol. 12775, pp. 236–245. Springer, Cham (2021). https://doi.org/10.1007/978-3-030-77685-5_19
26. Hysaj, A.: Group reports in the online platform: a puzzle, a ride in the park or a steep slope: a case study of multicultural undergraduate students in the United Arab Emirates. In: 2021 IEEE International Conference on Engineering, Technology & Education (TALE), pp. 745–750. IEEE, December 2021
27. Hysaj, A.: COVID-19 pandemic and online teaching from the lenses of K-12 STEM teachers in albania. In: 2021 IEEE International Conference on Engineering, Technology & Education (TALE), pp. 01–07. IEEE, December 2021
28. Hysaj, A., Hamam, D., Baroudi, S.: Efficacy of group work in the online platform: an exploration of multicultural undergraduates' attitudes in Online Academic Writing Classes. In:

Meiselwitz, G. (eds.) Social Computing and Social Media: Applications in Marketing, Learning, and Health. HCII 2021. LNCS, vol. 12775, pp. 246–256. Springer, Cham (2021). https://doi.org/10.1007/978-3-030-77685-5_20

29. Hysaj, A., Hamam, D.: Understanding the development of critical thinking through classroom debates and online discussion forums: a case of higher education in the UAE. J. Asia TEFL **18**(1), 373–379 (2021)

30. Hysaj, A., Hamam, D.: The Journal of Asia TEFL 2021

31. Hysaj, A., Khan, Z.R.: Understanding reasons students may plagiarize in online assessments. In: European Conference on Academic Integrity and Plagiarism, p. 38 (2021)

32. Hysaj, A., Hamam, D.: Dimensions of formative feedback during the COVID-19 pandemic: evaluating the perceptions of undergraduates in multicultural EAP classrooms. In: Meiselwitz, G. (eds.) Social Computing and Social Media: Applications in Education and Commerce. HCII 2022. LNCS, vol. 13316, pp. 103–114. Springer, Cham (2022). https://doi.org/10.1007/978-3-031-05064-0_8

33. Hysaj, A.: Exploring the impact of group video creation in multicultural students in the online platform. J. Asia TEFL **20**(1), 127–131 (2023)

34. Hysaj, A., Haroon, H.A.: Online formative assessment and feedback: a focus group discussion among language teachers. In: Meiselwitz, G. (eds.) Social Computing and Social Media: Applications in Education and Commerce. HCII 2022. LNCS, vol. 13316, pp. 115–126. Springer, Cham (2022). https://doi.org/10.1007/978-3-031-05064-0_9

35. Hysaj, A., Freeman, M., Khan, Z.R.: Theory of planned behaviour in higher education: exploring the perceptions of multicultural ESL students about cheating. In: Coman, A., Vasilache, S. (eds.) Social Computing and Social Media. HCII 2023. LNCS, vol. 14026, pp. 58–71. Springer, Cham (2023). https://doi.org/10.1007/978-3-031-35927-9_5

36. Hysaj, A., Farouqa, G., Khan, S.A., Hiasat, L.: Reducing stress through formative assessments: a case of the digital platform. In: Coman, A., Vasilache, S. (eds.) Social Computing and Social Media. HCII 2023. LNCS, vol. 14026, pp. 486–500. Springer, Cham (2023). https://doi.org/10.1007/978-3-031-35927-9_33

37. Hysaj, A., Hamam, D.: What does it take to develop critical thinking? The case of multicultural students in a digital learning platform. In: Coman, A., Vasilache, S. (eds.) Social Computing and Social Media. HCII 2023. LNCS, vol. 14026, pp. 49–57. Springer, Cham (2023). https://doi.org/10.1007/978-3-031-35927-9_4

38. Kacena, M.A., Plotkin, L.I., Fehrenbacher, J.C.: The use of artificial intelligence in writing scientific review articles. Curr. Osteoporos. Rep.1–7 (2024)

39. Kaplan, A., Haenlein, M.: Siri, Siri, in my hand: who's the fairest in the land? On the interpretations, illustrations, and implications of artificial intelligence. Bus. Horiz. **62**(1), 15–25 (2019)

40. Khan, Z.R., Hysaj, A., John, S.R., Khan, S.: Gateway to preparing K-12 students for higher education–reflections on organizing an academic integrity camp. In: European Conference on Academic Integrity and Plagiarism, p. 66 (2021)

41. Khan, Z.R., Balasubramanian, S., Hysaj, A.: Using the IEPAR framework-a workshop to build a culture of integrity in higher education. Concurr. Sess. **12**, 50 (2022)

42. Khan, Z.R., Hysaj, A., John, S.R., Khan, S.A.: Transitional module on academic integrity to help K-12 students in the UAE prepare for next stage of education. In: Bjelobaba, S., Foltýnek, T., Glendinning, I., Krásničan, V., Dlabolová, D.H. (eds.) Academic Integrity: Broadening Practices, Technologies, and the Role of Students. Ethics and Integrity in Educational Contexts, vol. 4, pp. 263–287. Springer, Cham (2022). https://doi.org/10.1007/978-3-031-16976-2_15

43. Kumar, R., Eaton, S.E., Mindzak, M., Morrison, R.: Academic integrity and artificial intelligence: an overview. In: Eaton, S.E. (eds.) Second Handbook of Academic Integrity, LNCS,

pp.1583–1596. Springer International Handbooks of Education. Springer, Cham (2024). https://doi.org/10.1007/978-3-031-54144-5_153

44. Lancaster, T.: Artificial intelligence, text generation tools and ChatGPT–does digital watermarking offer a solution? Int. J. Educ. Integr. **19**(1), 10 (2023)

45. Marzuki Widiati, U., Rusdin, D., Darwin Indrawati, I.: The impact of AI writing tools on the content and organization of students' writing: EFL teachers' perspective. Cogent Educ. **10**(2), 2236469 (2023)

46. Michel-Villarreal, R., Vilalta-Perdomo, E., Salinas-Navarro, D.E., Thierry-Aguilera, R., Gerardou, F.S.: Challenges and opportunities of generative AI for higher education as explained by ChatGPT. Educ. Sci. **13**(9), 856 (2023)

47. Moss, S.A., White, B., Lee, J.: A systematic review into the psychological causes and correlates of plagiarism. Ethics Behav. **28**(4), 261–283 (2018)

48. Motlagh, N.Y., Khajavi, M., Sharifi, A., Ahmadi, M.: The impact of artificial intelligence on the evolution of digital education: a comparative study of openAI text generation tools including ChatGPT, Bing Chat, Bard, and Ernie, pp. 3443–3463 (2023). arXiv preprint arXiv: 2309.02029

49. Nikolic, S., et al.: ChatGPT versus engineering education assessment: a multidisciplinary and multi-institutional benchmarking and analysis of this generative artificial intelligence tool to investigate assessment integrity. Eur. J. Eng. Educ. 1–56 (2023)

50. Ng, D.T.K., Lee, M., Tan, R.J.Y., Hu, X., Downie, J.S., Chu, S.K.W.: A review of AI teaching and learning from 2000 to 2020. Educ. Inf. Technol. **28**(7), 8445–8501 (2023)

51. Porter, A., Graham, S., Myles, F., Holmes, B.: Creativity, challenge and culture in the languages classroom: a response to the Ofsted curriculum research review. Lang. Learn. J. **50**(2), 208–217 (2022)

52. Sandu, N., Gide, E.: Adoption of AI-Chatbots to enhance student learning experience in higher education in India. In: 2019 18th International Conference on Information Technology Based Higher Education and Training (ITHET), pp. 1–5. IEEE, September 2019

53. Soler, R., Soler, J.R., Araya, I.: Subjects in the blended learning model design. Theoretical-methodological elements. Procedia-Soc. Behav. Sci. **237**, 771–777 (2017)

54. Sudlow, B.: Review of Joseph E. Aoun: Robot Proof: Higher Education in the Age of Artificial Intelligence, p. 187. The MIT Press, Cambridge, Massachusetts (2017). ISBN 9780262037280 2019

55. Suleymanova, S., Hysaj, A.: Undergraduate Emirati students' challenges of language barrier in meeting expectations of English medium university in the UAE. In: Meiselwitz, G. (eds.) Social Computing and Social Media: Applications in Education and Commerce. HCII 2022. LNCS, vol. 13316, pp. 199–209. Springer, Cham (2022). https://doi.org/10.1007/978-3-031-05064-0_15

56. Thacker, J.: The age of AI: artificial Intelligence and the Future of Humanity. Zondervan (2020)

57. Umbrello, S., Van de Poel, I.: Mapping value sensitive design onto AI for social good principles. AI Ethics **1**(3), 283–296 (2021)

58. Rahiman, H.U., Kodikal, R.: Revolutionizing education: artificial intelligence empowered learning in higher education. Cogent Educ. **11**(1), 2293431 (2024)

59. Rincón-Flores, E.G., López-Camacho, E., Mena, J., López, O.O.: Predicting academic performance with Artificial Intelligence (AI), a new tool for teachers and students. In: 2020 IEEE Global Engineering Education Conference (EDUCON), pp. 1049–1054. IEEE April, 2020

60. Van Leeuwen, J., Wiedermann, J.: The Turing machine paradigm in contemporary computing. Mathematics unlimited—2001 and beyond, pp. 1139–1155 (2001)

61. Vergara-Morales, J., Del Valle, M., Díaz, A., Matos, L., Pérez, M.V.: Motivational profiles related to the academic satisfaction of university students. Anales de Psicología/Ann. Psychol. **35**(3), 464–471 (2019)

62. von Garrel, J., Mayer, J.: Artificial Intelligence in studies—use of ChatGPT and AI-based tools among students in Germany. Humanit. Soc. Sci. Commun. **10**(1), 1–9 (2023)

63. Wang, Y., Liu, C., Tu, Y.F.: Factors affecting the adoption of AI-based applications in higher education. Educ. Technol. Soc. **24**(3), 116–129 (2021)

64. Wiener, J.B., Ribeiro, D.L.: Impact assessment: diffusion and integration. In: Comparative Law and Regulation, pp. 159–189. Edward Elgar Publishing, Cheltenham (2016)

65. Whittlestone, J., Nyrup, R., Alexandrova, A., Dihal, K., Cave, S.: Ethical and Societal Implications of Algorithms, Data, and Artificial Intelligence: A Roadmap for Research. Nuffield Foundation, London (2019)

66. Yang, S., Evans, C.: Opportunities and challenges in using AI chatbots in higher education. In: Proceedings of the 2019 3rd International Conference on Education and E-Learning, pp. 79–83, November 2019

67. Yang, X., et al.: A survey on detection of llms-generated content (2023). arXiv preprint arXiv: 2310.15654

68. Zalazar-Jaime, M.F., Moretti, L.S., García-Batista, Z.E., Medrano, L.A.: Evaluation of an academic satisfaction model in E-learning education contexts. Interact. Learn. Environ. **31**(7), 4687–4697 (2023)

Using AI Tools to Enhance Academic Writing and Maintain Academic Integrity

Ajrina Hysaj[1]($\boxtimes$) (ID), Mark Freeman[2] (ID), and Doaa Hamam[3] (ID)

[1] UOWD College, University of Wollongong in Dubai, Dubai, UAE
`Ajrinahysaj@uowdubai.ac.ae`
[2] University of Sydney, Sydney, Australia
`mark.freeman1@sydney.edu.au`
[3] Higher Colleges of Technology Dubai, Dubai, UAE
`dhamam@hct.ac.ae`

Abstract. AI tools have become an important part of our professional lives, whether on the business level or the academic level. They play a crucial role for students and teachers. This has created the need to explore undergraduate students' perceptions of such tools, as there is a need to know how and why students use these tools. Those perceptions should be considered when applying adaptations to the curriculum, aiming to ensure a constructive environment where students benefit from these tools and learn simultaneously. So, the focus of this study was to explore reasons and ways why multicultural students use paraphrasing and AI tools, as well as their opinions about plagiarism and academic writing. Two focus groups participated in the study, each comprising five undergraduate students whose first language was not English. Students were from different countries and backgrounds, and they also spoke different first languages. The focus groups aimed to explore undergraduate students' perceptions of plagiarism, academic writing, and the use of AI tools in Higher Education. The collected data was analysed using qualitative methods. Finally, recommendations for future research were presented.

Keywords: Academic writing · AI Tools · ESL · Academic Integrity · Skills · Plagiarism

1 Introduction

English as a second language instructors and educators are aware of the variety of academic and personal needs that learners of the English language have when attending academic writing classes in universities or any other discipline-related subjects, especially those that require extensive academic writing work. The academic writing difficulties of multicultural undergraduate students whose English is not their first language are mainly related to a lack of adequate academic vocabulary and grammar skills [1, 3, 4, 40, 51]. Furthermore, multicultural students may lack the understanding of how to conduct research and cite sources since these skills are not commonly taught in most schools worldwide. Lack of emphasis on research, referencing and mechanics of academic writing skills in general creates a vacuum in the existing knowledge present in undergraduate

A. Coman and S. Vasilache (Eds.): HCII 2024, LNCS 14704, pp. 57–66, 2024.
https://doi.org/10.1007/978-3-031-61305-0_4

students [2, 5, 27]. Therefore, undergraduates are expected to develop the skills required to complete academic writing tasks in universities parallelly with the skills required to complete other non-academic writing tasks in most discipline-related subjects. Although the number of non-writing tasks is generally equal to the number of academic writing tasks or slightly higher in the natural sciences disciplines and vice-versa in humanities, education and business-related degrees, undergraduates of all majors are resistant to the fact that academic writing is crucial for their academic writing assessment and consider it as irrelevant to their studies in general [5, 6, 8, 10, 11, 32].

Generally, undergraduates consider academic writing difficult mainly because they lack general English vocabulary and grammar. It is a common fact that they often ask others for help. In many cases, they may indulge in instances of plagiarism due to the lack of adequate knowledge of how to write academically and cite appropriately. Moreover, as the technology advances and the widespread of AI and paraphrasing tools take an unprecedented role, especially as the likes of AI tools like ChatGPT, it is not uncommon for undergraduates to direct their academic needs and often their shortcomings to these tools and explore ways of using them to their benefit [39]. Although the utilisation of such tools does not come without challenges, undergraduates are willing to explore them and subsequently use them to their benefit, and very often, they would consider this as legitimate because English is not their first language and studying in English medium universities is as hard as it can get [7, 8, 11–13].

Since academic writing in English language is unquestionably daunting for multicultural undergraduates and their involvement in the use of AI tools is prevalent, it becomes imminent to explore their perceptions about the use of such tools in completing academic writing tasks, as well as their perceptions about plagiarism and academic integrity in general [9–11, 31]. The focus of this paper was to explore these perceptions and utilise the opinions of students in adapting the curriculum of academic writing classes to bridge the gap between students' existing level of knowledge of academic writing, their personal beliefs about plagiarism and the reasons why AI tools are used by undergraduates as well as the ways that they have been utilised. The level of engagement that students have in academic writing classes could be an indication of the degree of confidence that they have in writing academically and completing assessment tasks that require the use of sophisticated language on a well-researched topic. One way of encouraging active engagement in academic writing classes is by involving undergraduate students in open discussions about difficulties that they face when writing academically. As pointed out in the study of Martin and Bolliger [36], students' active engagement has the potential to be translated into improved academic performance [12–14, 28, 29]. According to Moore's interaction framework, the ways that students are engaged in classrooms are learner-to-instructor, learner-to-learner and learner-to-content [15, 16, 36].

Since the purpose of this study was to explore reasons why undergraduates use paraphrasing or AI tools, the focus of the framework related to engagement was that of the learner to content, especially with the difficulties faced by undergraduate students when writing academically. Furthermore, the aim of this paper was to understand students' perceptions about AI tools and plagiarism through guided questions, which has proven to be generally very beneficial for students and can have implications for instructors and instructional designers alike [4–6, 11, 17, 18]. As mentioned in the study by Breen [6], discussions in focus groups have the potential to provide a rewarding learning experience for students because they encourage them to establish a connection between the topics that are discussed and the relevance that those topics have with the participants academic or personal ambitions [13, 14, 19]. Nevertheless, an ultimate disfavour is done when students are engaged in discussions that are irrelevant to their personal or academic goals. Engaging students in discussions about academic writing can empower them with thoughts of the utilisation of AI tools while complying with academic integrity rules and upholding academic integrity values [20, 29, 30, 54].

2 Literature Review

2.1 Using Focus Groups to Identify Students' Perceptions of What Constitutes Plagiarism

Research on plagiarism tends to define the concept of plagiarism from students' perspectives in a rather ambiguous way. Much of it relates to the notions of plagiarism from teachers' and institutional perspectives rather than the perspectives of those who are caught committing it, e.g., students. Moreover, such definitions of notions of plagiarism may be prescribed in a rather shallow fashion and do not necessarily include the variety of cultures, mother tongues and nations. The concept of culture is very important when considering the rate of self-reported cases of plagiarism since different cultures adhere to different value systems, and not all the students would therefore be comfortable in self-reporting plagiarism [5, 8, 11, 21, 23, 32, 52, 53]. Part of the problem may be connected with the aspect of shame of committing any wrongdoings present in some cultures or with the resistance towards accepting such wrongdoings. Furthermore, as mentioned in the works by Park [40] and Trushell, Byrne and Simpson [51], students of collective cultures may consider it right to help others, e.g., family and friends, even if not in every lawful means as far as the end result is passing a subject or maintaining a much-needed scholarship. Not only do students from collective cultures consider this kind of support as necessary, but they also feel that it is not breaking any moral rules despite breaking institutional rules and regulations in most countries [4, 22, 35, 37, 37, 50, 51].

Another aspect that tends to be neglected when discussing plagiarism in ESL classrooms is the perceptions of fairness and equality from the perspective of ESL students. Most ESL students feel that it is unfair that their intellectual abilities are put to the test when writing English academically [5, 7, 8, 11, 24, 32, 49]. They feel that most of the time, they are unaware of not only the mechanics of academic writing in the English language but also, they are short of ideas on how the language nuances may vary and how the thought could be developed in a cohesive and coherent fashion. Rettinger and Kramer [44] and Trost [50] stated that ESL students often fail to realise that they have committed plagiarism because they have an extremely hard time understanding the journal articles when reading them. Although such occurrence may as well be relevant to students whose first language is English, it is yet more prevalent in students whose first language is not English and, as such, is rightly related to the lack of receptive and productive skills in the English language [25, 33–35, 48]. Many ESL students would agree that they find it valuable to learn ways of avoiding plagiarism by improving their academic writing skills. Yet, they may not know how to do it, and their first language and culture may hinder recognition and avoid plagiarism rather than support it.

2.2 Exploring Reasons Students Use AI Paraphrasing Tools in Academic Writing

The prominence of academic writing in higher education is well-known, and so is the necessity to develop it when learning English as a second language and aiming to be enrolled in English medium universities [45–47]. Research in the discipline of English language teaching has generally focused on analysing teachers' perceptions, but not enough has been done to explore students' perceptions. The perceptions of students about academic writing and writing in general, relate to their perceptions of the use of paraphrasing or AI tools to write academically. According to a study by Ismail [31], when participating in focus groups, students tend to be open to exploring the perceptions of others about issues relevant to them and employ the newly constructed knowledge in the new encounters they have in newly constructed realities. Furthermore, the same study found that students were open to talking about their difficulties when writing academically, and it is important that teachers see their opinions as valuable and subsequently get included in the adaptations of the curriculum design. Understandably, awareness of students' needs is the steppingstone towards dealing with these needs and subsequently can lead to including them in the alignment of the curriculum design of academic writing skills classes [26–29, 43, 45].

Studies of theory and research in human psychology show that understanding students' needs and views can support the path towards supporting these needs and nurturing the process of broadening students' horizons in support of improved behaviour regarding teaching and learning and utilisation of paraphrasing and AI tools for learning academic writing [27, 30, 41, 42, 46, 48]. The thorough exploration of students' needs, which can be made possible through in-depth interviews or focus groups, could contribute to successful changes in the behaviour of students [15]. Questions asked in focus groups are formulated around themes that are generated from specific headings related to the topic in question; hence, analysing the findings from the focus groups through qualitative means looking into the depth of students' thoughts can consequently support the process of utilising the paraphrasing and AI tools to write academically while maintaining upholding academic integrity and maintaining adequate levels of academic writing proficiency [8, 9, 29, 31, 31, 40]. For instance, although students use paraphrasing or AI tools, they may feel confusion or fear when using them. These emotions may come from worries that they may have academic consequences of using them. In other words, despite the widespread use of paraphrasing or AI tools among students, it is valuable that educators investigate regulating such usage [27, 35, 47, 54]. The starting point of this regulation comes from recognising students' needs and acknowledging their use of the tools [29, 33, 38, 39, 45]. This exploration can potentially empower students with the understanding of the adequate use of the tools, and this can result in supporting teaching and learning rather than doing a disservice to the process as a whole.

3   Methodology

The study utilized qualitative methods and involved focus groups. The research focused on four aspects: 1) identifying students' perceptions of what constitutes plagiarism, 2) identifying reasons for using paraphrasing or AI tools, c) exploring students' perceptions of the usefulness of paraphrasing or AI tools and d) exploring students' perceptions of ways of using paraphrasing or AI tools. The approach taken in this study was that of deductive qualitative research that draws lessons from the theoretical approach and applies those to the collection and analysis of the data (Pearse, 2019, June). The rationale behind choosing this approach was connected with the potential that the deductive qualitative research provides a platform for addressing issues related to the thematic understanding of knowledge of behavioural and social processes connected with the utilisation of paraphrasing tools in students' academic writing and instances of plagiarism. Nevertheless, it is worth pointing out that since focus groups focus on in-depth questioning techniques, analysing the results is lengthy and complex.

Two focus groups, each with five student members, were chosen for the purpose of data collection. Students participating in the focus groups were from various countries and spoke different first languages. The language used during the focus groups was English. To ensure that the participants were equipped with the adequate language skills to elaborate on the themes chosen for the focus groups, purpose random sampling was chosen as adequate for this stage of the study, and all the students who participated in the first focus groups acquired an IELTS score of 5.5 and the second focus group, IELTS score was 6 or 6.5. This step was taken to ensure that participants had the linguistic abilities to provide sufficient information required to answer the research questions. Participants were all students enrolled in various undergraduate degrees at the time of the study and were all enrolled in multicultural universities in the UAE, Canada and Australia. Positions held by students were influenced by their perspectives, which contributed to the examination of the research questions. All the participants signed a consent form and were encouraged to express their opinions in a long, in-depth way, which, as a result, helped in extracting codes and categories to answer the research questions. The qualitative tool used to analyse the data generated from the focus group was NVivo. First, the themes that were more common in the discussion were singled out, and then the software was used to explore the degree to which these themes influence students' intention to self-report plagiarism and to use paraphrasing and AI tools to write academically. It is worth mentioning that this study is part of a larger-scale PhD thesis that aims to investigate the utilisation of paraphrasing tools to reduce instances of plagiarism based on the theory of planned behaviour.

4   Results

Based on data analysis, two key themes emerged from the data: inadequate vocabulary and grammar skills, lack of time management, and increased stress levels, which may result in increased instances of plagiarism.

4.1 Inadequate Vocabulary and Grammar Skills

Writing has always been perceived as the most bothersome and challenging skill to develop for most students. The difficulties related to writing depend on the degree of English language development in each student. This study found that students with weaker vocabulary and grammar skills used paraphrasing tools to increase their understanding of the topic and improve the degree to which they could use the new vocabulary and grammatical forms. Students with an IELTS score of 5.5 mentioned using the tools as beneficial to improve their linguistic abilities. One of the students mentioned that: "I use the tools as I feel my vocabulary is very limited". Another student mentioned that: "Although I try hard to express myself in writing, I feel that my sentences are short and not clear". One of the students mentioned that he used the tools very often: "The structure of my first language is different from the structure of the English language. In my language, verbs are added at the end of the sentences, and I always forget this when writing. The translation and paraphrasing tools help me with the sentence structure and help me stay focused". Another student mentioned: "I use the tools because I feel that my vocabulary is poor, and even if I try to use similar words, I use them wrong".

The difficulty experienced due to inadequate vocabulary and grammar skills was mainly noticed in the focus group, whose participants had achieved an IELTS score of 5.5, and was less prevalent in the focus group, where participants had achieved an IELTS score of 6.0 or 6.5. The qualitative analysis of the data showed that the challenges of vocabulary and grammar skills hindered students' learning and were highly connected with their academic satisfaction. All five students who scored 5.5 in IELTS mentioned that they were surprised when they started attending foundation-level subjects because they found the English language used in journal articles difficult to comprehend and thought it was even more challenging to write about. One of the students mentioned that: "I understand only a small amount of what I read in journal articles, and I feel I cannot write about it". "Most of what I read is very complex, and the sentences are long and confusing for me". Interestingly, two out of five students who pointed out that they had difficulty with vocabulary and grammar skills highlighted that: "It is nice when our English teacher explains the topic through activities in class". "I like it when my teacher encourages me to read articles and helps me to find them". It is worth mentioning that students who had received a lower IELTS score considered writing more important than students who had received a higher IELTS score. All the five students who had received an IELTS score of 5.5 stressed that: "English is very important for their studies in higher education".

4.2 Lack of Time Management and Increased Stress Levels and Increased Plagiarism Instances

Students in both focus groups mentioned that often, they are short of time and may opt to plagiarise. "We know that copying and pasting is wrong, but we do not have time to write appropriately", mentioned one of the students. Another student said "I procrastinate easily, and although I know that plagiarism is morally wrong, I feel it is the only way that I can finish assignments on time". One of the participants who aimed at receiving higher distinction in his assignments pointed out: "I research a lot before writing an assignment, and then I lose focus and try to finish my assignments on time". "Very often, I find myself less worried about plagiarism and more concerned about submitting on time and receiving an HD". Seven out of ten students who participated in the focus groups were of the opinion that most subjects have assignments at similar times and found it challenging to complete them simultaneously. They highlighted that in schools, it is different because teachers break down the tasks in the lessons, and they have small quizzes to take before the big tests, while in university, teachers expect them to be more independent and not focus very much on small tests that can prepare them for their English assignments.

5 Discussion

While the use of paraphrasing and AI tools and the widespread plagiarism instances continue to dominate the arena of higher education, involving students in the discussion and taking into consideration their voices seem the most suitable plan of action [32, 34, 36]. Consideration of students' voices not only supports the understanding of their perceptions but can also help teachers in designing better-aligned curricula. The results of this study agreed with those of Cotton, Cotton and Shipway [9], who pointed out that the most common issues that encourage the use of paraphrasing tools and, in many cases, involvement of students in plagiarism instances are related to lack of time management skills, inadequate knowledge of linguistic abilities in English language and the inability to write academically. Furthermore, this study found that irrespective of what happens on the technology side, it is valuable to consider all the technological advances that could be utilised in favour of teaching and learning, provided that we understand and utilize them appropriately. This finding also concurs with Cotton, Cotton and Shipway [9] and Nicolic et al. [39], who tend to view paraphrasing and AI tools as educational tools that could add value to teaching and learning and are understood appropriately and utilised accordingly.

6 Conclusion and Recommendations

In conclusion, while the findings of this study cannot be generalised because they were based only on two focus groups and the sample was limited, the findings do provide adequate information about changes required to take place in the way academic writing is taught in class and ways that it is assessed. In other words, it is important to break down the assessment tasks into smaller tasks and organise classroom activities to facilitate students' understanding. Another important step that should be taken is to start using paraphrasing tools, especially to improve the vocabulary and grammar skills of weaker students [14, 16, 17, 29, 36, 37]. Another valuable finding of this study is to include reflective tasks in academic writing classes so students can develop their critical and analytical thinking abilities while writing in a less formal format. Furthermore, teachers should aim to design classroom materials with more activities and tasks that support the teaching and learning of writing strategies, such as summarising, coherence, cohesion, unity, searching for information and paraphrasing. Finally, this study should be followed by studies that analyse the improvement in curriculum design and the inclusion of paraphrasing or AI tools in the process of teaching and learning academic writing skills.

References

1. Angell, L.R.: The relationship of impulsiveness, personal efficacy, and academic motivation to college cheating. Coll. Stud. J. **40**(1), 118–131 (2006)
2. Ansorge, L., Ansorgeová, K., Sixsmith, M.: Plagiarism through paraphrasing tools—the story of one plagiarized text. Publications **9**(4), 48 (2021)
3. Barnas, M.: "Parenting" students: applying developmental psychology to the college classroom. Teach. Psychol. **27**, 276–277 (2000)
4. Belter, R.W., DuPre, A.: A strategy to reduce plagiarism in an undergraduate course. Teach. Psychol. **36**(4), 257–261 (2009)
5. Blum, S.D.: My Word! Plagiarism and College Culture. Cornell University Press, Ithaca NY (2009)
6. Breen, R.L.: A practical guide to focus-group research. J. Geogr. High. Educ. **30**(3), 463–475 (2006)
7. Childers, D., Bruton, S.: "Should it be considered plagiarism?" Student perceptions of complex citation issues. J. Acad. Ethics **14**, 1–17 (2016)
8. Colnerud, G., Rosander, M.: Academic dishonesty, ethical norms, and learning. Assess. Eval. High. Educ. **34**(5), 505–517 (2009)
9. Cotton, D.R., Cotton, P.A., Shipway, J.R.: Chatting and cheating: ensuring academic integrity in the era of ChatGPT. In: Innovations in Education and Teaching International, pp.1–12 (2023)
10. Dinneen, C.: Students' use of digital translation and paraphrasing tools in written assignments on direct entry English programs. Engl. Aust. J. **37**(1), 40–51 (2021)
11. Engler, J.N., Landau, J.D., Epstein, M.: Keeping up with the joneses: students' perceptions of academically dishonest behavior. Teach. Psychol. **35**, 99–102 (2008)
12. Farouqa, G., Hysaj, A.: Active Learning in the lenses of faculty: a qualitative study in universities in the United Arab Emirates. In: International Conference on Human-Computer Interaction, pp. 77–90. Springer, Cham (2022)
13. Farouqa, G., Hysaj, A.: Exploring faculty members perception of utilizing technology to enhance student engagement in the United Arab Emirates: technology and the ICAP Modes of engagement. In: Meiselwitz, G. (eds.) Social Computing and Social Media: Applications in Education and Commerce, HCII 2022. Lecture Notes in Computer Science, vol. 13316, pp. 67–76. Springer, Cham (2022). https://doi.org/10.1007/978-3-031-05064-0_5
14. Fitria, T.N.: QuillBot as an online tool: Students' alternative in paraphrasing and rewriting of English writing. Englisia: J. Lang. Educ. Human. **9**(1), 183–196 (2021)
15. Gullifer, J., Tyson, G.A.: Exploring university students' perceptions of plagiarism: a focus group study. Stud. High. Educ. **35**(4), 463–481 (2010)
16. Hamam, D., Hysaj, A.: Technological pedagogical and content knowledge (TPACK): Higher education teachers' perspectives on the use of TPACK in online academic writing classes. In: Stephanidis, C., Antona, M., Ntoa, S. (eds.) HCII 2021. CCIS, vol. 1421, pp. 51–58. Springer, Cham (2021). https://doi.org/10.1007/978-3-030-78645-8_7
17. Hamam, D., Hysaj, A.: The aftermath of COVID 19: future insights for teachers' professional development in higher education. J. Asia TEFL **19**(1), 303 (2022)
18. Hysaj, A., Elkhouly, A.: Why do students plagiarize? The case of multicultural students in an Australian university in the United Arab Emirates. In: Integrity in Education for Future Happiness, pp.64–77 (2020)

19. Hysaj, A.: Group reports in the online platform: a puzzle, a ride in the park or a steep slope: a case study of multicultural undergraduate students in the United Arab Emirates. In: 2021 IEEE International Conference on Engineering, Technology & Education (TALE), pp. 745–750. IEEE (2021)

20. Hysaj, A.: COVID-19 pandemic and online teaching from the lenses of K-12 STEM teachers in Albania. In: 2021 IEEE International Conference on Engineering, Technology & Education (TALE), pp. 01–07. IEEE (2021)

21. Hysaj, A., Hamam, D., Baroudi, S.: Efficacy of group work in the online platform: an exploration of multicultural undergraduates' attitudes in online academic writing classes. In: Meiselwitz, G. (ed.) HCII 2021. LNCS, vol. 12775, pp. 246–256. Springer, Cham (2021). https://doi.org/10.1007/978-3-030-77685-5_20

22. Hysaj, A., Hamam, D.: Understanding the development of critical thinking through classroom debates and online discussion forums: a case of higher education in the UAE. J. Asia TEFL **18**(1), 373–379 (2021)

23. Hysaj, A., Hamam, D.: The Journal of Asia TEFL 2021

24. Hysaj, A., Khan, Z.R.: Understanding reasons students may plagiarize in online assessments. In: European Conference on Academic Integrity and Plagiarism, p. 38 (2021)

25. Hysaj, A., Hamam, D.: Dimensions of formative feedback during the COVID-19 pandemic: evaluating the perceptions of undergraduates in multicultural EAP classrooms. In: Meiselwitz, G. (eds.) Social Computing and Social Media: Applications in Education and Commerce. HCII 2022. Lecture Notes in Computer Science, vol. 13316, pp. 103–114. Springer, Cham (2022). https://doi.org/10.1007/978-3-031-05064-0_8

26. Hysaj, A., Haroon, H.A.: Online formative assessment and feedback: a focus group discussion among language teachers. In: Meiselwitz, G. (eds.) Social Computing and Social Media: Applications in Education and Commerce, HCII 2022. Lecture Notes in Computer Science, vol. 13316, pp. 115–126. Springer, Cham (2022). https://doi.org/10.1007/978-3-031-05064-0_9

27. Hysaj, A., Hamam, D.: What does it take to develop critical thinking? The case of multicultural students in a digital learning platform. In: Coman, A., Vasilache, S. (eds.) Social Computing and Social Media, HCII 2023. Lecture Notes in Computer Science, vol. 14026, pp. 49–57. Springer, Cham (2023). https://doi.org/10.1007/978-3-031-35927-9_4

28. Hysaj, A., Farouqa, G., Khan, S.A., Hiasat, L.: Reducing stress through formative assessments: a case of the digital platform. In: Coman, A., Vasilache, S. (eds.) Social Computing and Social Media, HCII 2023. Lecture Notes in Computer Science, vol. 14026, pp. 486–500. Springer, Cham (2023). https://doi.org/10.1007/978-3-031-35927-9_33

29. Hysaj, A., Freeman, M., Khan, Z.R.: Theory of planned behaviour in higher education: exploring the perceptions of multicultural ESL students about cheating. In: Coman, A., Vasilache, S. (eds.) Social Computing and Social Media, HCII 2023. Lecture Notes in Computer Science, vol. 14026, pp. 58–71. Springer, Cham (2023). https://doi.org/10.1007/978-3-031-35927-9_5

30. Hysaj, A.: Exploring the impact of group video creation in multicultural students in the online platform. J. AsiaTEFL **20**(1), 127–131 (2023)

31. Ismail, S.A.A.: Exploring students' perceptions of ESL writing. Engl. Lang. Teach. **4**(2), 73–83 (2011)

32. Jones, D.L.R.: Academic dishonesty: are more students cheating? Bus. Commun. Q. **74**(2), 141–150 (2011)

33. Kayaoğlu, M.N., Erbay, Ş, Flitner, C., Saltaş, D.: Examining students' perceptions of plagiarism: a cross-cultural study at tertiary level. J. Furth. High. Educ. **40**(5), 682–705 (2016)

34. Khadawardi, H.A.: Saudi learners' perceptions of academic writing challenges and general attitude towards writing in English. J. Lang. Teach. Res. **13**(3), 645–658 (2022)

35. Kwong, T., Ng, H.M., Mark, K.P., Wong, E.: Students' and faculty's perception of academic integrity in Hong Kong. Campus-Wide Inf. Syst. **27**(5), 341–355 (2010)
36. Martin, F., Bolliger, D.U.: Engagement matters: Student perceptions on the importance of engagement strategies in the online learning environment. Online Learn. **22**(1), 205–222 (2018)
37. McCabe, D.L., Trevino, L.K., Butterfield, K.D.: Cheating in academic institutions: a decade of research. Ethics Behav. **11**(3), 219–233 (2001)
38. Miranda, D.: The Impact of Paraphrasing Tools on Students Paraphrasing Skills (Doctoral dissertation, UIn Ar-Raniry) (2022)
39. Nikolic, S., et al.: ChatGPT versus engineering education assessment: a multidisciplinary and multi-institutional benchmarking and analysis of this generative artificial intelligence tool to investigate assessment integrity. Eur. J. Eng. Educ., 1–56 (2023)
40. Park, C.: In other (people's) words: Plagiarism by university students – literature and lessons. Assess. Eval. High. Educ. **28**(5), 471–488 (2003)
41. Pearse, N.: An illustration of deductive analysis in qualitative research. In: 18th European Conference on Research Methodology for Business and Management Studies, p. 264 (2019)
42. Powers, L.G.: University students' perceptions of plagiarism. J. High. Educ. **80**(6), 643–662 (2009)
43. Prentice, F.M., Kinden, C.E.: Paraphrasing tools, language translation tools and plagiarism: an exploratory study. Int. J. Educ. Integr. **14**(1), 1–16 (2018)
44. Rettinger, D.A., Kramer, Y.: Situational and personal causes of student cheating. Res. High. Educ. **50**, 293–313 (2009)
45. Roe, J., Perkins, M.: What are Automated Paraphrasing Tools and how do we address them? A review of a growing threat to academic integrity. Int. J. Educ. Integr. **18**(1), 15 (2022)
46. Rogerson, A.M.: 13 the use and misuse of online paraphrasing, editing and translation software. In: A Research Agenda for Academic Integrity, p. 163 (2020)
47. Stokel-Walker, C.: AI bot ChatGPT writes smart essays-should academics worry? Nature (2022). https://doi.org/10.1038/d41586-022-04397-7
48. Sulistyaningrum, S.D.: Employing online paraphrasing tools to overcome students' difficulties in paraphrasing. Stairs: Engl. Lang. Educ. J. **2**(1), 52–59 (2021)
49. Sulistyaningrum, S.D.: Utilizing online paraphrasing tools to overcome students' paraphrasing difficulties in literature reviews. J. Engl. Lang. Stud. **6**(2), 229–243 (2021)
50. Trost, K.: Psst, have you ever cheated? A study of academic dishonesty in Sweden. Assess. Eval. High. Educ. **34**(4), 367–376 (2009)
51. Trushell, J., Byrne, K., Simpson, R.: Cheating behaviours, the internet and education undergraduate students. J. Comput. Assist. Learn. **28**(2), 136–145 (2012)
52. Wang, Y.: University student online plagiarism. Int. J. E-Learn. **7**(4), 743–757 (2008)
53. Williams, K.M., Nathanson, C., Paulhus, D.L.: Identifying and profiling scholastic cheaters: their personality, cognitive ability, and motivation. J. Exp. Psychol. Appl. **16**, 293–307 (2010)
54. Wollny, S., Schneider, J., Di Mitri, D., Weidlich, J., Rittberger, M., Drachsler, H.: Are we there yet? - A systematic literature review on chatbots in education. Front. Artif. Intell. **4**, 654924 (2021). https://doi.org/10.3389/frai.2021.654924

Investigation on the Use of Mora in Assessment of L2 Speakers' Japanese Language Proficiency

Yuta Isshiki and Hung-Hsuan Huang[✉]

Faculty of Informatics, The University of Fukuchiyama, Fukuchiyama, Japan
hhhuang@acm.org

Abstract. This paper presents the analysis on the language use of non-native (L2) Japanese speakers with focus on their proficiency in group discussion conversations. Due to the demographic development the necessity to close the resulting gap with foreign employees/workers and thus, non-native speakers is increasing. This work is based on a corpus collected in an experiment which acquired multimodal sensory data in collaborative tasks with unbalanced mixed setup, composed of one none-native speaker and three native (L1) speakers. Each group was given the task to discuss two topics and find a joint decision. This work aims to find the insights how the proficiency of the speakers and the difference in being a native or non-native speakers changes the used vocabulary and decision-making process, which will later be a major issue to ensure an efficient work of such mixed groups. The analysis is based on findings of a total number of seven groups and thus seven L2 speakers. The analysis is on the mora duration of the participants during the discussion, the stability of L1 and L2 speakers are compared with overall statistical information. We also introduced the use of one-dimensional convolution neural networks to analyze micro characteristics of the sequence of moral durations. The results show that it is positive to adopt the characteristics in automatic assessment on the proficiency level of L2 speakers.

Keywords: Multiparty interaction · group discussion · multimodal interaction · L2 learner · conversation analysis · Japanese language education · convolutional neural network

1 Introduction

In developed countries, the declining birthrate and aging population are progressing. Especially in Japan, the ratio of the population over 65 years old has been already as high as 28.1% and is expected to over 1/3 by 2036. On the other hand, the total population is expected to continuously decrease to be less than 100 million from current 126.4 million by 2053 [2]. In order to supplement the decreasing working population, Japanese government has started to relax the regulations on introducing foreign workers. The increase of foreigner workers in Japanese society can be expected in near future. In such a situation, foreigner workers are the minority and have to collaboratively work with Japanese colleagues who are the majority. The working environment is optimized for the Japanese, the rules of the company were also established by the

Japanese. Not only the language barrier, but the differences in habits, the way of thinking, common ground, and the communication styles oriented from cultural backgrounds may inhibit efficient team work.

Under an unbalanced environment where non-native (L2) speakers have to work with native (L1) speakers who are in majority, the L2 speakers may show degraded performance on the task due to the burden of language and unfamiliarity of the local culture. This may further decrease the team efficiency. Our project is aiming to understand the issues which may occur in an unbalanced teamwork, based on the results we would like to develop supportive technologies to close the gap and improve the team efficiency. This work is based on the corpus collected in an experiment which acquired multimodal sensory data in collaborative tasks with unbalanced group setup: each group is composed of one L2 speaker and three L1 speakers. Each group discussed two topics and made joint decisions on them. One topic is a free brainstorming one and the other one is the ranking problem on a list of candidates. There are less limits in the vocabulary of the former one and it is supposed to be more difficult for a L2 speaker to join. The discussion on the later one is supposed to be surrounding the candidates and thus should be easier for the L2 speakers to join. Each session for one topic is 15 min long. Experiments with such mixed groups as well as homogeneous groups (all L1 Japanese speakers speaking in Japanese, all L1 Chinese speakers speaking in Chinese) are conducted. From our knowledge, there is no such corpus available and we believe the data collected can provide valuable resources for developing tools in supporting unbalanced groups.

The best way to improve the ability to speak a foreign language is by speaking a lot with its native speakers. However, it is generally difficult to get a native speaking conversation partner to practice conversation with a L2 speaker at a time and place of the L2 speaker's choice. Intelligent virtual agents which can simulate some specific communication style, including the language itself, gestures, facial expressions as well as cultural backgrounds are good examples of such tools [9, 15]. L2 speakers can then practice how to communicate with L1 speakers through the interaction with intelligent virtual L1 agents in a virtual environment where various situations can be simulated.

During the interaction, to help the L2 speaker to improve his/her speaking skill, the system needs to automatically assess the language proficiency level of the L2 participant and adjust the behaviors of the virtual agents according to the L2 speaker's level in runtime. Many factors like pronunciation, grammar, vocabularies, fluency and so on can be considered to assess the language proficiency of the L2 speakers. We previously analyzed the use of words of L2 speakers regarding their proficiency level [5]. We did find some characteristics which can be used as the features to assess L2 speakers' level, but they are not deterministic. In this specific paper, we report our exploration on the potential of using *mora* in the automatic assessment of L2 speakers' proficiency level.

Mora is a linguistic term that denotes a basic timing unit of a certain spoken language. A syllable is composed of one or multiple moras. Not all languages can be counted by moras, but the Japanese language is one of those mora languages. In Japanese, a mora is also called a *haku (beat)*. Its duration is usually the same as a Japanese kana but with some exceptions: a sokuon (lengthened consonant) itself does not involve voice production but is counted as one mora. It does not exist individually but must be surrounded by other sounds. A choon (long sound) is counted as two moras. L1 Japanese speakers are known to speak in nearly even mora durations while adult Japanese learners whose language abilities have already developed are influenced by their native language and cannot move their mouths and tongues so smoothly and precisely as L1 speakers. The instability of mora duration causes the unnatural perception of their pronunciation and is observed as a characteristic to assess L2 speaker's proficiency level [11, 13].

This paper reports the investigation of the research questions on a subset of the data corpus. Seven groups and thus seven L2 speakers are analyzed and are compared with 21 L1 speakers. The analysis is on the mora durations of L1 and L2 Japanese speakers. In addition to basic statistical metrics, we also conducted machine learning experiments based on one-dimension convolutional neural networks (CNN) [8]. Such 1D CNNs extracts the relationship among the neighboring elements of a sequential data in their contribution to the final learning results. We use this technique to find the reason for the consequent consonant-vowel-consonant-vowel-.... can distinguish L1 and L2 speakers. We also compare the characteristics of mora durations on the proficiency levels (low, middle, high).

1D CNNs extracts the relationship among the neighboring elements of a sequential data in their contribution to the final learning results. We use this technique to find the reason for the consequent consonant-vowel-consonant-vowel-.... can distinguish L1 and L2 speakers. We also compare the characteristics of mora durations on the proficiency levels (low, middle, high). In this paper, we investigated the following research questions:

RQ1: Are there any distinguishing characteristics of mora durations among proficiency levels in practical conversation?

RQ2: If the answer of RQ1 is "yes," is it possible to utilize mora durations in the assessment of proficiency levels?

RQ3: If the answer of RQ2 is "yes," what is the potential cause of the characteristics? Is it possible to use the information to support L2 learners?

The paper is organized as the follows, Sect. 2 introduces related works, Sect. 3 introduces the data corpus used in this work, Sect. 4 explains the procedure of how the analysis was conducted and discuss the analysis results, and Sect. 5 concludes the paper.

2   Related Works

In the computer science field, there have been research works on machine learning based on nonverbal features, including such features as speaking turn, voice prosody, visual activity, and visual focus of attention on the interaction of small groups. Aran and Gatica-Perez [1] presented an analysis of participants' personality prediction in small groups. Okada et al. [17] developed a regression model to infer the score for communication skill using multimodal features, including linguistic and nonverbal features: voice prosody, speaking turn, and head activity. Schiavo et al. [18] presented a system that monitors the group members' nonverbal behaviors and acts as an automatic facilitator. It supports the flow of communication in a group conversation activity. There are works in exploring the barriers of L2 speakers in group discussion [19] or on their behavior changes between the group discussion in L1 and L2 languages [20]. But most of them are about using English as the targeted language.

After two decades of intensive research activities, the technologies of intelligent virtual agents have been getting more and more mature and the agents are deployed in a large variety of applications [10]. Language training is not an exception. However, most of the works are targeted in English since it is a de facto international common language. Projects like InteLLA[1] which adopt state-of-art technologies like multimodal interaction and language skill assessment based on machine learning techniques are also being conducted in Japan for Japanese English learners. Not only for learning a foreign language, intelligent virtual agents are also adopted in the simulation of refugees and their non-native accent for the training of the personnels of welfare services [16]. On the other hand, Japanese language, as a relatively minor language, there are much less activities or applications available. The commercial product, "Aoi Speak" released by DeepBrain[2] is one of the few examples. Due to its commercial purpose and mobile phone platform, the interactions are limited. There is a 2D agent but the input/output (IO) are only limited to voice. The agent's turn and the user's turn are one after the other. The user always answers the agent with a specified sentence and has to press the *record voice* button. It does not perceive the user's nonverbal behaviors and does not respond with nonverbal behaviors, either. The practice of social interaction is not possible on these kinds of platforms.

Although there are a number of academic research works on Japanese language learning in the fields of linguistics and language education [12], we found few works from the computer science field. In the field of Japanese education, the influences on Japanese mora timing from the foreign learners' mother tongue have been investigated in detail. Nagai [13] investigated the duration compensation between consecutive vowels and consonants between English speakers and native Japanese speakers when they speak Japanese. Masuda [11] investigated the pronunciation of sokuon of English and Korean speakers when they speak Japanese. However, these works are only based on the records of specific and exactly the same words rather than a conversation.

This work distinguishes previous ones in the following aspects:

- Unbalanced composition of L1/L2 speakers in the members of small groups where L1 speakers are in majority and talk in the same language (Japanese). The influences emerged under the pressure of the conversation with native speakers as the majority in the group are expected to be observed.
- Comparable data of the sessions in Chinese-speaker/Chinese-speaker, Chinese-speaker/Japanese, and Japanese/Japanese combinations so that the behavior changes of both of Japanese and Chinese-speaker participants can be analyzed.
- Data corpus collection and analysis in Japanese as 2nd language in the computer science field where sensory data is recorded and meant for machine learning tasks.

---

[1] https://www.teai-waseda.jp/.
[2] http://deepbrain.jp/.

– Data corpus is recorded during natural conversation rather than a collection of specific individual words. The conversation is task oriented so that the participants are supposed to utter similar words. The data is therefore more controlled than a chat conversation.

3 Data Corpus

3.1 Experiment Design

In order to extract the characteristics of unbalanced groups, we conducted the experiment to compare unbalanced groups with homogeneous groups. Participants are formed to be groups in the following conditions:

Unbalanced groups: collaborative decision-making discussions were conducted by four participants, three native Japanese speakers and one native Chinese speaker who speaks Japanese as a second language. The language used is Japanese only. Chinese-speaking participants are required to be living in Japan for at least one year, pass Japanese Language Proficiency Test (JLPT) level N2, and be confident to talk in Japanese fluently.

Homogeneous groups: composed of native Japanese or Chinese speakers only. The languages used are the participants' native languages (Japanese or Mandarin Chinese).

Chinese speakers are chosen as the foreigner participant because they are the majority of foreigner students in Japan (Chinese and Taiwanese, 41% in 2018) [6]. Considering the potential wider range of foreign students and the ease for people in the same generation to talk, the range of the participants are limited to between 18 to 29. All groups are composed with equal numbers of male and female participants to prevent gender bias in the results.

In order to identify the causes of the differences of participants' behaviors, the following factors are considered in the selection of discussion topics: the categories and the knowledge level. For the categories of topics, we considered the factor of whether there are prior candidates to choose from in making the final decision. Following the previous work [14], two typical categories of topics were selected in investigating this factor, ranking style and brain-storming style of topics. Because each participant is invited to attend two experiments (unbalanced and homogeneous groups) if his/her schedule meets, two topics are prepared for each category.

Ranking Style Topics: Participants are asked to collaboratively rank the items from a given list based on their importance or goodness. The discussion is supposed to surround the items in the list, and the participants are supposed to recall the vocabulary in a more limited space. The topic in this category should be easier for a L2 speaker. The topics for discussion in this category:

– Ranking of anime titles: participants are asked to predict the top-five rankings from a list of 15 Japanese anime titles based on their popularity. The correct answers are the scores of these titles on a Japanese SNS site where its members can discuss and score anime titles[3]. On this site, popular titles have at least several hundreds of

[3] https://www.anikore.jp/pop_ranking/.

evaluations and can be considered as a reliable source. Because it is possible that some participants do not know the titles of the anime, we prepare the preview video clips of each title which has the duration around five minutes so the participants can prepare themselves before the discussion. There is no time limitation for the participants to watch the video clips, but they usually finish the preparation within 20 min.

- Winter survival exercise: this is a classic task in the research field of group dynamics [7]. The participants are asked to rank the top-five important ones from a list of 15 items with an assumption that they met an airplane crash in winter mountains. Item scores determined by experts are available for evaluating this task. Because the participants are not necessarily familiar with all of the items, the text descriptions of the functionalities of the items are provided to them.

Brain-Storming Style Topics: Participants are asked to collaboratively deliberate as many ideas as possible without prior candidates. In this work, the preparation of a debate is decided to be the brain-storming task. The participants are asked to discuss the supporting and defending points from a point of view where they are preparing to debate it with another team. Because reliable sources of the evaluation of group performance on this type of task are not available, the count of deliberated supporting/defending points can be used as an objective metric of group performance. Therefore, all experiment sessions have to be conducted with the same point of view on each topic. We set it to be the side of *positive* opinion of the topics. In such a task, the boundary of the vocabulary is supposed to be broader and should be more difficult for the L2 speakers to join.

- Deregulation for introducing foreign workers: the participants are instructed to discuss this issue from the view point of its effect on Japanese society.
- Justice of animal experiments: the participants discuss the trade-off between advances in medical technology and the rights of animals.

During the experiment, Chinese-speaking participants are expected to have some degree of handicaps in their communication with the Japanese language. We have a hypothesis: if there are manipulatable objects that can be used to convey the participants' ideas, the discussion may be facilitated to achieve better team performance.

The setup of the recording environment is shown in Fig. 1. The experiment participants sit around a 1.2 m × 1.2 m square table. Two video cameras are used to capture the overall scene. Every one of them had a dedicated WebCam (Logitech Brio Ultra HD) to capture his or her face in large size in 1920 × 1080 resolution at 60 Hz frame rate. Four additional WebCam (Logitech C920) are attached at diagonal direction of the table to compensate for the center ones in the case when the participants face to the sides. These cameras have 1920 × 1080 resolution and capture at 30 fps. For each trial the data set contains 15 min of four face camera recordings and four corner recordings. In addition to the eight WebCams, two high-resolution (4K) video cameras (Sony FDR AX-700) are used to capture.

The participants also wear motion capture suites (Noitom Perception Neuron 2.0), and their body movements including fingers are recorded. In five out of the 18 experiment sessions motion data was recorded at 60 fps with 33 sensors. The sensor data was interpreted with a human body model by the bundled Axis Neuron software and translated into a BVH file containing the 3D coordinates for 72 body parts at 60 Hz. Each participant wore a headset microphone (Audio-Technica HYP-190H) which was connected to an audio digitizer (Roland Sonar X1 LE).

Fig. 1. Setup of the data corpus recording experiment. The female participant who is facing the camera is the L2 speaker who is perceived highest level of Japanese proficiency (H1)

3.2 Experiment Procedures

All subjects were recruited in Kyoto University, nearly all of them are students with only one exception, an office staff. Nine native Chinese speakers (three males and six females, mean age: 25.1) and 33 Japanese participants (18 males and 15 females, mean age: 22.7) were recruited for the experiment. Considering the potential wider range of foreign students and the ease for people in the same generation to talk, the age range of the majority of the participants is from 18 to 29 with only two exceptions (one is 31 and one is 36). Chinese-speaking participants were required to have been living in Japan for at least one year, passed Japanese Language Proficiency Test (JLPT)[4] level N2 and above, and self-declared that they can communicate in Japanese fluently. The Chinese speaker participants come from various nationalities including China, Taiwan, Canada etc. but all of them speak Mandarin Chinese as their first language.

The experiment was conducted in an in-subject manner, that is, the participants participated in two experiments, in an unbalanced group and in a homogenous group (speak in Japanese or Chinese as their L1). These participants were formed into 17 groups: eight mixed ones, seven Japanese-only ones, and two Chinese speaker-only ones. All groups are composed of the participants in the same gender or equal number of male and female participants to prevent gender bias in the results. The differences of group dynamics may be caused by the balance of a member's cultural background and

---

[4] https://www.jlpt.jp/e/.

may be caused by the personal traits. After the introduction of the whole experiment, the big-five [4] personality test of each participant is conducted. They then discuss two assigned topics, one is a ranking style topic and the other one is in brainstorming style. Each discussion session is limited to 15 min. An alarm clock is placed in front of each participant to help them to conclude the discussion within the allowed time slot. After the experiment, they filled questionnaires which evaluate the performance of the group and the individual participants. As Fig. 1 shows, an alarm is placed in front of each participant so that they can be aware of how much time is remaining and try to finish their discussion within the allowed time slot. After each discussion session, the participants are asked to fill a questionnaire about the performance of the group, the other members, and themselves.

4   Analysis

4.1   Proficiency Levels of L2 Participants

For the work reported in this paper, a subset of the collected corpus, seven mixed groups and thus seven L2 speakers are analyzed and are compared with 21 L1 speakers. Although the conditions in recruiting the L2 participants, they all at least hold the level N2 of JLPT and all claimed that they are fluent in speaking Japanese, their actual proficiency levels are diverse. For the analysis, the L2 participants are divided into three levels, low, middle, and high according to the following criteria by the experimenter. The experimenter is not a native speaker of Japanese language but has been living in Japan for more than 20 years since his 20's and holds professor positions for 13 years in Japanese universities. He teaches in Japanese and works in the field of communication science.

High (H) : the participant may have some foreign accent in his/her pronunciation and may have some non-native choices occasionally, but those are able to be compensated by L1 participants implicitly. The participant speaks Japanese fluently and has no difficulties in capturing L1 speakers' vocabularies and speed. The discussion is smooth and there are no observable issues occurring due to one of the participants being a foreigner.

Middle (M) : the participant's proficiency level is perceived lower than the participants in the High group. The participant can speak Japanese fluently and can capture almost all of what the L1 speakers said. However, the participant's vocabulary is perceived to be limited. Sometimes the participant cannot figure out how to express his/her ideas and requires the assistance from the L1 speakers explicitly.

Low (L) : the participant's proficiency level is perceived lower than the participants in the High and the Middle group. The participant does not speak Japanese fluently and the vocabulary is even more limited. The participant is perceived not to be not able to fully engage the discussion.

According to the criteria above, three of the L2 participants are rated as in the High group, two in the Middle group, and two in the Low group.

4.2 Extraction of Mora Durations

From our knowledge, currently there is no tool which can extract mora duration directly from voice data. Therefore, the mora duration information was extracted by the following procedure:

1. Transcription: the video data is then sent to a professional service for manual transcription. Since the L2 participants sometimes did not pronounce some words correctly or used wrong words, these *errors* are annotated with the correct words that the participants are supposed to say in addition. Laughings and coughings which are observed in the data set are distinguished with utterances with specific tags. Since the segments of laughings and coughings cannot be identified, the utterances containing those tags are omitted from the dataset in this specific investigation.
2. Transformation to Kana representation: three types of characters, *hiragana*, *katakana*, and *kanji* are used in the Japanese writing system. Hiragana and Katakana are both syllabaries which are used to denote Japanese phonological units, that is, *mora*. These two variants are used in different situations and are generally called *kana*. Hiragana is usually used in denoting traditional Japanese terms, grammartic expressions, and the combination with kanji (Chinese characters). Katakana is usually used to denote a sound and is especially often used to denote the pronunciation of foreign languages. Kanjis, as the original Chinese characters are ideograms and are pronounced as one or more hiraganas in Japanese. The manual transcriptions of the video corpus contain all of the three types of denotations and are uniformly transformed to hiragana form with a tool, KAKASI[5]. The utterances with laughs are omitted from the analysis.
3. Phonological analysis and timing alignment: after transforming the transcriptions to hiragana representation, the speech recognition tool, Julius[6] is used for the phonological analysis and the timing alignments of phonemes and the sound files can then be determined. After getting the timing information of the phonemes, mora durations can be computed from the combination of consonant-vowel pairs.

4.3 Statistical Analysis of Mora Durations

The overall summary of the results of the procedures above is shown in Table 1. The L2 participants in the group 1 to 3 are judged as *high* proficiency level, where the ones in the group 4 and 5 are *middle*, and the ones in the group 6 and 7 are *low*. Since the dataset size is quite small (only two to three samples at each proficiency level), no obvious tendencies could be found from the distribution. On the other hand, the higher level does not necessarily introduce more utterances from the L2 speaker. How much the L2 participants spoke seems to depend more on the participants' personality. It appeared that L2 participants with intermediate or higher proficiency were able to communicate well enough with L1 participants in the aspects of the number of utterances. The L2 participants in group 1, 2, and 4 spoke considerably more than their L1 partners. But the L2 participants at low proficiency level did have difficulties in catching up with

---

[5] http://kakasi.namazu.org/index.html.en.
[6] https://github.com/julius-speech/julius.

their L1 partners. They could not acquire floors smoothly and therefore spoke much less. Interestingly, the utterance durations are similar between the L2 participant and L1 participants. This may be caused by the synchrony effect where the participants may have had an influence on each other and talked in a similar way. Also, it could be observed that L1 participants talked in a more common way than the L2 participants while the L1 participants had similar mora counts per word (standard deviation: 0.083) but the L2 participants had larger variety among each other (standard deviation: 0.203).

Table 1. Overall summary of the results of mora duration extraction. "C" columns show the data of the Chinese speaker in each group while the J columns show the data of the average values of the three Japanese participants in the same group. "Uttr." means an utterance and the mark, # denotes the number of that item. The unit of duration is second

Group	Uttr. #		Uttr. duration		Word #		Mora #		Mora #/Word	
	C	J	C	J	C	J	C	J	C	J
1 (H)	412.0	175.3	1.456	1.225	1,816.0	836.3	3,116.0	1,190.7	1.716	1.424
2 (H)	384.0	271.3	1.528	1.530	1,854.0	1,384.3	2,781.0	2,134.7	1.500	1.542
3 (H)	138.0	302.3	1.674	1.497	837.0	1,630.3	1,161.0	2,568.0	1.387	1.575
4 (M)	412.0	270.3	1.561	1.527	2,170.0	1,347.0	3,292.0	1,986.7	1.517	1.475
5 (M)	242.0	328.3	0.916	1.123	954.0	1,646.7	1,083.0	2,628.0	1.135	1.596
6 (L)	92.0	246.0	1.250	1.343	407.0	1,082.3	655.0	1,464.3	1.609	1.353
7 (L)	173.0	325.0	0.715	0.966	571.0	1,437.7	662.0	2,236.0	1.159	1.555
Average	264.7	274.1	1.300	1.316	1,229.9	1,337.8	1,821.4	2,029.8	1.432	1.503
Std. Dev.	126.7	49.1	0.333	0.204	650.1	269.9	1,098.4	496.7	0.203	0.083

The statistics of the mora durations of the Chinese speaker of each group and their native Japanese partners are further investigated. The results are shown in Table 2. Similar to the results in Table 1, there was no obvious tendency regarding to proficiency level found in this table, either. L1 speakers spoke in a more common way, their mora durations were more similar to each other than L2 speakers (standard deviation: 0.009 versus 0.020). When each individual speaker is considered, L1 speakers also controlled their mora duration significantly more steadily than L2 speakers (standard deviation: 0.100 versus 0.108, two sided t-test, $p < 0.05$). In addition, the mora durations of L1 participants are significantly shorter than L2 participants (0.114 s versus 0.138 s, two sided t-test, $p < 0.05$).

The results above verified the findings of previous studies where L1 speakers can control their pronunciation at a more stable level than L2 speakers in the aspect of mora duration. The results also provided positive answers to our RQ1. The absolute duration of mora as well as the stability of mora duration should be able to be used for detecting whether a person is a native Japanese speaker or not. The current dataset size is still small at each proficiency level and it is unclear whether the characteristics can have sufficient resolution to distinguish the three proficiency levels among L2 speakers.

Table 2. Statistics of the mora durations of the Chinese speaker of each group and their native Japanese partners. The values in "J" column are the average of the three native Japanese speakers. The unit of all cells is second

Group	Average		Std. Dev.		Max.		Min.	
	C	J	C	J	C	J	C	J
1 (H)	0.149	0.106	0.088	0.088	0.810	1.030	0.030	0.030
2 (H)	0.156	0.133	0.134	0.125	1.860	1.933	0.030	0.030
3 (H)	0.146	0.117	0.116	0.099	1.340	1.217	0.030	0.030
4 (M)	0.131	0.120	0.121	0.116	1.860	1.237	0.030	0.030
5 (M)	0.111	0.104	0.093	0.073	1.080	0.810	0.030	0.030
6 (L)	0.165	0.109	0.110	0.115	0.880	1.267	0.030	0.030
7 (L)	0.109	0.107	0.097	0.080	0.520	1.180	0.030	0.030
Average	0.138	0.114	0.108	0.100	1.193	1.239	0.030	0.030
Std. Dev.	0.020	0.009	0.015	0.018	0.481	0.320	0.000	0.000

Nevertheless, the closer to L1 speaker the level is higher, is a reasonable hypothesis, it should be possible when there is more data available

4.4 Analysis Based on 1D CNN

The analysis was based on the overall statistics, in order to further explore the characteristics of mora duration at a micro level, that is, the relationship between moras, we introduced the use of the 1D CNN model. During the learning phase of 1D CNN, the relationship among the neighboring elements of a sequential data in their contribution to the final learning results is stored in the form of filters. By investigating the weights of the filters, how the relationships in the mora sequence are reflected to the classification of proficiency level is expected to be found. We understand it should be difficult to predict proficiency level merely by mora durations, the main purpose is for the analysis not for a proposal of a complete automatics assessment model. We therefore introduced a relatively simple 1D CNN architecture for the purpose. The organization of the network is shown in Fig. 2. An 1D CNN layer is used to extract the relationship of a fixed length sequence of mora duration in multiple filters. The learning of the filters is like scanning the whole sequence of an utterance by shifting the filter. After the learning converges, appropriate weights of each element will be assigned to the filters. One filter is keeping one kind of relationship. We explored different settings on filter length, number of filters as well as other hyper parameters. The layer is followed by a max pooling layer, a flatten layer to transform data format to one vector, finally a fully connected layer and then the output layer.

We form the analysis as two classification problems as the follows:

Native/Non-native (L1L2): a two-class classification problem for detecting whether a Japanese speaker is a native one (L1) or a non-native one (L2).

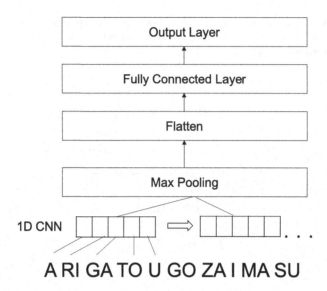

Fig. 2. Organization of the network used in the analysis

Low/Middle/ High/Japanese (LMHJ): a four-class classification problem for the assessment of three proficiency levels of L2 speakers and L1 speakers.

We adopted the same basic network organization for the two learning problems, and optimized their learning individually. Epoch number is fixed to 30, activation function of the fully connected layer is fixed to ReLU. And then all combinations of the filter length (3, 5, 7), filter number (16, 24, 32, 40, 48), and the size of the fully connected layer (16, 32, 40, 48) are explored. Since there are less L2 speakers than L1 speakers (7 versus 21), the dataset is an imbalanced one. SMOTE [3] algorithm is used to oversampling the data of L1 speakers. Recall rate of the Non-native class in L1L2 problem and the ones of Low/Middle/High class were used as the evaluation metrics, and leave-one-subject-out cross validation was adopted.

Filter length 5, 24 filters, and 16 neurons in the fully connected layer were found to achieve best classification results of the L1L2 problem. The recall of the L2 class is 0.574 which is higher than the chance level (0.5 for a two-class classification problem). Although the difference is not large, mora duration showed its effectiveness in distinguishing a L2 speaker from L1 speakers. Figure 3 shows the maps of all 24 filters trained with all available data and the settings above. We increased the width of the 1D filters to make them easier to be observed. The hidden variable values are shown in the vertical direction, from the top to the bottom, each horizontal line denoting the weight of one element, that is, one of five consecutive mora durations. Each map represents one template-like relationship of those mora durations, and data samples are matched with the templates to determine the final classification results. A completely white color denotes the maximum value (1.0) and a completely black color denotes the minimum value (0.0). A higher value means that element contributes more to the final classification results in that filter. The filter lengths were chosen to be an odd number (3, 5,

7) so that the relationships between the elements before and after the center one are observable.

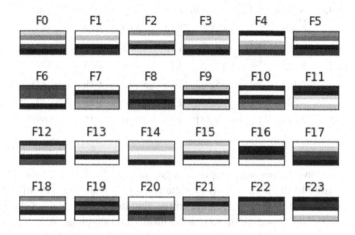

Fig. 3. Maps of all 24 filters learned L1L2 classification model

Each filter may have a different degree of influence on the final classification result. We measured the strength by compute the products of the weights through the path from each filter to each output neuron in the final output layer. Table 3 shows the weight products of each filter in the optimized L1L2 classifier for the L2 output. The filters with larger absolute values have stronger influence on detecting a sequence of mora duration as the pronunciation of a L2 speaker. The influences can be positive and negative, reflected in the sign of the values. From the table, we can find that the moras in front of a certain mora have stronger positive influence (F5 = 7.410, F8=5.767), but the moras behind it have stronger negative influence (F23=-12.687, F21=-10.321, F22=-9.079). These results show that when L2 speakers speak Japanese, the duration of the mora is affected by the previous mora, resulting in an unnatural pronunciation that distinguishes them from L1 speakers. Note that the range is until two previous moras, and the effect is stronger for the previous one than for the two previous ones.

On the other hand, filter length 3, 24 filters, and 40 neurons in the fully connected layer were found to achieve best average performance of the LMHJ problem. The average recall of low, middle, and high class is 0.247 while the precisions of three classes in this setting are 0.183, 0.288, and 0.270, respectively. Since the chance level of a four-class classification problem is 0.25, the performance of the learned network is not better than it. Therefore, it is unclear whether using mora duration is possible to distinguish the proficiency to three levels based on the current dataset. Since there are only three samples for the high group, and only two samples for the middle and the low group, respectively. Although the performance of the model for the LMHJ problem is not confirmed, we analyzed it following the same procedure of the L1L2 problem. Figure 4 shows all maps of the 24 filters. Tables 4, 5 and 6 show the weight products of each map for each output. There are no characteristics observable in the ones for middle output. But, the interesting finding is that the weights with large absolute values for high

Table 3. Weight products of each filter toward the L2 in the optimized model of the L1L2 classification problem

Filter	Weights	Filter	Weights	Filter	Weights	Filter	Weights
F0	2.269	F6	4.697	F12	−5.939	F18	1.060
F1	−4.058	F7	2.198	F13	5.321	F19	−0.081
F2	3.215	F8	5.767	F14	−0.137	F20	−4.576
F3	2.322	F9	−5.662	F15	5.610	F21	−10.321
F4	−2.102	F10	−3.796	F16	−4.842	F22	−9.079
F5	7.410	F11	−4.341	F17	1.730	F23	−12.687

and low outputs have values with opposite signs (F18, F23, F1, and F4). This imply that it may be able to distinguish two proficiency levels from the current dataset. To summarize the results for our research questions, the answers for both of the RQ2 and RQ3 are yes. Although it is difficult to use the mora duration alone, the results showed it is possible to distinguish L1 and L2 speakers from their control of mora duration. From the current dataset, three levels of proficiency could not be distinguished, though. However, some potential was found if the target number of levels is reduced to two. For the RQ3, the previous mora durations influenced the following one can cause unnatural pronunciation, this is consistent with previous studies.

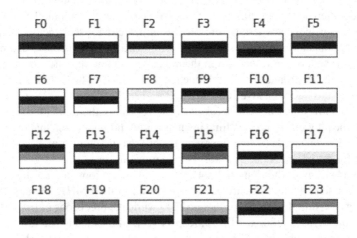

Fig. 4. Maps of all 24 filters of learned LMHJ classification model

Table 4. Weight products of each filter toward the Low output, 2in the optimized model of the LMHJ classification problem

Filter	Weights	Filter	Weights	Filter	Weights	Filter	Weights
F0	2.639	F6	4.079	F12	4.992	F18	−1.256
F1	4.331	F7	−0.556	F13	2.714	F19	4.702
F2	2.947	F8	3.455	F14	−0.006	F20	6.385
F3	−0.430	F9	−0.727	F15	0.365	F21	4.504
F4	−2.026	F10	1.724	F16	2.445	F22	4.128
F5	−0.117	F11	2.713	F17	1.631	F23	8.091

Table 5. Weight products of each filter toward the middle output, 2in the optimized model of the LMHJ classification problem

Filter	Weights	Filter	Weights	Filter	Weights	Filter	Weights
F0	4.851	F6	−0.488	F12	−1.168	F18	2.345
F1	1.506	F7	2.192	F13	4.766	F19	0.791
F2	1.445	F8	5.056	F14	2.030	F20	0.810
F3	1.808	F9	5.603	F15	0.138	F21	1.163
F4	4.064	F10	6.958	F16	1.259	F22	0.967
F5	1.707	F11	1.462	F17	3.756	F23	1.293

Table 6. Weight products of each filter toward the high output, 2in the optimized model of the LMHJ classification problem

Filter	Weights	Filter	Weights	Filter	Weights	Filter	Weights
F0	−2.839	F6	−1.533	F12	−3.339	F18	4.112
F1	−5.506	F7	−0.447	F13	−3.658	F19	−4.476
F2	0.869	F8	−1.992	F14	1.620	F20	−0.366
F3	−0.939	F9	0.286	F15	3.711	F21	1.753
F4	−5.598	F10	−1.489	F16	3.240	F22	−3.956
F5	−2.278	F11	−2.360	F17	2.713	F23	−5.264

5   Conclusions

This paper reports the investigation of the potential in using mora duration of L2 speakers' pronunciation to detect their proficiency level of Japanese language. We analyzed the statistics of L2 and L1 participants' mora durations based on a data corpus which was collected in unbalanced group discussion. The results showed that there are indeed characteristics distinguishing L1 and L2 speakers. The previous moras have influences on the following ones. We also did preliminary analysis on the dataset by using 1D CNN, the results were positive and we see the potential for adopting mora duration in the automatic assessment model development.

Further direction of this work is to find the what kinds of computer aided support can be realized in what kind of situations during collaborative work of unbalanced group members. A short-term goal is to find the moments where non-native speakers have difficulty in expressing their thoughts and provide handily hints in runtime. Also, the transcription part of this work relies on human annotation, since the exact meaning of the pronunciation is not critical for detecting correct pronunciation, we would like to develop an automatic assessment model directly from the voice of the users. In order to work on such detection task, the data corpus is still small, it is necessary for us to conduct more experiments to increase the number of groups for more generalized results.

References

1. Aran, O., Gatica-Perez, D.: One of a kind: inferring personality impressions in meetings. In: proceedings of 15th ACM International Conference on Multimodal Interaction (ICMI 2013). Sydney, Australia (2013)
2. Cabinet Office, G.O.J.: Annual report on the ageing society: 2019. Tech. rep. (2019)
3. Chawla, N.V., Bowyer, K.W., Hall, L.O., Kegelmeyer, W.P.: Smote: synthetic minority over-sampling technique. J. Artif. Intell. Res. **16**, 321–357 (2002)
4. Claes, L., Vandereycken, W., Luyten, P., Soenens, B., Pieters, G., Vertommen, H.: Personality prototypes in eating disorders based on the big five model. J. Pers. Disord. **20**(4), 401–416 (2006)
5. Huang, H.H.: Analysis on the language use of L2 Japanese speakers regarding to their proficiency in group discussion conversations. In: 15th International Conference on Social Computing and Social Media (SCSM 2023), held as part of the 25th HCI International Conference (HCII 2023). Lecture Notes in Computer Science, vol. 14025, pp. 55–67. Copenhagen Denmark (2023). https://doi.org/10.1007/978-3-031-35915-6_5
6. (JASSO), J.S.S.O.: Survey results of enrollment status of foreign students in fy2018. Tech. rep. (2019)
7. Joshi, M.P., Davis, E.B., Kathuria, R., Weidner, C.K.: Experiential learning process: exploring teaching and learning of strategic management framework through the winter survival exercise. J. Manage. Educ. **29**(5), 672–695 (2005)
8. LeCun, Y., et al.: Backpropagation applied to handwritten zip code recognition. Neural Comput. **1**(4), 541–551 (1989)
9. Li, X., Yamashita, N., Duan, W., Shirai, Y., Fussell, S.R.: Improving non-native speakers' participation with an automatic agent in multilingual groups. In: Proceedings of the ACM on Human-Computer Interaction, vol. Group, pp. 1–28 (2022)

10. Lugrin, B., Pelachaud, C., Traum, D. (eds.): The Handbook on Socially Interactive Agents – 20 Years of Research on Embodied Conversational Agents, Intelligent Virtual Agents, and Social Robotics, vol. 2: Interactivty, Platforms, Application. ACM (2022)

11. Masuda, K.: Influence of L1 on the acquisition of Japanese mora timing by native speakers of English and Korean. Nihongo Kyoiku **141**, 3–13 (2009)

12. Mori, Y., Hasegawa, A., Mori, J.: The trends and developments of L2 Japanese research in the 2010s. Lang. Training **54**(1), 90–127 (2020)

13. Nagai, K.: Compensatory lengthening by British learners of Japanese. Japan. Lang. Educ. Around Globe **8**, 87–97 (1998)

14. Nihei, F., Nakano, Y.I., Hayashi, Y., Huang, H.H., Okada, S.: Predicting influential statements in group discussions using speech and head motion information. In: 16th International Conference on Multimodal Interaction (ICMI 2014), pp. 136–143. Istanbul (2014)

15. Obremski, D., Brucker, E., Friedrich, P., Lugrin, B.: Behavioural adaptation towards foreign virtual agents in VR - the impact of non-native speech. In: Proceedings of the 23rd ACM International Conference on Intelligent Virtual Agents, pp. 1–3. Würzburg, Germany (2023)

16. Obremski, D., Hering, H.B., Friedrich, P., Lugrin, B.: Exploratory study on the perception of intelligent virtual agents with non-native accents using synthetic and natural speech in German. In: ICMI 2022: Proceedings of the 2022 International Conference on Multimodal Interaction, pp. 15–24. Bengaluru, India (2022)

17. Okada, S., Nakano, Y., Hayashi, Y., Takase, Y., Nitta, K.: Estimating communication skills using dialogue acts and nonverbal features in multiple discussion datasets. In: 18th ACM International Conference on Multimodal Interaction (ICMI 2016), pp. 169–176. Tokyo (2016)

18. Schiavo, G., Cappelletti, A., Mencarini, E., Stock, O., Zancanaro, M.: Overt or subtle? Supporting group conversations with automatically targeted directives. In: Proceedings of the 19th International Conference on Intelligent User Interfaces (IUI 2014), pp. 225–234 (2014)

19. Stroud, R.: Second language group discussion participation: a closer examination of 'barriers' and 'boosts'. In: Proceedings of the International Conference on Education and Learning (ICEL). Tokyo (2017)

20. Yamamoto, S., Taguchi, K., Ijuin, K., Umata, I., Nishida, M.: Multimodal corpus of multiparty conversations in L1and L2 languages and findings obtained from it. Lang. Resour. Eval. **49**, 857–882 (2015)

Modeling a Workflow-Based Design Specification for Learning with Flexibility Characteristics, Absence of Deadlocks, and Achievability of Each State in TEL Applications

Matías Iturrieta[1,2] , Juan Felipe Calderon[1,2](✉) , and Luis A. Rojas[1,2]

[1] Facultad de Ingeniería, Universidad Andrés Bello, Quillota 980, Viña del Mar, Chile
m.iturrietahernndez@uandresbello.edu, juan.calderon@unab.cl,
lrojasp1@docente.uss.cl
[2] Facultad de Ingeniería, Arquitectura y Diseño, Universidad San Sebastián, Bellavista 7,
8420524 Santiago, Chile

Abstract. Technology-enhanced learning (TEL) has profoundly transformed education in recent years. In this line, the TELs have made it possible to transport the pedagogical scenario to a virtual environment. However, as with face-to-face education, the remote format poses complex challenges due to its dynamic and unpredictable nature. In face-to-face classes, teachers have greater flexibility to adapt to possible emerging situations, which is not the case for remote lessons. In TEL, it is common for teachers to follow a predefined workflow to meet teaching objectives during classes. The problem lies in the fact that these workflows could be more flexible. Therefore, providing flexible and adaptable solutions to changing circumstances within a virtual classroom is necessary. Workflows are based on formal specifications that have rules and steps to follow. We propose a design specification for online learning that validates no deadlocks between the activities and that the workflow is entirely achievable, all in a real-time environment. The specification is tested on a workflow engine that automatically responds to events from an online learning platform. To put our approach in a broader context, we conducted a comprehensive and comparative study of various workflow modeling taxonomies. This analysis allows us to find existing modeling techniques in the field of workflow research with flexibility characteristics that can be adapted to the proposed specification. Our study concludes that an e-learning system that allows for emergent changes can substantially improve the effectiveness of TEL applications.

Keywords: flexible workflow · learning design · e-learning · model-checking

1 Introduction

Education and Learning Technologies (TELs) have proven valuable in many aspects of education, but effectively implementing these technologies in remote learning environments presents unique challenges. Synchronous learning, in which participants interact in real-time, requires high coordination and flexibility. These learning environments can be dynamic and unpredictable, as they are subject to various factors, such as variability in student engagement, differences in learning styles, and fluctuations in technology availability [1, 2].

Within this context, the technological platforms and tools that enable online and synchronous education must be flexible enough to allow real-time adaptations based on the emerging needs that may arise in a virtual classroom. Implementing EML, mainly through IMS-LD, has provided a solid basis for formalizing TEL applications. However, this implementation faces inherent limitations, especially in managing heterogeneity and flexibility in pedagogical planning [3].

Despite IMS-LD's ability to provide three levels of complexity, constraints have been identified for creating more heterogeneous and complex TEL applications. Attempts to address these issues have resulted in approaches that still rely on predefined workflows and offer no true flexibility in task descriptions or exception handling. Consequently, this research seeks to address these challenges by developing a more practical approach to implement flexibility in TEL applications, both in managing heterogeneity and real-time adaptations in pedagogical planning [4, 5].

2   Learning Design & Workflows

The learning design lays out the overall plan for the learning experiences. The concept refers to planning and structuring the learning activities mentioned above. It includes defining learning objectives, selecting and organizing content, identifying appropriate teaching and assessment strategies, and planning interactions between students and content. A diversity of learning design tools focus on different areas of the educational process. These areas include content delivery, student assessment, pedagogical planning, and authorship [6, 7].

An essential consideration in this area is the management of heterogeneity, especially about pedagogical planning and authorship. The diversity of pedagogical approaches, teaching styles, and learning needs demands that learning design solutions be flexible and adaptable. In other words, heterogeneity management must be aligned with how learning design is formally represented. This alignment ensures that the technologies employed in education are genuinely beneficial, able to support a variety of pedagogical approaches, and adapt to the individual needs of students [5, 8].

In education, workflows are activities to implement the established learning design. They provide structure and order for learning activities. Given the growing emphasis on incorporating technologies into teaching, the field of learning design has explored how these workflows can be optimized through the use of ELTs [9–11].

3   Educational Modeling Languages

Educational modeling languages (EMLs) are a family of modeling languages that seek to represent educational processes formally. It aims to provide a standardized, reusable way to describe the structure and sequence of learning activities, teaching strategies, and interactions. EMLs are generic and can be applied to a variety of pedagogical approaches. They can also be quite complex and abstract, as they seek to cover a wide range of educational scenarios [12, 13].

As mentioned above, IMS-LD is a specification of a particular educational modeling language developed by the IMS Global Learning Consortium. IMS-LD provides a standard for describing, exchanging, and implementing learning designs in online learning systems. IMS-LD aims to make learning designs more accessible, reusable, and shareable by providing a formal, standardized framework for their representation [3].

A vital aspect in this area is the integration of active and authentic learning principles, as highlighted in a study by Reilly and Reeves. These principles, rooted in sociocultural-constructivist approaches, emphasize the need for educational design that allows for active student participation in virtual environments [14].

Reilly and Reeves' study demonstrated how applying these principles can quantify and enhance active learning in online courses. Courses with high scores on authentic e-learning principles offered better opportunities for active learning, while those with lower scores had significant deficiencies. In addition, student surveys provided valuable data to refine these principles, highlighting the importance of adaptability and personalization in the design of online education.

Another study, focused on "Agency in Educational Technology," addresses the design of personalized EdTech for children, highlighting the importance of adapting the level of agency according to the cognitive and metacognitive development of the child. This study proposes an "agency personalization loop," adjusting the level of agency provided by technology to balance the free choice of learning content and the allocation of optimal range. This approach is crucial to avoid ineffective learning due to overestimating children's ability to manage their knowledge [15].

4 Flexible Learning Design Framework

This section integrates hypotheses, research objectives, and the methodological framework to overview the study's investigative and innovative approach comprehensively.

4.1 Hypothesis

The identification of critical problems in the execution of learning designs in SLI, particularly in terms of reachability and mutual locks in a framework of flexibility, leads to the proposal of two main hypotheses that will be tested throughout this research:

Hypothesis 1 (H1): It is proposed that an extension of a workflow specification with the integration of pedagogical constraints can support the problems of mutual locks and reachability in executing a learning design.

4.2 Objectives

The main objective of this research is to provide runtime flexibility features in a learning design specification, supporting the absence of mutual locks and reachability as compliance parameters.

To achieve the proposed general objective, the following specific objectives have been defined:

Specific Objective 1 (O1): To enable each state's absence of mutual locks and reachability in executing a learning design when flexibility features are built into its specification.

Specific Objective 2 (O2): Demonstrate the applicability of this approach in a real-time TEL application using a predefined scenario.

4.3 Methodological Framework

Concerning specific objective O1, to enable the absence of mutual locks and the attainability of each state in the execution of a learning design when flexibility features are incorporated into the specification, a formal approach is proposed. The proposed workflow specification shall be justified using an architectural design that supports workflows that meet the domain scenario's requirements for consistency, completeness, and correctness.

Finally, on the specific objective O2, Demonstrate the applicability of this approach in a real-time TEL application, using a predefined scenario, an experimental technical approach. Complementing the experimentation in (O2), simulations will be carried out utilizing the implemented system, according to (O2).

To meet both objectives, Design-Based Research supports the architectural design and implementation of the applicability scenario [16].

5 Results

In the first phase, a comprehensive literature review focused on different workflow taxonomies to identify those compatible with flexibility. In this research phase, YAWL (Yet Another Workflow Language) has been recognized as a critical reference for the design of flexible workflows. YAWL stands out for its advanced ability to handle complex processes, being particularly relevant for online learning, where adaptability is essential [17].

A core feature of YAWL is worklets, small work processes that are dynamically integrated into larger workflows. These worklets are selected using the Ripple Down Rules (RDR) technique, a case-based reasoning approach that adapts the workflow to changing conditions. This flexibility is crucial to respond to the varied situations in virtual educational environments [18].

Also, during the review, several flexible workflow approaches were identified that are relevant to online learning in a nutshell [19]:

Flexibility by selection: It allows the choice between different execution paths within a predefined process model, suitable for anticipated and mappable scenarios.

Flexibility by change: It allows process participants to change the process model at runtime. This approach is practical but requires users to possess experience in process modeling.

Flexibility by deviation: It offers the ability to deviate from the proposed execution paths during the execution time without modifying the process model, although it is less researched and has practical limitations.

Flexibility due to indeterminacy: It enables a partial process model with flexible builds built in both build and run time. It differs from flexibility by design, based on a complete process model, and determines the flexibility possible during construction time.

YAWL's worklets and RDR model have inspired this proposal, which is adapted to the specific needs of online learning design. Unlike the standard implementation in YAWL, where the worklets focus on general business processes, in this proposal, the worklets are designed to address specific virtual learning situations, for example, the assignment of activities depending on the students' performance. In addition, while YAWL uses RDR to select worklets in a business context, in this approach, RDRs are adapted to evaluate and respond to pedagogical variables, such as the number of members per group or the approved activities per student, for example.

Continuing from this base, the research delves into developing a structured formalism. This formalism, which will be the cornerstone of our approach, establishes a rigorous and coherent framework, providing the fundamental principles and structures that guide the design of online learning, including flexibility, absence of mutual lock-ins, and attainability.

5.1 Practical Application of the Design Specification

The previous section outlined the conceptual approach and proposed design specification for online learning environments, focusing on flexibility, absence of mutual lock-ins, and reachability. The next crucial step in our research has been to translate this theory into practical application, testing the effectiveness of the specification in a natural online learning environment. This process is essential to validating Specific Objective 2 (O2).

As shown in Fig. 1, a systematic and distributed approach was adopted to carry out this practical implementation, taking advantage of cloud computing resources to deploy and orchestrate services.

1. Bi-directional data flow process and modification in LMS

The LMS (Learning Management System) instance is the starting point where the course content and data originate.

The Bridging System acts as an intermediary, facilitating the transfer of information between the LMS instance and the flexible workflow. This system ensures that communication is bidirectional, allowing modifications made to the LMS to be reflected in the workflow and vice versa.

2. Runtime Workflow Modification Process

The Flexible Workflow Instance adjusts to the needs of the course in real time. This is where the New Rule generated by the Ripple Down Rules (RDR) is integrated and its conditions and worklet are managed.

– New Rule

When a change or need is detected in the learning environment, RDRs assess the situation and determine the best action to take, creating a "New Rule."

– Assignment completed (worklet and condition of the new rule)

The system's flexibility is enhanced by the ability to create and manage RDR through a "Web Platform for RDR Management." This platform enables the assignment of worklets and conditions in the new RDRs, providing a vital tool for tailoring the workflow to specific and emerging needs in a dynamic learning environment.

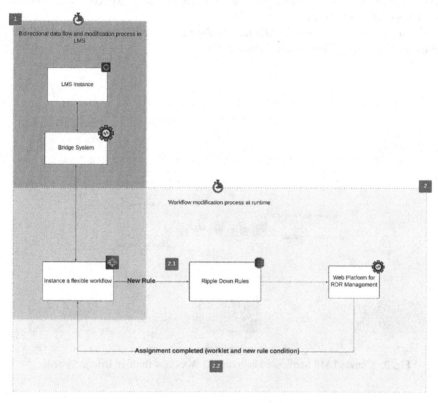

Fig. 1. General Architecture.

Delving into the data flow process between the Canvas LMS instance and the flexible workflow, the Bridging System stands as a critical element. When this system starts, it activates the corresponding procedures in AWS Step Functions, and if the workflow requires it, changes or information are requested from the Canvas LMS. The workflow in AWS responds to these stimuli by adapting tasks as needed.

The specific operation is deployed as follows:

1 Starting the Workflow in AWS: The Bridge System triggers the start of the workflow in AWS Step Functions.
2 Communicating with Canvas LMS: Throughout the workflow, if additional information needs to be obtained or adjustments made to the Canvas LMS, an action request is sent to the Bridging System.

3 Polling To the Canvas LMS API: The Bridging System executes a polling mechanism, querying the Canvas LMS API at regular intervals, defined as every X seconds. During this process, the workflow on AWS is kept waiting for a response.
4 Response and Subsequent Procedures: After receiving and validating the response from Canvas LMS, the Bridging System proceeds according to the nature of this response:
5 If yes, the AWS SDK's sendTaskSuccess method is used to notify AWS Step Functions of the operation's success.
6 If the answer is no, the sendTaskFailure method is applied. This can lead AWS Step Functions to initiate contingency actions.

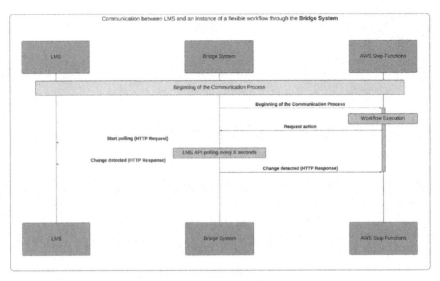

Fig. 2. Canvas LMS Sequence Diagram and Workflow through Bridge System.

On the other hand, the most innovative aspect of our overall architecture is the real-time workflow modification process, which plays a crucial role in improving the flexibility and adaptability of the system in online learning contexts. This innovative mechanism is triggered when the system identifies unforeseen situations during the workflow without a predefined protocol. In such cases, the system initiates an evolution process, creating a new Ripple Down Rule (RDR) that, in its initial state, has no associated criteria or worklet. This situation allows an expert, in this case a teacher, to intervene directly, customizing the RDR by assigning specific criteria and selecting the most appropriate worklet. In short, this process is integrated and operates within the system's structure through expert intervention, allowing for agile and precise adaptation in response to emerging needs (Figs. 2 and 3).

With a complete understanding of the system provided by the General Architecture, we now focus on meeting the specific O2 objective by presenting a practical example. This example is designed to demonstrate the practical application of our proposal in

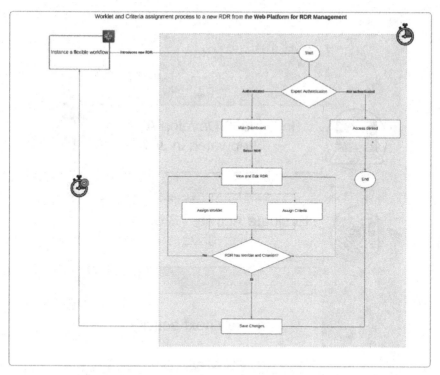

Fig. 3. Flowchart on Web System for RDR Management.

a scenario that simulates real situations that could arise in an online learning environment. Let's imagine the following scenario: assessments in a programming subject are project-based. As an initial requirement, students must form groups of three. The first evaluation is to develop a Java Stopwatch individually. The second activity is group work to create a prototype of the video game Hunt The Wumpus. To tackle this second task, all group members must have previously passed the individual Java Stopwatch activity. This workflow is illustrated in Fig. 4, summarizing it with a dot:

Initial requirement: Students are grouped in threes.

1 Individually, students develop the activity of programming a stopwatch in the Java programming language.
2 The teacher evaluates the activity of the stopwatch.
3 Depending on the result obtained by each student, the next activity, which can be individual or group, is assigned.
4 Finally, the teacher assigns the students' final grades.

In this context, "Assign Next Activity" acts as a worklet, and developing the Hunt The Wumpus activity is equivalent for now. Worklets are essentially workflows. As shown in Fig. 5, the worklet is a StartExecution action of AWS Step Functions, which essentially invokes another workflow. In this case, StartExecution triggers a worklet and always calls the same workflow to terminate the RDR.

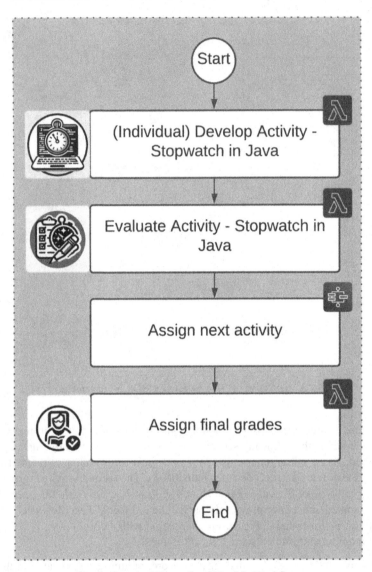

Fig. 4. Practical Example of Flexible Workflow.

This child workflow is responsible for identifying the rule that meets the conditions given by the running parent workflow. If an RDR satisfies these conditions, the worklet associated with this RDR is selected and returned to the main workflow (Fig. 6).

Under this premise, the Ripple Down Rules tree would have two nodes: a parent node whose criteria are always valid, with its default worklet to develop the Hunt The Wumpus activity, and another node that, if the groups are of three students and everyone has passed, also triggers the development of Hunt The Wumpus. If we leave the process at this point, we would have a workflow that monitors the status of student assessments,

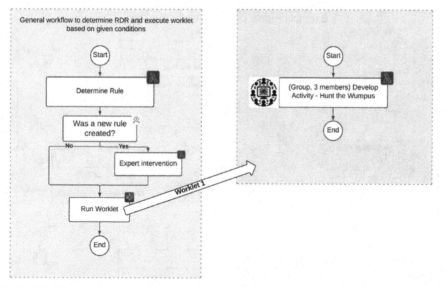

Fig. 5. Workflow to determine RDR and execute worklet based on data from the current context and default worklet.

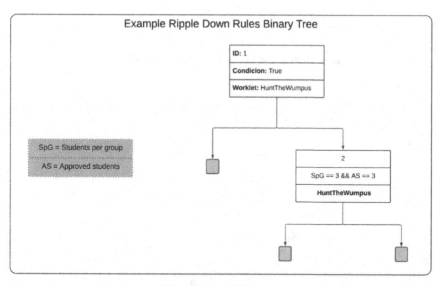

Fig. 6. Initial RDR tree.

in this case, the Timer in Java and the activity of Hunt the Wumpus, as long as everyone in the group has passed the Timer in Java. But a critical question arises: what happens if some student fails to pass the individual Stopwatch activity in Java? In this case, since the current conditions are not handled by any existing RDR, a new RDR is created, initiating the process shown in Fig. 7 for its subsequent assignment of worklets and criteria.

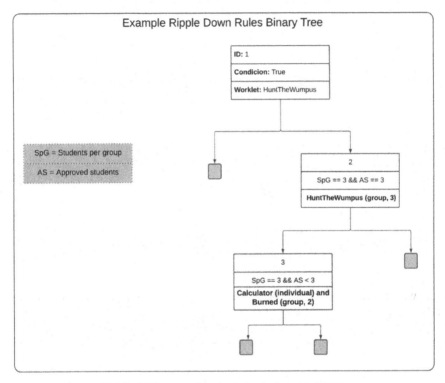

Fig. 7. RDR tree with new dynamically added RDR.

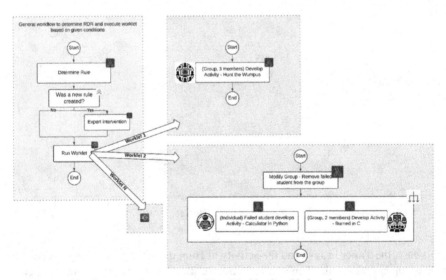

Fig. 8. Rendering a new worklet (Worklet 2) added to the system.

Consequently, as seen in Fig. 8, the teacher assigns a worklet (Worklet 2) to the new RDR, which removes the student who did not pass from the group and gives him an individual activity to develop a Python Calculator. The remaining two students in the group must now complete the C Burn Activity. With this example, we have demonstrated the applicability of our design specification in a real-time TEL application using a predefined scenario.

6 Conclusions

This paper addressed the challenge of modeling a design specification for online learning, focusing primarily on flexibility features. The research concentrated on developing a learning system that allows for emergent changes to improve the effectiveness of Teaching and Learning Technologies (TEL).

Regarding the specific objective O1, it was possible to construct a formal workflow specification that enables the absence of mutual blockages and achievability in executing the learning design. This specification was justified using an architectural design consistent with the domain scenario, satisfying requirements for consistency, completeness, and correctness. However, the need to develop the formalism further was identified to provide a more detailed grammar and semantics, allowing for a better understanding and application of the proposed model.

Therefore, concerning the specific objective O2, the applicability of this approach in a real-time TEL application using a predefined scenario was demonstrated. A systematic, distributed approach was adopted, utilizing cloud computing resources for service orchestration, and a dynamic process of modifying workflows in real time was implemented. Despite these advances, there was a need for further research into the integration of the specification into different learning environments and its scalability in broader contexts.

In terms of projections, this work suggests that using artificial intelligence tools could be crucial to advancing this field. For example, the information collected by the worklets' decision engine, based on the Ripple Down Rules (RDR), could be used to build a machine-learning model. This model would be able to automatically assign worklets with a certain percentage of certainty, reducing the need for constant expert intervention.

References

1. Martin, F., Parker, M.A., Deale, D.F.: Examining interactivity in synchronous virtual. In: The International Review of Research in Open and Distance Learning.
2. Bower, M.: Synchronous collaboration competencies in web-conferencing. Distance Educ. **32**(1), 63–83
3. Koper, R., Miao, Y.: Using the IMS LD standard to describe learning designs. In: Handbook of Research on Learning Design and Learning Objects: Issues, Applications, and Technologies, p. 45
4. Vesin, B., Mangaroska, K., Giannakos, M.: Learning in intelligent environments: user-centered design and analytics of an adaptive learning system. Smart Learn. Environ.

5. Pozzi, F., Asensio-Perez, J.I., Ceregini, A., Dagnino, F.M., Dimitriadis, Y., Earp, J.: Supporting and representing learning design with digital tools: in between guidance and flexibility. Technol. Pedagogy Educ. **29**(1), 21

6. Asensio-Pérez, J.I., et al.: Towards teaching as design: exploring the interplay between full-lifecycle learning design tooling and teacher professional development. Comput. Educ. **41**

7. Celik, D., Magoulas, G.D.: A review, timeline, and categorization of learning design tools. In: Chiu, D.K.W., Marenzi, I., Nanni, U., Spaniol, M., Temperini, M. (eds.) ICWL 2016. LNCS, vol. 10013, pp. 3–13. Springer, Cham (2016). https://doi.org/10.1007/978-3-319-47440-3_1

8. Persico, D., Pozzi, F.: Informing learning design with learning analytics to improve teacher inquiry. British J. Educ. Technol. **46**(2)

9. Hofmann, M., Betke, H., Sackmann, S.: Automated Analysis and Adaptation of Disaster Response Processes with Place-Related Restrictions

10. Agostinho, S., Bennet, S., Lockyer, L., Jones, J., Harper, B.: Learning designs as a stimulus and support for.

11. Macfadyen, L.P., Lockyer, L., Rienties, B.: Learning design and learning analytics: snapshot 2020. J. Learn. Analytics **7**(3), 18

12. Torres, J., Cardenas, C., Dodero, J.M., Juarez, E.: Educational modelling languages and service-oriented learning process engines. Mary Beth Rosson

13. Koper, R.: Modelling units of study from a pedagogical perspective: the Pedagogical metamodel behind EML. Open University of the Netherlands

14. Reilly, C., Reeves, T.C.: Refining active learning. Active Learn. High. Educ.

15. Brod, G., Kucirkova, N., Shepherd, J., Jolles, D., Molenaar, I.: Agency in educational technology: interdisciplinary. Educ. Psychol. Rev.

16. Hoadley, C., Campos, F.C.: Design-based research: what it is and why. Educ. Psychol.

17. v Aalst, W., d Hofste, A.: YAWL: Yet Another Workflow Language

18. Adams, M.: Usability Extensions for the Worklet Service

19. d Naturwissenschaften, D., Grumbach, L.: Flexible Workflows - A Constraint- and Case-Based Approach

The Edifying Impact of Blending Game-Based Learning with Educational Robotics: A Systematic Review of Empirical Evidence

Nicos Kasenides[(✉)] [ID], Andriani Piki [ID], and Nearchos Paspallis [ID]

University of Central Lancashire Cyprus, Larnaca, Cyprus
{nkasenides,apiki,npaspallis}@uclan.ac.uk

Abstract. Game-based learning is an effective pedagogical approach with a demonstrated capacity to activate learner engagement, inspire motivation, and enhance the overall learning experience. The application of educational robotics has also attracted a lot of attention in recent years across educational levels and domains. Despite their appeal and the positive learning outcomes associated with such innovative pedagogies, the synergistic edifying impact of blending them remains largely unexplored. The aim of this study is to present a synthesis of empirical evidence on game-based learning and educational robotics. A systematic literature review is conducted focusing on empirical research published between 2019 and 2023. The analysis reveals prevalent methodological approaches and pedagogical theories framing learning and instruction, as well as the most widely employed robotics and gaming platforms. The study sheds light not only on the benefits of embracing game-based learning and educational robotics, but also on the barriers and challenges associated with adopting such innovative pedagogies. Ultimately, the study attempts to portray the impact of these approaches on learning and transferable skills development.

Keywords: Educational Robotics · Game-Based Learning · Pedagogical Frameworks · Skills · Competencies · Empirical evidence

1 Introduction

The integration of robotics in learning activities has gained substantial momentum in recent years, with several studies revealing that embracing educational robotics (ER) in the classroom can result in considerable instructional benefits and learning gains [9,26,34]. Game-Based Learning (GBL) constitutes another prevalent innovating pedagogy increasingly employed in educational interventions [24]. Through GBL activities, learners are presented with genuine opportunities for tinkering and inquiry-based learning commonly associated with positive emotional, behavioural, and cognitive learning outcomes, such as increased learner engagement, enhanced understanding and knowledge acquisition, and transferable skills development [24,33].

© The Author(s), under exclusive license to Springer Nature Switzerland AG 2024
A. Coman and S. Vasilache (Eds.): HCII 2024, LNCS 14704, pp. 97–115, 2024.
https://doi.org/10.1007/978-3-031-61305-0_7

The present study explores the impact of blending game-based learning and educational robotics (abbreviated to *GBL-ER*), placing an emphasis on the development of transferable skills, abilities, and competencies. Even though both pedagogical territories stand strong in the realm of educational technology, very few studies have attempted to explicitly explore the interaction between GBL and ER and the synergistic impact this combination can have on transferable skills development. As a result, these two innovative pedagogies have remained largely separate in the past [26]. This illuminates an opportunity for leveraging each other's strengths to improve the learning outcomes and promote logical and critical thinking, problem solving, and social skills through playful and interactive activities [9,40]. Furthermore, although the application of GBL-ER can serve as a versatile platform for enriching both practical skills (such as design, engineering, and programming) and soft skills (like computational thinking, critical thinking [7], problem-solving, teamwork and collaborative learning [1], communication, and leadership [18]), more emphasis is often placed on the former. This presents a gap in understanding the full potential of blending the use of GBL with ER toward transferable skills development. The focus on competencies and soft skills development is motivated by this gap, and the growing need for continuous upskilling and reskilling in light of the ongoing digital transformations across all levels of education and in workplace settings alike. Hence, a systematic and critical analysis of recent literature is deemed essential for educational researchers, instructors, and practitioners to make informed decisions about leveraging ER in GBL contexts, and vice versa.

After defining the research aim, objectives and research questions, the paper presents the educational profile of GBL-ER, and the methodology employed for conducting the systematic review, followed by a synthesis of key research findings. The paper concludes with a discussion of avenues of future research.

2 Research Aim, Objectives and Research Questions

Given the diversity in methodological approaches employed in empirical research, the educational theories and pedagogical frameworks applied, the participants' characteristics and level of education, as well as differences in pedagogical design and implementation contexts, the present study aims to systematically review, evaluate, synthesise, and present empirical evidence drawing on recent literature on GBL-ER. To address the identified research gap, this study systematically reviewed empirical evidence in the field of GBL-ER across various educational levels and contexts. Two primary research objectives are being pursued:

1. To evaluate the most prominent research methods and methodologies; learning theories and pedagogical frameworks; robotics and games platforms; benefits (learning outcomes and positive impact) ascribed to GBL-ER as well as barriers (challenges or negative effects) that impede its effective implementation; and, ultimately, the impact of implementing GBL-ER on developing transferable skills, abilities, and competencies.

2. To identify avenues for future research towards establishing stronger theoretical foundations for GBL-ER, exploiting the constructive impact it can have on learners' knowledge, skills, behaviour and overall learning experience.

The following research questions were formulated based on the aforementioned research aim and objectives:

1. What methodological approaches are used in research exploring GBL-ER?
2. Which levels of education are empirically explored in GBL-ER research?
3. What are the underlying pedagogical theories framing GBL-ER activities?
4. What types of robotics platforms and games are used, and how are they combined to improve the educational experience?
5. What skills, abilities, and competencies are emphasised in empirical research employing GBL-ER?
6. What are the potential benefits (learning outcomes) and challenges (barriers) of GBL-ER?

The findings stemming from the analysis can serve as the cornerstone towards crafting a conceptual research framework for soft skills development through GBL-ER. This framework can guide future research endeavours leveraging and synthesising different strands of educational technology.

3   Educational Profile of GBL-ER

3.1   Game-Based Learning

Educational or serious games are widely employed in learning and skills development initiatives [10]. GBL involves learning through playing games [24], including massively multiplayer online games [5], mobile games [33], and immersive Virtual Reality (VR) games [43], amongst others. GBL approaches embrace a series of game mechanics including storytelling, narratives, role-playing, competitive tasks, points, badges, and reward systems to enrich the learning experience [32], make learning more fun, accessible, and 'seamless' [42,48].

GBL is frequently associated with positive outcomes including: triggering creative thinking, problem-solving, analytical and communication skills [24]; prompting imagination and curiosity-driven learning [5]; promoting wellbeing, happiness, joyful and playful experiences [24]; activating learner engagement, motivation, participation and social interactions [57]; encouraging tinkering and learning through trial-and-error [24]; promoting goal orientation and enhancing learners' communication skills; activating interest through the use of multimedia and multimodal content; improving students' cognitive, meta-cognitive, and social skills, and the ability to retain newly learned information, hence offering an alternative to the conventional focus on structural learning and memorisation [24]. By blending entertainment and learning elements, serious games constitute a powerful educational medium, which can improve learners' emotional, behavioural and cognitive engagement, augment the level of understanding and knowledge acquisition, and enhance skills development [33,42].

In addition to the vast array of benefits associated with GBL, there are still many barriers constraining their impact [33,44]. Key challenges include the need for customization and personalization of existing games to fit individual learners' needs, (dis)abilities, and preferences, the challenge educators have for monitoring progress and providing timely and relevant feedback, and the scarcity and rigid nature of most games making them difficult to adjust to diverse settings [44]. Therefore, future research and development should emphasise the importance of prioritising human factors in GBL initiatives [42].

3.2 Educational Robotics

Physical and virtual robots, robotic simulations, and robots' digital twins, are becoming increasingly more accessible and affordable, making their use plausible beyond industrial settings, infiltrating our households, classrooms and workplaces, and creating intelligent educational and work spaces. Recent studies have showcased innovative educational applications combining robotics with Artificial Intelligence (AI) and VR, including physical robotic heads encapsulating affective robots responding to emotional cues and context-driven interactions [35] and digital twins of physical robots embedded in VR environments for educational purposes [43]. The use of social robotics is also emerging in educational milieus [1,8,21,41,53] providing novel opportunities to promote Education for Sustainable Development (ESD), including efforts to improve learners' attitudes toward recycling [11] and child rights education [15].

The influence of ER is observable in diverse settings, ranging from classrooms to ambient assisted living and learning spaces for individuals with special needs, and across a variety of domains, extending from software project management and planning skills [9] to Science, Technology, Engineering, Arts, and Mathematics (STEAM) education [3,12,16]. Educational research employing ER focuses on an array of aspects ranging from technical specifications, usability, effectiveness, and aesthetics, to programmable features, Human-Robot Interaction (HRI) design, technology acceptance, user engagement, and social dynamics of ER [8,41]. While predominantly targeting K-12 students in the age group of 6–18 years [26], educators are increasingly employing a range of robotics technologies, ranging from platforms such as LEGO, Arduino Learner, and REV, to programmable humanoid or social robots (e.g., Nao, Pepper, QTRobot, Cozmo, etc.), in an attempt to tailor learning across a broad range of learner groups, including pre-K-12 [53] and higher education [1,7,9,34].

While recent research has illustrated the feasibility of ER, including social and humanoid robots [8], in diverse educational and training settings [7,9,40], it has also revealed that it is not always straightforward to obtain long-term interaction and engagement between robots and learners [53]. The key factors and conditions that may affect the impact of HRI on the overall learning experience include the length of deployment, the autonomy of robotic action, the duration of interaction time [53], the type of robot used [9], the task at hand [1], as well as the pedagogical models employed [34], among other factors. Therefore, further research is needed to continue exploring the realm of ER.

4   Methodology

4.1   Research Design

This research focuses on the edifying impact of game-based learning approaches and educational robotics on the learning experience. To address the research questions, a systematic literature review was performed using thematic and content analysis [57]. The empirical evidence was drawn from 56 journal articles and conference papers published in the 5-year period between January 2019 and December 2023. Employing a combination of content and thematic analysis was beneficial in the process of synthesising the extracted data into themes corresponding to each research question, while also capturing emerging patterns, prominent research clusters, as well as gaps in the literature. By using this approach, information from the studies included in the review was organised in thematic categories (e.g., level of education, pedagogical theory, gaming platform, robotics platform, etc.) which were subsequently analysed with the vision to inform future research, or identify specific areas where empirical evidence is limited and hence further case studies can be conducted.

4.2   Search Strategy

The present study investigated peer-reviewed academic articles published in conference proceedings or academic journals from 2019 to 2023 in three major bibliographic databases: Springer, IEEE Xplore, and Elsevier Scopus. During the search process, papers from these three databases that matched a set of search terms related to *educational robotics*, *game-based learning*, and *skills*, were extracted. The following search strings[1] were used to obtain results from these three databases:

- **Springer and IEEE Xplore**: (``educational robot'' AND ``game-based learning'') AND (skill* OR abilit* OR competenc*)
- **Elsevier Scopus** ((educational robot* AND game* based learning) AND (skill* OR abilit* OR competenc*))

4.3   Inclusion Criteria

The purposeful combination of GBL-ER with skills development yielded a total of 122 articles as follows: Springer (n=24), IEEE Xplore (n=6), and Elsevier Scopus (n=92). A set of inclusion criteria was used to ensure that the selection process was objective and that the final corpus of papers could be identified for subsequent analysis.

- The studies had to be empirical research papers, published in academic journals or conference proceedings between January 2019 and December 2023, and written in English.

---

[1] A common query string was used but was adapted to each database's search syntax.

- Studies employing different methodologies and research methods (qualitative, qualitative and mixed methods) were included.
- Studies conducted in all educational levels across the world were considered, including primary, secondary and higher education, and vocational training.
- Articles exploring game-based learning and/or educational robotics were included even if they did not explicitly combine both approaches, and were tagged accordingly.
- Papers matching variations of the keywords specified in the query strings, including plural keywords and synonyms were included (e.g., skill, skills, skillset; robot, robots, robotics; competence, competency, and competencies).
- No restrictions were applied on the journals and conference proceedings, in an attempt to capture diverse viewpoints since the broader field of GBL-ER is defined in the intersection of multidisciplinary areas such as Human-Computer Interaction (HCI), Information Systems (IS), Technology-Enhanced Learning (TEL), and Humanities and Social Sciences (HSS), among others.

4.4 Exclusion Criteria

The initial database search yielded a total of 122 publications which were considered for the second phase of the review. In this phase, the screening and selection steps were carried out based on a set of exclusion criteria. Initially, a table was created for each paper, including the paper's title, abstract, and keywords, and a unique ID was assigned to each entry. The authors then independently read the abstracts and tagged each entry with the respective label 'include', 'exclude', or 'indecisive', along with a short statement justifying the reasoning for their decision. The authors then compared their classifications to discuss any mismatches, to reach consensus on entries labelled as 'indecisive', and to eliminate researcher bias. The following studies were excluded (some studies were flagged on more than one criterion):

- Book chapters, books, theoretical articles, systematic reviews, bibliographic studies, meta-analyses, editorials, etc. (n=19);
- Studies referring to the use of robotics in sectors other than education (e.g., industrial robots) or generic technology applications (e.g., wearable devices) without reference to GBL-ER (n=47);
- Studies focusing on teachers rather than students (n=6);
- Studies focusing on the technology (e.g., game mechanics or robot's configuration) rather than learners/learning (n=9);
- Studies exploring gamification but not GBL (n=3).

Ultimately, out of the initial 122 papers, 66 were excluded following the collaborative screening phase, leaving 56 articles eligible for the third phase of the review. Figure 1 presents a flow chart summarizing the filtering, eligibility screening, and final inclusion process.

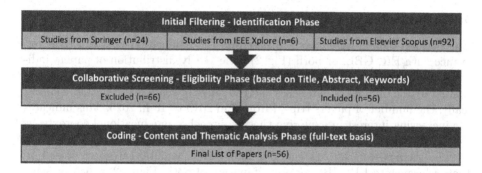

Fig. 1. The process of filtering, eligibility screening, and inclusion.

4.5 Coding and Data Analysis

At first, the authors independently analysed the final set of papers (n=56). During this process, key pieces of information relevant to the research questions were coded. The coding structure was recorded in a spreadsheet file, with rows representing the papers, and columns representing the codes (both deductively generated codes and emerging ones). These included the paper's ID, year of publication, type of study and research methodology, the level of education being studied, the pedagogical frameworks employed, relevance with robotics, humanoid robots, educational robotics, or GBL, combination of GBL-ER, reference to soft or hard skills addressed, and information on assessment strategies and intervention duration. Data analysis also included recording any surprising results or interesting observations in terms of student engagement and motivation, considerations regarding usability and accessibility, learning outcomes, and the potential benefits and challenges of each approach.

5 Results

This section presents our findings and attempts to provide insights into the research questions based on the results gathered by analysing the final set of 56 articles. To provide a high-level understanding of the research trends in this topic, we first analyse the chronological distribution of publications in the last 5 years. We then discuss findings related to the research methodologies used in studies addressing GBL and educational robotics. Furthermore, we present results on the level of education (where this was mentioned in the studies), the skills addressed, the pedagogical frameworks, assessment strategies, and the robotic platforms, games, and tools utilised in experimental evaluations. The impact of GBL and ER on the educational experience is further analysed by discussing profound benefits and barriers illuminated in the empirical studies under analysis.

5.1   Chronological and Thematic Distribution

The selected papers were classified based on the publication year and their relevance with ER, GBL, or both (Fig. 2). The yearly distribution of papers indicates an upward trend in the number of papers published per year, despite being limited by the number of databases and the range of years searched. More specifically, the number of papers tripled from 6 in 2019 to 18 in 2023. This indicates the increasing interest in exploring these approaches in educational contexts, as well as the widening utilisation of the underlying technologies.

The studies were also categorised into three thematic categories based on their relevance to ER, GBL, or a combination of both. Figure 2, which presents the number of papers in each of these categories in a chronological distribution, suggests that a substantial number of studies involves a combination of GBL-ER. A total of 34 papers (61%) utilised an approach combining educational robotics with game-based learning, whereas 18 papers used ER only (32%), and 4 papers (7%) used GBL only. In 2023, the vast majority of the analysed papers (78%) combined both fields in their empirical research. This observation suggests an upward trend not just in the total number of papers per year, but also in the number of papers combining both fields as a medium to improve the educational experience.

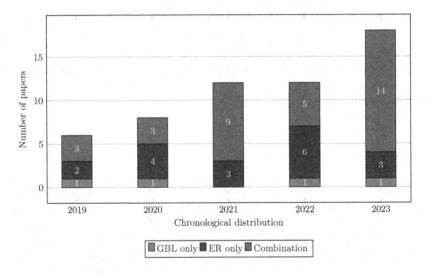

Fig. 2. Chronological and thematic distribution of selected papers.

5.2   Methodological Approaches Employed in Empirical Research

The first research question attempts to determine which methodological approaches have been used by the selected corpus of studies to explore GBL-ER. To this end, we have categorised the different methodologies used by researchers in order to determine which are the most widely used ones and, equally, to identify gaps in the research methodologies utilised in recent studies. The results shown in Table 1 present the set of research methodologies as reported by authors (where applicable), sorted by frequency of use. It is worth noting that one publication may have reported none, one, or mixed methods, hence the numbers recorded in the table refer to frequency rather than number of unique papers.

The results show that the majority of studies have used a quasi-experimental approach (60%). Analysis of previous works and proof of concept approaches were employed as part of mixed-methods studies (10%). Less frequently used approaches included interviews and focus groups, and observations of students and other study participants in small-scale studies. Only one paper used expert evaluation. It is also noteworthy that all of these approaches used a limited time-frame in terms of data collection, which was often constrained to a few weeks. This may suggest a lack of studies attempting to reveal the long-term effects of ER and GBL on the learning experience, as well as the impact of each approach on diverse target audiences. In addition to short-term, most of the empirical studies appear to be small-scale with an average of 57 participants per study and only 4 studies engaging more than 100 participants (min=2, median=50, and max=232 participants). This presents a gap in conducting qualitative, ethnographic, and experiential studies focusing on a particular group of learners, and the need to launch longitudinal, mixed methods studies involving learners from diverse backgrounds.

Table 1. Frequency distribution of research methodologies used.

Research methodology	Frequency
Quasi-experimental	34
Analysis of previous works	6
Concept paper	6
Interviews, focus groups	4
Observations	3
Expert evaluation	1

5.3 Level of Education

The second research question attempts to identify the levels of education in which ER and GBL are used. Figure 3 displays a distribution of the different levels of education identified through the studied articles. Various case studies have utilised technologies, tools, and methodologies related to ER and GBL in diverse classroom contexts, in special education, and as part of specialised training. The majority of the studies (46%) reports findings from K-12 education, followed by studies conducted at undergraduate university level (13%). Fewer studies were

conducted in special education contexts –mostly related to visual impairment–
(7%) and toward building specialised skills such as nursing, equipment training,
or aiding refugees (7%). Surprisingly, none of selected studies were conducted
in postgraduate education. This presents an empirical gap in GBL-ER research.
Finally, a large set of studies did not explicitly identify the educational level or
learners' background. It can be assumed that these studies attempted to address
multiple levels of education or engage a general audience.

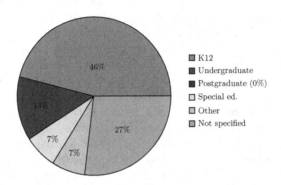

Fig. 3. Distribution of papers based on the level of education.

5.4   Pedagogical Frameworks

The pedagogical frameworks and learning theories employed to leverage GBL
or ER constitute the focus of the third research question. Theoretically framing
the educational process is an important consideration and can inform curriculum
design. It is noteworthy that the majority of the studies analysed did not explicitly mention any theoretical frameworks, neither provided any background information pertinent to the broader pedagogical approach. Only 24 (43%) papers
discussed the pedagogical approach framing the GBL or ER learning activities
employed in the studied context, including studies which have proposed and
evaluated new pedagogical approaches to address unique contexts of use.

Among the pedagogical approaches utilised, the most prominent are *social
constructivism, active, interactive, collaborative, situated*, and *project-based learning*, and *self-determination*. In addition, two of the studies mentioned the
GAFCC (Goal, Access, Feedback, Collaboration, Challenges) model [31], which
uses several theoretical constructs including *self-determination theory, goal setting theory, social comparison theory*, and *behavioral reinforcement theory*. A
small subset of studies also utilised the SMART goal-setting model [20]. Despite
the usefulness of these results, more research is needed to address the gaps which
are evident in the pedagogical realm regarding the use of GBL and ER, across all
levels of education. We argue that human-centred learning contexts employing
GBL-ER can significantly benefit from existing learning theory and pedagogical
frameworks, while novel theoretical explorations and pedagogical strategies can
help illuminate the full educational potential of GBL and ER.

5.5 Robotics Platforms and Games

The studied articles feature a diverse set of robotics platforms and gameful activities which have been used either independently or combined in an educational context. Some studies have used integrated educational robotics platforms such as LEGO Mindstorms EV3 or LEGO Mindstorms NXT [58]. These sets feature multiple components required to build a robot using LEGO technology, such as building blocks, sensors, motors, and other parts. Such platforms often utilise both text-based and block-based programming tools to provide more flexibility to the students and to address wider audiences across multiple educational levels. These are diverse, high-quality educational robotics sets with a lot of support for their design and programming software, as well as third-party robot-building instruction sets. Conversely, other studies have reported the reduced availability of such sets –especially regarding spare parts– as well as their high cost, as two important issues when such technologies must be implemented at a larger scale (i.e., in school-wide curricula) [25]. Alternatives to these technologies include Arduino devices which are available at a significantly lower cost and higher customizability [38,47].

The integration of various robotics platforms with other technologies was prevalent amongst the studied articles. Some studies utilised wearable devices like Myo armbands, while others employed mobile devices to provide a high-level GBL-ER platform [47]. The synergistic combination of multiple educational technologies seems to benefit learners. This illuminates avenues for future research leveraging the educational efficacy of mobile devices, AI, VR, and Augmented Reality (AR) [6] and combining them with robotics applications, or even capitalising on the immersive power of AR and VR in combination with Generative Pre-trained Transformers (GPTs) to enhance the user experience through simulated HRI or interactions with humanoid robots. Such technologies have leveraged commercial tools such as the Unity game engine, as well as commercially available platforms like the Metaverse. Given a particular problem context, any blend of technologies is plausible and may prove effective, as long as a strong emphasis is placed on human factors, skills development, and learner well-being.

The use of social robots has also been extensive, indicating the importance of HRI in providing a higher level of motivation and engagement, especially with younger audiences [11,19,21,23,28]. The combination of robotics and AI can potentially transform education, with the introduction of AI-assisted teaching [54] allowing a greater array of capabilities in addition to a higher level of HRI quality. Finally, only 12 out of the 56 studies (21%) considered the use of humanoid or social robots. While the analysed corpused of data is limited, we argue that this observation may instigate future research directions that take advantage of social and humanoid robots and their benefits to bring tangible results in terms of a more positive and engaging educational experiences [8,9,17].

From the perspective of GBL, several studies appear to utilise serious games in multiple contexts, including both general education and special education for visually impaired children, computing, mathematics, and languages, and training for skilled individuals such as nurses and athletes. It is evident that the use of visual programming languages like Scratch and Blockly [45] can significantly improve the level of interaction with the underlying robotics technologies, but also with the game itself, however these must be adapted to specific learning needs. Examples of serious games utilised include the iDo serious game [39] as well as game-based competitive environments that involve maze-solving and line-following activities implemented by educational robots [38,49]. Finally, some studies have also blended ER and GBL to offer simulations/games for specialised skills training for dangerous work environments, managing cyberattacks or computer networks, creating an IoT system, or building electronic circuits [37,47,56].

5.6   Skills Development

All articles except one, identified or explored at least one skill, competency, or ability. To address our fifth research question, we categorised the identified skills as either *soft skills* or *hard skills* and, in turn, computed the frequency of each skill per category with the aim to identify the skills emphasised in GBL-ER research. We extracted a set of 17 soft skills and 16 hard skills promoted through either GBL, ER, or both. Tables 2 and 3 display the soft and hard skills, respectively, sorted by frequency.

Table 2. Soft skills addressed in the reviewed publications, sorted by frequency.

Soft skills	Frequency
Computational thinking	14
Problem-solving	12
Teamwork, collaboration	8
Critical thinking	6
Creativity, originality	4
Green, environmental, sustainability skills	3
Engagement, attentiveness	3
Motivation	3
Exploration, experimentation	3
Navigation, spatial skills	3
Human rights education, equality	3
Self-regulated learning, self-efficacy	3
Decision-making	2
Empathy	2
Knowledge construction	1
Competitiveness	1
Flexibility	1

The most widespread soft skills, promoted in the articles reviewed, are computational thinking, problem-solving, teamwork, collaboration, and critical thinking, while creativity, sustainability skills, engagement, motivation and exploration, self-regulated learning and self-efficacy were also highlighted. Soft skills including decision making, empathy, flexibility, knowledge construction and competitiveness, were also captured, albeit to a lesser extent. Among the hard skills identified, the most popular was programming and computer science, followed by language skills, robotics, STEAM education, and design. Subject specific skills were also captured, such as mathematics and engineering, software testing and debugging, laboratory safety, nursing, computer networking, and others.

Table 3. Hard skills identified through the related works, sorted by frequency.

Hard skills	Frequency
Programming or computer science	14
Language, reading, speaking, vocabulary	11
Robotics	10
STE(A)M	6
Design	6
Mathematics	4
Engineering & mechanics	4
Software testing, debugging	2
Laboratory safety	2
Nursing	2
Object recognition	2
Computer networking	2
Computer-aided design	1
Computer-aided manufacturing	1
Data visualization	1
Cybersecurity	1

The analysis of the skills highlighted in the studied papers, reveals a pattern indicating that computing-related skills – both soft (computational thinking, problem solving) and hard skills (programming, robotics, design) – are among the most widely explored competencies. One plausible explanation for this observation is the close relationship between Computer Science and both educational robotics and Digital Game Based Learning (DGBL) [4,33]. Even though ER and GBL have been used in a wide variety of educational contexts and domains, their adoption still appears to be more prominent in the field of Computer Science due to their natural proximity. However, we argue that the benefits of ER and

GBL may transfer to, and transform, the educational settings of other fields, especially when coupled with new, innovative pedagogical strategies.

5.7   Benefits and Challenges

The final research question was formulated with the view to explore the potential benefits and challenges related to utilizing ER and GBL and their effectiveness as teaching and learning tools. GBL is characterised as an alternative learning method [13] which can promote *"active education"* [50] and facilitate *"learning achievement"* and *"progressive skill improvement"*. It is more *"effective"* compared to other methodologies [45]. Participants reported that GBL activities *"improved their understanding"* [2,50] and *"accelerated their learning proficiency"* [50] in various subjects. Furthermore, GBL was found to have a significant impact on children's *"skills and motivation"*, while also *"minimizing costs"*, and providing positive outcomes in terms of *"enjoyment"*, *"task accomplishment"* and *"learning comprehension"* [27,51].

ER has been used in conjunction with GBL to foster *"cooperation and critical thinking"* [29] and increase *"student engagement and concentration"* [36]. Learners perceived social robots as more trustworthy compared to other types of robots, and in some cases robots surpassed the popularity of human tutors [15,28]. Coupled with AI, VR/AR, and mobile or wearable technologies, blending GBL-ER can provide a truly *'engaging educational medium"* [30,52]. The findings stemming from our thematic and content analysis provide valuable directions for designing future learning spaces supported by these technologies, and guidelines for human-centred GBL-ER experiences in education [22], which can enable the desired transformation of the educational systems globally.

On the other hand, the current state of research in these domains reveals several shortcomings which must be addressed. A challenge regarding the adoption of these approaches – especially educational robotics – is the *"lack of qualified trainers, instructors, or teachers"* that can successfully deploy them [37,51] and effectively take advantage [14] of these educational technologies. Blending GBL-ER approaches requires a *"relatively high level of technology literacy"*, which means that training must be provided to educators in order for these to be utilised effectively. Furthermore, several studies have cited the *"lack of resources available"*, especially in the case of ER [36,51]. Given the variability of robot types and robotics platform to choose from, the diversity of game genres, types of games (digital, immersive, mobile, etc.,) and game mechanics, the often complex production methods, the limited availability of user files, instructions and regulations, and other instrumental factors, blending GBL with ER may be characterised as a *"resource-demanding and high-maintenance approach"*. Lastly, it appears that the interaction design of these methodologies has not yet been perfected. The findings stemming form the analysis of the studied literature suggest that these barriers may be alleviated by actively involving learners in co-creating learning spaces. Substantial work is needed to understand how different social, contextual, pedagogical, technological, emotional, and cognitive factors can affect student engagement and motivation [15,46,55], and the learning outcomes.

6 Conclusions

This paper has explored an emerging field of research defined by blending two technology-enhanced pedagogical approaches: Game-Based Learning (GBL) and educational robotics (ER). The synthesised corpus of empirical studies was critically reviewed and analysed, focusing on research methods and methodological approaches, theoretical models/constructs and pedagogical frameworks, robotics platforms and games platforms, benefits (learning outcomes and positive impact) and barriers (challenges or negative effects), and ultimately the impact of implementing the pedagogies on skills development. By reviewing and synthesising information from various related works, we have identified key methodological approaches, tools, pedagogical frameworks, and technological platforms used in these approaches. Our findings underscore the increasing interest in harnessing the combined benefits of GBL and ER, not only to enhance practical and subject-specific skills but also to foster soft and transferable skills, abilities and competencies such as problem solving, collaboration, communication, and creativity.

Our review has exposed empirical, methodological and theoretical gaps in studies addressing GBL-ER. Addressing these gaps is essential for understanding the full potential of integrating GBL and ER for transferable skills development. The findings revealed both the benefits as well as the challenges related to deploying these approaches. Despite the limited range of years studied and the study's scale and scope, our findings contribute to the broader conversation on innovation in educational methodologies and 'pedagogical engineering". It emphasises the role of human factors in technology-enhanced teaching and learning contexts, stresses the need for comprehensive skill development strategies through the combination of pedagogical frameworks and GBL-ER, and underlines the potency of the synergy between the two.

Looking ahead, it is crucial for researchers, practitioners, and educators to continue exploring these synergies. This may involve refining pedagogical models, crafting customised educational experiences, incorporating feedback from both learners and instructors, and also training them to blend various types of educational technologies. By doing so, we can better motivate and equip learners for the future workforce's demands and empower them with the varied skill sets needed for their success in an ever-changing digital world.

References

1. Ahtinen, A., Kaipainen, K., Jarske, S., Väänänen, K.: Supporting remote social robot design collaboration with online canvases: Lessons learned from facilitators' and participants' experiences. Int. J. Soc. Robot. **15**(2), 317–343 (2023)
2. Akdeniz, M., Özdinç, F.: Maya: an artificial intelligence based smart toy for preschool children. International J. Child-Comput. Interact. **29** (2021). https://doi.org/10.1016/j.ijcci.2021.100347
3. Alimisis, D.: Robotics in education & education in robotics: shifting focus from technology to pedagogy. In: Proceedings of the 3rd International Conference on Robotics in Education, vol. 9 (2012)
4. All, A., Castellar, E.P.N., Van Looy, J.: Assessing the effectiveness of digital game-based learning: best practices. Comput. Educ. **92**, 90–103 (2016)
5. Bawa, P., Watson, S.L., Watson, W.: Motivation is a game: massively multiplayer online games as agents of motivation in higher education. Comput. Educ. **123**, 174–194 (2018)
6. Bottega, J.A., et al.: Jubileo: an immersive simulation framework for social robot design. J. Intell. Robotic Sys. **109**(4), 91 (2023)
7. Buchem, I., Leiba, M.: Virtual exchange as an instructional design approach to promoting critical skills in higher education: a case study of project-based collaboration on "social robots in education'. In: EDULEARN 2022 Proceedings, pp. 6435–6440. IATED (2022)
8. Buchem, I., Lewe, C., Susanne, G.H., Sosta, S.: Learning agile estimation in diverse student teams by playing planning poker with the humanoid robot nao. results from two pilot studies in higher education. In: International Conference on Human-Computer Interaction, pp. 287–299. Springer (2023). https://doi.org/10.1007/978-3-031-34550-0_20
9. Buchem, I., Tutul, R., Jakob, A., Pinkwart, N.: Non-verbal sound detection by humanoid educational robots in game-based learning. multiple-talker tracking in a buzzer quiz game with the pepper robot. In: International Conference on Robotics in Education (RiE), pp. 185–196. Springer (2023). https://doi.org/10.1007/978-3-031-38454-7_16
10. Carrión12, M., Santorum12, M., Aguilar, J., Peréz, M.: iplus methodology for requirements elicitation for serious games (2019)
11. Castellano, G., De Carolis, B., D'Errico, F., Macchiarulo, N., Rossano, V.: Pepperecycle: improving children's attitude toward recycling by playing with a social robot. Int. J. Soc. Robot. **13**(1), 97–111 (2021). https://doi.org/10.1007/s12369-021-00754-0
12. Chaldi, D., Mantzanidou, G.: Educational robotics and steam in early childhood education. Adv. Mobile Learn. Educ. Res. **1**(2), 72–81 (2021)
13. Chen, Y.L., Hsu, C.C., Lin, C.Y., Hsu, H.H.: Robot-assisted language learning: integrating artificial intelligence and virtual reality into english tour guide practice. Educ. Sci. **12**(7) (2022). https://doi.org/10.3390/educsci12070437
14. Chevalier, M., Giang, C., Piatti, A., Mondada, F.: Fostering computational thinking through educational robotics: a model for creative computational problem solving. Inter. J. STEM Educ. **7**(1) (2020). https://doi.org/10.1186/s40594-020-00238-z
15. Chew, E., Khan, U.S., Lee, P.H.: Designing a novel robot activist model for interactive child rights education. Int. J. Soc. Robot. **13**(7), 1641–1655 (2021)

16. Conde, M.Á., Rodríguez-Sedano, F.J., Fernández-Llamas, C., Gonçalves, J., Lima, J., García-Peñalvo, F.J.: Fostering steam through challenge-based learning, robotics, and physical devices: a systematic mapping literature review. Comput. Appl. Eng. Educ. **29**(1), 46–65 (2021)

17. Dahiya, A., Aroyo, A.M., Dautenhahn, K., Smith, S.L.: A survey of multi-agent human-robot interaction systems. Robot. Auton. Syst. **161**, 104335 (2023)

18. Darmawansah, D., Hwang, G.J., Chen, M.R.A., Liang, J.C.: Trends and research foci of robotics-based stem education: a systematic review from diverse angles based on the technology-based learning model. Inter. J. STEM Educ. **10**(1), 1–24 (2023)

19. De Carolis, B., D'Errico, F., Rossano, V.: Pepper as a storyteller: exploring the effect of human vs. robot voice on children's emotional experience. LNCS, vol. 12933, pp. 471–480 (2021). https://doi.org/10.1007/978-3-030-85616-8_27

20. Doran, G.T., et al.: There'sa smart way to write management's goals and objectives. Manage. Rev. **70**(11), 35–36 (1981)

21. Egido-García, V., Estévez, D., Corrales-Paredes, A., Terrón-López, M.J., Velasco-Quintana, P.J.: Integration of a social robot in a pedagogical and logopedic intervention with children: A case study. Sensors (Switzerland) **20**(22), 1–19 (2020). https://doi.org/10.3390/s20226483

22. Engwall, O., et al.: Learner and teacher perspectives on robot-led l2 conversation practice. ReCALL **34**(3), 344–359 (2022). https://doi.org/10.1017/S0958344022000027

23. Estévez, D., Terrón-lópez, M.J., Velasco-quintana, P.J., Rodríguez-jiménez, R.M., Álvarez manzano, V.: A case study of a robot-assisted speech therapy for children with language disorders. Sustainability (Switzerland) **13**(5), 1 - 20 (2021). https://doi.org/10.3390/su13052771

24. Ferguson, R., et al.: Innovating pedagogy 2019: Open university innovation report, vol. 7 (2019)

25. Galvão, G., Neto, A.C., Araújo, C., Henriques, P.R.: The visual programming environment robi for educational robotics. vol. 104 (2022). https://doi.org/10.4230/OASIcs.SLATE.2022.14

26. Hovardas, T., Xenofontos, N., Pavlou, I., Kouti, G., Vakkou, K., Zacharia, Z.: Integrating educational robotics, game-based learning and inquiry-based learning: Pedagogical design and implementation. In: Innovate Learning Summit, pp. 343–357. Association for the Advancement of Computing in Education (AACE) (2020)

27. Hsu, T.C., Chang, C., Liang, Y.S.: Sequential behavior analysis of interdisciplinary activities in computational thinking and efl learning with game-based learning. IEEE Trans. Learn. Technol. **16**(2), 256–265 (2023). https://doi.org/10.1109/TLT.2023.3249749

28. Hsu, T.C., Chang, C., Wong, L.H., Aw, G.P.: Learning performance of different genders' computational thinking. Sustainability (Switzerland) **14**(24) (2022). https://doi.org/10.3390/su142416514

29. Hsu, T.C., Liang, Y.S.: Simultaneously improving computational thinking and foreign language learning: interdisciplinary media with plugged and unplugged approaches. J. Educ. Comput. Res. **59**(6), 1184–1207 (2021). https://doi.org/10.1177/0735633121992480

30. Hsueh, H.W., Hsu, T.C.: Game-based learning of ai image recognition on computational thinking and self-efficacy of undergraduates. **2**, 699–707 (2023)

31. . Huang, B., Hew, K.: Using gamification to design courses: lessons learned in a three-year design-based study. Educ. Technol. So **24**, 44–63 (01 2021)

32. Kapp, K.M.: The gamification of learning and instruction: game-based methods and strategies for training and education. John Wiley & Sons (2012)
33. Kasenides, N., Piki, A., Paspallis, N.: Exploring the user experience and effectiveness of mobile game-based learning in higher education. In: International Conference on Human-Computer Interaction, pp. 72–91. Springer (2023). https://doi. org/10.1007/978-3-031-35927-9_6
34. Leiba, M., Zulhian, T., Barak, I., Massad, Z.: Designing pedagogical models for human-robot-interactions–a systematic literature review (slr). In: International Conference on Human-Computer Interaction, pp. 359–370. Springer (2023). https://doi.org/10.1007/978-3-031-34550-0_26
35. Leon, K., Stipancic, T., Ricko, A., Orsag, L.: Multimodal emotion analysis based on visual, acoustic and linguistic features (2022)
36. Leoste, J., et al.: Using robots for digital storytelling. a game design framework for teaching human rights to primary school students. In: Lepuschitz, W., Merdan, M., Koppensteiner, G., Balogh, R., Obdržálek, D. (eds.) RiE 2020. AISC, vol. 1316, pp. 26–37. Springer, Cham (2021). https://doi.org/10.1007/978-3-030-67411-3_3
37. Lin, V., Chen, N.S.: Interdisciplinary training on instructional design using robots and iot objects: a case study on undergraduates from different disciplines. Comput. Appl. Eng. Educ. **31**(3), 583–601 (2023). https://doi.org/10.1002/cae.22601
38. Marouani, H.: Exploration of applying lego nxt and arduino in situated engineering teaching: a case study of a robotics contest at king saud university. International Journal of Robotics and Control Systems **2**(1), 67–78 (2022). https://doi.org/10. 31763/ijrcs.v2i1.508
39. Maskeliunas, R., et al.: Serious game ido: Towards better education in dementia care. Information (Switzerland) **10**(11) (2019). https://doi.org/10.3390/ info10110355
40. de Oliveira, D.S., Garcia, L.T., Gonçalves, L.M.: A systematic review on continuing education of teachers for educational robotics. J. Intell. Robotic Syst. **107**(2), 24 (2023)
41. Pachidis, T., Vrochidou, E., Kaburlasos, V.G., Kostova, S., Bonković, M., Papić, V.: Social robotics in education: State-of-the-Art and directions. In: Aspragathos, N.A., Koustoumpardis, P.N., Moulianitis, V.C. (eds.) RAAD 2018. MMS, vol. 67, pp. 689–700. Springer, Cham (2019). https://doi.org/10.1007/978-3-030-00232- 9_72
42. Piki, A., Markou, M.: Digital games and mobile learning for inclusion: perspectives from special education teachers. In: 10th IEEE International Conference on Behavioural and Social Computing (BESC 2023). IEEE (2023)
43. Piki, A., Nisiotis, L., Alboul, L.: A preliminary exploration of the learning and engagement potential of an intelligent virtual environment. In: 2022 IEEE 2nd International Conference on Intelligent Reality (ICIR), pp. 27–30. IEEE (2022)
44. Piki, A., Ştefan, I.A., Stefan, A., Gheorghe, A.F.: Mitigating the challenges of mobile games-based learning through gamified lesson paths. In: World Conference on Mobile and Contextual Learning, pp. 73–80 (2020)
45. Pou, A.V., Canaleta, X., Fonseca, D.: Computational thinking and educational robotics integrated into project-based learning. Sensors **22**(10) (2022). https:// doi.org/10.3390/s22103746
46. Psycharis, S., Theodorou, P., Spanidis, Y., Kydonakis, P.: Teaching programming skills to blind and visually impaired learners. In: Guralnick, D., Auer, M.E., Poce, A. (eds.) Innovations in Learning and Technology for the Workplace and Higher Education, pp. 270–279. Springer International Publishing, Cham (2022)

47. Serrano Pérez, E., Juárez López, F.: An ultra-low cost line follower robot as educational tool for teaching programming and circuit's foundations. Comput. Appl. Eng. Educ. **27**(2), 288–302 (2019). https://doi.org/10.1002/cae.22074

48. Ştefan, I.A., Gheorghe, A.F., Ştefan, A., Piki, A., Tsalapata, H., Heidmann, O.: Constructing seamless learning through game-based learning experiences. Inter. J. Mobile Blended Learn. **14**(4), 1–12 (2022). https://doi.org/10.4018/ijmbl.315625

49. Thanyaphongphat, J., Thongkoo, K., Daungcharone, K.: A micropython-based educational robotic maze approach: learning improvement to competition, pp. 138 - 142 (2023). https://doi.org/10.1109/ECTIDAMTNCON57770.2023.10139363

50. Thanyaphongphat, J., Thongkoo, K., Daungcharone, K., Areeprayolkij, W.: A game-based learning approach on robotics visualization for loops in programming concepts. In: 2020 Joint International Conference on Digital Arts, Media and Technology with ECTI Northern Section Conference on Electrical, Electronics, Computer and Telecommunications Engineering (ECTI DAMT & NCON), pp. 381–385 (2020). https://doi.org/10.1109/ECTIDAMTNCON48261.2020.9090770

51. Vathanakulkachorn, V., Pichitpreecha, S., Supakwong, S.: Enhancing sequence coding skills in lower primary school through affordable game-based learning: A case study in thailand. In: 2023 8th International STEM Education Conference (iSTEM-Ed), pp. 1–5 (2023). 10.1109/iSTEM-Ed59413.2023.10305796

52. Wee, C., Yap, K.M., Lim, W.N.: iprogvr: design of a virtual reality environment to improve introductory programming learning. IEEE Access **10**, 100054–100078 (2022). https://doi.org/10.1109/ACCESS.2022.3204392

53. Woo, H., LeTendre, G.K., Pham-Shouse, T., Xiong, Y.: The use of social robots in classrooms: a review of field-based studies. Educ. Res. Rev. **33**, 100388 (2021)

54. Wu, S.Y., Su, Y.S.: Behavior and cognition processing of educational tabletop coding games. J. Internet Technol. **22**(2), 363–370 (2021). https://doi.org/10.3966/160792642021032202011

55. Yang, Q.F., Lian, L.W., Zhao, J.H.: Developing a gamified artificial intelligence educational robot to promote learning effectiveness and behavior in laboratory safety courses for undergraduate students. Int. J. Educ. Technol. High. Educ. **20**(1), 18 (2023)

56. Yett, B., et al.: A hands-on cybersecurity curriculum using a robotics platform, pp. 1040 - 1046 (2020). https://doi.org/10.1145/3328778.3366878

57. Zainuddin, Z., Chu, S.K.W., Shujahat, M., Perera, C.J.: The impact of gamification on learning and instruction: a systematic review of empirical evidence. Educ. Res. Rev. **30**, 100326 (2020)

58. Zhang, X., Chen, Y., Li, D., Hu, L., Hwang, G.J., Tu, Y.F.: Engaging young students in effective robotics education: an embodied learning-based computer programming approach. J. Educ. Comput. Rese. (2023). https://doi.org/10.1177/07356331231213548

Verification of Evaluation Model for Speech Proactiveness in Foreign Language Conversations

Naoki Matsumura[1]([✉]) and Tomoko Yonezawa[1,2,3]

[1] Kansai University, 2-1-1, Ryozenji-Cho, Takatsuki, Osaka 569-1095, Japan
{k452174,yone}@kansai-u.ac.jp
[2] ATR Interaction Science Laboratories, 2-2-2, Hikaridai, Soraku-gun,
Kyoto 619-0288, Japan
[3] Keio University, 5322, Endo, Fujisawa, Kanagawa 252-0882, Japan

Abstract. The purpose of this study is to estimate the speech proactivity of Japanese foreign-language learners in foreign-language communication. First, we focused on intonation change, utterance time ratio, and average voice volume as parameters for evaluating speech proactivity. We assumed that higher values indicate the impression of proactivity. Based on this prediction, we defined a linear model to predict speech proactivity using these evaluation parameters as independent variables. We implemented the speech proactivity evaluation system that applied this mathematical model using Pure Data and Unity. To verify the validity and suitability of the evaluation parameters for the prepared speech proactivity evaluation model, was conducted an experiment with 24 Japanese students. The participants listened to short English conversations between foreigners and Japanese people and gave their impressions of Japanese-speaking attitudes. Multiple regression analysis was conducted using the degree of intonation change, utterance time ratio, and average voice volume obtained by the system as independent variables, and the impression of proactivity was obtained through the experiment as a dependent variable. The analysis yielded a significant regression model. We found that the degree of intonation change and the ratio of speech time had a positive causal relationship with the impression of proactiveness. The above shows that the parameter selection of each evaluation parameter of the speech proactivity evaluation model is generally appropriate.

Keywords: Foreign-language communication · Speech proactivity · Intonation · Speech Duration · Voice volume · Prosody

1 Introduction

Globalization in Japan has been progressing rapidly in recent years [8]. Amid these changes is an increasing trend in the number of companies and organizations seeking and nurturing people with high English-language proficiency.

The Japanese Ministry of Education, Culture, Sports, Science and Technology pointed out that foreign-language communication is necessary in various situations and has improved the foreign-language-education curriculum. In 2020, "foreign language" was introduced as a new subject in the curriculum for the elementary school upper grades [12,13].

In foreign-language classrooms in Japan, behavioral psychological learning approaches that focus on memorization of words and sentences and repetitive practice, such as pattern practice, are often adopted [19]. These learning approaches are called audio-lingual methods. This method emphasizes the accuracy of grammar and pronunciation. Several studies have shown that this approach improves grammatical and phonetic accuracy and fluency in foreign-language learners' speaking [20,21]. On the other hand, it is believed that the Japanese people are not positive in foreign-language communication because they emphasize accurate language use. In fact, it has been revealed that Japanese people have high language anxiety in conversations with native speakers due to lack of skills [23]. However, in actual communication, a positive attitude toward conversation impresses the interlocutor, even if formal accuracy, such as in grammar and pronunciation of spoken words, is lacking. Dufner and Krause found that speech behavior with four agential behaviors (leading, dominant, confident, and boastful) and four collaborative behaviors (polite, benevolent, warm, and friendly) during a conversation enhance the interlocutor's first impression [2]. Therefore, in this study, we consider the speech attitude with these characteristics and strongly believe the intention to interact with the interlocutor is the communication skill that the foreign-language learner should acquire. We also define the degree of the intention to convey to the interlocutor as proactiveness. The purpose of this study is to identify prosodic characteristics in speech with high proactiveness and to quantify it for communication skills training. Quantification of proactiveness in foreign-language learners' foreign-language speech provides an objective evaluation of learners' speech effort in terms of speech attitude. This makes it possible to construct a system that enhances communication skills. In this study, we examined a speech proactivity evaluation model applicable to foreign-language communication situations between Japanese people.

2   Related Research

2.1   Prosodic Characteristics and Speech Attitude

With the advances in speech processing technology, it has become possible to evaluate the rhythm and pronunciation of speech from the length and intonation of silence in speech [9]. Some studies have used prosodic features to analyze speakers' emotions and speech attitudes [16,22]. Mauchand and Pell investigated the neural processes involved in hearing spoken complaints. The verification showed that prosody was related to social relation factors (cultural identity, etc.) in the possibility that the listener sympathized with the speaker [14]. Monetta et al. found the difference in the recognition method of the speech prosody of the healthy subject and the Parkinson disease patient was clarified, and the possibility that the prosodic feature influences the impression of the confidence was shown [15]. Loveday also examined the impression of politeness and showed that pitch affects the impression of politeness in English [11]. Other studies have shown that intonation and volume affect the interlocutor's attitude [6]. This paper concerns the relationship between speech proactiveness and speech prosodic features, referring to these studies.

2.2   Communication Attitude Evaluation

Many attempts have been made to evaluate communication skills. As a manual evaluation method, the method using the evaluation scale is general. Various assessment scales have been developed, including the Communication Skills Attitudes Scale, Empathic Tendency Scale, Assessment of Communication and Interaction Skill, and Evaluation of Social Interaction. These scales have been shown to have some validity for evaluation [3,4,10,18]. However, professional qualifications may be required to use some of them [3]. Also, the skill level in the actual communication is unlikely to be evaluated because it is based on self-evaluation. In addition, there are some disadvantages, such as the labor and time required for evaluation, and continuous evaluation is not possible. On the other hand, researchers have attempted to construct an automatic scoring system for communication skills. Rasipuram and Jayagopi et al. proposed an evaluation system with high prediction accuracy using communication skills in interviews as cues, such as prosody, conversation activity, and facial expression, and showed the importance of attributes such as fluency, speaking speed, and persuasiveness/persuasiveness [17]. Also, we examine the system that estimates "positive" and "negative" speech attitudes based on prosodic features, such as F0 pattern and phoneme alignment, and head actions, such as "nod" and "tilt" [5]. In this paper, we try to estimate speech proactiveness from prosodic features such as intonation (change in f_0), volume, and speaking time, referring to these studies.

3   System

In this section, we describe a speech proactivity evaluation model and an implementation of the system for quantifying the proactivity of foreign-language learners when they speak based on the model. In the system, each evaluation viewpoint described below is used as a parameter, and the total score weighted by each value indicates the degree of proactivity.

3.1   Parameters for the Evaluation

Intonation Change. It is assumed that the more inflected the utterance, the more likely it is to give the impression of speaking positively. The evaluation value, I, of the intonation change degree is defined as the average of the absolute value of the amount of change between frames for the pitch, p_t, in T frames recorded in the speech interval estimated by speech interval detection as follows.

It quantifies the degree to which intonation is applied, and it is not an evaluation of the quality of foreign pronunciation.

$$I = \frac{\sum_{t=1}^{T} |p_t - p_{t-1}|}{T - 1} \tag{1}$$

Utterance Time Ratio. It is assumed that the more quickly the person responds to the utterance and the shorter the silence during the utterance, the greater the positive impression. Let $t_s d$ be the utterance duration and $t_r t$ be the response time, and define the evaluation value, U, of the utterance time ratio as follows. It does not distinguish whether it is an English utterance or a filler. For the section in which the user holds the speaking right, the longer the speaking time, the better the evaluation.

$$U = \frac{t_s d}{t_s d + t_r t} \tag{2}$$

Average Voice Volume. Assume that speech with a higher average volume feels more like active speech. The evaluation value, V, of the voice volume is defined as the average value of the volume, v_t, between the T frames recorded in the voice section estimated by the voice section detection as follows.

$$V = \frac{\sum_{t=1}^{T} v_t}{T} \tag{3}$$

Speech Proactivity Evaluation Formula. Using the above three evaluation values and the weighting factors a, b, and c, we define the evaluation value, P, of speech proactivity as follows.

$$P = aI + bU + cV \tag{4}$$

3.2 Implementation

We implement a system that conducts real-time acoustic analysis of sound input to a microphone and uses the data to evaluate proactiveness based on the above hypothesis. The system configuration and setting are described. The sound input to the microphone is a linear PCM with a sampling frequency of 16 kHz, 16-bit quantization, and 1 channel. Pure Data is used for prosodic information analysis, and Unity is used for control of proactiveness evaluation and the calculation of evaluation values. Data is sent and receive between Pure Data and Unity using the Open Sound Control format. Figure 1 shows the flow of the proactivity evaluation system. Pure Data conducts acoustic analysis, and Unity smooths the analyzed data, detects speech intervals, and evaluates proactiveness.

Acoustic Analysis. The user's voice is inputted to Pure Data, the sinusoidal wave analysis is conducted, and pitch and volume (dB) are calculated in real time. The volume was converted from dB to root mean square (RMS), and the data was sent to Unity.

Smoothing. Unity keeps the data sent from Pure Data in relation to the received time and averages the pitch and volume for each interval of 150 ms before and after (300 ms total). The obtained value is retained as voice data obtained 150 ms before the system time.

Voice Activation Detection. The voice activation detection determines whether this data is an utterance section. Use the smoothed volume data. An interval in which the state in which the RMS after smoothing exceeds the threshold continues for 150 ms or more is classified as a voice interval. If the volume falls below the threshold and then exceeds the threshold again before 300 milliseconds have passed, the system determines that the utterance is continuing in that interval. The input sound is assumed to be input to a microphone in a quiet environment, and the possibility of misdetecting long-term noise as sound is not considered.

Speech Proactivity Evaluation. Only prosodic information corresponding to the speech section is used for speech proactiveness evaluation. When it is determined that the utterance is finished, the proactiveness of the utterance is evaluated from the accumulated data.

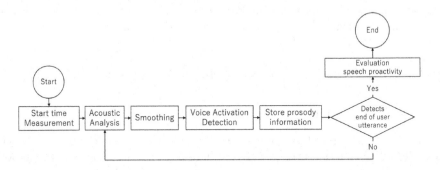

Fig. 1. The flow of the speech proactivity evaluation

4 Verification

4.1 Experimental Purpose

To confirm the validity and accuracy of a speech proactivity evaluation model. The purpose of this verification is to investigate the effect of various ways of speaking in English conversation on the impression of speech and to verify the hypothesis included in the speech proactivity evaluation model.

4.2 Experimental Hypothesis

We formulated hypotheses corresponding to each evaluation parameter of the speech proactivity evaluation model as follows:

H1 The greater the intonation change, the easier it is to feel proactivity.
H2 The greater the Utterance time ratio, the easier it is to feel proactivity.
H3 The higher the average volume, the more likely it is to feel proactivity.

4.3 Experimental Conditions

We set the following as the factors that affect the feeling of speech proactiveness. A total of eight within-subject experimental designs with two levels of each of three factors were established.

Factor A: Degree of intonation change (large/small).
Factor B: Utterance time ratio in the whole utterance turn (large/small).
Factor C: Voice volume (large/small).

4.4 Experimental Stimulus

Conversation audio corresponding to each factor was recorded. In the video, a foreigner speaks to the learner and a Japanese English-language learner responds to it. Two types of speech in Japanese were recorded in a soundproof room as evaluation speech and stimulus speech for each condition, speech with intonation and speech without intonation, for the evaluation part of each script. The recordings were made in an input environment with 2 channels, 24-bit quantization, and a 44.1 kHz sampling frequency. Next, the left and right volume balance of these voices was made uniform and normalized, and lip noise produced before and after the utterance was removed as much as possible. This audio was processed using Studio One 5 Artist. On the other hand, the foreigner's speech was made using the speech synthesis using Ondoku3. The speech was stereoized and normalized. The panning was set to 70 to the left. The speech after editing was written in 2 channels with 16-bit quantization in a 44.1-kHz wav format.

4.5 Evaluation Item

The participants gave their impression of the learner's English speech in each speech condition by subjective evaluation using the Visual Analog Scale method, which answers the following question items with integer values from 0 to 99 (0 = not completely true, 99 = completely true).

Q1 He spoke with confidence.
Q2 He was talking actively.
Q3 He was talking emotionally.
Q4 He was talking clearly.

4.6 Experimental Procedure

The experiment was conducted following the procedure below:

- The questionable points in the progress of the experiment by the experiment participant are solved, and the volume is adjusted.
- To familiarize them with the evaluation, they were asked to evaluate an experimental stimulus for practice created in the same way as the actual evaluation speech.
- A total of 24 trials were conducted. In each trial, the participants were asked to listen to the audio after checking the English script and the Japanese connotation in the audio and then asked to answer each evaluation item.

The order of presentation of the experimental conditions was determined using the Latin square method, considering the counterbalance [7]. The order of the conversation scripts was matched regardless of the experimental participants. To prevent the spread of COVID-19, the experiment was conducted with the experimenter and the experimental participant communicating remotely using Zoom.

4.7 Experimental Result

Method of Analysis. To verify the evaluation formula of speech proactiveness based on the hypothesis, multiple regression analysis was conducted to estimate the values of each evaluation item by setting each evaluation item as a dependent variable and intonation change degree, utterance time ratio and average voice volume as independent variables. In this analysis, the significance level was set at 5%. The analysis was conducted using the forced-input method without excluding the outlier. Each analysis included 576 samples. The numerical data used as independent variables were analyzed in the speech proactivity evaluation system of the proposed method. Tables 1 and 2 show the results of multiple regression analysis for each question.

Experimental Results of Q1. The analysis predicting the impression of speaking with confidence yielded a significant regression model ($p < .001$). Among the independent variables, the significance of the coefficient was confirmed in intonation change degree ($p < .001$) and mean voice volume ($p = .021$). With respect to these standardized coefficients (β), a positive causal relationship ($\beta = 0.431$) was confirmed between the intonation change and proactiveness. Therefore, the greater the intonation, the easier it was to feel that the speaker of English conversation was speaking with confidence in the third person. On the other hand, the mean vocal volume was negatively related ($\beta = -0.094$). Although the degree of influence was small, the lower the average voice volume, the higher the evaluation result. The causality of the utterance time ratio was not confirmed. The value of the adjusted coefficient of determination was low ($R^2 = 0.174$).

Experimental Results of Q2. In the analysis predicting the impression of the speaker's proactivity, a significant regression model was obtained ($p < .001$). All independent variables were significant ($ps < .05$). Regarding these standardized coefficients, the degree of intonation change was positively related to the evaluation value ($\beta = 0.431$), the utterance time ratio time was positively related ($\beta = 0.139$), and the volume of voice was negatively related ($\beta = -0.093$). Therefore, the shorter the non-utterance interval in the utterance turn and the more intonated the utterance, the higher the positive impression. On the other hand, the influence was small, but the lower the voice volume, the greater the positive impression. Also, the estimation accuracy is not high ($R^2 = 0.198$).

Experimental Results of Q3. In the analysis predicting the impression of emotional expression, a significant regression model was obtained ($p < .001$). As in the regression analysis of the impression of positivity, all the coefficients of the set independent variables were confirmed to be significant ($ps < .05$). Based on the standardized coefficients of these independent variables, we found a relatively strong positive relationship ($\beta = 0.643$) for the degree of intonation change, a negative relationship ($\beta = -0.177$) for the proportion of speaking time, and a negative relationship ($\beta = -0.117$) for the average voice volume. As in the other analyses, the degree of intonation change particularly affected the evaluation, and the more inflected the speech, the more affective it was felt. On the other hand, although the degree of influence was small, the speech time was short, and the evaluation result increased when the voice volume was low.

Experimental Results of Q4. Multiple regression analysis to predict brisk speech impressions produced a significant regression model ($p < .001$). The only independent variable that was significant was the intonation change ($p < .001$), which showed a positive relationship with the evaluation value ($\beta = 0.499$). Therefore, the more intonation the speech had, the easier it was to feel that they were speaking clearly. On the other hand, utterance time ratio and voice volume had no effect.

Support of Hypothesis. For all of the impressions tested in the present experiment, intonation change had a positive causal relationship. Therefore, H1 was supported. On the utterance time ratio, there was a positive causal relationship for the impression of proactivity. However, the impression of emotional speech was a negative causal relationship. Therefore, H2 was partially supported. The mean voice volume was negatively correlated with the impression of confidence, proactivity and emotional speech. Therefore, H3 was not supported.

5   Discussion

As a result of the verification, it was shown that the degree of intonation change, speech time ratio and average voice quantity were related to the impression of

Table 1. Results of multiple regression analysis for Q1 and Q2

Model	Q1					Q2					VIF
	B	SE	β	t	p	B	SE	β	t	p	
(Intercept)	30.852	4.264		7.236	< .001	23.801	3.932		6.053	< .001*	
Intonation change	735.039	66.984	0.430	10.973	< .001*	689.843	61.776	0.431	11.167	< .001*	1.067
Utterance time ratio	10.686	8.748	0.048	1.222	.222	28.842	8.068	0.139	3.575	< .001*	1.090
Average voice volume	-50.191	21.722	-0.094	-2.311	.021*	-46.660	20.033	-0.093	-2.329	.020*	1.141
R^2	0.174 ($p < .001$)					0.198 ($p < .001$)					

Note.*...$p < .05$

Table 2. Results of multiple regression analysis for Q3 and Q4

Model	Q3					Q4					VIF
	B	SE	β	t	p	B	SE	β	t	p	
(Intercept)	39.897	4.071		9.801	< .001*	40.811	3.844		10.617	< .001*	
Intonation Change	1226.015	63.952	0.643	19.171	< .001*	800.000	60.391	0.499	13.247	< .001*	1.067
Utterance time ratio	-28.885	8.352	-0.117	-3.458	.001*	-12.369	7.887	-0.060	-1.568	0.117	1.090
Average voice volume	-106.046	20.739	-0.177	-5.113	< .001	-17.682	19.584	-0.035	-0.903	.367	1.141
R^2	0.393 ($p < .001$)					0.235 ($p < .001$)					

Note.*...$p < .05$

the proactivity. In particular, the degree of change in intonation and the ratio of speaking time were positively correlated with proactiveness. Therefore, the selection of the evaluation parameter was generally appropriate. On the other hand, on the impression of the emotional speech in the utterance time ratio, there was some negative relation, though the effect degree was small. In addition, the average voice volume showed a negative relationship with the impression of confidence in speech, positivity, and emotional speech. As a cause of this, it is possible that when there was a certain level of fluency in English speech, it was evaluated by the consciousness that if they were confident, they would not speak with a loud voice. Next, The value of R^2 in the multiple regression model obtained in this analysis was not sufficient. As the cause, the setting of this experiment may have affected it. In the interpersonal communication, it is said that the communication is carried out through visual cues such as facial expression, gaze, gesture and posture as well as metrical information such as words, speech speed and voice volume. However, in this experiment, these visual cues were evaluated using only speech without presenting them to the evaluator, so the evaluation seems to be dispersed.

5.1   Limitation of this Study

The verification showed that the degree of intonation change, speech time ratio and average voice quantity were related to the impression of the proactivity. In particular, the degree of change in intonation and the ratio of speaking time were positively correlated with proactiveness. Therefore, the selection of the evaluation parameter was generally appropriate. On the other hand, in the impression of the emotional speech in the utterance time ratio, there was some negative relation, but the effect was small. In addition, the average voice volume had a negative relationship with the impression of confidence in speech, positivity and emotional speech. As a cause of this, it is possible that when there was a certain level of fluency in English speech, it was evaluated considering that if the speakers were confident, they would not speak with a loud voice. Next, the value of R^2 in the multiple regression model obtained in this analysis was not sufficient. As the cause, the setting of this experiment may have affected it. In the interpersonal communication, it is said that the communication is carried out through visual cues, such as facial expression, gaze, gesture and posture, as well as metrical information, such as words, speech speed and voice volume. However, in this experiment, these visual cues were evaluated using only speech without presenting them to the evaluator, so the evaluation seems to be dispersed.

5.2   Safety in Using the System

We discuss safety and ethical issues when applying this technology to AI agents with appearance. The actual reliability of AI may be far from the visual reliability. In the real world, the opponent's personality and speech attitude are often predicted from their appearance characteristics and behavior. For example, a certain level of politeness is required for customer service in shops regardless of the person. However, this technology does not take this into account. Therefore, the actual attitude the agent expresses becomes inappropriate, and as a result, the reliability may be damaged. On this point, the following countermeasures are considered.

- Set laws and standards for use by agents and the application of services.
- Implement a module to investigate the appropriate speaking attitude and proactiveness considering the usage scene and correct the speaking proactiveness evaluation.

In some cases, AI attitudinal statements fail to address discomfort or compliance in the metaverse. Agents created using this technology do not behave in the same way as humans and may evince problematic speech attitudes. The expression of the agent's attitude depends on the magnitude of the speaker's expression in interactions. In other words, there is a possibility of giving the speaker the unintended impression of, for example, a psychological attack, coercion, or harassment from the user with highly expressive speech. The following measures are considered for such noncompliance.

- Restrict use to users who understand the disclaimer.
- It also provides customer service to handle problems.
- To pursue responsibility for AI agents by deleting agents and suspending their use for output adjustment.

In social skills training using this speech proactivity evaluation, learners may acquire incorrect skills. The present speech proactivity evaluation system conducts the evaluation, ignoring the speech partner and situation. In particular, consideration for personal space and social manners of the person to be spoken to are not considered. For example, in cross-cultural exchange, it has been reported that the sense of politeness of the speaker differs between native and non-native speakers from the viewpoint of prosodic features of speech [1]. Also, the act of speaking with intonation and gestures larger than necessary without considering the difference of the position with the conversation partner may violate one's personal space and social manners. In the real world, active speech does not necessarily give a positive impression. However, the system may output high ratings for such inappropriate conversational behavior, which may lead learners to acquire incorrect social skills. Researchers will need to evaluate speech proactivity by adding this point as a parameter.

In the metaverse space, it can be used to learn how to make a good impression on the opponent. When speech proactivity increases, it is easy to make a good impression on the person to talk to and to establish a good relationship. This means that they can learn to manipulate the other person's impression of them and intentionally help them. For example, the speech proactivity evaluation model that fits the conversation partner is made, and the speech training using it is carried out. Therefore, it seems that the communication skill that can manipulate the impression for the specific individual is mastered. As a result, it may be used for misdeeds, such as manipulation of relationships, fraud and multilevel marketing. It will be necessary to establish guidelines such as using speech proactiveness evaluation optimized for individuals under the same strict control as personal information.

6   Conclusion

The purpose of this study was to quantify the speech proactivity of Japanese foreign-language learners in foreign-language communication. We examined an evaluation model for estimating speech proactiveness based on evaluation parameters (intonation change, utterance time ratio, average voice volume) to determine whether evaluation parameters contribute to speech proactiveness. As a result of the verification, the examined parameters affected the impression of speech proactiveness. Specifically, we found that the degree of intonation change strongly influenced the impression of speech proactiveness. Therefore, the selection of parameters was almost appropriate. On the other hand, the evaluation model's estimation accuracy remained low. Therefore, it is difficult to say that the present model is practicable considering estimation accuracy.

In the future, the prediction accuracy will be examined considering other metrical information, such as speech speed, and modalities, such as gesture, facial expression and gaze, which were not the object this time. We believe that by further increasing the estimation accuracy, the learner's positivity and eagerness, which are not dependent on the evaluator's subjectivity, are quantified, and it is applied to the game, which enhances the communication skill.

Acknowledgments. This study was supported in part by JSPS KAKENHI 19K12090, 23K11202, 23K11278, 21K11968; the Kansai University Fund for Supporting Young Scholars in 2023; Sharing Music Experience using Empathetic Agent; and the JST Moonshot R&D Program (Grant Number JPMJMS2215). JPMJMS2215 supported the investigation of the proposed system's safety and security, and the other funds supported the system implementation and the experiment.

References

1. Cao, J.: Prosody influence on (im) politeness perception in Chinese-German intercultural communication. J. Polit. Res. (0) (2023)
2. Dufner, M., Krause, S.: On how to be liked in first encounters: the effects of agentic and communal behaviors on popularity and unique liking. Psychol. Sci. **34**(4), 481–489 (2023)
3. Fisher, A., Griswold, L.: Evaluation of Social Interaction (ESI). Three Star Press, Fort Collins (2010)
4. Forsyth, K., Lai, J.S., Kielhofner, G.: The assessment of communication and interaction skills (acis): measurement properties. Br. J. Occup. Ther. **62**(2), 69–74 (1999)
5. Fujie, S., Ejiri, Y., Matsusaka, Y., Kikuchi, H., Kobayashi, T.: Recognition of paralinguistic information and its application to spoken dialogue system. In: 2003 IEEE Workshop on Automatic Speech Recognition and Understanding (IEEE Cat. No. 03EX721), pp. 231–236. IEEE (2003)
6. Gelinas-Chebat, C., Chebat, J.C.: Effects of two voice characteristics on the attitudes toward advertising messages. J. Soc. Psychol. **132**(4), 447–459 (1992)
7. Grant, D.A.: The latin square principle in the design and analysis of psychological experiments. Psychol. Bull. **45**(5), 427 (1948)
8. Gui, Q., Liu, C., Du, D.: Globalization of science and international scientific collaboration: a network perspective. Geoforum **105**, 1–12 (2019)
9. Hsieh, C.N., Zechner, K., Xi, X.: Features measuring fluency and pronunciation. In: Automated Speaking Assessment, pp. 101–122. Routledge, Abingdon (2019)
10. Kocak, C., Onen, A.S.: Emphatic tendency scale for student teachers: validity and reliability studies. Educ. Sci. Theory Pract. **13**(2), 958–964 (2013)
11. Loveday, L.: Pitch, politeness and sexual role: an exploratory investigation into the pitch correlates of English and Japanese politeness formulae. Lang. Speech **24**(1), 71–89 (1981)
12. Machida, T.: How do Japanese junior high school English teachers react to the teaching English in English policy. JALT J. Res. J. Jpn. Assoc. Lang. Teach. **41**(1), 5–26 (2019)
13. MacWhinnie, S.G., Mitchell, C.: English classroom reforms in Japan: a study of Japanese university EFL student anxiety and motivation. Asian-Pac. J. Second Foreign Lang. Educ. **2**, 1–13 (2017)
14. Mauchand, M., Pell, M.D.: Listen to my feelings! how prosody and accent drive the empathic relevance of complaining speech. Neuropsychologia **175**, 108356 (2022)
15. Monetta, L., Cheang, H.S., Pell, M.D.: Understanding speaker attitudes from prosody by adults with Parkinson's disease. J. Neuropsychol. **2**(2), 415–430 (2008)
16. Pervaiz, M., Khan, T.A.: Emotion recognition from speech using prosodic and linguistic features. Int. J. Adv. Comput. Sci. Appl. **7**(8), 1–7 (2016)

17. Rasipuram, S., Jayagopi, D.B.: Automatic assessment of communication skill in interface-based employment interviews using audio-visual cues. In: 2016 IEEE International Conference on Multimedia & Expo Workshops (ICMEW), pp. 1–6. IEEE (2016)
18. Rees, C., Sheard, C.: Evaluating first-year medical students' attitudes to learning communication skills before and after a communication skills course. Med. Teach. **25**(3), 302–307 (2003)
19. Sakamoto, M.: Moving towards effective English language teaching in Japan: issues and challenges. J. Multiling. Multicult. Dev. **33**(4), 409–420 (2012)
20. Sidabutar, U.: The effect of the audio lingual method on students' speaking achievement. Jurnal Suluh Pendidikan **9**(1), 56–65 (2021)
21. Sukarman, E.P., Algiovan, N.: The use of audio-lingual method in improving speaking accuracy of Indonesian EFL learners. Int. J. Multicult. Multirelig. Understand. **9**(2), 734–740 (2022)
22. Vainio, M., Suni, A., Šimko, J., Kakouros, S.: The power of prosody and prosody of power: an acoustic analysis of finnish parliamentary speech. arXiv preprint arXiv:2305.16040 (2023)
23. Woodrow, L.: Anxiety and speaking English as a second language. RELC J. **37**(3), 308–328 (2006)

Evaluating the Student eXperience: A Scale that Includes Cultural Dimensions

Nicolás Matus[1]([✉]) [iD], Virginica Rusu[2] [iD], Cristian Rusu[1] [iD], and Federico Botella[3] [iD]

[1] Pontificia Universidad Católica de Valparaíso, Valparaíso, Chile
nicolas.matus.p@mail.pucv.cl, cristian.rusu@pucv.cl
[2] Universidad de Playa Ancha, Av. Playa Ancha 850, Valparaíso, Chile
virginica.rusu@upla.cl
[3] Universidad Miguel Hernández de Elche, Elche, Spain
federico@umh.es

Abstract. Student eXperience (SX) is a particular case of Customer Experience (CX). SX refers to all perceptions and reactions, both physical and emotional, that a student or future student experiences in response to interaction with the various products, systems or services provided by a Higher Education Institution (HEI). Proper SX management allows increasing student satisfaction, which is related to student retention and satisfaction, in addition to the HEIs perceived quality ultimately related to their strategic advantage. It is for this reason that the SX evaluation is of great relevance. It is precisely for this reason that we have proposed to develop an evaluation scale to detect the HEI's main strengths and weaknesses considering cultural aspects, which are not usually considered when analyzing the undergraduate student's journey. The development of our scale is based on dimensions of SX and national culture models. This work details the development and validation process of this tool. The validation consists of expert's feedback as well as with statistical methods. Experts were from multiple cultural contexts, areas of specialization and gender. Furthermore, by working based on theoretical models we make sure that the approach proposed to the diagnostic processes for students was appropriate.

Keywords: Student eXperience · Evaluation Scale · Customer eXperience · HCI · Culture · Cultural Aspects · Higher Education · Higher Education Quality

1 Introduction

Student eXperience (SX) and the consequent student satisfaction are important factors to ensure student well-being as well as the perceived Higher Education Institution (HEI) quality. If we incorporate the cultural factor into SX solutions, it is possible to extend that satisfaction to students from cultural contexts with different expectations and perceptions about the services and products offered by HEIs.

There are various tools to manage Customer eXperience (CX). One of these tools is diagnostic in nature and allows us to have a general overview of an organization's current situation to help make decisions. To contribute to student satisfaction and integration in

© The Author(s), under exclusive license to Springer Nature Switzerland AG 2024
A. Coman and S. Vasilache (Eds.): HCII 2024, LNCS 14704, pp. 129–142, 2024.
https://doi.org/10.1007/978-3-031-61305-0_9

higher education, we have proposed the development of an SX evaluation methodology incorporating cultural aspects.

As part of developing our holistic SX methodology, we set out to develop an evaluation scale focused on student perceptions considering inherent aspects of the student's culture. This evaluation scale is based mainly on two theoretical models referring to SX (Matus et al., 2023) [1] and culture (Hofstede et al., 2010) [2, 3]. The instrument has been developed in two iterations under the supervision of experts. Its validation consists of expert judgment, statistical validation, and pilot tests in different cultural contexts. This document details the development, refinement and validation process of this tool.

2 Experiences and Culture

2.1 User eXperience

User experience (UX) concept directly relates a user to a product, system, or service to be used. The ISO standard 9241–210 defines UX as the "person's perceptions and responses resulting from the use and/or anticipated use of a product, system or service" [4]. The UX concept is relevant to our proposal, given that, as a client, students use the services, products, and systems offered by HEIs. UX incorporates transversal elements of any higher education student, such as emotions, personal beliefs/preferences/thoughts, perceptions, physiological/psychological responses, behaviors, and the achievement of activities that occurred before, during, and after using a product or service. As students use more than a single educational product or service throughout their career, to holistically analyze their behavior and perceptions it is necessary to approach it from a Customer eXperience (CX) point of view. This explores the consumer's interactions with all the products, systems and services provided throughout their customer journey [5].

2.2 Customer eXperience

The CX term arises in marketing and is considered a UX theoretical extension. Although the term CX has been widely discussed, it needs a more precise and standardized definition. Among the most used CX definitions is that of Hill et al. (2007) who defines it as "the physical and emotional experiences that occur through interactions with the products and/or services offered by a brand/company from the point of first direct and conscious contact, considering the total journey, until the post-consumption stage" [6].

Regarding the factors specific to CX, Gentile et al. (2007) considered that CX has six dimensions: i) emotional, ii) sensory, iii) cognitive, iv) pragmatic, v) lifestyle, and vi) relational [7]. The emotional component appeals to the consumer's affective system, analyzing moods, feelings and emotions throughout the "consumer journey" [8]. The sensory component is related to the sensory stimulation of consumers. The cognitive component is associated with the conscious mental processes of consumers. The pragmatic component relates to the practical results of consumers' actions. The lifestyle component is associated with consumers' moral values, pre-established beliefs, and adopting certain lifestyles and behaviors. The relational component involves the subject, his social context, and the dynamics of his interpersonal relationships. It has been observed that proper CX management leads to a strategic advantage in organizations [9]. Certainly, HEIs can benefit strategically by holistically analyzing the perceptions and reactions of their students.

2.3 Student eXperience

Student eXperience (SX) is a relatively new concept that has been defined in multiple ways [10, 11]. Even so, it is possible to consider it a particular case of CX, in which students are the clients of HEIs. This client/student-company/HEI relationship is ubiquitous and maintained outside the classroom, as students remain in contact with educational services even at home [12, 13]. The SX has been defined as "all the physical and emotional perceptions and reactions that a student or future student experiences in response to interaction with the products, systems, or services provided by a HEI, and interactions with people related to the academic field, both inside and outside of academic space" [14]. Its analysis and correct administration are directly related to the needs raised by many governments that seek to improve the quality of higher education.

It should be noted that higher education has been considered at the forefront of the UNESCO Sustainable Development Goals (SDGs) [15]. SX solutions like the one proposed in this article can affect multiple SDGs such as Quality Education, Gender Equality, and Reduced Inequalities [16]. This is considering that our diagnostic instrument, in addition to detecting HEI's strengths and weaknesses, contemplates cultural aspects that, in turn, are related to, e.g., gender aspects. Additionally, solutions focused on increasing student satisfaction often impact the HEIs perceived quality [12, 17]. This shows the importance of developing SX solutions to achieve international educational quality and integration goals and improve the HEIs' general results.

2.4 Culture

Culture is a fundamental element in societies. Its analysis allows us to visualize the individuals' social dynamics, understand their internal and external stimuli reactions, and anticipate their behavior to a certain extent. According to Hofstede (2001), culture refers to "the collective programming of the mind that distinguishes the members of one group or category of people from another" [2]. How individuals react to specific stimuli usually depends on the culture in which they have grown. Analyzing the cultural factor in the student-HEI relationship allows us to visualize the positive and negative aspects of their university experience regardless of students' perceptions from another culture. Additionally, the cultural factor is evident in students' adaptation and re-adaptation processes in a foreign cultural environment [18, 19]. This is especially relevant for immigrant or exchange students.

To develop the proposed evaluation scale, we used Hofstede's national culture model [2, 3]. This considering that this model is recognized as one of the most relevant regarding people's cultural behavior. In the model proposed by Hofstede, he has identified six dimensions of national cultures: (i) Power distance (PD), (ii) Uncertainty avoidance (UA), (iii) Individualism/collectivism (IDV), (iv) Masculinity/Femininity (MAS), (v) Long/short term orientation (LTO), and (vi) Indulgence/restraint (IVR). This cultural model was used to develop the theoretical model that supports the development of the methodology and the evaluation scale.

2.5   Evaluating the Student eXperience

In the preliminary phases of our proposal, we have developed a systematic literature review (SLR) on the SX concept, its dimensions, and its evaluation methods [14]. We were able to propose a definition of SX with a focus on CX and detail its three dimensions. By observing the need for more cultural studies in the area, we proposed incorporating the cultural factor into an evaluation methodology. To understand how cultural aspects influence students' multiple experiences, we develop a theoretical SX-Cultural model based on the cultural dimensions proposed by Hofstede [1].

- The preliminary proposal for evaluation methodology incorporates an evaluation scale as a diagnostic method to apply to students [20]. The items of this instrument refer to each of the 3 SX dimensions and six national culture dimensions. It is important to mention that the method focuses exclusively on evaluating undergraduate students' perceptions of higher education. Both the instrument and the theoretical base do not consider other educational levels.

3   Developing a Scale for Student Experience Evaluation with Cultural Aspects

The conceptual analysis that we have previously carried out on SX, its dimensions and its evaluation methods allowed us to observe the lack of methods that incorporate cultural aspects [14]. Although there are evaluation scales that address cultural aspects, no integration with factors related to student interactions from a CX focus has been observed. Our scale is being developed considering several iterations:

1. A preliminary version of our scale was developed based on literature, adapting two tools already available. One focused on SX and the other on cultural aspects.
2. Our scale was evaluated by experts, academics, and undergraduate students.
3. The scale was refined based on their feedback.
4. The scale was validated through a pilot test.
5. The final version of the scale will be applied to undergraduate students from multiple cultural backgrounds and will be statistically validated.

   - Rodríguez-Rivero et al. (2007) proposed a scale in higher education environments, that includes questions based on the cultural dimensions proposed by Hofstede [21]. Based on the SX-cultural model [1] proposed by us, we selected and adapted questions to be applied in Latin America and Spain and included them in a section focused on cultural aspects of SX. Additionally, we included questions adapted from the National Student Survey (NSS) [22, 23] as well as an open question in the section focused on SX.
   - Our proposal grouped 31 questions and is focused on being a support method for the evaluation process of a broader methodology. We believe that with the perceptions provided by the students and with the observations of the HEIs staff it will be possible to suggest technically reliable improvements to increase student satisfaction considering their cultural background.

3.1 Preliminary Scale

We created the first version of our scale based on widely known student satisfaction surveys [22, 23] and a student survey with cultural background applied in Spain and Latin America [21]. The questions were adapted to Spanish to apply to the countries under analysis. The scale was divided into two parts. The first included 19 items grouped in the 3 SX dimensions: i) Social, ii) Educational, and iii) Personal. Item 19 is an open question so it was not included in the statistical analysis.

The second part included 12 items, grouped in the 6 National Culture dimensions proposed by Hofstede (2 items per dimension): i) Indulgence vs Restraint (IVR), ii) Individualism vs Collectivism (IDV), iii) Masculinity vs Femininity (MAS), iv) Uncertainty Avoidance (UA), v) Long-Term Orientation vs. Short-Term Orientation Term Orientation (LTO), and vi) Power Distance (PD).

The scale development was supervised by three UX/CX experts with computer science and statistics backgrounds, and items were refined based on their feedback. The demographic data included in the survey had questions regarding age, nationality, gender, promotion, and career.

- This version of the scale was applied to a group of 31 undergraduate students from Chile and 38 undergraduate students from Spain. It should be noted that in the group of students from Spain there were students who identified with various nationalities, such as Argentina, Belarus, Bulgaria, Chile, Spain, France, Mexico, Romania, and Uruguay. The scale reliability for each model (SX/Culture) were analyzed with Cronbach's Alpha [24] (Table 1 and Table 2). After analyzing the UX/CX experts' group, the survey was proposed to undergo another expert judgment in a second iteration.

Table 1. Cronbach's Alpha test for data collected in the pilot scale.

Model	Cronbach's Alpha
SX	0.887
Cultural	0.711
Cronbach Alpha's acceptable range	>0.700

Based on the reliability of the results (Table 1 and Table 2), we adapted items IDV22, IDV23, MAS25, UA27, PD30, and PD31 from the cultural section. It was decided to reformulate the item questions to avoid inverted scale elements that could confuse the test subjects.

Subsequently, in the refinement stage, it was decided to additionally reformulate item MAS24 based on the value of Cronbach's Alpha and the experts' feedback.

Table 2. Cronbach's Alpha test for data for each item.

Model	Dimension	Item	Cronbach's Alpha eliminating item
SX	Educational	ED01	0.879
		ED02	0.885
		ED03	0.885
		ED04	0.878
		ED05	0.879
		ED06	0.874
		ED07	**0.897**
		ED08	0.881
		ED09	0.883
	Social	SO10	0.880
		S011	0.881
		SO12	0.880
		SO13	0.880
		SO14	0.877
		SO15	0.876
		SO16	0.884
	Personal	PE17	0.886
		PE18	0.874
Cultural	IVR	IVR20	0.672
		IVR21	0.657
	IDV	IDV22[a]	0.697
		IDV23[a]	0.710
	MAS	**MAS24**	**0.753**
		MAS25[a]	0.685
	UA	UA26	0.689
		UA27[a]	0.680
	LTO	LTO28	0.697
		LTO29	0.705
	PD	PD30[a]	0.663
		PD31[a]	0.683

[a]inverted scale element

3.2 Refining the Scale Based on Experts' Feedback

After developing the first version of the scale and with the supervisors' approval, we set out to refine the instrument through expert judgment. The scale was quantitatively and qualitatively examined in mid and late 2023 by:

- Four usability experts who work in the academic and private sectors.
- Eight academics from Chile, Colombia, and Italy.

The participants were asked to evaluate each of the 31 items using a 5-point Likert scale [25], where 1 is not appropriate and 5 is very appropriate. They were also asked to comment on items and the scale (Table 3).

Table 3. Overall opinions on the preliminary scale.

	Min	Max	Average	S.D
Experts	2	5	4.54	0.76
Academics	1	5	4.46	0.93

Based on the analysis of Cronbach's Alpha by dimensions and the comments of experts and academics, we decided to modify two items (Table 4). The item MAS24 "For students, their university career is more important than their social circle" was selected to be adapted because the experts mentioned that the item can be ambiguous and difficult to interpret.

Another item to adapt is LTO29 "When it comes to preparing for assessments, students plan from day one". Like the other item, this one was also considered ambiguous with respect to what a student can consider "day one". Additionally, the subjectivity of the question was criticized, making it unclear whether a student was referring to her personal situation or what was observed regarding their classmates.

All items of the SX dimensions were kept. Although Cronbach's Alpha increases slightly when item ED07 is eliminated, expert opinion supports its existence. Regarding the items referring to the cultural dimensions, 2 previously mentioned elements (MAS24 and LTO29) were adapted based on expert comments, clarifying their meaning and/or better focusing to be less ambiguous for students.

- As part of Hofstede's work on the dimensions of national culture, scores ranging from 0 to 100 were developed for each cultural dimension [26]. In this way, each country has a score for each culture dimension, which oscillates between 2 opposite attitudinal poles. Values below 50 are considered low and values above 50 are considered high in relation to the distinctive attributes of each cultural dimension. These scores were used to comparatively describe data from the culture section of our scale for the Chilean and Spanish student groups (Table 5).

Table 4. Quantitative evaluation of the preliminary scale.

Model	Dimension	Item	Average	S.D	Action
Student eXperience Model	Educational Dimension	ED 01: The courses developed by the teachers are interesting	4.42	0.79	Keep
		ED 02: The courses challenge me to give my best by being demanding	4.50	0.67	Keep
		ED 03: My courses have given me the opportunity to explore ideas or concepts in depth	4.83	0.39	Keep
		ED 04: My courses have given me opportunities to apply what I have learned	4.75	0.62	Keep
		ED 05: Course evaluations have been fair	4.50	0.80	Keep
		ED 06: Courses are organized in a way that they run smoothly	4.50	0.67	Keep
		ED 07: The course schedule is appropriate for me	4.08	1.08	Keep
		ED 08: The university resources and facilities have helped me in my learning	4.17	0.94	Keep
		ED 09: I have been able to access specific resources and facilities when I needed them	4.33	1.07	Keep
	9 ED Items				
	Social Dimension	SO 10: I have received useful comments on my academic work	4.33	1.23	Keep
		SO 11: I have been able to contact university staff when I needed it	4.75	0.62	Keep
		SO 12: I have received sufficient guidance regarding my courses	4.75	0.62	Keep
		SO 13: I feel part of a university community	4.75	0.62	Keep

(*continued*)

The data in the table are complemented by the data in Table 6, where the Mann-Whitney U test was applied to check the existence of significant differences [27]. This

Table 4. (*continued*)

Model	Dimension	Item	Average	S.D	Action
		SO 14: I have had adequate opportunities to work with other students as part of my courses	4.58	0.51	Keep
		SO 15: University staff value student opinions	4.42	0.90	Keep
		SO 16: The student center/delegation/association effectively represents the academic interests of students	4.58	0.90	Keep
	7 SO Items				
	Personal Dimension	PE 17: I have had adequate opportunities to provide feedback on my courses	4.67	0.49	Keep
		PE 18: I am satisfied with the quality of my courses	4.83	0.39	Keep
	2 PE Items				
National Culture Model	IVR	IVR 20: Students have a positive view of the university, considering that it is possible to have fun there	4.42	0.79	Keep
		IVR 21: Both teachers and students gladly accept questions in class, fostering a participatory environment	4.75	0.87	Keep
	IDV	IDV 22: The feeling of individual competitiveness among students is low; teachers encourage teamwork	4.27	1.27	Keep
		IDV 23: There is a sense of collective identity; students care about overall course assessment results	4.25	1.22	Keep
	MAS	**MAS 24: For students, their university career is more important than their social circle**	**3.75**	**1.22**	**Adapt**

(*continued*)

Table 4. (*continued*)

Model	Dimension	Item	Average	S.D	Action
		MAS 25: The university offers resources for less fortunate students	4.83	0.39	Keep
	UA	UA 26: Students know exactly how they will be evaluated; They have exams from previous years or precise information about the evaluations	4.25	1.14	Keep
		UA 27: Bureaucracy at the university is a problem that consumes a lot of students' time	4.67	0.78	Keep
	LTO	LTO 28: Courses focus on the professional development of students based on current content in engineering/science/business	4.92	0.29	Keep
		LTO 29: When it comes to preparing for assessments, students plan from day one	**3.42**	**1.44**	**Adapt**
	PD	PD 30: There are mechanisms for students to express their opinion and influence university decisions	4.58	0.79	Keep
		PD 31: The treatment of the teachers is quite distant. They are considered an unquestionable authority	4.45	0.69	Keep
	2 Items per cultural nation dimension				

is in consideration of the ordinal nature of the results that make it necessary to use a non-parametric test. In this test a p-value of 0.05 was used as decision rule.

Considering the low number of test subjects and the lower cultural homogeneity of the group of students from Spain the results could distort to a certain extent. This could certainly be a limitation of our pilot test. To reduce the heterogeneity of the data the results have been reduced to the two largest groups of each test (Chile and Spain). This is also considering that the cultural scores proposed by Hofstede were documented for individual nations, not regions.In Table 5 we present the averages of the items referring to cultural dimensions together with the cultural dimension scores presented by Hofstede, differentiated by the country where the results were collected.

Table 5. Cultural differences comparison for each group of students.

Item	Country	Average	S.D	Hofstede's Cultural Score
IVR 20	**Chile**	**3.26**	**0.93**	**IVR:** **68 (Chile)** **44 (Spain)**
	Spain	**2.59**	**1.19**	
IVR 21	Chile	3.61	0.84	
	Spain	3.70	0.95	
IDV 22[a]	Chile	2.35	1.20	IDV: 49 (Chile) 67 (Spain)
	Spain	2.52	0.98	
IDV 23[a]	Chile	3.16	1.44	
	Spain	3.26	0.94	
MAS 24	**Chile**	**2.71**	**1.13**	**MAS:** **28 (Chile)** **42 (Spain)**
	Spain	**2.04**	**0.98**	
MAS 25[a]	Chile	2.81	1.11	
	Spain	2.41	1.15	
UA 26	Chile	3.03	1.05	UA: 86 (Chile) 86 (Spain)
	Spain	3.07	1.04	
UA 27[a]	Chile	3.48	0.93	
	Spain	3.30	1.10	
LTO 28	**Chile**	**3.52**	**0.96**	**LTO:** **12 (Chile)** **48 (Spain)**
	Spain	**2.89**	**1.25**	
LTO 29	Chile	2.74	1.06	
	Spain	2.56	0.93	
PD 30[a]	Chile	3.48	1.12	PD: 63 (Chile) 57 (Spain)
	Spain	3.22	1.09	
PD 31[a]	Chile	2.74	1.18	
	Spain	2.59	0.97	

[a] inverted scale element

The elements that have more differentiated averages have a margin of 0.67 points. This can be seen between the results of Chile and Spain for items IVR20 and MAS24. In Table 6 we observe that there is evidence to consider significant differences for items IVR20, MAS24, and LTO28 considering the hypothesis Ha: μ Chile $\neq \mu$ Spain.

In the IVR20 item we observe that the average differences are consistent with their cultural scores for the IVR dimension. This could indicate that our instrument could detect cultural differences. In the case of item MAS24, the difference is contrary to the cultural scores for the MAS dimension. Considering the results of Cronbach's Alpha (Table 2), the experts feedback (Table 4), and the results of the Mann-Whitney U test (Table 6), we have chosen to modify the question in item MAS24.

– Item LTO28 present a difference that is not explained by the cultural score for the corresponding dimensions. Considering the nature of the sample and the feedback from the experts, we have decided to keep the item.

Table 6. Mann-Whitney U test for cultural differences Chile-Spain.

Item	p-value
IVR20	**0.033**
IVR21	0.642
IDV22	0.376
IDV23	0.835
MAS24	**0.025**
MAS25	0.157
UA26	0.764
UA27	0.487
LTO28	**0.038**
LTO29	0.536
PD30	0.256
PD31	0.733

Item MAS24 has been modified. The version shown to the experts indicates "For students, their university career is more important than their social circle." Considering the feedback from the experts, the question presents a binary scenario that can lead to errors. Additionally, they indicated that the social circle could include social interactions that occur within the university. For these reasons we have decided to modify the question to "For students, it is acceptable to reduce their social interactions in order to improve their academic results."

– Item LTO29 has also been modified. The version shown to the experts indicates "When it comes to preparing for assessments, students plan from day one." Considering the experts' feedback, this question is far too personal, being ambitious make a student speak for a general group of people. Additionally, they indicated that the term "day one" can be very ambiguous. For these reasons we have decided to modify the question to "When it comes to preparing for assessments I plan ahead."

4   Conclusions & Future Work

The theory on which our proposal is based shows the lack of research and the importance of incorporating cultural aspects into SX solutions. Within these solutions we believe that an evaluation methodology is the most appropriate to satisfy the HEI's needs considering its flexibility. It is as a method of these methodology that we have proposed the scale presented in this work.

- Our scale was developed based on literature and a SX-Cultural model. The incorporated items refer to both the 3 SX dimensions and the 6 national culture dimensions proposed by Hofstede. It has 31 questions and was then evaluated by 12 experts/scholars/professionals from different areas, national contexts, and gender. The instrument was refined in 2 stages under the supervision of experts in the UX/CX area; 2 items were adapted, and 29 items were kept unchanged.
- Considering the limited number of participants in the preliminary scale, we believe that it is too ambitious to do an in-depth analysis of the cultural differences between the participants. Even so, after the massive application of the consolidated scale, this analysis is imperative.

In the future we will use structural equation modeling (SEM) to check the underlying model of our scale. We intend to use the scale in future surveys in conjunction with other methods within the framework of an evaluation methodology that incorporates cultural aspects. We do not rule out an additional iteration of refinement of the instrument after statistically analyzing the results of its application in students from different educational and cultural contexts.

Acknowledgments. The authors would like to thank the School of Informatics Engineering of the Pontificia Universidad Católica de Valparaíso (PUCV) and the Universidad Miguel-Hernández de Elche (UMH). Nicolás Matus is a beneficiary of ANID-PFCHA/Doctorado Nacional/2023–21230171, in Chile.

References

1. Matus, N., Rusu, C., Botella, F.: Proposing a SX model with cultural factors. Appl. Sci. **13**(6), 3713 (2023)
2. Hofstede, G., Hofstede, G.J., Minkov, M.: Cultures and Organizations: Software of the Mind. McGraw Hill, New York (2010)
3. Hofstede, G.: Culture's Consequences: Comparing Values, Behaviours, Institutions, and Organizations Across Nations, 2nd edn. Sage, London (2001)
4. ISO 9241-210. Ergonomics of Human-system Interaction—Part 210: Human-centered Design for Interactive Systems. International Organization for Standardization (2010)
5. Nielsen Norman Group. How Channels, Devices, and Touchpoints Impact the Customer Journey. https://www.nngroup.com/articles/channels-devices-touchpoints/. Accessed 14 Dec 2023
6. Hill, N., Roche, G., Allen, L.: Customer Satisfaction. The Customer Experience Through the Customer's Eye, 1st edn. Cogent Publishing, Abingdon (2007)
7. Gentile, C., Spiller, N., Noci, G.: How to sustain the customer experience: an overview of experience components that co-create value with the customer. Eur. Manag. J. **25**, 395–410 (2007)
8. Lemon, K.N., Verhoef, P.C.: Understanding customer experience throughout the customer journey. J. Mark. **80**, 69–96 (2016)
9. Sujata, J.: Customer experience management: an exploratory study on the parameters affecting customer experience forcellular mobile services of a telecom company. Procedia Soc. Behav. Sci. **133**, 392–399 (2014)
10. Haselgrove, S.: The Student Experience. Open University Press, London (1994)

11. Bates, E.A., Kaye, L.K., McCann, J.J.: A snapshot of the student experience: exploring student satisfaction through the use of photographic elicitation. J. Furth. High. Educ. **43**, 291–304 (2019)

12. Harvey, L., Knight, P.T.: Transforming Higher Education: Society for Research into Higher Education. Open University Press, London (1996)

13. Arambewela, R., Maringe, F.: Mind the gap: staff and postgraduate perceptions of student experience in higher education. High. Educ. Rev. **44**, 63–83 (2012)

14. Matus, N., Rusu, C., Cano, S.: Student eXperience: a systematic literature review. Appl. Sci. **11**(20), 9543 (2021)

15. UNESCO. Higher Education and the SDGs. https://www.iesalc.unesco.org/en/the-contribut ion-of-higher-education-to-the-sdgs/. Accessed 14 Dec 2023

16. UNESCO. The 17 Goals: Sustainable Development. Available online: https://sdgs.un.org/ goals. Accessed 14 Dec 2023

17. McInnis, C.: Studies of student life: an overview. Eur. J. Educ. **39**, 383–394 (2004)

18. Lysgaard, S.: Adjustment in a foreign society: norwegian fulbright grantees visiting the United States. Int. Soc. Sci. Bull. **7**, 45–51 (1955)

19. Gullahorn, J.T., Gullahorn, J.E.: An extension of the u-curve hypothesis. J. Soc. Sci. **19**(3), 33–47 (1963)

20. Matus, N., Rusu, C., Botella, F.: Towards well-being and inclusion in the educational system: a preliminary methodology for evaluating student eXperience considering cultural factors. In: Coman, A., Vasilache, S. (eds.) Social Computing and Social Media. HCII 2023. Lecture Notes in Computer Science, vol. 14026. Springer, Cham (2023). https://doi.org/10.1007/978-3-031-35927-9_8

21. Rodríguez-Rivero, R., Ortiz-Marcos, I., E. Patiño-Arenas, V.: Exploring the influence of culture in the present and future of multicultural organizations: comparing the case of Spain and Latin America. Sustainability **14**(4), 2327 (2022). https://doi.org/10.3390/su14042327

22. National Student Survey. https://www.thestudentsurvey.com/. Accessed 14 Dec 2023

23. Office for Students UK. Questionnaires for NSS 2023 and 2022. https://www.officefor students.org.uk/media/4bbda46a-b4b8-498d-8797-67d66dd2d910/nss-2023-annex-a-nss-2023-and-nss-2022-core-questionnaires-december-2022.pdf. Accessed 14 Dec 2023

24. Cronbach, L.J.: Coefficient alpha and the internal structure of tests. Psychometrika **16**(3), 297–334 (1951)

25. Likert, R.: A technique for the measurement of attitudes. Arch. Psychol. **22**(140), 55 (1932)

26. The Culture Factor Group. Country Comparison Tool. https://www.hofstede-insights.com/ country-comparison-tool/. Accessed 14 Dec 2023

27. Mann, H.B., Whitney, D.R.: On a test of whether one of two random variables is stochastically larger than the other. Ann. Math. Stat. **18**, 50–60 (1947)

The Impact of a Mechanism Where a Stacked Book Provides Memories of Its Purchase on Buyer's Interest

Haruto Nomoto[1], Masayuki Ando[2], Kouyou Otsu[3], and Tomoko Izumi[3](✉)

[1] Graduate School of Information Science and Engineering, Ritsumeikan University,
1-1-1 Noji-Higashi, Kusatsu 525-8577, Shiga, Japan
[2] Ritsumeikan Global Innovation Research Organization, Ritsumeikan University,
1-1-1 Noji-Higashi, Kusatsu 525-8577, Shiga, Japan
[3] College of Information Science and Engineering, Ritsumeikan University, 1-1-1 Noji-Higashi,
Kusatsu 525-8577, Shiga, Japan
izumi-t@fc.ritsumei.ac.jp

Abstract. The focus of this paper is addressing the problem associated with "Tsundoku", a condition where a book is left unread (hereinafter referred to as "stacked book"). We investigate an approach to rekindle interest in and enhance a motivation to read stacked books, which are feelings that wane after purchase. In this study, we verify the hypothesis that "Presenting memories of when a stacked book was purchased by itself enhances the buyer's interest in it and motivation to read it". We developed an augmented reality (AR)-based experimental system to display messages from a book in the form of speech balloon text on a smartphone screen. In the experiment, we compared the effects of presenting three types of information from a stacked book: a book's title, third-party opinions such as product reviews, and memories of when the book was purchased. The experimental results show that presenting memories from books has no significant effect on reading motivation or interest when compared to providing third-party opinions. However, it was demonstrated that the information presentation method, in which an anthropomorphic book discusses its past purchase memories, is effective in increasing buyer's interest and motivation to read the book.

Keywords: Stacked books · Tsundoku · Memory-based information · Recommendation system · Conversational Agent · Anthropomorphization · Media-Equation

1 Introduction

Do you ever leave a book you bought unread? A book in such a state is called "Tsundoku" (stacked books) in Japan because it arises from being accumulated and piled up without being read. This term was featured in the BBC News article in 2018 [1], and the concept of "Tsundoku" has gained international recognition and resonance beyond Japan. Book lovers tend to accumulate books because they aspire to read many, but often lack the time [2]. Moreover, as time passes, the motivation and interest in purchasing a book fade, and people often forget about the book's presence. Thus, although they may have an interest in the contents of the stacked books, they can still not clear out the stacks of unread books. Hereinafter, we refer to a "Tsundoku" book as a "stacked book."

In this research, we consider a support method for enhancing interest in and reading motivation for stacked books. Our approach focuses on reviving buyer's original memories of a book at the time of its purchase as a potential means to achieve this goal. When a buyer decides to buy a book, there is usually some reason for doing so. Therefore, reminding buyers of their initial emotions and some of their book purchasing experiences may enhance their interest and bring the books back to mind.

From this perspective, to increase interest in stacked books, we consider a method to present memories of the books' purchase. Additionally, this study focuses on a conversational approach with agents for presenting purchase memories. In the field of conversational agents research, design methods that transform everyday items into agents have been proposed and demonstrated to effectively capture the user's attention [3]. Therefore, personifying a book purchased by a buyer and presenting it as a narrator of its own purchase memories could be an effective strategy for capturing the buyer's attention and evoking its presence.

This study aims to clarify whether the mechanism by which a stacked book presents memories of being purchased can help to increase the buyer's reading motivation. As a first step toward achieving this goal, we established a prototype environment in which a stacked book itself presents memories of being purchased to the buyer as a text message. We then examined, in a laboratory-controlled setting, how such memory-based information affects buyers' reading motivation.

2 Related Research

2.1 Relationship Between Memory About Items and Attachment to Them

In the field of consumer psychology, several studies have been conducted on the effects of people's memories of artifacts on their impressions of them. In particular, the relationship with people's attachment to artifacts has been discussed. For example, Kino [4] showed that long-term ownership of a target artifact and having memories of it are major reasons for attachment to the artifact. They also suggested that the artifacts to which a person becomes attached tend to be personified as the person themselves or a familiar person. Additionally, another study by Hatori [5] examined the factors enhancing attachment to one's possessions, focusing on bicycles. They showed that recalling memories about one's own bicycles enhances the sense of attachment to them and that persons with a higher sense of attachment are more likely to refrain from neglecting the bicycles. These studies suggest that memories of a person's own artifacts may enhance feelings of attachment to them. However, these studies focus only on investigating the factor of attachment to a person's own artifacts, without intending to generate interest in or desire to use artifacts.

2.2 Conversational Agent Based on Anthropomorphism of Objects

In the research field of conversational agents, several studies have been conducted on the design method of presenting information in the form of talking from artifacts themselves by anthropomorphizing them as a conversational agent. These studies suggest the potential of the method for attracting users' attention to artifacts. Unconscious perception of artifacts as human is known as the concept of Media-Equation [6] or Theory of Mind [7]. In terms of agent design, these studies investigate the mechanism of encouraging human attention based on the knowledge that humans have a cognitive tendency to treat artifacts like humans. For example, Osawa et al. [3] proposed a design method to attach eyes and hands to an artifact and make the artifact itself an anthropomorphic agent. They experimented by comparing a proposed case in which anthropomorphized artifacts talk about themselves with a control case in which an interactive agent independent of artifacts talks about the artifacts. From their findings, a system design in which the anthropomorphized artifacts themselves talk effectively attracts user's attention to the artifacts. Additionally, there is a study focused on speech expressions to make people feel anthropomorphic when designing these anthropomorphized artifacts [8]. It is shown that first-person expression is an important factor in forming the sense that an artifact itself is speaking independently. Moreover, the interaction with other anthropomorphic elements, such as informal wording and emotional reaction, is important for enhancing the feeling of affinity. These findings suggest that communicating information from anthropomorphic artifacts is useful in eliciting users' interest in the artifacts.

2.3 Our Study

The purpose of this study is to clarify whether the mechanism of presenting past memories about stacked books from the books themselves can trigger the recollection of their presence and raise the interests of buyers. As mentioned in Sect. 2.1, several studies have suggested that recalling memories about artifacts in daily life can increase the sense of attachment to them. Thus, it is conceivable that recalling experiences with artifacts may trigger a re-examination of the relationship between an owner and the artifacts. Therefore, presenting the relationship and memories between a buyer and stacked books might make the buyer more aware of them and also be useful in increasing the buyer's interest in the books.

To encourage owners to recall memories of artifacts where their attention has waned, such as stacked books, it is necessary to consider strategies to attract their attention to the artifacts. For example, presenting visual information such as the design of book covers might effectively remind the buyer of the books' existence. However, such visual information might not motivate them to read the books because the spines of stacked books are always visible, yet the books remain unread. So, in this study, we further consider an effective strategy to attract attention to books by having them talk about past memories themselves. The literature referred to in Sect. 2.2 suggests that narratives from anthropomorphized artifacts effectively elicit owner's interest in the artifacts. In addition to those presented in the previous section, some interfaces to help people reflect on past memories have been proposed, such as [9, 10]. However, these studies focused on supporting memory recall about life events or behaviors in life. Therefore, as in this study, an interface that focuses on supporting the recall of a memory related to specific artifacts and using it to address specific issues in daily life has not been extensively studied. Our study presents a case of assisting in recalling memories about specific objects to address issues related to the objects in the context of the issue of stacked books.

3 Our Proposal

3.1 Design Concept

In this study, we propose an information presentation framework that provides a user's memory of purchasing a book in the form of narration from the book itself. To recall memories about artifacts that are out of the owner's interest or consciousness, such as stacked books, it is necessary to draw attention to the artifacts. The framework is designed to draw attention to a stacked book by making the book itself the narrator to recount memories of the purchase, inspired by the findings about anthropomorphized agents described in Sect. 2.2. In this framework, the books themselves narrate stories encouraging users to recall the books, such as "You found me on that day when you were looking for a popular novel in the store, right?" The user's purchase experience can be considered as a memory for the book itself. In designing this framework, we consider it important for the book itself to speak to the user to attract their attention and to present sympathetic information about the book itself. The design to present the experience shared with a user from a book's point of view is derived from these two requirements. Therefore, providing information based on the framework is expected to attract users' attention and encourage users to re-examine the relationship between artifacts and users.

3.2 Experimental System

To realize this concept faithfully, it is necessary to consider a concrete presentation method for when and how a book itself should interact with a user. However, there are many points to consider, such as how speech from a book itself should be represented, what type of presentation is most convenient for a user, and what voice and tone of books should be applied. It is difficult to address all these issues at once. Therefore, this study focuses solely on the question, "Does presenting a buyer's memories from a stacked book attract the buyer's attention and make the buyer want to read it again?," which is the core idea of the proposed method. Consequently, in this study, we investigate the effect of presenting a message related to memory to a user under a controlled and limited situation where the message is presented as text on the screen of a smartphone. During the experiment, the user's impression when reading the text is evaluated.

For this evaluation, we developed an AR-based information presentation system wherein the book's speech is displayed in a speech bubble on a smartphone screen when the phone's camera is held up to the book. This system is a smartphone application built in Unity. When the camera captures the spine of a book, a speech balloon is visualized, emerging from the spine to create the appearance that the book itself is speaking. The speech bubble contains a text message generated by system, giving the impression that the book is conveying the message.

Fig. 1. Experimental setup. Smartphones on the left present book information, while the PC on the right controls smartphone contents and provides a questionnaire answering function.

We conducted experiments to identify useful information for enhancing interest in stacked books and motivation to read them by comparing various types of texts presented on the system display. Details of the texts compared in the experiment, their methods, and evaluation items are presented in Sect. 4. However, the details of the systems used in the experiment are described here in advance.

In the experiment, we employed Thurston's pairwise comparison method [11] to evaluate the impressions of the presented messages. This survey method asks participants to choose the most appropriate option from two given choices of a given question while viewing two contents simultaneously. To conduct the experiment using this method, we established an evaluation environment to facilitate the smooth running of the pairwise comparison process. Figure 1 illustrates the evaluation environment, which consists of two smartphones placed in front of the books running the experimental application and a PC for controlling the displayed contents on these devices and collecting participants' responses. Participants can provide their choices for the given questions on the PC while viewing the contents displayed on the smartphones.

In the PC, the list of question items and the presenting messages on the smartphones are registered in advance. Participants can proceed with the experimental procedure based on the pairwise comparison method by answering questions on the PC while comparing the displays of the two smartphones. At this time, the messages displayed on the smartphones and the question messages on the PC screen are dynamically updated along with the participants' answer status. In the pairwise test, for each question, participants compare all possible pairs of messages that a book talks about. The answers for each pair are recorded in a log file on the PC. After the participants answer all pairs in all questions, the screen is automatically closed. In this system, the order of the combinations of messages displayed on the smartphone is set to be random for each participant.

4 Experiment

4.1 Purpose and Hypothesis

In this experiment, our aim is to examine whether our proposed method, wherein a stacked book itself recounts past memories of its purchase, is effective in eliciting the buyer's interest in the book. As mentioned in the introduction, interest in and motivation to read a purchased book are typically higher at the time of purchase. Therefore, it is expected that recalling the event of the purchase might enhance a motivation to read it. Additionally, existing research suggests that speech from artifacts themselves attracts owner's attention to the artifacts. Based on this, we formulated the hypothesis: "Presenting a past experience when a book was purchased by the book itself enhances the buyer's interest in and motivation to read the book." This experiment aims to verify this hypothesis.

4.2 Outline of the Experiment

In this experiment, we established laboratory-controlled settings that closely resemble the use case of the proposed method. Specifically, to verify the effectiveness of the proposed method under controlled conditions, the experiment was designed to simulate the experience of purchasing a book and then evaluate the information presentation for the selected book after a period of time.

The experiment was conducted over two days and comprised two phases: a book selection phase and an evaluation phase. During the book selection phase (Day 1), participants were asked to select books on an online shopping site and share their selection process and impressions in an interview. The evaluation phase (Day 2) involved participants experiencing a system that provided information about the selected book. Notably, participants had no opportunity to interact with the selected book between Days 1 and 2. Day 1 corresponded to the book-buying phase, while Day 2 corresponded to remembering the books while using the system. Days 1 and 2 were separated by approximately a week to evaluate the selected book's information after the participant's memories and feelings of the selected books had faded. In the following sections, we describe the content of each experimental day.

4.3 Day 1: Book Selection and Interview

The book selection phase on Day 1 was designed to simulate conditions similar to stacked books, remaining unread. Participants were tasked with choosing three books they wished to read from the shopping website Amazon.com using a provided PC. During the book selection process, participants were informed via a note (Fig. 2) about the limited categories of books they could choose from, such as literature, criticism, nonfiction, and business books. The screen was recorded during the book selection for use in the post-interview. It is important to note that participant only selected books they wanted to read but did not purchase them during the experiment.

After the book selection phase, we conducted a narrative interview [12] to obtain information about their selection processes and subjective feelings. Participants were

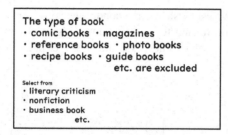

Fig. 2. Note outlining exclusion criteria in the book selection process.

Table 1. Questions for the additional interview. IQ7 is asked at the end of the interview.

No	Question
IQ1	What made you interested in this book?
IQ2	What did you think when you saw that information?
IQ3	Why did you decide to search with this search term?
IQ4	Why did you decide to select in this category?
IQ5	What was the deciding factor in selecting the book?
IQ6	Is there anything I forgot to say or additional things about this book?
IQ7	Please rank the three books you selected in the order you want to read. Please also tell me the reason for that ranking

asked to explain their selection processes and feelings orally in chronological order while watching the video recorded during the selection process. The purpose of this interview was to collect data that could be used to present information as their memories of the purchase experiences in the experiment on the second day. Subsequently, the experimenter conducted an additional interview to further explore the participant's experiences based on their responses from the narrative interview. Table 1 outlines the questions asked during the interview.

4.4 Day 2: Experimental Methods and Comparison Conditions

In the evaluation phase on Day 2, participants were tasked with comparing and evaluating the text messages concerning the books selected on Day 1, as described in Sect. 3.2. Day 2 was separated by approximately one week from Day 1. During Day 2, participants engaged with the AR-based experimental system to view speech bubbles containing messages about one of the books they had selected on Day 1. In this experiment, participants evaluated for one of the books they selected on Day 1, which is chosen by the experimenter. We utilized Thurstone's pairwise comparison method [11] to assess the impression of three types of information about a book. Participants were instructed to simultaneously view two randomly selected text messages from the three types and rate which they deemed the most appropriate answer to the questionnaire using the experimental system. We established three conditions corresponding to the three types of presented information related to stacked books. Figure 3 depicts examples of the application screens, while Table 2 shows sample messages presented for each condition.

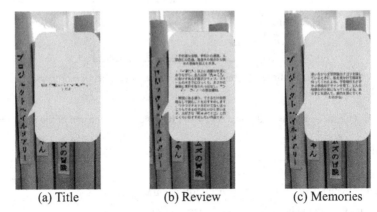

| (a) Title | (b) Review | (c) Memories |

Fig. 3. Example screens of the experimental system used in the study. Each image in (a)-(c) corresponds to the displayed content for the respective condition described in the main text.

Table 2. Example of displaying information in each condition about the book selected by the participant. These contents are translated into English from the text depicted in the image shown in Fig. 3. The [Book title] and [Author] represent the title and author of the book handled in the experiment, and [Title of another book] represents the title of another book.

Condition	Example of displaying information
(a) Title	I'm "[Book title]"
(b) Review	- A strange experience. Exploring the unknown. The crisis of human existence. A world beyond imagination, viewed in life-size - Even though the situation is more severe than in [Title of another book], the main character is as positive as in [Title of another book], I was surprised at the grandeur. The unexpected development has been mind-boggling. That is worthy of [Author's name] 's reputation - As described in the explanation, we recommend that you read without prior information as much as possible. We think it will give you not only excitement but also warmth. I would recommend it as much as my favorite [Title of another book]
(c) Memories	I know you saw me and became interested in me when you were searching the Literary Criticism category. When you saw the design of my cover where the astronauts float, it seemed to me that you were wondering what kind of story it was. Did I capture your interest after you read the synopsis?

- **Title condition:** Presenting the book title only.
- **Review condition:** Presenting third-party reviews obtained from Amazon.com as a message from the book.
- **Memories condition:** Presenting each participant's memories in the selection process obtained from the interview as a message from the book itself.

One possible reason for the decline in motivation to read stacked books could be that people forget about the books' existences or loose interested in them. Therefore, we introduced the title condition to investigate whether presenting the book's existence or a specific memory associated with it could be effective. Additionally, we set the review condition to assess whether presenting memories, rather than just information that simply attracts users' interest, would be effective.

In the Title condition, the book title is presented as a form of self-introduction, such as "I am [book title]," as shown in (a) of Table 2. The Review condition presents three reviews of a book randomly extracted from Amazon.com with at least three stars, as shown in (b) of Table 2. Thus, the review condition incorporates third-party opinions about the book into the message. The obtained original review comments are presented in bullet points within the message. We selected reviews within 100 words, excluding information unrelated to the evaluation of the book, such as the book's condition or spoilers about the content. Moreover, we eliminated reviews containing first-person expressions, which is terms referring to the reviewer, such as "I" because it might be whether such terms refer to the reviewer or the book itself in this experiment. However, a few reviews containing first-person expressions were displayed. Reviews viewed during the book selection were not used because these reviews may reside in the participants' memories and trigger unintended recall.

The messages in the Memories condition were designed based on a summary of the narrative interview on Day 1, expressing the participant's experience chronologically from the book's perspective in about 100 words, as shown in (c) of Table 2. The approach involved writing in first person 'I', focusing solely on events directly related to the book in spoken language, and aiming to personalize the memories as if the book itself were recounting them. This ensures that the shared memories with the book are presented as comfortably as information that the book itself conveys.

4.5 Day 2: Experimental Bookshelf

In this experiment, we used the experimental system outlined in Sect. 3.2 to display messages about a book on a bookshelf simulating stacked books. The system presents dialogue in a speech balloon text from the spine of book in AR format on the smartphone screen, creating the illusion that the stacked books themselves are speaking. We constructed the bookshelf with 11 books, including one selected by the participants, secured between bookends (see Fig. 1). To closely simulate a stacked book scenario, we included 10 other books in addition to the participant's selected book. Although the actual books selected on Day 1 were not used in this experiment, we prepared dummy books covered in white book covers labeled with their titles on the spines to create the appearance that the actual book is present.

4.6 Procedure and Evaluation Items

On Day 1, we first conducted informed consent with the participants before starting the experiment. Following consent, we instructed the participants to select books they wished to read on Amazon using the provided PC. The procedure on Day 1 is detailed in Sect. 4.3.

On Day 2, participants were tasked with comparing the information from the selected book presented on two smartphones using Thurstone's pairwise comparison method, as described in Sect. 3.2. They responded to pairwise comparison questions, as outlined in Table 3, which asked about their impressions, repeatedly for all pairs of the three patterns. Following the pairwise comparison, participants completed a questionnaire containing the questions detailed in Table 4. These questions were based on a 5-point Likert scale (5 being most positive) and were designed to assess participants' impressions of each of the three pieces of information individually. During this questionnaire, participants viewed each information from the selected book individually in order and responded to questions about it. This process was repeated three times, with participants looking at one piece of information and answering questions about it each time. The order of presentation varied depending on the participant.

5 Results

5.1 Results from Pairwise Comparison Phase

Figure 4 shows the scales generated from the results of the questionnaire responses in the pairwise comparison. To create these scales, we constructed a choice ratio matrix for each pair of information based on the participants' responses. Subsequently, we calculated the mean Z-scores of the choice ratios in each condition from the matrix and determined the scale values accordingly.

Table 3. Three questions used in the pairwise comparison.

No	Question
Q1–1	Which text message increased your interest in the book?
Q1–2	Which text message did you remember wanting to read more?
Q1–3	Which text message made you more eager to read this book?

Table 4. Questions in the additional questionnaire to ask about the impression of information individually.

No	Question
Q2–1	My motivation to read the book was increased by viewing the information
Q2–2	I felt that the book was talking to me while using this system
Q2–3	I felt the presented information on this system is interesting

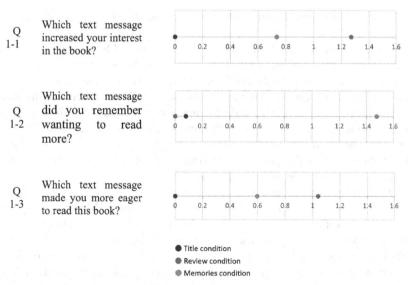

Q 1-1 — Which text message increased your interest in the book?

Q 1-2 — Which text message did you remember wanting to read more?

Q 1-3 — Which text message made you more eager to read this book?

● Title condition
● Review condition
● Memories condition

Fig. 4. Scales generated from the results of the questionnaire in the experiment (N = 19).

These questions are evaluated using Thurston's pairwise comparison method.

In Q1–1, "Which text message increased your interest in the book?", the Title condition scored the lowest, while the Review condition scored the highest. These results were consistent for Q1–3 as well. Additionally, the Memories condition scored higher than the Title condition in both Q1–1 and Q1–3. Therefore, it can be concluded that the Memories condition tends to enhance participants' interest and reading motivation compared to the Title condition. In Q1–2, "Which text message did you remember wanting to read more?", the Review condition scored the lowest, while the Memories condition scored the highest. The distances between the Memories and the other two conditions in Q1–2 were notably large. This result suggests that the Memories condition's effect on reminding participants that they wanted to read a book is significantly higher compared to the other conditions.

The results from Q1–2 suggest that presenting memories of purchasing the book helps participants recall their past motivation to read the book. Additionally, the results of Q1–1 and Q1–3 suggest that interest in and motivation to read the books tend to increase when memories of the purchasing the books are presented. However, the degree of increase is greater when reviews are presented.

5.2 Results from the Questionnaire in Post Impression Evaluation Phase

Figure 5 depicts box-and-whisker plots illustrating the trends of responses to the questionnaire which was rated on a 5-point Likert scale as detailed in Table 4. Each question was answered individually for each condition to evaluate impressions of information presented from the books without comparison. The Friedman test was performed to examine differences between the averages of the three conditions for each question, with results being significant ($p < .05$) for all questions. Subsequently, multiple comparisons tests using the Bonferroni method were conducted for all questions. These results are shown in Fig. 5.

In Q2–1, "My motivation to read the book was increased by viewing the information," the mean scores are higher for the Review > Memories > Title condition. Multiple comparison tests confirm significant differences between the Title-Review condition and the Title-Memories condition. There are no statistical differences between the Review and Memories conditions. Therefore, the Memories condition does not show a tendency to increase reading motivation significantly compared with the Review condition. However, because the Memories condition also has statistically higher scores than the Title condition, it is suggested that providing information about the memories of the purchase may enhance the motivation to read the books.

In Q2–2, "I felt that the book was talking to me while using this system," the mean scores are higher for Memories > Title > Review condition. Multiple comparisons reveal significant differences between all combinations. Therefore, participants tend to feel that the books are talking to them when the books discuss memories. Additionally, only the Review condition results in significantly lower scores than the other conditions. This suggests that presenting reviews reduces the feeling that the books are talking to the participants compared to presenting other information.

In Q2–3, "I felt the presented information on this system is interesting," the mean scores are higher for the Memories > Review > Title condition. The results for multiple comparisons are significant between the Title-Review and the Title-Memories condition. This suggests that participants tend to feel interested when introduced to third-person reviews about the books and their memories of the purchase, compared to presenting only the book's title. In other words, introducing content about the books themselves may affects the results. Regarding the differences in the contents of the Memories and Review conditions, there is no statistical difference between them. However, the average value is slightly higher in the Memories condition than the Review condition. Therefore, it is suggested that presenting memories tends to feel relatively more interesting than the other information.

Fig. 5. Box-and-whisker plots of questionnaire results for each condition (*: p < 0.05, **: p < 0.01)

6 Discussion

Based on the experimental results, we evaluated whether the hypothesis presented in Sect. 4.1, "Presenting a past experience when a book was purchased by the book itself enhances buyer's interest in and motivation to read the book" is supported. As described in Sect. 5.1, focusing on the composed scale in Q1–2, the score of the Memories condition is higher than in the Title and Review conditions. This fact suggests that presenting past memories when the book was purchased from the book's perspective may be useful in enhancing the recall of the buyer's feelings of wanting to read the book at the time of purchase. However, in Q1–1 and Q1–3, the scores of the Review condition are higher than the Memories condition, and the scores of the Memories condition are higher than the Title condition. This suggests that presenting the past experience of the purchase tends to increase the buyer's interest in and motivation to read it, rather than presenting the book title, but the degree of this increase is not greater than presenting reviews. Therefore, the pairwise comparison test results do not support the hypothesis.

In the impression survey for each condition described in Sect. 5.2, for Q2–1, the mean scores in the Review condition are higher than the Memories and Title conditions. Therefore, the results of individual impression survey questionnaires for each condition also do not support the hypothesis. However, the difference in mean scores between the Review and Memories condition is slight and not significant from the result of multiple comparison tests for Q2–1 and Q2–3. Additionally, for Q2–1 and Q2–3, the mean scores in the Review and Memories conditions are significantly higher than the Title condition. From the results, presenting the purchase memories or reviews tends to increase the interest in and motivation to read the books compared to presenting the book title only.

The results for Q2–2 suggest that presenting memories may increase the feeling that the books are talking to the participants, while reviews may reduce it. As described in Sect. 4.4, the messages in the Title and Memories condition incorporate anthropomorphic expressions, with the book itself speaking using first-person representation, "I." In contrast, the messages in the Review condition lack anthropomorphic expressions, as they consist of review texts obtained from online shopping websites. Therefore, it is suggested that incorporating anthropomorphic expressions of the books makes it easier to feel that the books are talking to the participants. Additionally, the Review condition tends to contain more text than the other conditions, which may also affect the feeling.

Although the hypothesis is not supported in this experiment, our findings suggest that presenting memories of the purchase in the form of books themselves talking to users may have a positive effect on users' interest in and motivation to read the books.

7 Conclusion

In this study, we focused on addressing the phenomenon of "Tsundoku" (i.e., stacked books), which refers to the condition in which books are left unread. Our objective was to explore methods to rekindle buyers' interest in stacked books that had waned after purchase and to increase their motivation to read the books. For this purpose, we proposed a system that provides information about the book's memories of when a user purchased it, as if the book itself is talking.

We hypothesized that "Presenting a past experience when a book was purchased by the book itself enhances buyer's interest in and motivation to read the book" and conducted an experiment to verify it. To conduct the experiment, we developed an AR-based experimental system capable of displaying messages from a book in the form of speech balloon text on a smartphone screen. We then compared the effects of presenting three types of information − the book title, book reviews, and memories of the book purchase − in a written message as a narrative from the book.

Through the results of pairwise comparisons and questionnaires, it was suggested that presenting purchase memories was useful in reminding participants of their desire to read the book at the time of purchase. Additionally, it was confirmed that memory information significantly increased participants' interest in and motivation to read the book compared to the book title alone. However, although there was no significant difference between memories and reviews, the increase in interest and motivation was larger when presenting reviews than memories. Therefore, the results of this experiment did not support the hypothesis. Nevertheless, it was suggested that the presentation method, in which the anthropomorphic book itself narrates memories of the purchase, may have a positive effect on the interest and motivation to read the books.

Our future work will focus on designing how to anthropomorphize books to apply the proposed method to actual stacking book situations. Additionally, we plan to re-examine the effects of the proposed method in settings where the interval between the experiences of purchase and recalling books is longer. In this experiment, Day 1 and Day 2 were separated by about a week. It is possible that the short interval between experiments allowed participants to remember the book well, potentially reducing the effect of the presentation by the system.

Acknowledgements. This work was supported in part by Tateisi Science and Technology Foundation, KDDI foundation, JSPS KAKENHI (Grant Number 23K16931 and 22K21096), and Ritsumeikan Global Innovation Research Organization(R-GIRO), Ritsumeikan University. We would like to thank Editage (www.editage.jp) for English language editing.

References

1. Tsundoku: The art of buying books and never reading them. BBC UGC & Social News, https://www.bbc.com/news/world-44981013. Accessed 5 Dec 2023
2. Tsundoku: The Art of Buying Books and Never Reading Them. https://basmo.app/tsundoku-buying-books-never-reading/. Accessed 5 Dec 2023
3. Osawa, H., Osawa, R., Imai, M.: Using attachable humanoid parts for realizing imaginary intention and body image. Int. J. Soc. Robot. 1(1), 109–123 (2009)
4. Kino, K., Iwaki, T., Ishihara, S., Dekihara, H.: An analysis of the attachment to artifacts: a study using the analogy of interpersonal relationships. J. Japan Soc. Kansei Eng. 6, 33–38 (2006)
5. Hatori, T., Fukuda, D., Mikiya, S., Fuji, S.: The effect of retrieving memories of possessions on attachment to objects: attachment to bicycle and problem of illegal bicycle parking. Stud. Sci. Technol. 1(2), 107–114 (2012)
6. Reeves, B., Nass, C.I.: The Media Equation: How People Treat Computers, Television, and New Media Like Real People. Cambridge (1996)

7. Carlson, S.M., Melissa, A.K., Madeline, B.H.: Theory of mind. Wiley Interdisc. Rev. Cogn. Sci. **4**(4), 391–402 (2013)
8. Otsu, K., Izumi, T.: An investigation of user perceptions of anthropo-morphic linguistic expressions in guidance from home appliances. Int. Conf. Appl. Hum. Fact. Ergonom. **21**, 37–43 (2022)
9. Fukuda, N., Yasumura, M.: Memory extractor: extracting memories from data using RFID. IPSJ SIG Tech. Rep. **2004**(51), 33–37 (2004)
10. Shigi, M., Ando, M., Otsu, K., Izumi, T.: Laughter map: supporting system for re-calling pleasant memories based on the recording and visualization of laughter experiences. In: Kurosu, M., Hashizume, A. (eds.) Human-Computer Interaction, HCII 2023. Lecture Notes in Computer Science, vol. 14012, pp. 279–292. Springer, Cham (2023). https://doi.org/10.1007/978-3-031-35599-8_18
11. Thurstone, L.L.: A law of comparative judgment. Psychol. Rev. **34**(4), 273–286 (1927)
12. Nukariya, H., Suwa, M.: A method of interviewing to constructively generate a narrative through interactions between interviewer and interviewee - a case study to examine creative thoulghts of an architectural student –. Mater. Type II Study Group Japan. Soc. Artif. Intell. **2011**, 1–6 (2011)

Professor Experience in Higher Education Institutions, Considering Cultural Factors: A Literature Review

Oriella Ortiz[1]([envelope]) [ORCID], Ayaka Ito[2] [ORCID], Nicolás Matus[3] [ORCID], and Cristian Rusu[3] [ORCID]

[1] Universidad de Valparaíso, Blanco 951, 2361891 Valparaíso, Chile
oriella.ortiz@uv.cl
[2] Reitaku University, 2-1-1, Hikarigaoka, Kashiwa 2778686, Chiba, Japan
ayitou@reitaku-u.ac.jp
[3] Pontificia Universidad Católica de Valparaíso, Avenida Brasil 2241, 2362807 Valparaíso, Chile
nicolas.matus.p@mail.pucv.cl, cristian.rusu@pucv.cl

Abstract. In a context where organizations are customer oriented, maintaining customer satisfaction becomes a primary and ongoing mission. This translates into satisfying customer needs, which, when fulfilled, can directly manifest itself as a competitive advantage. Customer Experience (CX) studies the relationship between a company and its customers. It takes into account the emotional and physical factors that customers experience when interacting with the products, systems and services provided by the company/organization. This research delves into the Professor's Experience (PX) in Higher Education Institutions (HEIs), which is a specific subset of CX. In this case, the academic/professor is understood as a type of customer of the products, systems and services offered by HEIs.

Although the literature indicates the existence of several studies related to the professor's experience, most of them are oriented to students and their experience. Because of this lack, the following research questions are generated: what is PX (in HEIs), what are the dimensions/attributes/factors that influence PX, what methods are used to evaluate PX, and how cultural factors influence PX. Among the various approaches that can be used when studying PX, culture represents one of the most significant. It has a direct impact on academic and personal pursuits throughout life.

Keywords: Professor Experience · Customer Experience · Culture · Higher Education

1 Introduction

Presently, organizations increasingly emphasize meeting customer needs, considering it a primary strategy for achieving a competitive and comparative advantage in the market. Some organizations have even incorporated strategies for customer satisfaction by also focusing on employee satisfaction. Customer Experience (CX) addresses the aforementioned by studying the relational aspects between an organization and its customers, considering emotional and physical factors that customers undergo when interacting with the products, systems, and/or services offered by the organization.

A. Coman and S. Vasilache (Eds.): HCII 2024, LNCS 14704, pp. 158–173, 2024.
https://doi.org/10.1007/978-3-031-61305-0_11

CX is defined as a multidimensional construct that focuses on the cognitive, emotional, behavioral, sensory, and social responses customers have towards an organization's offerings throughout the entire customer journey, pre purchase, during, and post purchase [1].

In this research we study the Professor's Experience (PX), understanding it from a CX perspective, where this user is a customer of the various products, systems and/or services that can be offered by various institutions, such as the university where he/she works, scientific organizations, state institutions, other universities, conferences, publishing houses, research centers, among others.

The significance of investigating this role lies in the fact that the Professor Experience (PX) involves an analysis that encompasses much more than just teaching practices. It entails understanding the perceptions, emotions, and realities that shape educational work. Therefore, investigating this experience involves comprehending the intrinsic motivations driving their commitment to teaching, exploring the complex interactions between pedagogical skills of different professors, the changing needs of students, as well as understanding how institutional and cultural dynamics shape their identity as educators, influencing teaching and experience. Studying PX not only enriches the understanding of teaching but also opens doors to continuous improvement in educational quality and experience optimizations. However, for the purposes of this research, PX is analyzed solely within Higher Education Institutions (HEIs).

Preliminary findings indicate a scarcity of research focused on PX within HEIs, reflecting a significant gap in the holistic understanding of the educational environment, acknowledging the professor as a fundamental element in education. This lack of attention to the entangled network of perceptions, challenges, and successes that shape a professor's life limits the ability to fully understand the challenges they face in their daily work. The lack of dedicated research to this particular role leads to a limited understanding of how institutional decisions, changes in the educational environment, social expectations, and cultural differences directly affect motivation, teaching quality, and emotional well-being of professors. Therefore, this research has a cultural focus on PX within HEIs, aiming to provide insights into the professor's experience and its essential nature in developing more effective and targeted strategies that promote more enriching educational environments for both professors and students.

As such, we conducted a bibliographic review of the main published studies addressing PX in HEIs from the last 13 years, from 2010 to 2023. The aim was to understand existing definitions of PX, the dimensions, attributes, and/or factors influencing PX, methods for evaluating PX, and identifying how cultural factors influence PX. Search strings such as "Professor Experience," "Teacher Experience," and "Academic Experience" in Web of Science and Science Direct databases.

From this search, we found that most research is oriented towards the academic experience of students, focused on primary and secondary education rather than higher education, and tends to be unidisciplinary. But several surveys evaluating PX were identified.

Regarding definitions of PX, there isn't a generally accepted one with a holistic focus solely on professors. Hence, this research proposes a definition to serve as a foundation for future studies exploring PX.

The rest of the document is organized as follows: a background review is developed in Sect. 2, to know what the terms used below refer to, the methodology of this research is explained in Sect. 3, the research questions are answered in Sect. 4, and conclusions and proposals for future work are given in Sect. 5.

2 Background

The most relevant terms that shape this research are presented below. And the relationship of each term in relation to the others and to the analysis itself is explained.

2.1 Customer Experience

Customer Experience (CX) refers to the customers' response to any direct or indirect interaction with an organization. Direct contact usually occurs during the purchasing process, while indirect interactions happen through unplanned encounters with a company's products, services, or brands. Another definition of CX describes it as spontaneous and non-deliberate responses and reactions to specific stimuli [2].

However, CX encompasses the entire interaction process, from before, during, and after the user engages with the organization, analyzing their touchpoints (TP) [3]. This refers to the identification and analysis of key sequence points within the analyzed processes of the user organization relationship, focusing on one or multiple products, systems, or services.

It is established within an organization based on perceived quality, satisfaction, trust, and convenience for customers. It may encompass aspects such as customer service, product quality, ease of use, personalization, consistency, and empathy displayed by the organization, among others.

Most importantly, CX is essential for customer loyalty, recommendations, and building lasting relationships, as a positive experience can generate an emotional bond with the brand and differentiate it in a competitive market [4].

Accordingly, the following is a subset of CX, the PX, in which the professor is understood as a customer of the systems with which he/she interacts, and which are necessary to carry out his/her teaching functions.

2.2 Professor Experience

In this research, the professor is considered as an educator who teaches in Higher Education Institutions (HEI), a professional who is highly qualified and specialized in a specific area of knowledge. Some of their functions include generating knowledge, conducting research as they wish or as required by the HEI, and guiding students during their university education [5].

But, in addition to conducting classes (which is understood to be their main task), the feelings of HEI professors can also vary and affect them considerably. They may also face high expectations, as there is a perception towards them about being considered knowledge facilitators, knowledge managers or transformational leaders [6]. However, they also have great challenges, such as heavy workload, pressure to publish, academic expectations, time management, keeping up with new technologies, cultural variations, changes in higher education, among others.

Among the aforementioned, considered as one of the greatest challenges, culture plays a fundamental role, since it influences the whole life of the professor and has a direct impact on his or her doings and relationships.

2.3 Culture

Culture refers to the set of values, beliefs, norms, traditions, and behaviors shared by a specific group within a society or environment. This can specifically exist within an HEI, as they often contain a vast array of cultural variations. This is due to the educational system being immersed in information rich, globalized, multicultural, and continuously changing society [7].

Hofstede [8] proposes that culture can be manifested in different dimensions, which are shown in the following table (Table 1).

Table 1. Research Questions in the Literature Review

Dimension	Description
Power distance	Corresponds to the acceptance and expectations of inequality within a society. In cultures with high power distance, a clear hierarchical structure and greater separation between leaders and followers is expected. In cultures with low power distance, a more equal distribution of power and less difference between leaders and subordinates is sought
Individualism versus collectivism	Refers to the degree to which a culture values individual independence over group interdependence and cohesion. Individualistic cultures tend to focus on personal achievement and autonomy, while collectivistic cultures prioritize group well-being and social relationships
Uncertainty avoidance	It deals with the tolerance that a society may have towards uncertainty and risk. Cultures with high uncertainty avoidance tend to seek clear structures, strict rules and avoid ambiguous situations, but cultures with low avoidance are more tolerant of ambiguity and show greater flexibility in the face of the unknown
Masculinity versus femininity	This dimension describes the distribution of gender roles in a society. More "masculine" cultures value competition, ambition and the pursuit of success, while "feminine" cultures prioritize cooperation, modesty and quality of life

(continued)

Table 1. (*continued*)

Dimension	Description
Long term versus short term orientation	This dimension focuses on the time perspective of a culture. Long term-oriented cultures value perseverance, long term planning and adaptation to change, while short term-oriented cultures focus on tradition, respect for the past and compliance with established social norms
Indulgence versus restraint	Added later, this dimension refers to the degree to which a culture permits the gratification of human impulses and desires. Indulgent cultures accept the satisfaction of personal needs and desires, while cultures of restraint tend to regulate and control these impulses more

Which can influence the way people (professors in this case study) perceive the world, the way they relate to each other and their behavior in different contexts [8].

This research examines culture from the perspective of HEI professors, which can result in variations in teaching styles, academic expectations based on cultural backgrounds, collaboration styles, and teamwork. It acknowledges a culture distinct from professors who come from a different country than the one where they currently teach, having studied for a significant period in another country and its culture, or having spent time in another country for any reason, thereby experiencing and assimilating another culture.

Therefore, deepening PX within the framework of CX emerges as to improve the quality of education and the work environment. By deeply understanding the interactions, challenges, and motivations shaping the professor's experience, pedagogical effectiveness and professional well-being can be optimized. Identifying positive elements within this experience can unveil key factors such as institutional support, professional development, classroom autonomy, and job satisfaction, all pivotal for talent retention, educational excellence, and the creation of a conducive learning atmosphere.

3 Research Method

A literature review can serve as an effective means to comprehend the context surrounding a research topic, especially when research questions exist. It is applicable across disciplines and can offer an overarching view of a particular subject or research problem, potentially generating a new conceptual model or theory. This method proves valuable in evaluating a field of research within a specified timeframe [9].

According to Snyder, this method involves four phases:

- Designing the review
- Conducting the review
- Analysis
- Drafting the review

3.1 Research Questions

Within this literature review, we address the following topics: (1) Definitions of PX, (2) Identification of dimensions, attributes, and/or factors influencing PX, (3) Methods used to evaluate PX, and (4) How cultural factors impact PX. These topics lead to the formulation of the following research questions (Table 2).

Table 2. Research Questions in the Literature Review

ID	Research Questions (RQ)
RQ1	What is PX (in HEIs)?
RQ2	What dimensions/attributes/factors influence PX?
RQ3	What methods are used to evaluate PX?
RQ4	How do cultural factors influence PX?

3.2 Literature Search

This literature review was conducted by extracting publications from the last 13 years, spanning from 2010 to 2023, aiming to obtain a more comprehensive understanding of recent educational contexts. The consulted databases included Web of Science and Science Direct, using search strings containing the following keywords:

- "Professor Experience"
- "Teacher Experience"
- "Academic Experience"

The search yielded the following quantity of articles (Table 3):

Table 3. Total Identified Research per Database

Databases	Number of publications	% of participation
Web of Science	812	62,17%
Science Direct	494	37,83%
Total	1.306	100%

Figure 1 shows the percentage shares of publications found in the selected databases, in which a considerable difference can be seen between the high number of PX related articles in Web of Science and approximately half of those found in Science Direct. Only 96 publications are found in both databases.

Figure 2 indicates the area of knowledge to which the publications in the Science Direct database belong. Most of them belong to the Social Sciences and a smaller number to Computer Science.

% of publications by database

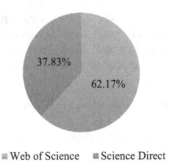

■ Web of Science   ■ Science Direct

Fig. 1. Percentage of publications in scientific databases used.

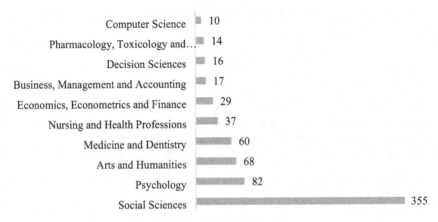

Fig. 2. Science Direct Subject Area.

Figure 3 also contains the areas of knowledge of the publications but corresponding to the Web of Science database. In contrast to Science Direct, the majority belongs to Education Educational Research and the minority corresponds to Information Science Library Science.

Figure 4 shows that in the Science Direct database there has been a considerable increase per year in the number of publications. And the drop recorded in 2024 occurs because the cutoff date was at the end of 2023.

The Web of Science database also shows a steady increase in the number of publications, with a peak in 2022. Represented in Fig. 5.

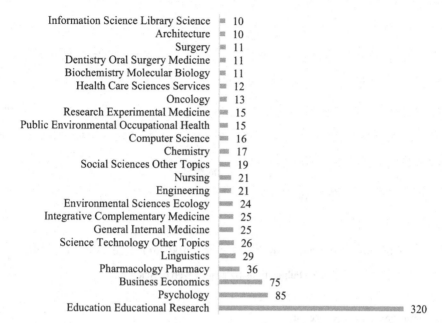

Information Science Library Science	10
Architecture	10
Surgery	11
Dentistry Oral Surgery Medicine	11
Biochemistry Molecular Biology	11
Health Care Sciences Services	12
Oncology	13
Research Experimental Medicine	15
Public Environmental Occupational Health	15
Computer Science	16
Chemistry	17
Social Sciences Other Topics	19
Nursing	21
Engineering	21
Environmental Sciences Ecology	24
Integrative Complementary Medicine	25
General Internal Medicine	25
Science Technology Other Topics	26
Linguistics	29
Pharmacology Pharmacy	36
Business Economics	75
Psychology	85
Education Educational Research	320

Fig. 3. Web of Science Subject Area.

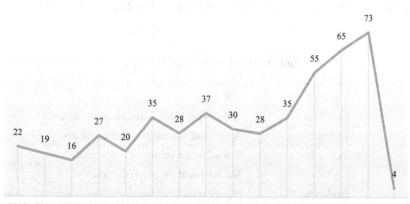

2010 2011 2012 2013 2014 2015 2016 2017 2018 2019 2020 2021 2022 2023 2024

22 19 16 27 20 35 28 37 30 28 35 55 65 73 4

Fig. 4. Publications by year in Science Direct.

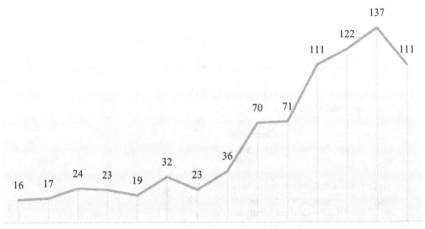

Fig. 5. Publications by year in Web of Science.

3.3 Study Selection Criteria

Although interdisciplinary publications on PX were considered, selection criteria were applied to define the studies to be analyzed in this research. The criteria presented below (Table 4):

Table 4. Publication Selection Criteria

ID	Category	Criteria
IN1	Inclusión	Articles published between 2010 and 2023
IN2	Inclusión	Articles addressing research questions
IN3	Inclusión	Regarding the professor's experience
EX1	Exclusión	Studies not at the university level
EX2	Exclusión	Highly specific technical cases on a topic
EX3	Exclusión	Article about student experience

By way of explanation, IN1 considers only articles within that publication year range to maintain a manageable and updated dataset. IN2 selects articles that are related to the research questions, at least in one aspect. The final inclusion criterion specifies that only articles studying the professor's experience, not any other role, are accepted. As for exclusion criteria, EX1 excludes articles from educational levels other than university. EX2 excludes those addressing highly specific issues that may not be replicable. Lastly, EX3 excludes articles focusing on student perceptions.

The search criteria were as follows (Table 5):

Table 5. Publication Selection Criteria

Databases	Search string
Web of Science	ALL = ("Professor Experience" OR"Teacher Experience" OR"Academic Experience")
Science Direct	"Academic Experience" OR "Professor Experience" OR "Teacher Experience"

And due to the large number of investigations related to PX, which, in this case, with a cutoff date in December 2023, were 1,306 only in the two databases. It is that a complete analysis of the literature has not yet been carried out, that is, a systematic review of the literature, and that becomes the main limitation of our study. And the selection of research was carried out subjectively to articles that responded in their abstract to the first three research questions.

4 Answering the Research Questions

4.1 What is PX (in HEIs)?

In this literature review, various research works have been analyzed with the aim of finding definitions of PX in HEIs. However, this search has not been able to find definitions of this term. Overall, the identified studies deal with the academic experience of students, which is directly related to them and their experiences within educational institutions. Some studies focus on the teaching experience with students having certain very specific characteristics, and the research revolves around these student characteristics.

Given the low number of studies focused on professors (with a total focus on their roles) and the nonsystematic review, the definition of PX in another study cannot be ruled out. However, for the purposes of this study, no formal definitions were found, considering that the search was conducted using the terms 'Professor Experience,' 'Teacher Experience,' and 'Academic Experience.'

Regarding the definition of PX, it can be said that the teaching profession imposes great demands on professors from an emotional, cognitive, social, and physical standpoint [10]. However, based on the findings, it can be said that initially, academia was founded on traditional, patriarchal, conservatives' values [11]. There might be many factors influencing PX, with one being variations according to the professional stage of the professor. For instance, for professors midway through their careers, high productivity and influence are attributed since it is considered that most academic achievements can be attained during this stage, such as obtaining leadership and management positions. However, these can become challenges and barriers if not managed properly along with other responsibilities. They also tend to perceive low levels of accomplishment in terms of labor justice perception, professional development, and job satisfaction. Additionally, when analyzing the teaching experience in the mid-career stage, it becomes more challenging when it coincides with middle age, encompassing significant processes like changing careers, aging, marriage, and having children, among others. These aspects might be relevant when balancing work and personal life, leading to decisions on where to focus predominantly. This generates a scenario where, mostly, white, cisgender, heterosexual men might achieve more success in their academic progression, unlike female professors who generally undertake assumed supportive functions, leaving them with less time to concentrate on their work (or it is assumed so). Therefore, it can be noted that female academics might be affected by ideal worker norms, maternal norms, and social norms [12].

Another gender-focused study also points out that there is an expectation of care and service in female professors, who may inherently be professors and administrators, while leadership roles are intrinsic to male professors, which may explain why men tend to occupy higher leadership positions in academia. In addition, female professors tend to combine their work with other commitments, roles and identities, which may be perceived negatively by their colleagues as an additional effort. However, when a professor combines work and family responsibilities, it is considerably valued [13]. The above is directly related to the Masculinity versus femininity dimension in which Hofstede points out the roles of what is understood as masculine and feminine in the culture.

While several studies focus on teaching experiences, examining women and their roles, there are also some on non-heterosexual individuals and how their context might affect their teaching career. A study in Chinese HEIs showed that, in general, universities exhibit institutional heteronormativity directly linked to the level of leadership non-heterosexual individuals can achieve. This led non-heterosexual individuals down three intertwined paths: entering heterosexual marriages or relationships, distancing themselves from others on campus, and showcasing outstanding professional performance to fit within the institution's structure and the country's customs [14].

Regarding teaching experience, it is stated that with the emergence of neoliberalism and managerialism, HEI professors grapple with an excessive work culture, assuming they must fulfill a wide range of work commitments, potentially explaining why some professors focus more on research than on teaching [14]. It's understood that professors can be teaching academics, research academics, and teaching research academics [12].

Consequently, an essential component for optimal school functioning is professor well-being, directly impacting students. This can be explained by professor resilience, where maintaining a focus on resilience can enhance professor well-being. Understanding education as evolving and encountering challenging situations.

Negative teaching experiences and work-related stress can be generated by expectations imposed by others or those set by professors themselves, leading to a departure from teaching. This explains the importance of resilience as well-being and its relationship with teaching effectiveness [15].

Therefore, it should be understood that the aforementioned elements might help define what the Professor Experience entails. However, all experiences are subjective and contextual to what happens in each HEI. Nevertheless, at a general level, it can be explained as the set of experiences, skills, and knowledge acquired throughout the teaching profession in HEIs, including not only experiences directly related to teaching but also those explained by the relationship a professor has with colleagues, students, the institution, other institutions, which can be directly influenced by personal factors such as gender, age, sexual orientation, culture, among others.

4.2 What Dimensions/Attributes/Factors Influence PX?

The PX may be explained by many dimensions/attributes/factors that can directly or indirectly affect it. This literature review considers some of these dimensions described below, but it should be noted that there may be more. The dimensions may pertain to a particular issue that some research focuses on, a specific discipline, or even a cultural context. However, these dimensions seem to recur in more than one study. Therefore, to establish these dimensions, a holistic and interdisciplinary approach is necessary.

One of the analyzed studies aiming to relate professors' figurative language to understand professor resilience conducted a systematic literature review to better comprehend professor resilience. It identified four general dimensions: motivational, professional, social, and emotional. Information was gathered by administering surveys containing questions about professors' careers, experiences as educators, relationships with other professors, students, parents (where applicable), administration, specific tasks as educators, job concerns, and work challenges [15].

Another research endeavor focusing on culture employed a questionnaire querying the work experience of Arab American pharmacy professors, revealing three dimensions: 'participants' overall satisfaction with their academic experience related to Diversity, Equity, and Inclusion (DEI) issues,' 'demographics,' and 'professional characteristics.' The first dimension inquired about negative experiences concerning well-being, evaluation, academic progression, funding, research resources, practice sites, promotions, and tenure. The second dimension queried about country of origin, citizenship, and religion. The third dimension investigated academic titles, disciplines, appointments, academic rank, and work history [16].

From this, it can be deduced that when comparing two studies on PX, one being general and the other culturally focused, the dimension of professional characteristics appears in both. Overall, both studies inquire about professional and relational experiences.

4.3 What Methods Are Used to Evaluate PX?

Given that, according to the compiled information, it can be stated that a holistic and interdisciplinary definition of PX has not been found, we can indicate that a centralized methodology to assess PX has not yet been established. However, all the analyzed research is qualitative, with the majority collecting direct information from professors through different data collection methods.

For instance, a study focusing on mid-career female academics applied semi structured interviews developed based on research objectives, literature, and modifications from previous phases guiding these interviews. These interviews included open ended questions to establish relationships with participants (validated by the Human Research Ethics Committee at Curtin University). The interviews were recorded, conducted face to face or online, later transcribed verbatim, analyzed, and the preliminary results were reviewed by the interviewees [12].

Another research endeavor aiming to relate figurative language to professor resilience gathered data through semi structured surveys from academics participating in a project on the same research topic. A total of 42 professors teaching at different academic levels and in various subjects participated. This data collection process commenced with distributing a participation form that participants needed to accept, corresponding to consent. The surveys lasted approximately 20 min and were anonymous. Subsequently, they were transcribed, coded, categorized, and analyzed [15].

Additionally, a research study on professor experience with a gender focus was carried out through narrative reviews in six steps: (1) Systematic definition of criteria, defining research questions, inclusion and exclusion criteria, (2) Literature exploration, database search, term identification, and study selection, (3) Quality assessment using the Critical Appraisal Skills Program, (4) Data extraction and presentation, (5) Data synthesis, and (6) Review of findings, reflections on the process, and future work generation [13].

Another research project examining female professors in cultures different from their own utilized a distinct research methodology called a story dialogue. Participants with foreign backgrounds (who had studied or worked at least once at a university different from their home country) and English-speaking abilities were recruited for a workshop. The workshop was conducted via Zoom, preceded by sending the professors an article for discussion and questions about the Story Dialogue Method (a set of questions to foster discussions and reflections). The workshop discussions were recorded, anonymized, and analyzed [17].

Finally, another research study focusing on culture and aiming to understand the work experience of Arab American pharmacy professors conducted an online questionnaire via Qualtrics. This questionnaire had a cross sectional design with multiple choice and open response items. After being sent to participants, reminders were sent every two weeks, totaling three reminders in the end (the questionnaire was approved by the institutional review board of Creighton University). To reach the final questionnaire, individuals of interest were selected, and this questionnaire was administered over six weeks with three repetitions, where keywords were identified and subsequently applied to six professors of Arab descent. Additionally, participants were asked for consent and acceptance before responding. This questionnaire consisted of 49 evaluation items [16].

In conclusion, we can identify that two of these methods were semi structured surveys, one through narratives, another through dialogue, and a questionnaire. However, the common thread among them is the direct collection of information from professors and the formalization of data collection through consent agreements. Additionally, the majority sent preliminary results to participants for comments. One of the most adaptable methodologies to the current research being conducted is the first mentioned in this section, which analyzes professor experience with a gender focus and involves six steps similar to the current study.

4.4 How Do Cultural Factors Influence PX?

According to the gathered information, it can be identified that there is a deficit in research on cultural themes related to PX, as most studies address other topics such as gender or specific disciplines. However, an observation we can make about cultural research is that it often focuses on a specific culture and/or country. Therefore, the aim of this research is to adopt a holistic approach that can be adaptable to any culture. To achieve this, some recurring and constant cultural factors are identified below.

Some of the most relevant cultural factors include language and the limitations it brings regarding teaching. Religion is another dominant factor, as many individuals choose to study in places that share the same religion to feel comfortable and free to practice it. Stigmas are also an important element, as people tend to generalize negative experiences they may have had with individuals from the same culture. Additionally, it's found that local professors are unwilling to learn about non local academics in terms of managing international classrooms [18].

In a study on Arab professors, they indicated feeling ignored and consequently missing out on opportunities. Some experienced stereotypes, microaggressions, and racism. They also mentioned that treatment varies depending on where they teach; for instance, individuals working in the Southern United States are more likely to experience discrimination, which could be linked to historical events in the area. Additionally, in this research, women have a lower perception of experiencing racism than men. However, despite more women being surveyed, there's a lack of women in high leadership positions. Concerning religion, Muslim academics believe that racism remains a significant issue due to historical negative stereotypes, exacerbated by the events of September 11, 2001, according to respondents [16].

The above can be complemented by the study mentioned in Sect. 4.1 on non-heterosexual professors in Chinese HEIs, where they indicate that gender issues not only affect informal interactions with colleagues but are deeply rooted in institutional practices such as employment, promotion, and unions. This can directly affect performance and result in high stress, which is directly related to traditional Chinese culture, as per the research [19].

Understanding that all contexts may have differences, when there's academic mobility, it can bring both opportunities and limitations. Opportunities may include developing useful and appreciated skills, contributing new ideas, enhancing sociocultural communication approaches, and adaptability. Limitations might involve social exclusion in the workplace, isolation, experiences of rejection, and feelings of otherness. Therefore, receiving support from employers and colleagues can help improve a sense of belonging, work facilitations, and adaptation [17].

Another research study highlights aspects that are repetitive across different cultural adaptations, such as language differences, a sense of otherness related to ethnic identity and cultural customs, performance pressures, biases, and professional marginalization. Additionally, differences and gender inequalities between cultures can exist. These issues can be mitigated with the help of a mentor to guide the cultural adaptation experience [17].

Therefore, it can be said that regardless of the culture professors need to adapt to, there are certain consistent factors. Clearly identifying these factors can lead to better approaches to mitigate them or leverage the benefits that cultural diversity may bring.

5 Conclusions and Future Work

Given the nature of this literature review, we cannot definitively state that there is no formal definition of the term 'Professor Experience.' However, based on the review conducted in this research, we can preliminarily note that it is not defined. But with the increasing number of studies related to PX in recent years, it's necessary to formalize a definition of the term. This will provide a foundation for future research as the importance of understanding this role's experience in educational institutions seems to be growing.

Additionally, we must consider that most of the research gathered from the selected databases referred to students' academic experience, not covering HEIs (which is the focus of this research), or delved into very different topics unrelated to education while investigating these individuals' academic experience. Therefore, it remains a subject with limited research yet should be explored further, recognizing that professors hold a fundamental role worldwide in fostering people's knowledge. This identifies an opportunity for deeper investigation into this topic.

Thus, we developed a definition based on some identified research that addressed PX from specific problematic perspectives or considered cultural factors. Preliminarily, it appears to be an under researched approach, yet several studies mention its relevance in PX.

Furthermore, we also identified dimensions/attributes/factors that can impact PX and, according to the findings, are consistent across various studies. These dimensions encompass not only academic aspects but also personal factors, considering that professors continue to exist outside their work. The most relevant dimensions/attributes/factors identified for understanding PX are motivational, professional, social, and emotional. To include a cultural factor, it's essential to add participants' overall satisfaction with their academic experience related to Diversity, Equity, and Inclusion, based on the findings of previous research.

Regarding the types of methods to assess PX, all identified methods were qualitative and directly related to Regarding the types of methods to assess PX, all identified methods were qualitative and directly related to Regarding the types of methods to assess PX, all identified methods were qualitative and directly related to Regarding the types of methods to assess PX, all identified methods were qualitative and directly related to Regarding the types of methods to assess PX, all identified methods were qualitative and directly related to Regarding the types of methods to assess PX, all identified methods were qualitative and directly related to professors.

Moreover, we identified how cultural factors influence PX, finding that it's a highly relevant element in PX and can directly impact teaching methods and the academic lifestyle. And that it can be directly related to the dimensions of culture proposed by Hofstede.

Therefore, as future work, we propose to conduct a systematic literature review in more databases to address the same research questions and directly relate culture according to Hofstede to what is found in the literature.

References

1. Lemon, K.N., Verhoef, P.C.: Understanding customer experience throughout the customer journey. J. Mark. **80**(6), 69–96 (2016)
2. Meyer, C.: Comprendiendo la experiencia del cliente. Harv. Bus. Rev. **85**(2), 89–99 (2007)
3. Verhoef, P.C., Lemon, K.N., Parasuraman, A., Roggeveen, A.L., Tsiros, M., Schlesinger, L.A.: Customer experience creation: determinants, dynamics and management strategies. J. Retail. **85**(1), 31–41 (2009)
4. Homburg, C., Jozić, D., Kuehnl, C.: Customer experience management: toward implementing an evolving marketing concept. J. of the Acad. Mark. Sci. **45**, 377–401 (2017)
5. Kini, T., Podolsky, A.: Does Teaching Experience Increase Teacher Effectiveness? A Review of the Research. Palo Alto: Learning Policy Institute (2016)
6. Pedraja-Rejas, L.: Desafíos para el profesorado en la sociedad del conocimiento. Ingeniare. Revista chilena de ingeniería **20**(1), 136–144 (2012)
7. Ríos, F.X.C., Del Mar Lorenzo Moledo, M., Rego, M.A.S.: Diversidad cultural y escenarios migratorios. Un estudio sobre formación de profesores. Educar **55**(1), 19–37 (2019)
8. Hofstede, G.: Culture's consequences: Comparing values, behaviors, institutions, and organizations across nations. Coll. Aviat. Rev. **34**(2), 108 (2016)
9. Snyder, H.: Literature review as a research methodology: an overview and guidelines. J. Bus. Res. **104**, 333–339 (2019)
10. Verešová, M., Malá, D.: Stress, proactive coping and self- efficacy of teachers. Procedia Social Behav. Sci. **55**, 294–300 (2012)
11. Blackburn, H.: The status of women in STEM in higher education: a review of the literature 2007–2017. Sci. Technol. Libr. **36**(3), 235–273 (2017)
12. Phillips, M.J., Dzidic, P., Roberts, L.D., Castell, E.: "All we have to do, is do it all": exploring middle-career women's academic identities in Australian higher education using foucauldian discourse analysis. Womens Stud. Int. Forum **96**, 102679 (2023)
13. Phillips, M.J., Dzidic, P., Castell, E.: Exploring and critiquing women's academic identity in higher education: a narrative review. SAGE Open **12**(2), 215824402210961 (2022)
14. Si, J.: Higher education teachers' professional well-being in the rise of managerialism: insights from China. Higher Educ. **87**, 1121–1138 (2023)
15. Peel, K., Kelly, N., Danaher, P.A., Harreveld, B., Mulligan, D.: Analysing teachers' figurative language to shed new light on teacher resilience. Teach. Teach. Educ. **130**, 104175 (2023)
16. Alsharif, N. Z., Chahine, E. B., Attarabeen, O. F., Mohamed, I., Halat, D. H.: An exploratory study of Arab American pharmacy educators' work experience with diversity, equity, and inclusion. Am. J. Pharmaceut. Educ. **87**(3), ajpe9038 (2023)
17. Pajalić, Z., et al.: What are the disadvantages of having a foreign background as a female academic and working at a university in Europe? Social Sci. Human. Open **8**(1), 100551 (2023)
18. Trahar, S.: 'This is Malaysia. you have to follow the custom here': narratives of the student and academic experience in international higher education in Malaysia. J. Educ. Teach. **40**(3), 217–231 (2014)
19. Cui, L.: "I had to get married to protect myself": gay academics' experiences of managing sexual identity in China. Asian J. Soc. Sci. **50**(4), 260–267 (2022)

Academic Assessment: Usability Evaluation of an Integrated Platform for Students with Disabilities

Luis A. Rojas[1]([✉]), Juan Felipe Calderon[2], John W. Castro[3,4], and Claudio Álvarez[5]

[1] Facultad de Ingeniería, Arquitectura y Diseño, Universidad San Sebastián, Bellavista 7, 8420524 Santiago, Chile
lrojaspl@docente.uss.cl

[2] Facultad de Ingeniería, Universidad Andrés Bello, Quillota 980, Viña del Mar, Chile
juan.calderon@unab.cl

[3] Departamento de Ingeniería Informática y Ciencias de La Computación, Universidad de Atacama, Copiapó, Chile
john.castro@uda.cl

[4] Centro Interuniversitario de Envejecimiento Saludable (CIES), Talca, Chile

[5] Facultad de Ingeniería y Ciencias Aplicadas, Universidad de los Andes, Santiago, Chile
calvarez@uandes.cl

Abstract. This paper presents a usability evaluation of a novel educational platform for students and teachers, focusing on exam creation and monitoring. Employing a quasi-experimental design, the study assessed effectiveness, efficiency, and user satisfaction in alignment with ISO-9241-11 standards. Both students and teachers demonstrated 100% task effectiveness, highlighting the platform's adaptability and inclusivity. Task completion times, while generally acceptable, revealed variability, emphasizing the need for optimization. Usability questionnaire results indicated positive perceptions of Ease of Learning and Satisfaction, affirming the platform's user-friendly design. The platform effectively facilitates accessible assessments, demonstrating its potential in fostering inclusive educational environments. Future work aims to optimize task times, enhance accessibility features, and refine the user interface, ensuring continuous improvement and broader applicability across diverse educational institutions.

Keywords: Educational Technology · Usability Evaluation · Inclusive Assessments · Exam Creation

1 Introduction

Equal access to education is a fundamental principle supported by international legal and ethical frameworks [1]. Despite this acknowledgment, the educational landscape does not always ensure equitable conditions for all students [2]. Individuals with visual and physical disabilities encounter significant challenges in their participation in educational assessments. Accessibility limitations, both in physical and virtual environments, have created barriers to their full integration and academic performance [2, 3].

Human-Computer Interaction (HCI) has become a crucial field in addressing these barriers [4]. This interdisciplinary approach focuses on the interaction between humans and computer systems, aiming to enhance technology's efficiency, ease of use, and adaptability for users [5]. In an educational context, HCI plays a vital role in striving for the creation of accessible and inclusive environments, enabling students with disabilities to effectively interact with educational material and assessment tools.

In response to the increasing need for inclusive educational environments, this research focuses on the development of an integrated assessment platform specifically designed to cater to students with visual and/or physical disabilities in secondary and higher education settings. The primary motivation is to address existing barriers to the equitable participation of students with disabilities in academic assessments, facilitating equitable access and supportive learning tools.

The objectives of this research are centered on creating an accessible environment that allows students with disabilities to effectively undertake assessments. Additionally, the aim is to empower teachers to manage educational material and assess student activities, while ensuring that students themselves have access to this material and can review corrections made by teachers.

A user-centered design approach [6] will be implemented, considering universal accessibility guidelines and feedback from potential users, including both students and teachers. The methodology involves the development and implementation of the platform, followed by practical tests with representative users, including students and teachers with visual and physical disabilities.

Preliminary findings demonstrate that the integrated platform meets expectations for accessibility and ease of use for students and teachers with disabilities. Students were able to access material, conduct assessments, and review corrections effectively, while teachers successfully managed content and assessed activities with ease.

This research showcases the potential of technology to eliminate barriers in education, fostering an inclusive environment for students and teachers with disabilities. The implications go beyond accessibility, impacting equitable participation and the quality of teaching in educational settings. Possible areas for improvement are identified, and suggestions for future research in human-computer interaction, focusing on accessibility and inclusion, are proposed.

2 Proposal

Students with disabilities often encounter significant challenges when attempting to access technologies that facilitate accessible and comprehensive assessments [7, 8]. This situation perpetuates the constant need for students to seek alternatives and adapt to fully participate in the various educational platforms used today [9, 10]. The lack of specific tools designed to address the individual needs of these students complicates their educational experience, highlighting the importance of implementing solutions that promote inclusion and equal opportunities in the educational sphere.

As mentioned earlier, students with special needs may encounter significant obstacles in utilizing mainstream educational technologies, particularly when it comes to participating in assessments, due to a lack of tools that are designed with their unique requirements in mind. Line with this issue, this work aims to improve the assessment process by introducing a new platform at our university. The primary purpose of this initiative is to provide students experiencing difficulties related to literacy, due to disability situations, the opportunity to carry out their assessments easily. To achieve this, various accessibility tools tailored to the specific needs of these students will be implemented, contributing to the creation of an inclusive and equitable educational environment.

The platform's structure delineates three essential roles: administrator, teachers, and students. Administrators play a crucial role in creating profiles for teachers and students, enabling them to access the platform. Admitting these two participants into the system involves a prior analysis of the needs and abilities of students with disabilities. This process is essential to ensure that individual characteristics are compatible with the application.

A concrete example of this approach is the consideration of students' verbal communication skills. The application requires verbal responses in assessments, so students' ability to communicate in this way is assessed. Furthermore, the choice to allow access to the platform is based on the justification that the students' disability situation merits the use of this tool; consequently, certain disabilities or levels of disability are considered exclusionary.

Additionally, it is a requirement that students have previous experience using the internet. This criterion is implemented to ensure that familiarity with technology is not a hindrance when using the application. In summary, the platform's configuration is based on a rigorous approach that seeks compatibility and suitability of participants, ensuring an effective and accessible experience for all involved.

In the platform, teachers play a crucial role in assessing students with disabilities. They initiate the process by adding the necessary courses and assigning students to these courses from an available list. Subsequently, they upload educational material, following instructions to ensure clear presentation to students with disabilities.

When teachers add assessments to the courses, after students respond, they conduct detailed corrections. In addition to indicating the correction, they provide detailed feedback on the correct and incorrect aspects of the answers and assign scores. The system automatically calculates the student's final grade based on these scores.

As for students, their main activity on the platform is to complete assessments. During this process, they have on-screen tools that facilitate their responses. After completing the assessment, they must wait for teachers to make corrections and provide feedback, thus completing the evaluation process. The fundamental purpose of the platform is to make it easier for students with visual and/or physical disabilities to carry out their written assessments.

2.1 Main Functions

The platform has been designed with an intuitive and efficient approach, providing specific tools for each of its key users: administrators, teachers, and students. Below, we detail the main features that enable an inclusive and effective educational experience for all.

Administrator.

- Create User Profile: Allows the administrator to input users, distinguishing between students and teachers, assigning specific functions to each profile.
- Create Periods: Facilitates organization by enabling the creation of periods indicating the year and semester in which a course will take place.
- Create Majors: Allows the categorization of courses according to the major to which they belong.
- *Teacher:*
- Create Course: Enables the teacher to add a new course to the platform, including the uploading of content accessible to students.
- Add Materials: Facilitates the inclusion of study documents and assessments for students to access.
- Add Students: Allows the teacher to select and add students to the courses they teach.
- Grade Assessments: Provides the ability to provide detailed feedback and grade assessments conducted by students.
- Generate Reports: Allows the teacher to create an Excel report that includes student data and grades.
- *Student:*
- Take Assessments: Enables students to view and respond to assessment questions.
- Use Accessibility Tools: Facilitates access through visual and verbal tools, such as font size enlargement, reading guides, and the ability to respond verbally through a microphone and speaker.
- Access Corrections: Allows students to review feedback and grades provided by teachers for completed assessments.

2.2 User Interfaces

Initially, prototypes were created with the goal of validating and capturing the essential requirements of end users. Throughout this process, usability was prioritized, considering a minimalist design that displays only the essential functions on the screen. This approach focuses on facilitating user navigation, specifically by providing the necessary functions for activities related to taking and completing assessments.

A key aspect in creating the prototypes was to ensure that tasks followed a logical order and required the fewest possible steps. To achieve this, all platform options were integrated into the navigation bar, allowing users to directly access the functionality they desire.

The prototypes prominently incorporate the use of modals, pop-up windows that appear when selecting a specific function. These structures, overlaying other elements on the screen, capture the user's attention, providing precise guidance on the activity they need to perform.

Regarding the color palette chosen for the prototypes, shades ranging from white and purple to sky blue and blues have been selected. This choice aims to convey sensations of honesty, harmony, security, trust, calmness, and intelligence to users. The underlying purpose is to create an environment in which students feel at ease when facing the process of taking their assessments.

Examples of the final interfaces are presented here, starting with the "Add Material" interface (see Fig. 1). This is displayed on the screen when the teacher selects the corresponding option. In the associated modal, the fields that the teacher must complete are presented: name and type. The type can be material or assessment. In addition to this data, the teacher is required to choose and upload a specific file to the platform. It is worth noting that this particular view is activated when selecting that the material type is an assessment.

Fig. 1. User Interface for the Addition of New Materials by Professors.

In Fig. 2, the interface designed for teachers to review and correct student responses is presented. The screen includes distinctive buttons to mark answers as correct or incorrect, providing an effective correction tool. Additionally, there is an input field for comments and scoring, allowing detailed and personalized feedback from the teacher.

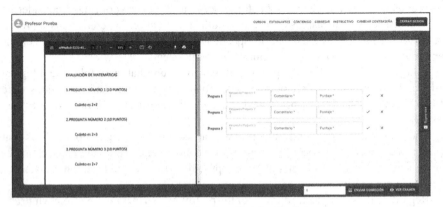

Fig. 2. Correction Interface for Teachers.

In Fig. 3, the "Instructions" interface designed for teachers is presented. This visual section provides detailed guidelines on the required format for the files that will be uploaded to the platform. Its main objective is to guide the teacher in the uploading process, ensuring that the files meet the established requirements. This tool is essential to guarantee the consistency and compatibility of the documents, thus contributing to an efficient and seamless user experience. By accessing this interface, the teacher obtains crucial information that facilitates the correct utilization of the platform and optimizes the process of uploading materials.

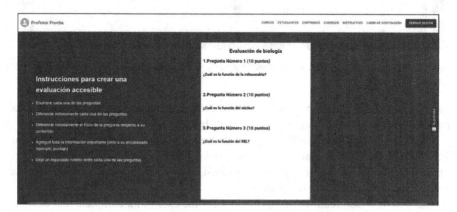

Fig. 3. Interface "Instructions" for Teachers.

Figure 4 presents the interface designed for students to carry out evaluations. The primary objective of this interface is to offer students an accessible and functional environment for responding to questions. Specifically designed to support students, including those with visual and/or physical disabilities, the aim of this interface is to streamline the process of completing written assessments. The desired outcome is that students can effectively answer questions using the accessibility tools provided by the platform.

The utility of the interface lies in the clear visualization of the document with questions and the presence of inputs that allow students to respond using various accessibility tools.

The interface offers options to listen to the text of the assessments, providing an auditory reading function that enhances accessibility. Additionally, functionalities are provided for writing and responding through voice, expanding interaction options for those students who can benefit from unconventional methods of text input. In summary, Fig. 4 focuses on improving the assessment experience for all students, regardless of their needs or abilities.

Figure 5 shows the interface designed for students to view the corrections made by the teacher in their evaluations. The main goal of this interface is to furnish detailed and personalized feedback, aiming to enhance the student's comprehension of their performance. Through this interface, students gain insights into their strengths and areas for improvement, fostering a deep understanding of their academic progress. The desired

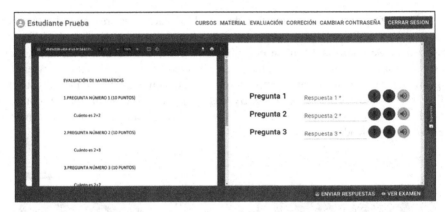

Fig. 4. Interface for Student Evaluation.

outcome is that students, upon viewing this interface, can review and reflect on the provided feedback, facilitating their continuous learning.

The utility of this interface lies in the clear presentation of the corrected evaluation. Each question includes comments from the teacher, the evaluation made, and the score obtained. Additionally, the final grade is included, offering the student a comprehensive view of their performance in the evaluation.

The interface also features an option to view the exam in a complete and detailed manner, giving students the opportunity to review every aspect of the evaluation. In summary, Fig. 5 aims not only to inform about the final grade but also to enrich the educational process by providing constructive and accessible feedback.

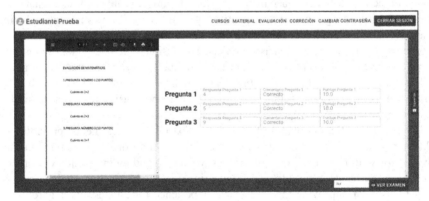

Fig. 5. Interface for Students' Evaluation Correction.

3   Usability Analysis: Evaluations with Students and Teachers

In this section, the comprehensive usability evaluation process conducted with students and teachers actively using the proposed platform is detailed. The applied methodology encompassed both secondary and university-level students as well as educators, delivering a thorough assessment of the user experience in various educational contexts.

3.1   Student Evaluation

The primary aim of the experimental investigation was to examine and assess the usability of the proposed technological platform. To avoid any biases resulting from a random selection of study groups, a quasi-experimental design was implemented, specifically choosing the study group from an environment closely related to the researcher.

This experiment was meticulously crafted to fulfill the three key usability conditions (effectiveness, efficiency, and satisfaction) outlined in the ISO-9241-11 standard [11].

Identification of Variables and Research Questions: In alignment with the principal objective of the experimentation, the study defined both the variables and the research inquiries. Independent variables encompassed the number of tasks performed by users, the total time users expended to complete tasks, participant characteristics (age and gender), and users' responses to the usability questionnaire.

Conversely, dependent variables were aligned with the three usability conditions specified in the ISO-9241-11 standard, namely effectiveness, efficiency, and satisfaction. Effectiveness gauges the level of success users achieve in task execution, measured as the percentage of task accomplishment. Efficiency quantifies the time users require to complete each task, measured in seconds. Lastly, satisfaction denotes the subjective perception of usability with the proposed platform, assessed through the average value of users' responses to the questions in the usability questionnaire. As previously mentioned, the questionnaire utilized is primarily based on the USE questionnaire [12], with some adaptations derived from Davis's Perception of Utility and Ease of Use questionnaire [13], as well as the Purdue Usability Questionnaire [14].

Research questions have been formulated to address the three dependent variables:

- RQ1: What is the effectiveness demonstrated by students in carrying out tasks related to exam creation and monitoring using the proposed platform?
- RQ2: What is the efficiency demonstrated by students in carrying out tasks related to exam creation and monitoring using the proposed platform?
- RQ3: What is students' perception of usability regarding the proposed platform?

Participants. A total of 5 students actively engaged in the evaluation of the proposed platform (see Table 1). The participant group comprised 2 males and 3 females, with ages ranging from 15 to 22 years ($M = 19.6$, $SD = 2.79$).

Tasks. Below is the sequential list of tasks performed by students during the platform evaluation phase. It is important to note that the defined tasks have a direct influence on the evaluation process, so functions that were not relevant at this stage were excluded; an example of this is the password change.

- Log in (T1): Requires the user to access the system using the credentials assigned beforehand.

Table 1. Demographic Profile of Students with Disabilities.

ID	Age	Gender	Disability Type	Educational Level
Student 1	21	Female	Physical	Higher
Student 2	21	Female	Visual	Higher
Student 3	19	Female	Physical	Middle
Student 4	15	Male	Visual	Middle
Student 5	22	Male	Physical	Higher

- Enter the course (T2): Asks the user to access a specific course.
- Access the evaluation (T3): Urges the user to enter the corresponding evaluation section.
- Perform evaluation (T4): Requests the user to complete the evaluation using all available accessibility tools.
- Submit answers (T5): Requires the user to submit the evaluation once finished.
- Access corrections (T6): Asks the user to enter the section housing all corrections for evaluations in a specific course.
- View corrections (T7): Invites the user to review the corrections made in a specific evaluation.

Results Obtained. The results are presented in accordance with the research questions.

- RQ1: What is the effectiveness demonstrated by students in carrying out tasks related to exam creation and monitoring using the proposed platform?

Effectiveness is measured through the task completion percentage. A 100% effectiveness is achieved, indicating that students successfully completed all seven tasks related to exam creation and monitoring. This underscores a consistent and successful performance across various platform functions.

- RQ2: What is the efficiency demonstrated by students in carrying out tasks related to exam creation and monitoring using the proposed platform?

Efficiency is gauged by the time students take to perform the seven tasks. Table 2 presents descriptive statistics for seven tasks undertaken by users during the usability experimentation with the technological platform. Each task is identified from T1 to T7, corresponding to specific platform functionalities.

The task that took the most time was "Perform evaluation" (T4), with an average of 1 min and 14 s. The variability in times suggests potential challenges for some users, emphasizing the importance of investigating the reasons behind these discrepancies to enhance overall efficiency.

In contrast, "Access the evaluation" (T3) was the task that took the least time, with an average of 2 s. The consistency in times indicates notable efficiency in this function.

The completion times fall within the accepted usability standards, according to the guidelines of ISO-9241-11. However, the variability in the completion times for the

Table 2. Students: Task Completion Times (in seconds) on the Technological Platform.

Descriptive Statistics	Tasks						
	1	2	3	4	5	6	7
Average	22	4	2	74	2	14	2
Standard Deviation	4	1	1	22	1	6	1
Minimum	17	2	2	44	2	8	2
Maximum	27	5	4	104	3	24	4

"Perform evaluation" task suggests that it might be beneficial to explore ways to reduce this variability and enhance performance consistency.

- RQ3: What is students' perception of usability regarding the proposed platform?

Figure 6 presents the results of the platform's usability assessment through a questionnaire, measuring four key variables: Utility, Ease of Use, Ease of Learning, and Satisfaction. These metrics are crucial to understanding the user experience and their overall perception of the platform.

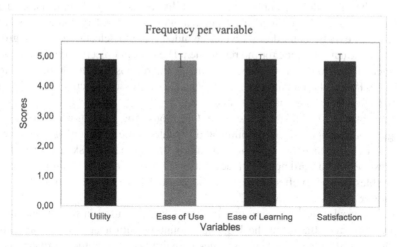

Fig. 6. Students: Results of Usability Assessment through Questionnaire.

Each variable was assessed on a scale of 1 to 5, with 5 being the highest rating. The total score is the average of the four variables, providing a comprehensive view of the platform's usability. Additionally, the usability questionnaire included two open-ended questions aimed at capturing users' perspectives on both positive and negative aspects of the platform.

Ease of Learning leads with an outstanding score of 4.93, indicating the platform's ability to be quickly adopted by users. Although Satisfaction has the lowest score at 4.87, it remains a notable rating, highlighting the overall quality of the user experience.

The results reflect a highly efficient and satisfactory platform for users. The high score in Ease of Learning emphasizes its accessibility, while ratings in Utility and Ease of Use solidify the platform as a valuable and user-friendly tool. Continued attention to user satisfaction could further enhance the experience, but overall, the results support the quality and usefulness of the evaluated platform.

Regarding the open-ended questions in the usability questionnaire, it is noteworthy that users expressed an overall positive perception of the platform. One of the most prominent aspects is the comfort and intuitiveness in using the interface, reflecting a successful design in terms of accessibility and user-friendliness.

A relevant point identified in the positive responses is the platform's utility in academic contexts, with users noting its ease of learning and the value it brings to those with physical or visual disabilities. This recognition underscores the positive impact the platform has on inclusion and diversity.

Concerning the negative aspects, most users did not find significant drawbacks, describing the platform as "providing exactly what is needed and nothing more". However, some suggestions hint at the possibility of expanding accessibility for individuals with different disabilities, indicating an opportunity for increased inclusion.

3.2 Teacher Evaluation

Following the methodology applied in the usability assessment of students, a parallel investigation was conducted focusing on educators from secondary and university levels. The quasi-experimental design, which avoided random selection of study groups, ensured contextual relevance for the researcher. The overall objective remained consistent: a meticulous examination of the usability of the proposed technological platform. Adhering to ISO-9241-11 standards, the experiment addressed effectiveness, efficiency, and satisfaction as primary usability conditions.

Identification of Variables and Research Questions: The replication of variables and investigations from the student usability study speaks to the methodological coherence of the research. Independent variables, including the number of tasks performed, total time investment, and participant characteristics, remained constant. Similarly, dependent variables, linked to effectiveness, efficiency, and satisfaction, continued to be the foundation of the investigation.

It is noteworthy that the same usability questionnaire used in the student evaluation was employed. Based on the USE questionnaire with adaptations from Davis's Perception of Utility and Ease of Use questionnaire, as well as the Purdue Usability Questionnaire.

Adapting the research to the teacher group, the research questions were adjusted:

- RQ4: What effectiveness do teachers demonstrate in performing tasks related to exam creation and monitoring using the proposed platform?
- RQ5: What efficiency do teachers demonstrate in performing tasks related to exam creation and monitoring using the proposed platform?
- RQ6: What is the usability perception of teachers regarding the proposed platform?

Participants. A total of 5 teachers participated in the usability evaluation of the proposed platform (see to Table 1). The group consisted of two males and three females, with ages spanning from 25 to 58 years ($M = 40.8$, $SD = 12.26$). They work across different levels of education, with two teachers engaged in middle education and three in higher education (Table 3).

Table 3. Participants' Profile: Teachers in Usability Evaluation.

ID	Age	Gender	Level of Education They Work With
Teacher 1	25	Female	Middle
Teacher 2	43	Male	Higher
Teacher 3	40	Female	Higher
Teacher 4	58	Female	Higher
Teacher 5	38	Male	Middle

Tasks. Following is the sequential list of the twelve tasks performed by teachers during the platform evaluation phase. It is worth noting that the tasks outlined have a direct impact on the students' evaluation process; therefore, functions that were not relevant to this stage were excluded, such as changing the password or uploading non-evaluated material.

- Log in (T1): User is required to log in to the system with previously assigned credentials.
- Read instructions (T2): User is prompted to access the Instructions section to read guidelines on how to use the system and create exams.
- Add course (T3): User is prompted to create a new course using default data.
- Enter the course (T4): User is prompted to enter the course created in the previous task.
- Add exam-type material (T5): User is prompted to add an exam to the course using default data and files.
- Review material (T6): User is prompted to verify if the material has been uploaded correctly.
- Search for a student (T7): User is prompted to search for users in a specific course.
- Add student (T8): User is prompted to add a student to a specific course.
- Access corrections (T9): User is prompted to look for pending corrections in a specific course.
- View answers (T10): User is prompted to access the answers given by a specific student.
- Correct answers (T11): User is prompted to provide feedback and a score for each answer in the evaluation.
- Generate report (T12): User is prompted to generate a report for a specific student.

Results Obtained. Similar to the student results, these findings are presented in alignment with the research questions.

- RQ4: What effectiveness do teachers demonstrate in performing tasks related to exam creation and monitoring using the proposed platform?

Effectiveness is gauged by the task completion percentage, and a remarkable 100% effectiveness is attained. This indicates that teachers adeptly executed all twelve tasks associated with exam creation and monitoring, showcasing a uniform and proficient performance across diverse platform functions.

It is noteworthy that assistance was required for two tasks, T9 and T11. T9 records a 15.2% assistance time, attributed to its time-constrained nature. On the other hand, T11 exhibits a higher assistance percentage, reaching 34%, as correcting responses demanded more time.

Despite the need for assistance in these specific tasks, it is crucial to emphasize the overall exceptional results achieved. Nevertheless, a comprehensive 100% effectiveness underscores the teachers' commendable mastery of the platform's functionalities.

- RQ5: What efficiency do teachers demonstrate in performing tasks related to exam creation and monitoring using the proposed platform?

Efficiency is measured based on the time it takes for teachers to complete the twelve tasks. Table 4 presents task completion times for teachers on the proposed technological platform, providing insights into their efficiency in performing tasks related to exam creation and monitoring.

The average completion times vary across tasks, reflecting the efficiency of teachers in navigating and utilizing the platform. Notably, tasks T6 and T10 demonstrate the shortest completion times, with averages of 4 s and 3 s, respectively. These tasks involve relatively simple actions, such as reading instructions and accessing student responses.

On the other hand, tasks T11 and T3 have the longest average completion times, standing at 43 s and 32 s, respectively. Task T11, involving correcting responses, understandably requires more time due to its complexity and the detailed nature of the evaluation process. Task T3, related to adding a new course, also demands a substantial investment of time.

The tasks with the least variability in completion times are T10 and T6, with minimum and maximum times consistent with the averages. Conversely, tasks T4 and T11 exhibit higher standard deviations, indicating greater variability in the time teachers spent on these activities.

- RQ6: What is the usability perception of teachers regarding the proposed platform?

Figure 7 presents the crucial findings derived from the usability evaluation conducted with teachers who participated in the use of the proposed platform. This analysis focused meticulously on four fundamental variables: Utility, Ease of Use, Ease of Learning, and Satisfaction, providing a comprehensive view of the user experience.

Particularly, the Ease of Learning variable achieved the highest score, reaching an impressive 4.63. This result clearly and strongly indicates that teachers perceive the platform as highly accessible and easy to learn.

Despite this success, the Satisfaction variable obtained the lowest score, registering a 3.83. However, the standard deviation of 0.87 reveals variability in the responses, indicating that specific aspects influence user satisfaction and deserve closer attention.

Table 4. Teachers: Task Completion Times on the Technological Platform.

Tasks	Average	Standard Deviation	Minimum	Maximum
T1	17	9	11	33
T2	33	11	20	45
T3	32	18	20	62
T4	28	8	4	25
T5	46	6	39	53
T6	4	2	2	8
T7	12	6	7	22
T8	14	12	4	35
T9	11	4	8	17
T10	3	2	2	6
T11	43	19	20	72
T12	19	5	13	26

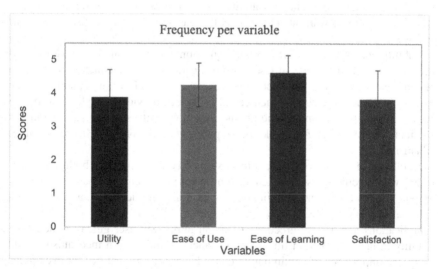

Fig. 7. Teachers: Results of Usability Assessment through Questionnaire.

In summary, teachers assess the platform as highly user-friendly, emphasizing its effectiveness for efficient adoption. Although variations in satisfaction have been identified, this specific aspect requires more detailed attention to enhance the overall user experience. Overall, these results support the overall effectiveness of the platform while providing valuable insights into specific areas that can be continuously improved.

Regarding the open-ended questions, most users highlight the ease of understanding and using the application. Simplicity is repeatedly mentioned as a positive aspect, and some users praise its intuitiveness, allowing them to use it without additional instructions. On the other hand, one user mentions the difficulty in immediately confirming or corroborating actions, pointing out the lack of quick access previews as an area for improvement.

Overall, the responses suggest a positive experience, emphasizing simplicity and ease of use as key strengths. Improvement suggestions focus on action confirmation and the implementation of additional features, indicating specific areas for the development team's attention.

4 Discussion

The comprehensive usability evaluation conducted with students and teachers using the proposed platform yielded significant insights into the user experience in diverse educational contexts.

Both students and teachers demonstrated 100% effectiveness in performing tasks related to exam creation and monitoring, showcasing the platform's adaptability to diverse user needs and fostering an inclusive and accessible environment.

Efficiency, measured by task completion times, was generally acceptable for both groups, with some observed variability in certain tasks. Specifically, the "Perform evaluation" task for students exhibited variability, indicating potential areas for improvement. Further investigation is warranted to uncover the reasons behind these discrepancies and refine overall efficiency.

Usability perception, assessed through questionnaires, revealed positive ratings in variables such as Utility, Ease of Use, Ease of Learning, and Satisfaction for both students and teachers. While Satisfaction scores were generally positive, some variability was noted among teachers. Open-ended responses provided insights into positive aspects, such as ease of understanding and use, along with suggestions for improvement, including the need for quick access previews and more effective confirmation mechanisms.

Overall, the results support the platform's general effectiveness for both students and teachers, with specific areas identified for continuous improvement. Consistent feedback from both groups emphasizes the importance of addressing identified areas to achieve an optimal user experience.

Implications and future directions focus on improving user guidance, addressing variability in task completion times, and enhancing confirmation mechanisms. Additionally, the importance of continuing to expand accessibility features for even greater inclusion is emphasized. The findings provide valuable patterns and directions for the ongoing development and improvement of the platform.

5 Conclusions and Future Work

The comprehensive evaluation of the proposed technological platform for conducting accessible assessments reveals promising results and key areas for ongoing development. The findings suggest that the platform achieves its primary goal of facilitating the participation of students with disabilities in educational settings while providing teachers with effective tools for assessment creation and review.

The demonstrated effectiveness by both students and teachers, reaching 100% in the completion of specific tasks, underscores the adaptability and overall usability of the platform. Users have shown a strong ability to leverage the provided features, supporting the vision of an inclusive environment.

Task completion times, although mostly acceptable, suggest potential areas for optimization. Variability in the times of some tasks, especially the "Perform evaluation," highlights the importance of further research to address potential challenges that may arise for certain users.

Usability assessments through the questionnaire reveal high scores in Ease of Learning and Satisfaction from both students and teachers. These results support the notion that the platform meets accessibility and simplicity requirements, promoting an inclusive and user-friendly educational environment.

Based on the results obtained and the identified areas for improvement, several directions for future work are outlined:

Optimization of Specific Task Times: A detailed investigation will be conducted on variabilities in task completion times, especially in the "Perform evaluation" task. This will help identify potential obstacles and optimize the workflow for overall efficiency.

Expansion of Accessibility Features: Efforts will continue to expand accessibility features to address diverse needs. The implementation of additional tools, such as enhanced screen readers and simplified navigation options, will contribute to even greater inclusion.

Integration of Formal Methods for User Prioritization in Proposal Design: An additional avenue for future work involves integrating formal methods to prioritize user preferences systematically [15, 16]. This enhancement aims to formally capture end-users' priorities during the design phase, ensuring that the proposed platform aligns closely with their needs and expectations.

Refinement of User Interface: Based on user feedback, improvements to the user interface will address the need for quick access previews and clearer confirmation mechanisms. This will ensure a smoother and more satisfying experience for all users.

Expansion of Testing with Multiple Institutions: To further validate the effectiveness and adaptability of the platform, pilot tests are planned with multiple educational institutions. Feedback from a variety of educational environments will contribute to the continuous evolution of the platform.

References

1. Keates, S.: Universal access: the challenges ahead. In: Antona, M., Stephanidis, C. (eds.) HCII 2019. LNCS, vol. 11572, pp. 100–112. Springer, Cham (2019). https://doi.org/10.1007/978-3-030-23560-4_8
2. Lazar, J., Goldstein, D.F., Taylor, A.: Ensuring digital accessibility through process and policy. Morgan kaufmann (2015). Accessed 29 Oct 2023. https://books.google.com/books?hl=es&lr=&id=YepDBAAAQBAJ&oi=fnd&pg=PP1&dq=Ensuring+Digital+Accessibility+through+Process+and+Policy&ots=vTkS4wzmbv&sig=SNXQauWOpINxvQuYv3lkJTUWtEw
3. Márton, S.M., Polk, G., Fiala, D.R.C.: Convention on the Rights of Persons with Disabilities. USA U. N. (2013). Accessed 29 Oct 2023. https://www.refworld.org/pdfid/5280d17a4.pdf

4. Mahdi, Z.A., Naidu, V.R., Kurian, P.: Analyzing the role of human computer interaction principles for E-learning solution design. In: Al-Masri, A., Curran, K. (eds.) Smart Technologies and Innovation for a Sustainable Future: Proceedings of the 1st American University in the Emirates International Research Conference — Dubai, UAE 2017, pp. 41–44. Springer International Publishing, Cham (2019). https://doi.org/10.1007/978-3-030-01659-3_6

5. Sinha, G., Shahi, R., Shankar, M.: Human computer interaction. In: 2010 3rd International Conference on Emerging Trends in Engineering and Technology, pp. 1–4. IEEE (2010)

6. Rojas, L.A., Macías, J.A.: An agile information-architecture-driven approach for the development of user-centered interactive software. In: Proceedings of the XVI International Conference on Human Computer Interaction, pp. 1–8 (2015)

7. McNicholl, A., Casey, H., Desmond, D., Gallagher, P.: The impact of assistive technology uses for students with disabilities in higher education: a systematic review. Disabil. Rehabil. Assist. Technol. 16(2), 130–143 (2021)

8. Lopez-Gavira, R., Moriña, A., Morgado, B.: Challenges to inclusive education at the university: the perspective of students and disability support service staff. Innov. Eur. J. Soc. Sci. Res. 34(3), 292–304 (2021)

9. Batanero-Ochaíta, C., De-Marcos, L., Rivera, L.F., Holvikivi, J., Hilera, J.R., Tortosa, S.O.: Improving accessibility in online education: comparative analysis of attitudes of blind and deaf students toward an adapted learning platform. IEEE Access 9, 99968–99982 (2021)

10. Zhang, H., Babar, M.A., Tell, P.: Identifying relevant studies in software engineering. Inf. Softw. Technol. 53(6), 625–637 (2011)

11. Din, E.: 9241-11. Ergonomic requirements for office work with visual display terminals (VDTs)–Part 11: Guidance on usability. Int. Organ. Stand. (1998)

12. Lund, A.M.: Measuring usability with the use questionnaire12. Usabil. Interface 8(2), 3–6 (2001)

13. Davis, F.D.: Perceived usefulness, perceived ease of use, and user acceptance of information technology. MIS Q. 13, 319–340 (1989)

14. Lin, H.X., Choong, Y.-Y., Salvendy, G.: A proposed index of usability: a method for comparing the relative usability of different software systems. Behav. Inf. Technol. 16(4–5), 267–277 (1997)

15. Rojas, L., Olivares-Rodriguez, C., Alvarez, C., Campos, P.G.: OurRank: a software requirements prioritization method based on qualitative assessment and cost-benefit prediction. IEEE Access 10, 131772–131787 (2022). https://doi.org/10.1109/ACCESS.2022.3230152

16. Rojas, L.A., Macías, J.A.: Toward collisions produced in requirements rankings: a qualitative approach and experimental study. J. Syst. Softw.Softw. 158, 110417 (2019)

Teachers' Perspectives on Transatlantic AI Implementation in K-12 and University Classrooms

Jennifer Smith[✉]

Illinois State University, Normal, IL 61790, USA
jsmit54@illinois.edu

Abstract. Artificial intelligence is not new to education, but recent advancements, such as the creation of Chat GPT have placed AI into the educational spotlight. The primary aim of this paper is to provide a case study of the experiences of teachers engaged in transatlantic collaboration with the aim of incorporating AI in their classrooms. Using semi-structured interviews, I found that teachers sought transatlantic collaboration for projects such as AI implementation in order to share their experiences as well as learn from the experiences of others. The teachers incorporated a variety of AI tools into their practice to develop lesson plans, assess students, and teach students how to use AI. The collaboration was a source of inspiration and support for teachers, even though their contexts varied in terms of both the content and age levels of students.

Keywords: Artificial Intelligence · Transatlantic · Collaboration

1 Introduction

Artificial intelligence (AI) has held a space in education for the past few decades. As the incorporation of computers and personal computing devices has become almost ubiquitous in the classroom, AI has also occupied these classroom spaces in the form of a variety of online interactives and even in programs that may be easy to overlook, such as spellcheck. Recent technological advancements and innovations, such as the creation of Chat GPT, have brought new changes to education and have placed AI into the educational spotlight.

Considering these advancements, educators have been faced with the challenge of learning how to navigate these new forms of AI, first as learners themselves and second as educators. Educator training on the topic of AI varies greatly from school to school both in the United States and abroad. Educator attitudes toward AI are also varied, with some teachers fully embracing it while others are more wary [1]. For educators who are willing and able to implement AI into their classrooms, having the opportunity to collaborate with and learn from other educators who are also strategically implementing AI presents a unique opportunity for support and growth. The Transatlantic Educator Dialogue (TED) Fellowship through the European Union Center at the University of Illinois Urbana-Champaign is an example of a program designed to facilitate transnational

A. Coman and S. Vasilache (Eds.): HCII 2024, LNCS 14704, pp. 191–200, 2024.
https://doi.org/10.1007/978-3-031-61305-0_13

collaborative experiences for educators. As the use of AI in classrooms has increased, the participants in the 2023–2024 TED Fellows program have collaborated to better understand its implications for their classrooms.

The purpose of this qualitative study is to examine the ways in which teachers navigate transatlantic collaboration to implement AI in their classrooms. Furthermore, this study explores AI's ability to empower both teachers and students to meaningfully interact across continents, grade levels, and content areas. The research questions guiding this study are:

1. What techniques do teachers use to implement AI in their classrooms?
2. How does transatlantic collaboration impact teachers' use of AI in the classroom?

2   Literature Review

2.1   Brief History of AI in the Classroom

Artificial Intelligence has been defined and described in several different ways. For the purposes of this study, I employ the definition provided by Popenici and Kerr, "computing systems that are able to engage in human-like processes such as learning, adapting, synthesizing, self-correction, and the use of data for complex processing tasks" [2, p. 2]. Mechanical devices which required students to select the correct answer from multiple choices before they could move to the next question, or "teaching machines" were developed by Sidney Pressey, and these precursors to AI were used in education in the 1920s [3]. While these mechanical devices had been in use of a couple of decades, the term "artificial intelligence" is credited to have first been used in publication by McCarthy, Minsky, Rochester, and Shannon in 1955 in a research proposal aimed at exploring ways to write programs for machines to help them use language and solve problems [4]. Around the same time, Newell and Simon created a computer program, Logic Theorist, designed to prove mathematical theorems [5]. Working with James Moore, Newell created Merlin, an automated tutoring system, though it did not achieve the level of success Newell had desired [6]. While Merlin was not considered a success at the time, Intelligent Tutoring Systems began impacting education in the 1960s and 1970s [7]. By the 1980s, AI in education had become an established research field [8]. As the technology driving computers advanced, so did the incorporation of AI. Naturally then, as computers became more widely available in K-12 classrooms, the incorporation of AI followed suit, providing teachers with greater opportunities to incorporate AI into their classrooms.

2.2   Uses of AI in the Classroom

Early forms of AI were developed by cognitive scientists who used AI in classrooms both as learning aids and to study human cognition [6]. Current research on AI in the classroom includes systematic reviews regarding its implementation in the classroom. For instance, one study identified planning, implementation, and assessment as critical areas where teachers utilized AI [1]. A systematic literature review yielded similar results, identifying three central themes of AI use in education including "connecting to pedagogies (e.g., gaming, personalization), administration (e.g., diagnostic tools), and subject content" [9]. Implementing AI in the classroom can be an intimidating process for teachers. As such, researchers recommended that teachers be provided with time, expertise, funds, and resources to help them better understand and explore the applications of AI in education [10].

2.3 Transatlantic Collaboration in Education

Collaboration between teachers can be a driving force in professional growth and can take on a variety of forms. The effectiveness of professional learning communities housed in the same school or district has been widely studied. While some teachers may prefer face-to-face learning environments, a variety of online tools can be used to facilitate communities of practice in the online environment [11]. Communities of practice (CoPs) are an example of the type of groups educators may choose to work in to explore new pedagogies as they allow for ongoing interactions regarding a topic that the group members are passionate about pursuing [12].

These communities may be especially valuable when they include teachers from different backgrounds and cultures, such as those that can be found in transatlantic collaborations. Transatlantic collaboration provides a unique opportunity to gain insights from differing perspectives and can come with its own set of unique challenges as group members navigate cultural and contextual differences. These challenges can be navigated through various acts of translation as participants establish shared understandings, build relationships, and decenter personal, cultural, and institutional assumptions [13].

3   Methodology

Qualitative methods in the form of a case study were utilized in this study to gain insight into the ways that teachers engage in transatlantic collaboration, because qualitative methodologies produce data that lead to deeper understandings of social phenomena [14, 15]. Utilizing qualitative methods requires the researcher to play an integral role in both data collection and analysis, so it is important to delineate the researcher's positionality [16]. As such, constructivism is the theoretical perspective through which I approached this study [17]. It is also important to note that prior to conducting this study, I was a participant in the TED program. After a year of participating in the program, I stepped into the facilitator role for the TED Alumni program. I am currently the facilitator for the TED Fellows program. I am also an American educator in the public school system in the United States.

3.1 Participants

For this case study, exploring the ways in which transatlantic collaboration between teachers can facilitate the implementation of AI in the classroom, it was important to identify a sample of participants with experience in collaborating with teachers in transatlantic contexts. For this purpose, I sought study participants who are TED Fellows. The European Union Center housed at the University of Illinois Urbana-Champaign sponsors TED, a program aimed to foster collaborative efforts between educators in the United States and Europe by providing an online space for them to come together synchronously for shared exploration and examination of a variety of educational topics, such as global collaboration, supporting diverse learning needs, parental involvement, and technology in the classroom. Educators who successfully participate in the program are invited to continue their collaborations in subsequent years as TED Fellows. TED Fellows provides alumni of the TED program with an opportunity to collaborate on global projects, discuss salient education-related topics with an international group of colleagues, and expand their professional network. Fellows of the TED program meet as a cohort synchronously via Zoom once a month to plan and conduct a variety of ongoing projects, as such TED Fellows have significant experience in planning and conducting transatlantic collaborations.

The participants in this study include five educators who are active members of the TED Fellows program. The countries represented by the participants include Italy, Greece, Poland, Portugal, and the United States. The participants are all educators working with students at different age levels and content areas. One educator teaches English as a foreign language to students ages 4–12. A second educator instructs 10–12-year-old students in social studies. A third educator teaches math and science to students who are between the ages of 11 and 14. The fourth educator teaches psychology to 17 and 18-year-olds. Finally, one participant is a university instructor who teaches courses on the culture and history of English-speaking countries to students between the ages of 17 and 23.

3.2 Procedures

To conduct this case study, I recruited volunteer participants from the TED Fellows program via email. Volunteers were provided with detailed information about their participation in the study and completed consent forms. After obtaining consent, I reached out to each of the participants individually to schedule a semi-structured interview. The interviews were conducted via Zoom, as the study participants were not in the same state or country as the researcher. The interview questions invited participants to describe the ways in which they implement AI in their classroom contexts, the manner in which they collaborate with other educators to implement AI, the challenges they have encountered in transatlantic collaboration, and recommendations they have for other educators who are interested in implementing AI in collaborative contexts. The interviews took an average of twenty minutes, were conducted in English, and were recorded. After the interviews were conducted, the recordings were transcribed for coding.

3.3 Data Analysis

Initial coding was completed by hand for the first cycle analysis of each of the five interviews [18]. This initial coding was conducted on a line-by-line basis of the interview transcripts. These codes emphasized the key aspects of the interview in terms of the types of AI the educators noted interacting with, the ways they described interacting with AI in their classrooms, and the ways in which they collaborated with other educators.

In vivo coding was also used in the first cycle of coding to retain the voices of the participants [18]. Since the interviews were conducted in English, which is not the primary language for all the participants, there may have been instances in which it was challenging to select terms that fully conveyed the intended ideas. Once the first round of coding was complete, pattern coding was used during the second cycle of coding to build toward identifying themes in the data [18]. Pattern coding revealed key similarities among all the interviews, which led to the identification of themes that could be used to answer the research question regarding the techniques teachers used to incorporate AI into their classrooms as well as yielding insights into the research question about transatlantic collaboration.

4   Results

4.1   Use of AI in the Classroom

Each of the participants in the study utilized AI in their classrooms for a variety of purposes, though to varying degrees. When asked to describe the types of AI they used in their classrooms, three of the five educators listed specific AI programs by name. One theme that emerged in examining the way teachers were incorporating AI into their classrooms was that the AI was used to complete administrative type tasks. For instance, three of the five educators commented that they utilized generative AI to create lesson plans and to develop and implement student assessments. These uses included the use of AI in making modifications to existing curricular materials as well as the creation of entirely new materials. The participants utilized AI to create and deliver online versions of assessment for students in addition to generating assignment prompts. One participant taught students how to utilize AI as a source of feedback for written assignments.

The other theme that emerged when examining the ways in which the participants incorporated AI into the classroom was through explicit instruction on how the AI was trained. For instance, two of the participants described using AI programs to explain how the AI provided information requested by users. One of those educators specifically worked with students to train an AI program how to identify specific body movements as they related to sports.

4.2   Techniques for Incorporating AI into the Classroom

Surprisingly, when asked to describe the types of techniques they used to incorporate AI into the classroom, only two of the five participants responded directly to the question. One participant explained that they use "active learning" in their student-centered classroom and that they employ a "large range of tools and strategies" when implementing any idea into their classroom. The other participant noted that when implementing AI, they did not do "anything special or different from other content that we teach."

While not in response to the question about implementation, all of the participants noted that they explained some of the downsides of AI to their students when implementing it into the classroom. Primarily these downsides included the potential lack of reliability of generative AI, prompting the participants to note that they also taught students how to verify the information received via AI. While they did not explicitly state this need for teaching students how to verify AI-generated information as a technique for implementing AI in the classroom, based on my second cycle coding, I included it as such.

4.3 Identity and AI

As I reviewed the coded data, another theme that emerged related to teacher identity and, more broadly, human identity in juxtaposition to AI. One participant noted that some of the teachers they worked with outside of the TED Fellows program were afraid of AI because they thought it would be used to replace them. This notion of identity was also brought up by another participant who noted that when they teach students about the uses of AI, they have discussions about the ways that students should be thinking critically about their use of AI in terms of how they can set themselves apart from others in a world where everyone can use AI. For example, the participant explained that they ask students to think about the characteristics that make them unique in a way that would encourage an employer to hire them.

A sense of identity and self-awareness was also present when the participants discussed their implementation of AI. When asked about their implementation of AI, one participant noted, "maybe I'm not an expert, but I'm good enough." Another participant noted that they are "from a country of navigators" when detailing the importance of confidence when facing challenges when using AI in transatlantic collaborations. A third participant noted that they felt as though they were still in the early stages of implementing AI and were "dabbling" in its use.

4.4 Conditions for Collaboration

Another theme that emerged from the data was the conditions necessary in order for collaboration to occur. The interviews revealed that the participants in the study faced challenges in identifying collaborative partners in their buildings and districts. For instance, when asked about how they collaborated with others to implement AI in their classrooms, none of the participants identified working collaboratively with peers in their building as a source of inspiration or assistance.

One of the participants serves as a teacher trainer in addition to working with students. This participant noted that many of the teachers they work with are afraid of using AI and that there are not many teachers who are open to implementing it. Another participant noted that their institution did not hold meetings about A, and they were not aware of anyone in the institution who was consciously utilizing AI as an educational tool. Similarly, another participant noted that fewer than half of their colleagues are implementing AI, while another noted that their colleagues viewed AI as more of a problem than an opportunity. The participant from the United States recalled an in-service training from a previous school year during which the teachers were shown how to utilize AI in the form of a lesson plan generator but noted that they were not actively collaborating with anyone in their district to utilize AI.

While there may have been challenges in collaborating with local peers on AI implementation, the participants noted that TED Fellows had provided them with the opportunity to engage in supportive collaboration with others centered on the implementation of

AI. When speaking about their collaboration with other fellows, participants noted that their fellow colleagues were, "eager to learn and experiment with AI tools" and "have the same concerns" for implementing AI. This demonstrates that while the participants in TED Fellows had concerns regarding implementing AI, they were not afraid to try using it in their classrooms. One participant found more acceptance in the TED group because "we shared a common goal." Another participant noted that having the opportunity to collaborate with other educators regarding AI, "taught me as seeing different approaches and also seeing well, the difficulties, but also the opportunities that are available." This exchange of ideas was valuable to the fellows as one remarked that, "even though we teach like very different ages, some of them teach primary school, I teach college, but still, you know, a lot of the tools that we use actually can be adopted, adjusted", noting that the collaboration served as "a well of inspiration" for them.

The collaboration that took place within the TED Fellows program was not without its challenges. One challenge identified by the participants was the need for a leader. This participant noted that within a collaborative group it was important for someone to step up and take charge. Another major challenge that participants faced was time. Educators participating in transatlantic collaboration need to be cognizant of the time zone differences, which can make synchronous collaboration difficult, especially during the school day. Participants noted that, at times, culture and language could pose challenges during collaboration, primarily in minor misunderstandings or miscommunications. Asking for clarity and providing examples during collaboration were methods the participants used to navigate some of these challenges.

4.5 Challenges to AI Implementation

During the interviews, the participants also identified a variety of challenges they faced when working to implement AI in their classrooms. Some of these challenges were structural in nature. For instance, one of the participants noted that some of the AI programs they wanted to use were blocked by the internet filters in their school district. A similar challenge identified by a different participant was that many AI programs require a login that is tied to an email address, which their students did not have because of their young ages. While none of the participants faced this challenge themselves, one participant noted that lack of access to technology could be a hinderance to utilizing AI in the classroom and one participant noted that their implementation was hindered by paywalls.

Reliability and bias were two additional AI challenges that the participants referenced. In their interviews, several participants noted concerns regarding the reliability of work created through AI. While they acknowledged the concern, it did not prevent them from pursuing the use of AI. Rather, the concern caused them to double check products created using AI and some participants mentioned that they taught their students how to verify the accuracy of AI generated materials as well. Regarding the challenge of bias in AI, one of the participants from Europe commented that bias was very strong in AI tools and that it was difficult for people from North America to see because AI is a tool that was generated based on North American culture.

5 Discussion

The first research question in this study is: What techniques do teachers use to implement AI in their classrooms? To answer this question, it is important to first review the ways that teachers are implementing AI in their classrooms. Similar to previous studies, the participants in this study primarily utilized AI for planning and assessment purposes [1] though one participant explicitly taught students how to use AI. The participants were excited to describe the ways they implemented AI, many times including the names of the programs they used and even sending URL links so I could access their projects. Atypical to previous work though is the fact that the participants used AI in a variety of content areas, rather than primarily in math [19].

When asked specifically to share information about the techniques they used to incorporate AI, the participants responded by explaining that they used student-centered approaches or that they utilized similar pedagogical methods for AI as they did for the other types of tools they used. One participant identified that they did stop to think about their purpose for using different types of AI programs, commenting on the importance for teachers to think critically about the utility of a program and its purpose rather than just trying new ideas just to try them. Another technique that the participants identified when discussing the implementation of AI was determining the reliability of the information generated by AI. Participants explained that they taught students how to use additional sources of information to confirm the information they received from AI. While not stated explicitly, the participants in this study also demonstrated a willingness to use AI in their classrooms, sometimes juxtaposing themselves with their colleagues who were afraid of AI. This willingness to implement new pedagogical tools is, in a way, also a technique for implementing AI as none of the participants claimed to be experts in using AI but instead, demonstrated a curiosity and desire to move forward with implementation ideas. Networking with other teachers to learn more about the ways in which they were using AI was another technique utilized by multiple participants in the study.

The second research question for this study is: How does transatlantic collaboration impact teachers' use of AI in the classroom? All of the participants in the study noted a lack of collaboration around AI with the colleagues in their buildings. While not all of the reasons for this lack of collaboration are clear, it was clear that there are several teachers who are not yet ready to work toward implementing AI in their classrooms. The data from this study demonstrates that the participants sought out collaboration with peers through the TED Fellows program and found the network to be a helpful way to learn about AI programs and the ways other teachers were implementing the programs in their classrooms. The willingness of the TED Fellows to share their ideas and work together toward a common goal of learning more about AI was beneficial to the study participants. The participants felt supported and understood by their transatlantic colleagues.

While this study yielded helpful perspectives on the implementation of AI in the classroom, it is also limited. One limitation of this study is its small sample size, which may not be representative of the general population of teachers. Additionally, the participants in the study both regularly use online tools in their classrooms and have extensive experiences in interacting with and collaborating with educators from different countries, which may not be characteristic of a general sample of educators.

6   Conclusion

As we become a more global society, the value of transatlantic collaboration should not be overlooked. Collaborating with peers across the Atlantic can provide teachers with new insights about pedagogy as well as nuanced cultural perspectives. This study illustrates the ways in which transatlantic collaboration can fill gaps in local collaboration and serve to help teachers grow their understanding and implementation of topics they are interested in. The educators in this study were eager to learn more about AI and to pursue its use in the classroom. As they incorporated AI into the classroom, they leveraged student-centered pedagogies in addition to explicitly teaching students about key features of the AI. For example, the educators explained the importance of verifying the accuracy of AI generated products, much as they emphasize the importance of verifying information found using internet searches.

This study was limited in scope and, as such, future research into the differences between local collaboration and transatlantic collaboration regarding the implementation of AI could provide insight into the collaborative aspects that best facilitate the implementation of new technologies. As AI advances, further research could explore both the commonalities in teachers who are working toward AI integration as well as the techniques they find most successful during implementation.

Disclosure of Interests.   The author has no competing interests to declare that are relevant to the content of this article.

References

1. Celik, I., Dindar, M., Muukkonen, H., et al.: The promises and challenges of artificial intelligence for teachers: a systematic review of research. TechTrends **66**, 616–630 (2022). https://doi.org/10.1007/s11528-022-00715-y
2. Popenici, S.A.D., Kerr, S.: Exploring the impact of artificial intelligence on teaching and learning in higher education. Res. Pract. Technol. Enhanc. Learn. **12**(1), 1–13 (2017). https://doi.org/10.1186/s41039-017-0062-8
3. Watters, A.: Teaching Machines: The History of Personalized Learning. MIT Press, Cambridge (2021)
4. McCarthy, J., Minsky, M.L., Rochester, N., Shannon, C.E.: A proposal for the Dartmouth summer research project on artificial intelligence, August 31, 1955. AI Mag. **27**(4), 12 (2006). https://doi.org/10.1609/aimag.v27i4.1904
5. Newell, A., Simon, H.: The logic theory machine–a complex information processing system. IRE Trans. Inf. Theory **2**(3), 61–79 (1956). https://doi.org/10.1109/TIT.1956.1056797
6. Doroudi, S.: The intertwined histories of artificial intelligence and education. Int. J. Artif. Intell. Educ. **33**(4), 885–928 (2023). https://doi.org/10.1007/s40593-022-00313-2
7. Alkhatlan, A., Kalita, J.: Intelligent tutoring systems: a comprehensive historical survey with recent developments (2018)
8. Williamson, B., Eynon, R.: Historical threads, missing links, and future directions in AI in education. Learn. Media Technol. **45**(3), 223–235 (2020). https://doi.org/10.1080/17439884.2020.1798995
9. Crompton, H., Jones, M.V., Burke, D.: Affordances and challenges of artificial intelligence in K-12 education: a systematic review. J. Res. Technol. Educ. **56**(3), 248–268 (2024). https://doi.org/10.1080/15391523.2022.2121344

10. Antonenko, P.: Abramowitz, B: In-service teachers' (mis)conceptions of artificial intelligence in K-12 science education. J. Res. Technol. Educ. **55**(1), 64–78 (2023)

11. Gunawardena, C., Hermans, M., Sanchez, D., Richmond, C., Bohley, M., Tuttle, R.: A theoretical framework for building online communities of practice with social networking tools. Educ. Media Int. **46**(1), 3–16 (2009). https://doi.org/10.1080/09523980802588626

12. Wenger, E.: Communities of Practice: Learning, Meaning, and Identity. Cambridge University Press, Cambridge (1998)

13. Harris, H., Hatcher, S.J., Kampschulte, L.: Perceptions of possibilities: an exploration of transatlantic collaboration. J. Museum Educ. **46**(1), 86–92 (2021). https://doi.org/10.1080/10598650.2020.1834750

14. Creswell, J.W.: Qualitative Inquiry and Research Design: Choosing Among Five Traditions. Sage, Thousand Oaks (1998)

15. Plano Clark, V.L., Creswell, J.W.: Understanding Research: A Consumer's Guide. Pearson, Boston (2010)

16. Patton, M.: Qualitative Research and Evaluation Methods, 3rd edn. Sage, Thousand Oaks (2002)

17. Crotty, M.: The Foundation of Social Research. Sage, Thousand Oaks (1998)

18. Saldana, J.M.: The Coding Manual for Qualitative Researchers, 3rd edn. SAGE Publications, Thousand Oaks (2015)

19. Moore, R.L., Jiang, S., Abramowitz, B.: (2023) What would the matrix do? a systematic review of K-12 AI learning contexts and learner-interface interactions. J. Res. Technol. Educ. **55**(1), 7–20 (2023). https://doi.org/10.1080/15391523.2022.2148785

EPICommunity Platform: Towards an Academic Social Network Designed for Researchers by Researchers

Iakovos Stratigakis[1] , Christos Katsanos[1(✉)] , Anouk Tso[2], Dimitrios Kovaios[1],
and Thrasyvoulos Tsiatsos[1]

[1] Aristotle University of Thessaloniki, Thessaloniki, Greece
{iakovosds,ckatsanos,tsiatsos}@csd.auth.gr, koveos@agro.auth.gr
[2] University of Amsterdam, Amsterdam, The Netherlands
a.n.tso@uva.nl

Abstract. Existing academic social networks for researchers do not currently address the multitude of their tasks and diverse needs. This paper presents the EPICommunity platform, a social network for researchers designed by researchers. The EPICommunity platform aims to support researchers, particularly early career researchers, to connect with peers, showcase their work and collaborate and create groups. To this end, it provides unique features compared to existing systems, such as Europass profile interoperability, recommendations for researchers with similar interests based on various criteria, gamification mechanics, analytics to monitor researchers' own progress and a multi-dimensional set of researchers' assessment criteria, both quantitative and qualitative. The EPICommunity platform follows a human-centered development model. This paper presents its first iteration. Real-world user requirements were produced from three workshops with 17 researchers from 8 European Universities. Prototypes were also developed and evaluated in these workshops. Finally, a formative expert-based usability evaluation study was conducted. To this end, the heuristic evaluation method was employed involving five experienced usability experts.

Keywords: Academic Social Networks · Computer Supported Cooperative Work · Human-centered Software Development · Heuristic Evaluation

1 Introduction

Academic researchers are working in an increasingly demanding context; not only are they expected to be productive and impactful, they are also expected to undertake their work in collaborative settings within and beyond their affiliated organization, and to be able to explain how their results will benefit society. Their work reflects on their publications and academic activities, and they often need to collaborate with other researchers in many different countries and time zones.

Researchers often engage in online digital communities to achieve such goals. The most used such communities are the different social networks (e.g., Facebook, Twitter,

LinkedIn). For example, researchers might share their latest published paper in one or more social networks, a practice also encouraged by publishers, in an attempt to increase its visibility, engage other researchers in discussions, find researchers with similar interests that might be potential collaborators in future research endeavors and so forth. As another example, researchers might create or respond to posts in social networks for partnerships with people having specific expertise in the context of writing research proposals, co-authoring research papers, preparing the syllabus for a new course and so forth.

Academic social networks, like ResearchGate and Academia, are similar to the classic social networks but they are built to accommodate the research community, mainly exchanging information in the form of updates for publications and project involvement. However, researchers typically perform multiple other tasks, such as finding fellow researchers to collaborate with, institutions and organizations to partner with on proposals writing or as contractors, teams to join for postdoctoral research and so forth. They need ways to perform these tasks effectively and efficiently. However, existing academic social networks provide rather limited support for many of their needs, or researchers have to use multiple different platforms to achieve their goals.

This paper presents the EPICommunity platform (https://epicommunity.auth.gr), an academic social network for researchers to connect with peers, showcase their work and collaborate and create groups. This platform is being developed in the context of the European Partnership for an Innovative Campus Unifying Regions (EPICUR, https://epicur.edu.eu) Research project (EPICUR-Research) with the support of the Horizon 2020. EPICUR is a first-generation European University Alliance, dedicated to shaping European Society in Transition through the development of collaborative inter- and transdisciplinary teaching and learning. The EPICommunity platform follows a human-centered development model and this paper reports on the design and evaluation of its first version, hereafter EPICommunity-v1 platform or system.

2   EPICommunity Platform Design and Implementation

The EPICommunity platform is designed to serve as a registry, allowing for the easy discovery of high-quality research profiles. Like LinkedIn, the members of EPICommunity are the competitive advantage of the platform. The selection of specific features on a researcher's profile (e.g., publications, projects, skills, badges) gives our members the opportunity to effectively research future collaborators.

On a second level, our members can make use of community-like features, such as creating and participating in groups. This way they can have a quick way of coordinating for a common goal, such as co-authoring a scientific publication or preparing a project proposal. On the third level, the platform is trying to engage or kickstart such communications and collaborations by recommending to its members material and contacts relevant to them.

It is worth noting that the platform also implements an innovative framework for researchers' peer assessment (EPIQAssess framework) and a unique gamification framework that can actively recognize, reward and motivate researchers in their activities (EPIGame framework). These frameworks are delineated in the following.

2.1 Objective and Typical Users

The EPICommunity serves as a platform dedicated to establishing a European Social Network of researchers, with a focus on fostering academic matchmaking and collaboration. The primary user base comprises early career researchers, postdoctoral students, and professors. Although the main focus is on European researchers, the platform can be used by any researcher in the world. Additional users can be managers and supervisors of research units, researchers' assessment committees, and university leaders.

The EPICommunity platform provides a specialized environment that encourages networking and collaboration, facilitating meaningful connections within the research community. It is a dynamic space where researchers can engage in collaborative endeavors, exchange ideas, and contribute to the advancement of academic knowledge.

2.2 Software Design Process

The development of the EPICommunity academic social network follows the human-centered design for interactive systems [1]. In this paper, we present the results of its first iteration, the EPICommunity-v1 system.

We worked in close collaboration with researchers, and particularly early career researchers. In specific, 17 researchers from 8 European Universities at 5 different counties (Austria, France, Germany, Greece, Poland) were involved. These researchers form the EPICUR Researchers Board and include six PhD students, nine post-doctoral researchers, and two faculty members (one Assistant and one Associate Professor).

Real-world user requirements were produced from three workshops with the EPICUR Researchers Board. Prototypes were also developed and evaluated in these workshops, which also redefined some of the initial user requirements. Finally, a heuristic evaluation was conducted to investigate the usability of the EPICommunity-v1 system. We chose to employ heuristic evaluation at this phase of the EPICommunity system design because we were interested in a discount usability evaluation method that could also provide qualitative insights on how to improve the system before engaging in a user testing study.

2.3 EPIQAssess: Assessment Framework for Researchers

EPIQAssess [2] is a new, flexible and dynamic framework for researcher assessment principles and practices developed in the context of the EPICUR-Research project and used by the EPICommunity-v1 platform.

The EPIQAssess researchers' assessment framework aims to offer a practical tool for individual researchers, managers and supervisors of research units, researchers assessment committees, and university leaders to help develop and deploy ways in which staff performance is recognized and rewarded. A key feature of EPIQAssess is to focus on the actual deployment and practical implementation of the framework in real-life situations.

The assessment framework considers the entire life cycle of researchers' career paths based on four key dimensions: Learning & Teaching (LT), Research (R), Innovation (I) and Interaction with Society (S). The model framework is flexible and can be adapted to specific needs of individual users from all scientific disciplines, while proposing both quantitative and qualitative assessment criteria. These criteria are grouped into the following three categories: a) core criteria, b) specific criteria, c) personal qualities.

EPIQAssess builds upon ongoing discussions focusing on fostering research careers in national and European contexts, including the recent Council of the European Union's conclusions entitled "Deepening the European Research Area: Providing researchers with attractive and sustainable careers and working conditions and making brain circulation a reality" [3]. EPIQAssess had been initially drafted in close consultation with an Expert Group, comprising researchers and senior staff of all eight EPICUR partner universities, as well as members of the EPICUR Researchers Board. In addition, internal consultations within EPICUR partner universities have taken place and all feedback received has been considered.

2.4   EPIGame: Gamification Framework for Researchers

Games are designed in a way to provoke immersion and engagement in the player. Gamification is the integration and use of various game design elements in non-game contexts [4, 5].

Various studies in an academic context [6–8] have shown that gamification affects motivation and engagement in a positive way. Both tutors and learners seem to be more active in courses [9]. Moreover, the academic performance seems to be enhanced either to technological-based or non-technological-based courses [10]. In the EPICommunity-v1 platform, gamification is employed to actively recognize, reward and motivate researchers in their academic activities.

A properly designed gamification framework should rely on well-established theoretical models. We used the Self-Determination Theory (SDT) [11] as such a theoretical model. SDT posits that goal-directed behaviors are driven by three innate psychological needs in every human being: autonomy (i.e., the need to feel ownership of one's behavior), competence (i.e., the need to produce desired outcomes and to experience mastery), and relatedness (i.e., the need to feel connected to others). These needs can be linked to certain game design elements [8] that can increase users' motivation and engagement. The most common such elements employed are points, badges, leaderboards, and levels. These elements are categorized as achievement and progression-oriented elements. Only one of these game elements is not enough to motivate every user, so an environment with multiple game elements is recommended.

Based on the SDT and these popular types of gamification elements, we drafted a list of potential gamification mechanics for the EPICommunity-v1 platform, hereafter the EPIGame gamification framework [12]. EPIGame was discussed with the EPICUR Researchers Board in two working sessions in order to ensure its relevance and usefulness for researchers. The board members supported the key principles of the proposed gamification framework and provided various suggestions and ideas. For instance, they strongly argued that gamification should stimulate more collaboration and less competition among the platform users. They also preferred peer-to-peer-based assessments and rewards which could be implemented by each member of the EPICommunity, instead of competition-based judging panels.

The EPIGame framework includes 25 gamification mechanics. Table 1 presents representative examples of these elements.

Table 1. Representative examples of the EPIGame gamification mechanics.

Type	Title	Description	SDT [11] needs
Progress	User profile completion	Having filled out all the required profile entities (publications, courses, projects, positions)	Autonomy
Levels	User top categories	The top categories in profile level based on annotations (hashtags)	Competence
Score	User profile score	An aggregation of comments, likes and profile views	Competence
Badge	Opinion maker of the month [in Category]	The user with the higher impact in the [category] per month	Competence
Fixed reward	Profile caretaker	Update the profile once per month for at least six consecutive months	Autonomy
Badge	Most liked publication	A badge given to the users, who have a publication in the top 10% of the most liked publications	Relatedness
Badge	Most active group	A badge given to the group members for the most active group, when the aggregation of comments, likes and views is the higher in the EPICommunity	Relatedness
Badge	Excellence in service role	EPIQAssess Score > 85% of the total score in the society aspect	Competence
Progress	Reputation as Researcher in the Community	EPIQAssess Score based on peer assessment in the Researcher Role aspect	Relatedness
Physical Reward	Nomination for SciLink Course	User with the smaller EPIQAssess score	Relatedness

2.5 User Roles and Main Tasks

The EPICommunity-v1 platform offers a lot of functionality. This functionality is different based on the user's role. The user roles in the platform are the following: guest, subscriber, member, moderator, administrator. In the following, we present the main tasks per user role.

Anyone can access parts of the information on the platform as a guest. Guests use the public website to access general purpose informative pages and generic platform metrics (e.g., number of projects, number of groups).

Subscribers sign into the community component of the platform. They may be managers and supervisors of research units, researchers' assessment committees, and university leaders. They can search and access researchers' profiles (Fig. 1) and related content entities (e.g., publications, courses, projects, positions), as well as view groups and their associated information. They are not researchers themselves and thus they do not have their own researcher profile, they cannot conduct peer assessments of other users, neither join nor create a group.

Fig. 1. An example of the EPICommunity-v1 user interface for viewing a researcher profile. The "Badges" section presents the researcher's badges earned based on the EPIGame gamification framework [12].

Fig. 2. An example of the EPICommunity-v1 user interface for creating a researcher profile. The researcher can use the "Import from Europass" functionality to populate most of the fields.

Users with the member role have increased rights in comparison to the guest and subscriber roles as they can interact with the platform instead of just consuming content. They are researchers, which is the primary target group of the platform. They can search, access and interact with (e.g., endorse, comment) other researchers' profiles and associated content entities (e.g., publications, courses, projects, positions), create their own research profile (Fig. 2) and add content entities, use the academic matchmaking and recommendations capabilities (Fig. 3), use chat messages for communicating with other researchers, create and manage groups for their own purposes (e.g., collaborate on co-authoring a publication) (Fig. 4), conduct peer assessments of other researchers based on the EPIQAssess framework (Fig. 5), monitor analytics about their own progress (Fig. 6) and benefit from all the gamification mechanics of the EPIGame framework (Fig. 1 shows the badges that a researcher has earned). Users with the member role can additionally have the moderator role when they have created a group.

Fig. 3. An example of the EPICommunity-v1 user interface with recommendations for researchers with similar interests.

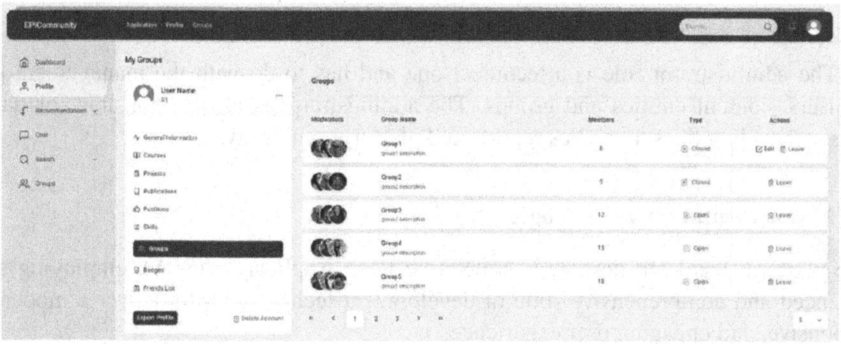

Fig. 4. An example of the EPICommunity-v1 user interface for managing user-created groups.

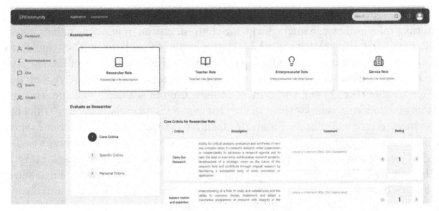

Fig. 5. An example of the EPICommunity-v1 user interface for peer assessing of other researchers based on the EPIQAssess framework [2].

Fig. 6. An example of the EPICommunity-v1 user interface for monitoring analytics about researcher's own progress.

The administrator role is a technical one and has to do with the management of all users, content entities and groups. The administrator is also responsible for data consistency, bug fixes, analytics reports and platform reliability.

2.6 Implementation Technologies

The platform has been designed as a Single Page Application (SPA), employing an advanced and comprehensive suite of development technologies to deliver a modern, responsive, and engaging user experience.

Regarding the EPICommunity-v1 frontend, Vue.js and Tailwind CSS are used. Vue.js is a progressive JavaScript framework for front-end development known for its simplicity and reactivity. The EPICommunity-v1 platform employs it to create dynamic and interactive SPAs, efficiently updating content without necessitating full page reloads. Tailwind CSS, a utility-first CSS framework, complements Vue.js by streamlining the styling process, facilitating the creation of a visually appealing and modern aesthetic for the EPICommunity-v1 platform.

Regarding the EPICommunity-v1 backend, Laravel, a robust PHP framework, forms the backbone of the backend infrastructure. Its elegant syntax, extensive feature set, and developer-friendly tools make it an ideal choice for crafting scalable and maintainable server-side logic. The Inertia.js library is used to connect the frontend Vue.js components with the Laravel backend seamlessly. This library allows developers to create powerful server-driven SPAs, eliminating the need for a separate API layer. Its integration with Laravel enhances the cohesion between the client and server, providing a smooth development workflow.

In addition, the EPICommunity-v1 backend employs Soketi, a WebSocket library, for real-time chat services and notifications. For managing relational database requirements, MariaDB has been incorporated into the technological stack. This open-source relational database management system ensures data integrity, high performance, and reliability. EPICommunity-v1 also leverages Redis as a caching mechanism to enhance performance and minimize database load. Redis accelerates response times, providing users with a more responsive experience. This approach not only optimizes resource utilization but also contributes to scalability.

The integration of Vue.js, Tailwind CSS, Laravel, Inertia.js, Soketi, and MariaDB forms a cohesive, cutting-edge technological stack. This approach optimizes user interactions, reduces load times, and ensures a responsive, visually appealing, and functionally rich academic social network.

2.7 System Architecture

Figure 7 presents an abstract overview of the EPICommunity-v1 architecture. Here is a brief description of each depicted component:

- EPICommunity Frontend: a single page web application with the interface that the user interacts with.
- Load balancer: ensures optimal resource utilization, enhances performance, prevents downtime, and ensures seamless scalability for users.
- Auth Service: manages user authentication, facilitates new user sign-up, and prevents unauthorized access to services or resources (EPICommunity Entities: publications, courses, projects, positions), ensuring secure and regulated system interactions. The Auth Service is accessible for everyone while the protected services can only be used by authenticated users.
- Search Service: enables users to search for other researchers, publications, projects, positions, courses and user groups.
- Recommendation Service: implements the matchmaking functionality of the platform. It runs once a day and finds new or updates existing associations between the following pairs: researchers–researchers, researchers–groups, researchers–courses, and researchers–positions. Based on the results, the EPICommunity platform recommends the top five closest matches for each pair to the user.

- Notification Service: provides real time notifications to the users, which is a pre-requisite for any modern social networking platform. This service informs users for actions that have a potential interest for them. For example, users receive a notification when they have an incoming message from another user. Users also receive a notification right after someone interacts (e.g., endorses, comments) with their content (e.g., publications, courses, projects, positions). Users are also notified when another user completes the evaluation process of their profile.
- Evaluation Service: implements the EPIQAssess researchers' assessment framework. This service enables researchers to conduct peer assessments of other researchers. The Evaluation Service communicates with the Gamification Service (see in the following) in order to calculate scores, show progress and identify weak/strong characteristics of a user.
- Gamification Service: implements the EPIGame gamification framework. The platform awards with a badge (e.g., "most endorsed course") exceptional users or groups once every month and once a year. This service also calculates the analytics for every profile. The analytics are metrics that not only show the progression of a user profile but also the impact that a user has in a specific topic, even in the whole EPICommunity.
- Chat Service: provides real time user-to-user communication, which is particularly important in any networking platform. This service is responsible for securely delivering messages between users.
- Replicate Service: regularly backups the EPICommunity production database to an external secondary database.
- EPICommunity Entities: includes the basic data models that the services of the EPICommunity platform have access and interact with.

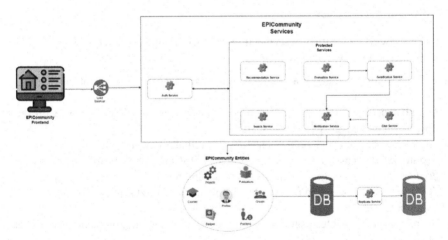

Fig. 7. Abstract overview of the EPICommunity-v1 platform architecture.

3   Usability Evaluation Study

A heuristic evaluation was conducted to investigate the usability of the EPICommunity-v1 platform. Heuristic evaluation [13–15] is the most popular usability inspection method. It has been effectively applied to many different types of software, such as websites and web applications [16, 17], games [18–20], mobile applications [21], and robotic applications [22–24]. We employed this method because we were interested in collecting qualitative insights on how to improve the EPICommunity platform during this initial design phase.

3.1   Methodology

Participants. Five experienced usability experts, 1 female and 4 male, conducted the heuristic evaluation of the EPICommunity-v1 platform. Three to five experts should be involved in a heuristic evaluation according to the literature [13, 25]; thus our study had an adequate number of experts.

All involved experts have undergraduate and postgraduate studies in Computer Science and extensive experience in the design and evaluation of interactive systems. Two evaluators have a PhD on HCI, and three evaluators have an MSc and are currently PhD candidates on interactive technologies. The coordinator of the evaluation process, who participated himself as an evaluator, is an Assistant Professor of HCI.

The evaluators are also researchers themselves. This means that they are double-experts for the evaluated system, thus having a higher chance to detect usability problems [26, 27]. These experts had not been involved in the design of the EPICommunity-v1 platform.

Procedures and Materials. First, the set of heuristics to be used was defined. For this evaluation, the 10 Nielsen heuristics as described in [28] were used (see also Table 2). Next, the evaluators were informed about the system goal, its representative users and their typical tasks. In addition, the development team of the system communicated the design goals and expectations.

Subsequently, each evaluator conducted a heuristic evaluation of the system. To this end, they were provided with the web address of the system. The evaluators created an account themselves and familiarized themselves with the system by exploring its functionality. After this initial exploration, they inspected the system, identified usability problems, and good usability points, and produced an individual report according to a pre-defined evaluation template.

According to this template, the evaluators noted the violated heuristic and rated its severity on a scale from 1 to 5 (1 = a little important, it does not significantly affect the user interaction, 5 = extremely important, catastrophic problem that may result in unsuccessful task) for each usability problem they identified. When evaluating the severity of a usability problem, they were asked to take into account the following factors [29]: a) the frequency with which the problem occurs, b) the impact of the problem if it occurs, and c) the persistence of the problem. Finally, each evaluator was asked to provide a design suggestion for resolving the identified usability problem.

After each individual evaluation, the experts participated in three online meetings to produce the final list of unique problems and good usability points, discuss on the final severity ratings (in most cases it was the average value of all ratings) and provide proposals for solutions. The meetings lasted approximately 10 h in total and were mediated by the Zoom conferencing tool. Finally, the evaluation team produced the final usability evaluation report for the system.

3.2 Results

Table 2 presents the number of unique usability problems found by the five experts grouped by heuristic number and problem severity. Results identified 120 unique usability problems for the EPICommunity-v1 platform. This number of usability problems might appear to be rather high, but one should consider that the evaluated system offers a lot of functionality and that this was the first iteration of its development cycle.

Results show that most (59%) usability problems were related to violations of the following heuristics: "2. Match between the system and the real world" (18%), "5. Error prevention" (17%), "1. Visibility of system status" (12%), and "10. Help and documentation" (12%). Regarding problem severity, the mean severity (2.8/5.0) of the identified usability problems is characterized as average. However, the number of severe problems (rated 4 and 5) was rather high (38). The problems with the highest severity ratings were related to the following three heuristics: "9. Help users recognize, diagnose and recover from errors" (3.8/5.0), "5. Error prevention" (3.6/5.0) and "10. Help and documentation" (3.4/5.0).

Representative examples of the identified usability problems are provided in the following. Due to space constraints, the experts' description of each usability problem has been considerably shortened (i.e., we picked one or two verbatim sentences from the description in their report) and any additional accompanying information (e.g., screenshot of the user interface showcasing the problem) has not been included here.

1. "Throughout the platform, links are not easy to identify compared to simple text."
2. "If users use the Europass import functionality to update their profile after they have created it, then the information from the Europass profile is not imported, despite a message (falsely) indicating that the profile has been updated."
3. "Users are not notified of friend requests, friend acceptances from other users, new messages, group member requests, or acceptance as a member of a group."
4. "In the Chat, there is no indication that a new message has arrived."
5. "After the users create an account, they are redirected to a rather lengthy procedure to complete their profile. If for any reason they do not complete the procedure all of their progress is lost."
6. "While creating a group, the users are provided with an option to select if the group belongs to one of three types (EPICluster, EPIConnect, EPICradle). However, it is unclear what these types mean."
7. "While creating/editing a group, it is unclear what properties are made private by selecting the group to be private."
8. "The "Log out" button is placed at the bottom of the side main menu. This is a rather unexpected position but more importantly the button is not always visible above the fold."

Table 2. Summary of the heuristic evaluation results for the EPICommunity-v1 platform. The unique usability problems found by the five experts are presented grouped by heuristic number and problem severity.

Heuristic [28]	Usability problems	Usability problems per severity					Mean severity of problems
		1	2	3	4	5	
1. Visibility of system status	14	2	5	4	1	2	2.7
2. Match between the system and the real world	21	5	6	3	3	4	2.8
3. User control and freedom	10	3	3	2	2		2.3
4. Consistency and standards	13	6	4	3			1.8
5. Error prevention	20	1	4	3	7	5	3.6
6. Recognition rather than recall	8	1	1	3	1	2	3.3
7. Flexibility and efficiency of use	4		1	2		1	3.3
8. Aesthetic and minimalist design	12	7	3	2			1.6
9. Help users recognize, diagnose, and recover from errors	4		1		2	1	3.8
10. Help and documentation	14	2	2	3	2	5	3.4
Total	120	27	30	25	18	20	2.8

9. "Throughout the platform, there are frames (examples in the screenshots below) that when the cursor hovers over, an animation appears and the cursor changes from default to pointer. This gives the (false) impression that some action will be performed, but there isn't any such action associated with these frames."
10. "If users delete any item (course, publication etc.) then it is removed without any warning from the system."
11. "There is an option in the Groups section of another user's profile to edit or leave a group in which the user is not a member. This shouldn't be possible."
12. "During peer assessment, if users choose to leave the assessment page without submitting it, then their input is lost."
13. "When users press "Finish" to create their profile, they may get some error messages that are related to previous steps/screens."

14. "When users apply to join a group, this information is not somewhere visible. They need to remember their applications in the various groups as they only get an error if they apply again to the same group."
15. "If users add a new item (course, publication etc.) then a dummy entry with various dummy texts is created and the users then have to edit it and delete all dummy texts to create the actual entry. This process includes many unnecessary steps and given that this is a task that is repeated many times, it is expected to have a substantial impact on the user interaction efficiency."
16. "In the search results, there should be functionality to sort the entries (e.g., for the Publications one may sort by Creator, Year etc.)"
17. "There are instances of screens using background and foreground colors that do not have enough contrast (examples in the following screenshots). This also creates an accessibility problem for people with visual disabilities."
18. "While users try to upload a profile picture that exceeds the required size an error page shows up, with no information related to the cause of the error and with language that is hard to understand by users."
19. "In the user profile, there is a "Badges" section. However, users are not provided with any information regarding these badges e.g., what badges can be earned, what are the required actions to earn a badge etc."
20. "There is no explanation in Profile Progression for what the roles represent and how these calculations are made."

Regarding good usability points, the experts agreed that the EPICommunity-v1 platform provides a lot of functionality to address the needs of the intended users. Moreover, a minimal and simple interface with consistent style and color codes is used across the system. Furthermore, EPICommunity-v1 provides efficient ways for importing user data (e.g., from a Europass account). In this context, the experts argued that it would be useful to add functionality to import publications from other online databases (e.g., Google scholar, Scopus etc.). Such mechanisms are expected to motivate potential users to use the system in their practices.

4   Conclusion

This paper presents the first iteration of the design and evaluation of the EPICommunity platform, an academic social network designed for researchers by researchers. The main aim of the platform is to support academic matchmaking and collaboration, particularly for early career researchers.

In the EPICommunity-v1 platform, researchers can perform various tasks, such as present their publications, upload courses that they teach, showcase their projects, create groups to collaborate with researchers that have similar interests, and provide peer assessments for people they have worked with. In contrast to existing systems, the EPICommunity-v1 platform offers unique features like the ability to easily integrate Europass profiles, automated recommendations for researchers who share similar interests, gamification mechanics, tracking of researchers' own progress through analytics, and peer-reviewing of researchers based on an innovative research's assessment framework with four dimensions (Learning & Teaching, Research, Innovation, Interaction with Society).

A heuristic evaluation involving five experienced usability experts was employed to investigate the usability of the proposed academic social network. The experts used the platform following an open exploration protocol, noted usability problems according to the Nielsen's 10 heuristics [28], rated the severity of these problems on a scale from 1 to 5, provided design suggestions for resolving the usability problems, and listed good usability points of the system. After each individual evaluation, the experts conducted three meetings to produce their final usability evaluation report. All in all, they identified 120 usability problems with a mean severity of 2.8/5.0.

The next iteration of the EPICommunity platform has already started and the majority of the identified usability problems has been resolved by the development team. Immediate future work includes conducting a user testing study for the next version of the platform. In addition, future research could investigate how the effectiveness of the platform's gamification framework is affected by factors such as the individuality of each person, the effect of each element, etc. Future work could also involve an evaluation of user emotional experience with the system, such as measuring stress based on physiological and self-reported data [30–36]. Finally, the use of conversational agents in the EPICommunity platform that enrich synchronous collaboration between researchers could be investigated, given their success in other contexts, such as participation in online courses [37], and the recent improvements in large language models, such as ChatGPT.

Acknowledgments. This research has been conducted in the context of EPICUR Research project, which has received funding from the European Union's Horizon 2020 research and innovation programme under Grant Agreement No 101016926.

Disclaimer. It should be noted that these results reflect only the authors' view and that the European Commission Research Executive Agency is not responsible for any use that may be made of the information it contains.

References

1. International Organization for Standardization: Ergonomics of human-system interaction. Part 210: Human-centred design for interactive system (2019). https://www.iso.org/standard/77520.html
2. Tso, A.: EPIQAssess - EPICUR qualitative researchers' assessment framework. European Partnership for an Innovative Campus Unifying Regions (EPICUR) Research project (EPICUR-Research) (2022). https://epicommunity.auth.gr/deliverable/assessment
3. Council of Europe: Deepening the European Research Area: Providing researchers with attractive and sustainable careers and working conditions and making brain circulation a reality, Council conclusions (2021)
4. Deterding, S., Canossa, A., Harteveld, C., Cooper, S., Nacke, L.E., Whitson, J.R.: Gamifying research: strategies, opportunities, challenges, ethics. In: Proceedings of the 33rd Annual ACM Conference Extended Abstracts on Human Factors in Computing Systems, pp. 2421–2424. ACM, New York (2015). https://doi.org/10.1145/2702613.2702646
5. Deterding, S., Dixon, D., Khaled, R., Nacke, L.: From game design elements to gamefulness: defining "gamification." In: Proceedings of the 15th International Academic MindTrek Conference: Envisioning Future Media Environments, pp. 9–15. Association for Computing Machinery, New York (2011). https://doi.org/10.1145/2181037.2181040

6. Lister, M.C.: Gamification: The effect on student motivation and performance at the post-secondary level. Issues Trends Learn. Technol. **3** (2015). https://doi.org/10.2458/azu_itet_v 3i2_lister

7. Majuri, J., Koivisto, J., Hamari, J.: Gamification of education and learning: a review of empirical literature. In: Proceedings of the 2nd International GamiFIN Conference, GamiFIN 2018. CEUR-WS (2018)

8. Zainuddin, Z., Chu, S.K.W., Shujahat, M., Perera, C.J.: The impact of gamification on learning and instruction: a systematic review of empirical evidence. Educ. Res. Rev. **30**, 100326 (2020). https://doi.org/10.1016/j.edurev.2020.100326

9. Mohammed, Y.B., Ozdamli, F.: Motivational effects of gamification apps in education: A systematic literature review. BRAIN Broad Res. Artif. Intell. Neurosci. **12**, 122–138 (2021). https://doi.org/10.18662/brain/12.2/196

10. Yıldırım, İ, Şen, S.: The effects of gamification on students' academic achievement: a meta-analysis study. Interact. Learn. Environ. **29**, 1301–1318 (2021). https://doi.org/10.1080/104 94820.2019.1636089

11. Ryan, R.M., Deci, E.L.: Self-determination theory and the facilitation of intrinsic motivation, social development, and well-being. Am. Psychol. **55**, 68–78 (2000)

12. Tso, A.: EPIGame - Researchers gamification framework. European Partnership for an Innovative Campus Unifying Regions (EPICUR) Research project (EPICUR-Research) (2022). https://epicommunity.auth.gr/deliverable/gamification

13. Nielsen, J.: How to conduct a heuristic evaluation. https://www.nngroup.com/articles/how-to-conduct-a-heuristic-evaluation/

14. Nielsen, J.: Enhancing the explanatory power of usability heuristics. In: Proceedings of the SIGCHI Conference on Human Factors in Computing Systems. pp. 152–158. ACM, New York, NY, USA (1994). https://doi.org/10.1145/191666.191729

15. Nielsen, J., Molich, R.: Heuristic evaluation of user interfaces. In: Proceedings of the SIGCHI Conference on Human Factors in Computing Systems, pp. 249–256. ACM, New York (1990). https://doi.org/10.1145/97243.97281

16. Chen, S.Y., Macredie, R.D.: The assessment of usability of electronic shopping: a heuristic evaluation. Int. J. Inf. Manag. **25**, 516–532 (2005). https://doi.org/10.1016/j.ijinfomgt.2005. 08.008

17. Sutcliffe, A.: Heuristic evaluation of website attractiveness and usability. In: Johnson, C. (ed.) DSV-IS 2001. LNCS, vol. 2220, pp. 183–198. Springer, Heidelberg (2001). https://doi.org/ 10.1007/3-540-45522-1_11

18. Barnett, J.S., Taylor, G.S.: Usability of wearable and desktop game-based simulations: a heuristic evaluation. Im: United States Army Research Institute for the Behavioral and Social Sciences (2010)

19. Desurvire, H., Caplan, M., Toth, J.A.: Using heuristics to evaluate the playability of games. In: CHI 2004 Extended Abstracts on Human Factors in Computing Systems, pp. 1509–1512. ACM, New York (2004). https://doi.org/10.1145/985921.986102

20. Pinelle, D., Wong, N., Stach, T.: Heuristic evaluation for games: usability principles for video game design. In: Proceedings of the SIGCHI Conference on Human Factors in Computing Systems, pp. 1453–1462. ACM, New York (2008). https://doi.org/10.1145/1357054.1357282

21. Korhonen, H., Koivisto, E.M.I.: Playability heuristics for mobile multi-player games. In: Proceedings of the 2nd International Conference on Digital Interactive Media in Entertainment and Arts, pp. 28–35. ACM, Perth (2007). https://doi.org/10.1145/1306813.1306828

22. Adamides, G., Christou, G., Katsanos, C., Xenos, M., Hadzilacos, T.: Usability guidelines for the design of robot teleoperation: a taxonomy. IEEE Trans. Hum.-Mach. Syst. **45**, 256–262 (2015). https://doi.org/10.1109/THMS.2014.2371048

23. Clarkson, E.C., Arkin, R.C.: Applying heuristic evaluation to human-robot interaction systems. In: Proceedings of the Twentieth International Florida Artificial Intelligence Research Society Conference, pp. 44–49 (2007)

24. Elara, M.R., Calderon, C.A.A., Zhou, C., Yue, P.K., Hu, L.: Using heuristic evaluation for human-humanoid robot interaction in the soccer robotics domain. In:Presented at the Second Workshop on Humanoid Soccer Robots at IEEE-RAS International Conference on Humanoid Robots (2007)

25. Nielsen, J.: Usability Inspection Methods. Wiley, New York (1994)

26. Nielsen, J.: Finding usability problems through heuristic evaluation. In: Proceedings of the SIGCHI Conference on Human Factors in Computing Systems, pp. 373–380. ACM, New York (1992). https://doi.org/10.1145/142750.142834

27. Nielsen, J., Landauer, T.K.: A mathematical model of the finding of usability problems. In: Proceedings of the INTERACT 1993 and CHI 1993 Conference on Human Factors in Computing Systems, pp. 206–213. ACM, Amsterdam (1993). https://doi.org/10.1145/169 059.169166

28. Nielsen, J.: 10 usability heuristics for user interface design. https://www.nngroup.com/art icles/ten-usability-heuristics/

29. Nielsen, J.: Severity ratings for usability problems. http://www.nngroup.com/articles/how-to-rate-the-severity-of-usability-problems/

30. Liapis, A., Faliagka, E., Katsanos, C., Antonopoulos, C., Voros, N.: Detection of subtle stress episodes during UX evaluation: assessing the performance of the WESAD bio-signals dataset. In: Ardito, C., Lanzilotti, R., Malizia, A., Petrie, H., Piccinno, A., Desolda, G., Inkpen, K. (eds.) INTERACT 2021. LNCS, vol. 12934, pp. 238–247. Springer, Cham (2021). https://doi.org/10.1007/978-3-030-85613-7_17

31. Liapis, A., Katsanos, C., Karousos, N., Xenos, M., Orphanoudakis, T.: User experience evaluation: a validation study of a tool-based approach for automatic stress detection using physiological signals. Int. J. Hum.-Comput. Interact. 37, 470–483 (2021). https://doi.org/10.1080/10447318.2020.1825205

32. Liapis, A., Katsanos, C., Sotiropoulos, D., Xenos, M., Karousos, N.: Recognizing emotions in human computer interaction: Studying stress using skin conductance. In: Abascal, J., Barbosa, S., Fetter, M., Gross, T., Palanque, P., Winckler, M. (eds.) INTERACT 2015. LNCS, vol. 9296, pp. 255–262. Springer, Cham (2015). https://doi.org/10.1007/978-3-319-22701-6_18

33. Liapis, A., Katsanos, C., Sotiropoulos, D.G., Karousos, N., Xenos, M.: Stress in interactive applications: analysis of the valence-arousal space based on physiological signals and self-reported data. Multimed. Tools Appl. 76, 5051–5071 (2017)

34. Liapis, A., Katsanos, C., Karousos, N., Sotiropoulos, D., Xenos, M., Orphanoudakis, T.: Stress heatmaps: a fuzzy-based approach that uses physiological signals. In: Marcus, A., Rosenzweig, E. (eds.) HCII 2020. LNCS, vol. 12202, pp. 268–277. Springer, Cham (2020). https://doi.org/10.1007/978-3-030-49757-6_19

35. Liapis, A., Katsanos, C., Karousos, N., Xenos, M., Orphanoudakis, T.: UDSP+: stress detection based on user-reported emotional ratings and wearable skin conductance sensor. In: Adjunct Proceedings of the 2019 ACM International Joint Conference on Pervasive and Ubiquitous Computing and Proceedings of the 2019 ACM International Symposium on Wearable Computers, pp. 125–128. ACM, New York (2019). https://doi.org/10.1145/3341162.3343831

36. Liapis, A., Katsanos, C., Sotiropoulos, D., Xenos, M., Karousos, N.: Subjective assessment of stress in HCI: a study of the Valence-Arousal scale using skin conductance. In: Proceedings of the 11th Biannual Conference on Italian SIGCHI Chapter, pp. 174–177. ACM, New York (2015). https://doi.org/10.1145/2808435.2808450

37. Tegos, S., et al.: Enriching synchronous collaboration in online courses with configurable conversational agents. In: Kumar, V., Troussas, C. (eds.) Intelligent Tutoring Systems: 16th International Conference, ITS 2020, Athens, Greece, June 8–12, 2020, Proceedings, pp. 284–294. Springer International Publishing, Cham (2020). https://doi.org/10.1007/978-3-030-49663-0_34

Social Media in Business and eCommerce

Research on Relationship Between Mental Accounting and Consumer Purchase Behavior

Mika Ezawa[✉] [iD] and Tomoaki Tabata [iD]

Tokai University, Tokyo, Japan
0cjm1220@mail.u-tokai.ac.jp

Abstract. The number of purchase points in ID-POS data approximates the number of decisions made by consumers at the time of purchase, which is an important indicator for elucidating consumer behavior. According to Belk (1975) [1], there are several factors that influence the purchase behavior of consumers, such as "physical environment," "social environment," "time," "task," and "antecedent state. Among these, changes in purchasing behavior due to issues, antecedent state, and time can be considered as a type of framing effect in psychology. Mental Accounting, which is based on the framing effect, is a theory proposed by Thaler (1985) [2] that shows that purchasing behavior changes depending on the psychological situation at the time of purchase. Miyatsu and Sato (2015) [3] conducted a quantitative study of Mental Accounting. Here, they constructed a model in which consumers' Mental Accounting is switched based on the threshold of each consumer's psychological pressure, and clarified the mechanism by which the number of purchase points is generated. However, consumers' psychological load does not change before and after the threshold, but is considered to be a change in three states: a state of reduced psychological load, a state of no psychological load, and a state of weighted psychological load. In this study, the two-state switching model based on mental load and threshold is extended to a three-state switching model based on mental pressure and two thresholds to clarify a more realistic mechanism of occurrence.

Keyword: Mental Accounting · Consumer Purchase Behavior · Hierarchical Bayesian Threshold Poisson Regression Models

1 Introduction

Mental Accounting is the concept that money is substitutable and can be freely used for any purpose, but the way people use money changes depending on their purposes due to their unconscious labeling of money. This chapter describes Mental Accounting after explaining the "framing effect," which is necessary to explain Mental Accounting.

1.1 Framing Effect

The framing effect is a phenomenon in which preferences are reversed and decision-making outcomes differ due to changes in viewpoints caused by differences in linguistic expressions describing the decision-making problem, even for the same decision-making problem. This can be interpreted as a phenomenon in which the outcome of decision-making differs depending on differences in the mental framework for understanding the decision-making problem, i.e., the decision frame. Tversky and Kahneman (1981) [4] explain how decision frames are constructed, especially in money-related decision making, using the concept of mental accounting.

1.2 Mental Accounting

Mental Accounting is an unconscious act of "labeling money" by humans, which leads to behavior that belies rational behavior in economics. And experiments have shown that humans behave irrationally due to Mental Accounting. Here, we introduce an experiment conducted by Tversky and Kahneman (1981).

They asked 200 subjects the question (1) in the lost ticket condition and 183 subjects the question (2) in the lost cash condition.

1. "Imagine the following scene. You decide to go see a movie, purchase a ticket for $10, and go to the movie theater. As you enter the theater, you realize that you have lost the ticket. Would you buy the ticket again?
2. "Imagine the following situation. You decide to go to see a movie and go to the theater. The ticket costs $10. As you enter the theater, you realize that you have lost $10 in cash. Do you buy the ticket?

The results of the question showed that 46% of the subjects in the lost ticket condition said they would buy the ticket, while 88% of the subjects in the lost cash condition said they would buy the ticket. Tversky and Kahneman explain that the results in the lost-ticket and lost-cash conditions differed because of the different nature of mental accounting. That is, in the lost-ticket condition, the ticket expenditure had to be paid for once more from the ticket expenditure account, whereas in the cash-lost condition, the cash and ticket expenditures were accounted for separately, so that the pain of buying a ticket twice was not felt, which could be interpreted as a higher intention to buy a ticket. Thus, Mental Accounting is more likely to be done on a topic-by-topic basis rather than on an overall evaluation of money.

2 Previous Studies

This chapter introduces the research of Miyatsu and Sato (2015) on consumer behavior considering the concept of Mental Accounting and the research of Terui and Dahana (2006) [7] as a reference for the model constructed in this study.

2.1 Miyatsu and Sato (2015)

Using ID-POS data, they model the mechanism of the occurrence of the number of purchase points, taking into account the Mental Accounting of each consumer. Assuming that consumers' mental status changes with each purchase occasion, we model the mechanism of the occurrence of purchase points within the framework of a hierarchical

Bayesian threshold Poisson regression model. The modeling is based on the assumption that mental load is defined as a latent variable with the payday of each consumer in mind, and that Mental Accounting switches based on it.

$$
\begin{cases}
l = 1 \Rightarrow & \text{From the 25th of the previous month} \\
 & \text{to the 24th of the current month} \\
l = 2 \Rightarrow & \text{From the 5th of the previous month} \\
 & \text{to the 4th of the current month} \\
l = 3 \Rightarrow & \text{From the 17th of the previous month} \\
 & \text{to the 16th of the current month}
\end{cases}
\tag{2.1}
$$

Cumulative purchase aggregation period

$$
cumm_{i,t_i,l} = \begin{cases} \sum_{j=1}^{trans^l(t_i)-1} M_{i,j,l} & , trans^l(t_i) \neq 1 \\ 0 & , trans^l(t_i) = 1 \end{cases}
\tag{2.2}
$$

In Eq. (2.1), we introduce a symbol for each corresponding cumulative purchase aggregation period. Equation (2.2) includes a symbol for the aggregation period of consumer i in the period covered by the aggregation l The Eq. (2.2) shows the cumulative amount of purchases up to the purchase opportunity t_i (2.2) shows the cumulative amount of purchases made by consumers up to the $trans^l(t_i)$ is the cumulative purchase amount until the consumer's i in the period covered by the aggregation for the consumer l indicates the number of store visits from the starting date to t_i indicates the number of store visits from the starting date to the $M_{i,j,l}$ indicates the number of visits by consumers i in the aggregation period of consumers l represents the amount of purchases made by the consumer during the aggregation period.j represents the amount of purchases made by the consumer during the period of the aggregation. The mental load is defined as the combination of the three cumulative purchase amounts in Eq. (2.3).

$$
CummM_{i,t_i} = \alpha_i^{*(1)} cumm_{i,t_i,1} + \alpha_i^{*(2)} cumm_{i,t_i,2} + \alpha_i^{*(3)} cumm_{i,t_i,3}
\tag{2.3}
$$

$\alpha_i^{*(k)} (k = 1, 2, 3)$ is a satisfying parameter that satisfies the constraints of $0 \leq \alpha_i^{*(k)} \leq 1$ and $\sum_{k=1}^{3} \alpha_i^{*(k)} = 1$, denoted $\alpha_i^* = \left(\alpha_i^{*(1)}, \alpha_i^{*(2)} \right)$.

$CummM_{i,ti}$ is small, it represents a state of reduced mental load, and its larger value represents a state of weighted mental load, respectively.

In this study, it is assumed that a single threshold parameter switches between two psychological situations, but in reality, it is considered to be a change between three states: a situation with reduced psychological load, a situation with no psychological load, and a situation with a weighted psychological load.

2.2 Terui and Dahana(2016)

Using a brand choice model with heterogeneous price threshold parameters, we investigate a three-region piecewise linear stochastic utility function. To identify the consumer's utility function, we assume a reference price and two price thresholds that consumers have for a brand, and define a utility function divided into three regions-gain, price acceptance, and loss. A threshold probit model with heterogeneous price thresholds and hierarchical Bayesian modeling are used to model consumers' utility for brand choice.

3 Proposal

In this chapter, we propose a two-state switching model of Mental Accounting by mental pressure and threshold proposed by Miyatsu and Sato (2015), which aims to clarify the mechanism of occurrence that more represents reality by extending the model to a three-state switching model by mental pressure and two thresholds.

3.1 Research Methods

Miyatsu and Sato (2015) constructed a model in which consumers' Mental Accounting is switched based on the threshold of each consumer's psychological pressure, and clarified the mechanism that generates the number of purchase points. When consumers' psychological pressure is lower than the threshold, their willingness to purchase increases, and in other words, they tend to purchase more items. On the other hand, when consumers' willingness to purchase tends to decrease, i.e., they tend to purchase fewer items, when their psychological pressure is greater than a threshold value. However, consumers' willingness to purchase does not change before and after the threshold, but rather changes among three states: "willingness to purchase increases," "willingness to purchase decreases," and "neither of the three states". Therefore, we construct a three-state switching model using a model based on Terui and Dahana's (2004) utility function divided into two thresholds and three regions.

3.2 Model

The proposed model divides each consumer's purchase opportunity into regimes based on the relationship between mental load and two threshold parameters, and models the generation mechanism of the number of purchase points per store visit. Each regime has a corresponding evaluation function. The observed structure is modeled in the framework of a Poisson regression model (threshold Poisson regression model) with different regression coefficients for each regime assigned by the threshold. The same model (Eq. 2.3) as in Miyatsu and Sato (2015) is used to model psychological load. The intra-individual and inter-individual models are shown in Sects. 3.2.1 and 3.2.2, respectively.

Intra-individual Model (Observation Model). Consumer i Purchasing Opportunities by t_i and the number of purchase points in y_{i,t_i} then the threshold parameters of mental load and consumer i and the consumer's threshold parameter $\gamma_i^{(1)}, \gamma_i^{(2)}$ We assume that a switch in the generation mechanism of Y_{i,t_i}. The three regimes are defined as follows. Regime 1 for situations with an aggravated psychological load. ($CummM_{i,t_i} > \gamma_i^{(1)}$), Regime 2 for situations with no psychological load. ($\gamma_i^{(1)} \geq CummM_{i,t_i} > \gamma_i^{(2)}$), Regime 3 for situations with reduced psychological load. ($CummM_{i,t_i} \leq \gamma_i^{(2)}$).In this case, each regime has a different evaluation function. In this chapter, we follow the model of Miyatsu and Sato (2015), and use the following equation y_{i,t_i} is count data, we formulate a within-individual model using a Poisson distribution. Equation (3.1) is the within-individual model that takes Mental Accounting into account.

$$Pr\left(Y_{i,t_i} = y_{i,t_i} \mid \lambda_{i,t_i}^{(1)}, \lambda_{i,t_i}^{(2)}, \lambda_{i,t_i}^{(3)}, \gamma_i^{(1)}, \gamma_i^{(2)}, \alpha_i^*, cummi_{i,t_i}\right)$$

$$= \begin{cases} \dfrac{\left(\lambda_{i,t_i}^{(1)}\right)^{y_{i,t_i}} \exp\left(-\lambda_{i,t_i}^{(1)}\right)}{y_{i,t_i}!} & , CummM_{i,t_i} > \gamma_i^{(1)} \\[2ex] \dfrac{\left(\lambda_{i,t_i}^{(2)}\right)^{y_{i,t_i}} \exp\left(-\lambda_{i,t_i}^{(2)}\right)}{y_{i,t_i}!} & , \gamma_i^{(1)} \geq CummM_{i,t_i} > \gamma_i^{(2)} \\[2ex] \dfrac{\left(\lambda_{i,t_i}^{(3)}\right)^{y_{i,t_i}} \exp\left(-\lambda_{i,t_i}^{(3)}\right)}{y_{i,t_i}!} & , CummM_{i,t_i} \leq \gamma_i^{(2)} \end{cases} \tag{3.1}$$

$\lambda_{i,t_i}^{(k)}(k = 1, 2, 3)$ denotes the non-negative mean (variance) parameter for each regime, and $\lambda_{i,t_i}^{(k)}$ log transformation of the regimes is structured as in Eq. (3.2).

$$\log\left(\lambda_{i,t_i}^{(k)}\right) = x_{i,t_i}^{(k)t} \beta_i^{(k)}, k = 1, 2, 3 \tag{3.2}$$

$x_{i,t_i}^{(1)} = \left(x_{i,t_i,1}^{(1)}, x_{i,t_i,2}^{(1)}, \ldots, x_{i,t_i,p}^{(1)}\right)^t, \beta_i^{(1)} = \left(\beta_{i,1}^{(1)}, \beta_{i,2}^{(1)}, \ldots, \beta_{i,p}^{(1)}\right)^t, x_{i,t_i}^{(2)} = \left(x_{i,t_i,1}^{(2)}, x_{i,t_i,2}^{(2)}, \ldots, x_{i,t_i,p}^{(2)}\right)^t, \beta_i^{(2)} = \left(\beta_{i,1}^{(2)}, \beta_{i,2}^{(2)}, \ldots, \beta_{i,p}^{(2)}\right)^t$ denotes the explanatory variables and regression coefficients for each regime. is the dimension of the explanatory variable, with $k = 1, 2, 3$ to distinguish each regime. The details of the explanatory variables are explained in Sect. 4.1. $R^{(k)}\left(\gamma_i^{(1)}, \gamma_i^{(2)}, CummM_{i,t_i}\right), k = 1, 2, 3$, denotes the set of purchase points of each consumer assigned to which regime he or she is in.

$$p\left(y_i \mid \beta_i^{(1)}, \beta_i^{(2)}, \beta_i^{(3)}, \gamma_i^{(1)}, \gamma_i^{(2)}, \alpha_i^*, x_i, cumm_i\right)$$

$$= \prod_{k=1}^{3}\left\{\prod_{t_i \in R^{(k)}\left(\gamma_i^{(1)}, \gamma_i^{(2)}, CummM_{i,t_i}\right)} \left(\frac{\left(\lambda_{i,t_i}^{(k)}\right)^{y_{i,t_i}} \exp\left(-\lambda_{i,t_i}^{(k)}\right)}{y_{i,t_i}!}\right)\right\}$$

$$\propto \prod_{k=1}^{3}\left\{\prod_{t_i \in R^{(k)}\left(\gamma_i^{(1)}, \gamma_i^{(2)}, CummM_{i,t_i}\right)} \left(\left(\exp\left(x_{i,t_i}^{(k)t} \beta_i^{(k)}\right)\right)^{y_{i,t_i}} \exp\left(-\exp\left(x_{i,t_i}^{(k)t} \beta_i^{(k)}\right)\right)\right)\right\} \tag{3.3}$$

Consumers i During the entire period of the n second purchase opportunity y_{i,t_i} explicitly $t_{i,n}$ and the total number of purchase opportunities is N_i and the total number of purchase opportunities is x_i is the total number of purchase opportunities $x_{i,t_{i,n}} = \left(x_{i,t_{i,n},1}^{(1)}, x_{i,t_{i,n},2}^{(1)}, \ldots, x_{i,t_{i,n},p}^{(1)}, x_{i,t_{i,n},1}^{(2)}, x_{i,t_{i,n},2}^{(2)}, \ldots, x_{i,t_{i,n},p}^{(2)}\right)^t$ and using $x_i = \left(x_{i,t_i,1}, x_{i,t_i,2}, \ldots, x_{i,t_i,N_i}\right)^t$.

Similarly, when $y_{i,t_i} = \left(y_{i,t_i,1}, y_{i,t_i,2}, \ldots, y_{i,t_i,N_i}\right)^t$ is the total number of purchase opportunities. In addition, when $cumm_{i,l} = \left(cumm_{i,t_i,1,l}, cumm_{i,t_i,2,l}, \ldots, cumm_{i,t_i,N_i,l}\right)$ and

$cumm_i = (cumm_{i,1}, cumm_{i,2}, cumm_{i,3})$ are the same as in (3.3). Furthermore, assuming that consumers are independent from each other, we can formulate the overall likelihood for all consumers($i = 1,2,...,H$) The overall likelihood for all consumers shown in Eq. (3.4) can be formulated (Table 1).

$$p\left(\{y_i\}|\{\beta_i^{(1)}\}, \{\beta_i^{(2)}\}, \{\beta_i^{(3)}\}, \{\gamma_i^{(1)}\}, \{\gamma_i^{(2)}\}, \{\alpha_i^*\}, \{x_i\}, cumm_i\right)$$

$$= \prod_{i=1}^{H} \prod_{k=1}^{3} \left\{ \prod_{t_i \in R^{(k)}\left(\gamma_i^{(1)}, \gamma_i^{(2)}, CummM_{i,t_i}\right)} \left(\frac{\left(\lambda_{i,t_i}^{(k)}\right)^{y_{i,t_i}} \exp\left(-\lambda_{i,t_i}^{(k)}\right)}{y_{i,t_i}!} \right) \right\} \quad (3.4)$$

$$\propto \prod_{i=1}^{H} \prod_{k=1}^{3} \{$$

$$\prod_{t_i \in R^{(k)}\left(\gamma_i^{(1)}, \gamma_i^{(2)}, CummM_{i,t_i}\right)} \left(\left(\exp\left(x_{i,t_i}^{(k)t} \beta_i^{(k)}\right)\right)^{y_{i,t_i}} \exp\left(-\exp\left(x_{i,t_i}^{(k)t} \beta_i^{(k)}\right)\right) \right) \}$$

Table 1. Symbols used in models

Symbols	meaning
t_i	Buying opportunities for consumer i
$trans^l(t_i)$	Number of visits from the aggregate starting date to t_i in the aggregate target period l for consumer i
$M_{i,j,l}$	Amount of purchases at purchase opportunity j in consumer i's aggregate period l
$\alpha_i^{*(k)}(k = 1, 2, 3)$	Parameters to consider for payday
$\gamma_i^{(1)}, \gamma_i^{(2)}$	Threshold parameters for consumer i
$\lambda_{i,t_i}^{(k)}(k = 1, 2, 3)$	Non-negative mean (variance) parameter for each regime

Inter-individual Model (Hierarchical Model). This subsection presents a hierarchical model that shows the structure of commonality behind heterogeneous parameters for each consumer. This subsection presents a hierarchical model that shows the structure of commonality behind heterogeneous parameters for each consumer. The regression coefficients of the Poisson regression $\beta_i^{(k)}$, $k = 1, 2, 3$ and the logarithm of the threshold parameter $\gamma_i^{(k)}$, $k = 1, 2$ together with the logarithm of the threshold parameter $\theta_i = \left(\beta_i^{(1)}, \beta_i^{(2)}, \beta_i^{(3)}, \log\left(\gamma_i^{(1)}\right), \log\left(\gamma_i^{(2)}\right)\right)$ is defined as the logarithm of the The parameter vector before the logit transformation of the component parameters of the psychological load model, i.e., the α_i^* The parameter vector before the logit transformation of $\alpha_i = \left(\alpha_i^{(1)}, \alpha_i^{(2)}\right)$ and the logarithm of the threshold parameter where α_i is defined as the inverse transformation of $\alpha_i^{*(k)} = \frac{\exp\left(\alpha_i^{(k)}\right)}{1+\sum_{l=1}^{2}\exp\left(\alpha_i^{(l)}\right)}$, $k = 1, 2, 3$ is defined as the inverse transformation of In this case, Eqs. (3.5) and (3.6) are the hierarchical model of consumer i.

The model is a hierarchical model of consumers.

$$\boldsymbol{\theta}_i = z_i^t \boldsymbol{\Delta}_\theta + \boldsymbol{\epsilon}_i^\theta, \boldsymbol{\epsilon}_i^\theta \sim N(0, \boldsymbol{\Sigma}_\theta) \tag{3.5}$$

$$\boldsymbol{\alpha}_i = z_i^t \boldsymbol{\Delta}_\alpha + \boldsymbol{\epsilon}_i^\alpha, \boldsymbol{\epsilon}_i^\alpha \sim N(0, \boldsymbol{\Sigma}_\alpha) \tag{3.6}$$

θ_i, α_i is an attribute variable of the consumer i attribute variables $z_i = (z_{i,1}, z_{i,2}, \ldots, z_{i,q})^t$ and the coefficient matrix Δ_θ, Δ_α and is expressed as a linear combination of q are the dimensions of the attribute variables, and Σ_θ, Σ_α is the variance-covariance matrix of each. In addition, the prior distribution of Δ_θ, Δ_α, Σ_θ, Σ_α The prior distribution of the In setting the prior distribution, we use the relation $p(\Delta_\theta, \Sigma_\theta) = p(\Delta_\theta|\Sigma_\theta)p(\Sigma_\theta)$, $p(\Delta_\alpha, \Sigma_\alpha) = p(\Delta_\alpha|\Sigma_\alpha)p(\Sigma_\alpha)$ is the multivariate normal distribution, and $p(\Delta_\theta|\Sigma_\theta)$, $p(\Delta_\alpha|\Sigma_\alpha)$ assumes a multivariate normal distribution and $p(\Sigma_\theta)$, $p(\Sigma_\alpha)$ is assumed to be the inverse Wishart distribution. The hyperparameters in Eqs. (3.7) and (3.8) are set as in Terui (2008) [7] to represent a diffuse prior distribution.

$$\begin{aligned} \boldsymbol{\delta}_\theta = vec(\boldsymbol{\Delta}_\theta) \sim N\left(\overline{\boldsymbol{\delta}}_\theta, \boldsymbol{\Sigma}_\theta \otimes A_\theta^{-1}\right), \boldsymbol{\Sigma}_\theta \sim IW\left(\upsilon_{\theta,0}, V_{\theta,0}\right) \\ \overline{\boldsymbol{\delta}}_\theta = 0, A_\theta = 0.001I, \upsilon_{\theta,0} = 17, V_{\theta,0} = \upsilon_{\theta,0}I \end{aligned} \tag{3.7}$$

$$\begin{aligned} \boldsymbol{\delta}_\alpha = vec(\boldsymbol{\Delta}_\alpha) \sim N\left(\overline{\boldsymbol{\delta}}_\alpha, \boldsymbol{\Sigma}_\alpha \otimes A_\alpha^{-1}\right), \boldsymbol{\Sigma}_\theta \sim IW\left(\upsilon_{\alpha,0}, V_{\alpha,0}\right) \\ \overline{\boldsymbol{\delta}}_\alpha = 0, A_\alpha = 0.001I, \upsilon_{\alpha,0} = 6, V_{\alpha,0} = \upsilon_{\alpha,0}I \end{aligned} \tag{3.8}$$

Algorithm. The posterior distribution of the proposed model is presented and the estimation algorithm for the model based on it is outlined. Figure 1 shows the Directed Acyclic Graph (DAG) derived from the proposed model for consumer i Fig. 1 shows the Directed Acyclic Graph (DAG) derived from the proposed model for consumers. Based on the DAG shown in Fig. 1, and assuming independence among consumers, we can derive the posterior distribution in Eq. (3.9).

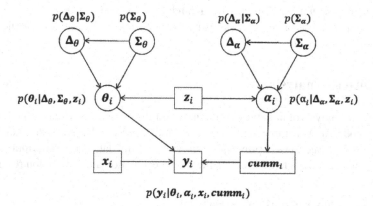

Fig. 1. DAG of the proposed model

$$\begin{aligned} p(\boldsymbol{\Theta}, \mathcal{A}|\boldsymbol{Y}, \boldsymbol{X}, \boldsymbol{Z}, M) &\propto p(\boldsymbol{\Delta}_\theta|\boldsymbol{\Sigma}_\theta)p(\boldsymbol{\Sigma}_\theta)p(\boldsymbol{\Delta}_\alpha|\boldsymbol{\Sigma}_\alpha)p(\boldsymbol{\Sigma}_\alpha) \\ &\times \prod_{i=1}^{H} p(\boldsymbol{y}_i|\boldsymbol{\theta}_i, \boldsymbol{\alpha}_i, \boldsymbol{x}_i, \boldsymbol{cumm}_i)p(\boldsymbol{\theta}_i|\boldsymbol{\Delta}_\theta, \boldsymbol{\Sigma}_\theta, \boldsymbol{z}_i)p(\boldsymbol{\alpha}_i|\boldsymbol{\Delta}_\alpha, \boldsymbol{\Sigma}_\alpha, \boldsymbol{z}_i) \end{aligned} \tag{3.9}$$

$\Theta = (\theta_1, \theta_2, \ldots, \theta_H)^t, \mathcal{A} = (\alpha_1, \alpha_2, \ldots, \alpha_H)^t, Z = (z_1, z_2, \ldots, z_H)^t, X = (x_1, x_2, \ldots, x_H)^t, Y = (y_1, y_2, \ldots, y_H)^t, M = (cumm_1, cumm_2, \ldots, cumm_H)^t$. The proposed model includes $\Theta, \mathcal{A}, \Delta_\theta, \Delta_\alpha, \Sigma_\theta, \Sigma_\alpha$ is a parameter that differs from consumer to consumer. $\Theta, \mathcal{A}$ is a parameter that is different for each consumer, and Δ_θ, $\Delta_\alpha, \Sigma_\theta, \Sigma_\alpha$ are parameters that are common among consumers. These parameters are estimated using the Markov Chain Monte Carlo (MCMC) method. The estimation algorithm is based on Eq. (3.9). $\Theta, \mathcal{A}$. The parameters in the hierarchical parameter set are non-conjugate, so the random walk Metropolis Hastings (random walk M-H) method is used for their sampling. On the other hand, the hierarchical parameter $\Delta_\theta, \Delta_\alpha, \Sigma_\theta, \Sigma_\alpha$ are conjugate, they are sampled using a standard Gibbs sampler.

θ_i, α_i are sampled by the random walk M-H method algorithm with Eqs. (3.10) and (3.11) as the kernel of the posterior distribution, respectively.

$$p\left(y_i | \theta_i, \alpha_i, x_i, cumm_i\right) p(\theta_i | \Delta_\theta, \Sigma_\theta, z_i)$$

$$\propto \prod_{k=1}^{3} \left\{ \prod_{t_i \in R^{(k)}\left(\gamma_i^{(1)}, \gamma_i^{(2)}, CummM_{i,t_i}\right)} \left(\left(\exp\left(x_{i,t_i}^{(k)t} \beta_i^{(k)}\right) \right)^{y_{i,t_i}} \exp\left(-\exp\left(x_{i,t_i}^{(k)t} \beta_i^{(k)}\right)\right) \right) \right\}$$
$$\times \exp\left\{ -\tfrac{1}{2}\left(\theta_i - z_i^t \Delta_\theta\right)^t \Sigma_\theta^{-1}\left(\theta_i - z_i^t \Delta_\theta\right) \right\}$$

$$(3.10)$$

$$p\left(y_i | \theta_i, \alpha_i, x_i, cumm_i\right) p(\alpha_i | \Delta_\alpha, \Sigma_\alpha, z_i)$$

$$\propto \prod_{k=1}^{3} \left\{ \prod_{t_i \in R^{(k)}\left(\gamma_i^{(1)}, \gamma_i^{(2)}, CummM_{i,t_i}\right)} \left(\left(\exp\left(x_{i,t_i}^{(k)t} \beta_i^{(k)}\right) \right)^{y_{i,t_i}} \exp\left(-\exp\left(x_{i,t_i}^{(k)t} \beta_i^{(k)}\right)\right) \right) \right\}$$
$$\times \exp\left\{ -\tfrac{1}{2}\left(\alpha_i - z_i^t \Delta_\alpha\right)^t \Sigma_\alpha^{-1}\left(\alpha_i - z_i^t \Delta_\alpha\right) \right\}$$

$$(3.11)$$

θ_i, αi generates candidate samples by a random walk and determines probabilistically whether to adopt or reject them using the adoption probabilities constructed by Eqs. (3.10) and (3.11), respectively.

4 Empirical Analysis

The empirical analysis of this study is conducted for the two-state-switching model (conventional model) and the three-state-switching model (proposed model) using supermarket ID-POS data. Section 4.1 provides an overview of the data and a description of the model variables, and Sect. 4.2 presents the model evaluation and estimation results.

4.1 Data Summary and Model Variables

The empirical analysis of this study was conducted using supermarket ID-POS data. The analysis included 4,145 consumers who had made at least 50 purchases in the target year and at least one purchase each month. The average age of the target consumers was 51.8 years, 82% were female (18% male), the average purchase amount was 23,927 yen/month, and the average purchase frequency was 9.2 times/month. The distribution

of the target consumers is shown in Appendix 1. The model variables used in this study
include those variables used in Miyatsu and Sato (2015), except for the ratio of products
discounted by 15% or more. A table of variables is shown in Table 2.

4.2 Results and Discussion

In this study, the total number of MCMC iterations was 50,000 and the burn-in sample
was 45,000.

Table 2. Model Variables

level		symbol
Consumer i × Opportunities t_i (x_{i,t_i})	y_{i,t_i}	Number of purchase points (objective variable)
	$CNST$	Constant: 1
	$DRTN_{i,t_i}$	Number of days elapsed since last purchase Number of days elapsed since last purchase opportunity
	$TIME1_{i,t_i}$	Dummy for time of visit: 9am-1pm = 1, other = 0
	$TIME2_{i,t_i}$	Dummy for time of visit: 2-6pm = 1, other = 0
	$WKND_{i,t_i}$	Visiting time dummy:Weekend = 1, Weekday = 0
Consumer i (z_i)	$LAGE_i$	Age vs Gender dummies: female = 1, male = 0 Number of annual purchase opportunities vs
	$GNDR_i$	Cumulative annual purchases vs
	$OPPT_i$	Age vs Gender dummies: female = 1, male = 0 Number of annual purchase opportunities vs
	$SPND_i$	Cumulative annual purchases vs

Model Evaluation. To evaluate the proposed model, a comparative evaluation of the
two-state switching model (conventional model) and the three-state switching model
(proposed model) was conducted using the Bayes factor. The Bayes factor is defined by
Eq. (4.1), *where M_0 is the two-state switching model (conventional model), and M_1 is
the two-state switching model (conventional model).*

$$B_{01} = \frac{p(y|M_0)}{p(y|M_1)} \tag{4.1}$$

In this study, Kass and Raftery (1995) [2] (Table 3) was used as the Bayes factor criterion. $B_{01} = 123.52$. The result is that the Bayes factor is $M1$ (3-state switching model), which is better than the 2-state switching model.

Table 3. Criteria of Kass & Raftery (1995)

BF(B_{01})	Support for M1
BF < 1	M0 is better
1 < BF < 3	Not so much
3 < BF < 12	affirmative
12 < BF < 150	strong
150 < BF	Very strong

Table 4 shows the threshold parameters $(\gamma^{(1)}, \gamma^{(2)})$ and the component parameters of psychological load$(\alpha^{*(1)}, \alpha^{*(2)}, \alpha^{*(3)})$ Table 4 shows the basic statistics for the posterior means of the posterior mean of the threshold parameter for switching from regime 3 (high willingness to buy) to regime 2 (neither willingness to buy) is 12,749 yen, and the average monthly cumulative purchase amount of consumers is 23,927 yen, indicating that consumers switch from Mental Accounting with high willingness to buy to Mental Accounting with low willingness to buy when the average cumulative purchase amount is over 53%. The consumers switch from the Mental Accounting with high purchase motivation to the Mental Accounting with neither motivation. Similarly, the posterior mean of the threshold parameter for switching from regime 2 (neither willingness to buy) to regime 1 (low willingness to buy) is 13,608 yen, so consumers switch from the Mental Accounting with high willingness to buy to the Mental Accounting with neither willingness to buy when the threshold exceeds 57% of the average accumulated purchase amount. When consumers' Mental Accounting is expressed in three levels, the two switching points differ by only about 1,000 yen and have a large standard deviation, suggesting that consumer heterogeneity is large.

Table 5 shows the estimated results for one consumer. The consumer is male, 26 years old, makes 175 purchases per year, and spends 290,000 yen per year. The estimation results show that the construct parameters of mental load $\alpha = (0.0015, 0.9972)$ The estimated results are as follows: the component parameters of mental load, the threshold parameter $\gamma = (16,370, 13,675)$ The switching from a low to a high Mental Accounting occurs when the average monthly purchase amount exceeds 68%, and the switching from a low to a high Mental Accounting occurs when the average monthly purchase amount exceeds 57% (Fig. 2).

Table 4. Basic statistics of the estimates ($N = 4{,}145$)

classification	statistic	$\beta_1^{(k)}$	$\beta_2^{(k)}$	$\beta_3^{(k)}$	$\beta_4^{(k)}$	$\beta_5^{(k)}$
Regime1 ($k = 1$)	Mean	−0.0094	0.0312	0.0391	0.0518	0.156
	median	−0.011	0.0298	0.0583	0.035	0.1409
	Max	4.7959	5.1902	4.6259	5.2672	6.6884
	Min	−6.7314	−5.9617	−5.0265	−5.0558	−4.8629
	SD	1.2782	1.2912	1.2625	1.2985	1.3887
Regime2 ($k = 2$)	Mean	−0.0026	0.0133	0.0407	0.0101	0.0042
	median	−0.0076	0.0144	0.0235	0.0157	0.013
	Max	5.5274	4.8834	5.2494	5.1701	6.0234
	Min	−4.6435	−6.4269	−4.4497	−4.1543	−4.8522
	SD	1.2833	1.3019	1.2799	1.2586	1.2606
Regime3 ($k = 3$)	Mean	0.0149	0.0665	0.2189	0.3761	1.8233
	median	0.0273	0.0338	0.238	0.3557	1.8992
	Max	5.1973	3.0578	5.3235	6.1483	6.0531
	Min	−6.5451	−3.5272	−8.0301	−4.7164	−3.0248
	SD	1.1085	0.3913	1.2483	1.1216	0.9576

Table 5. Basic Statistics for Estimates($N = 4{,}145$)

statistic	$\gamma(1)$	$\gamma(2)$	$\alpha * (1)$	$\alpha * (2)$	$\alpha * (3)$
Mean	13,607.99	12,749.00	0.3867	0.4023	0.2110
median	12,525.91	11,938.60	0.0082	0.0099	0.0031
Max	104,057.90	43,004.25	0.9993	0.9992	0.9975
Min	173.66	1150.11	0.0003	0.0002	0.0003
SD	14,268.37	12,818.92	0.4735	0.4766	0.3925

As an example of a marketing measure that could be considered from the results of the empirical analysis, we can expect an increase in the number of items purchased by increasing the number of sale items just before the three typical payday periods, when emotional load is weighted, compared to the normal period. The average number of items purchased tends to be larger in Regime 1, which is a state of low willingness to purchase, than in Regime 2, which is a state of neither high nor low willingness to purchase. This is because consumers are more inclined to purchase inexpensive products when they are under psychological pressure, and as a result, the number of items purchased, including sale items and other inexpensive products, tends to be larger than in normal times.

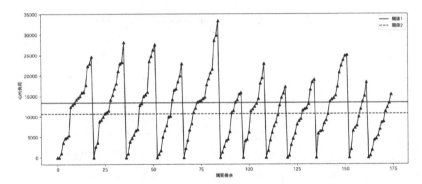

Fig. 2. Example of Estimation

5 Conclusion

In this study, we consider that consumers' willingness to purchase does not change before and after the threshold, but changes in three states: "the state in which willingness to purchase is increasing, the state in which willingness to purchase is decreasing, and the state in which neither state is occurring". The Miyatsu–Sato model, which models the mechanism of the occurrence of purchase point generation in the framework of a hierarchical Bayesian threshold Poisson regression model, is extended to a three-state switching model. In the empirical analysis, the regression coefficients of the three regimes and the two switching points were estimated for each consumer using supermarket ID-POS data, and the average difference between the two threshold parameters was about 1,000 yen, suggesting that consumer heterogeneity is large in the three-state switching model. Based on the results of the empirical analysis, a possible marketing measure is to increase the number of sale items during the period of high psychological pressure, which is just before payday.

The following three issues are considered for the future.

1. Since the estimation results for the two threshold parameters are not significantly different, the prior distribution is reexamined. Since the prior distributions used in this study were set up identically to those of Miyatsu and Sato, it is necessary to consider appropriate prior distributions when extending the model to a three-state switching model.
2. Given that the number of significant parameters estimated for regime 3 is lower than for the other regimes, we revisit the model with reduced mental load. Since regime 3 is a model with reduced emotional load, consumer heterogeneity is considered to be large. Therefore, we consider a model that takes the above into account.
3. Capturing qualitative changes in purchased products. In this study, the unit price of the purchased products is not taken into account, so that a customer who buys three ice cream products for 100 yen and a customer who buys three ice cream products for 300 yen will have the same behavior. Therefore, it is necessary to capture qualitative changes in the model in order to account for them.

References

1. Belk, R.W.: Situational Variables and Consumer Behavior (1975)
2. Thaler, R.: Mental accounting and consumer choice. Mark. Sci. **4**, 199–214 (1985)
3. Miyatsu, K., Sato, T.: Modeling the relationship between psychological wallets and purchasing behavior: a proposal for a hierarchical bayesian threshold poisson regression model. Appl. Stat. **44**, 161–182 (2015)
4. Tversky, A., Kahneman, D.: The framing of decisions and the psychology of choice. Science **211**(4481), 453–458 (1981)
5. Kahneman, D., Tversky, A.: Prospect theory: an analysis of decision under risk. Econometrica **47**(2), 263–291 (1979)
6. Kojima, S.: The psychology of price: what do consumers use as a "Measure" in making purchase decisions. In: Diamond Sales Editorial Planning (1986). (in Japanese)
7. Terui, N., Dahana, W.D.: Research note—estimating heterogeneous price thresholds. Mark. Sci. **25**(4), 384–391 (2006)

Twitch Consumer Behavior and the Importance of Streaming Habits

Cristóbal Fernández-Robin[(✉)], Diego Yáñez, and Joaquina Miranda

Departamento de Industrias, Universidad Técnica Federico Santa María, Av. España 1680, Valparaíso, Chile

`{cristobal.fernandez,diego.yanez}@usm.cl, joaquina.miranda@sansano.usm.cl`

Abstract. The boom of live audiovisual content broadcasting is closely related to the development of social media applications. Twitch is among the most widespread live streaming platforms, and has experienced significant growth. In 2022, it had more than 2.5 million daily spectators and more than 7 million streamers who shared their content through more than 92,000 channels. This study analyzes the factors influencing the use continuance intention of the current Twitch users through an online survey (n=297) conducted on SurveyMonkey. The findings of this study confirmed that multiple factors from the proposed hypothetical model, which was based on the UTAUT2 and the Hassanein and Head model, explained the Behavior Intention (BI) of use continuance. Some of these factors are the variables of Habit, Social Presence, Price Value and Effort Expectancy. As a result, the natural and automatic adaptation of users when using the platform, their capacity to connect and get close to other users through Twitch, the available paid benefits, and the ease of use associated with the platform contribute to increase the disposition of users to continue using the platform when they want to access live content via streaming. Based on the implications of this study, suggestions are made for companies in the live streaming world and for all the associated brands that want to invest in advertisement on these platforms.

Keywords: Twitch · Live streaming · Hedonic Motivation · Habit

1 Introduction

The use of technology has become essential to society, especially in recent years. This has given rise to companies that have taken advantage of this behavior change and of the explosive increase in the use of these new technologies, which have established their business models based on the development of ICTs drawing the attention of varied audiences, among which are live streaming platforms.

Live streaming is a "term that refers to online transmission means, recorded and broadcast in real time" [1]. According to the 2023 Annual Study on Social

Networks conducted by IAB Spain [16], users spend most of their time on apps such as Spotify, Twitch and Discord, with an average use of 1 h and 33 min, 1 h and 28 min, and 1 h and 27 min, respectively. The increasing popularity of social networks is evident, particularly on live streaming platforms like Twitch, which generates even more interest in their study.

Twitch, a live stream platform owned by Amazon, has become the main audiovisual medium, especially for young audiences that seek video game-related content. Millions of people around the world follow diverse streamers and enjoy live transmissions that are comparable to massive television events. Twitch comprises a wide range of content and is known as the "other way to watch television" [13]. In addition to video games, the platform supports the transmission of radio content thanks to tools that foster interaction and sharing in the community. This content diversity attracts users of different ages and tastes, facilitating the access to any person with basic knowledge about technology and providing opportunities for any individual interested in enjoying live streaming content.

Twitch is a space that gathers renowned content creators and enables a direct relationship between them and their followers, which represents a valuable opportunity for brands seeking new audiences. Although YouTube is the platform of choice for a la carte content, Twitch maintained its success in 2023 by offering a close connection between streamers and their followers, according to a study on digital trends [16]. Furthermore, a distinctive characteristic is that the growth of Twitch does not rely on algorithms, as opposed to its main competitor, YouTube.

This study aims to delve into the study of Twitch, which is still growing and will probably continue being successful over the years and with the advent of new technologies, becoming the new entryway for brands interested in new audiences, and aims to understand which factors influence the behavior intention of this platform's users.

2 Literature Review

The boom of live audiovisual content broadcasting is closely related to the development of social media applications [20]. Live streaming is considered an evolution of the classic broadcasting format offered by television [21]. Three platforms stand out as exponentially growing in the live streaming industry: Twitch, YouTube and Facebook [1].

Forecasts for the video marketing and live streaming industries are favorable. Statista, a statistics website, predicts that the live streaming market will reach 137.7 billion dollars in 2027 [25]. During the second quarter of 2020, live streaming continued its global expansion, with a change in the content consumption trend, in which not only eSports and video games became predominant, but music and performing arts as well [1].

The Twitch platform has experienced significant growth. In 2022, it had more than 2.5 million daily spectators and more than 7 million streamers that share their content through more than 92,000 channels [22]. Despite the competition in the live streaming field, Twitch has managed to maintain its position as the unarguable giant of the streaming world.

One of the success factors of Twitch is its way of giving dividends to live streaming creators. This platform monetizes the success of streamers based on advertising done, number of subscribers of the streamer's channel and other forms of donation from the audience of the streamer [14]. This system has caused content creators from other platforms to migrate to Twitch in the pursuit of better income [13]. This monetization strategy has significantly contributed to the consolidation of the leading position of Twitch in the live streaming world, and has created an ecosystem where both creators and the platform can prosper.

The model of the Unified Theory of Acceptance and Use of Technology has been employed on multiple occasions in technology adoption and dissemination research for empirical studies about user intention and behavior. The theory was developed based on the review and integration of 8 theories and dominant technology acceptance models, and therefore is attributed a great explanatory capacity. The model comprises four main constructs (Effort Expectancy, Performance Expectancy, Social Influence and Facilitating Conditions) that directly determine behavior intention and behavior as such [23]. Altogether, the UTAUT model offers a solid and complete structure to understand how people adopt and use new technologies in diverse contexts.

The Unified Theory of Acceptance and Use of Technology 2 (UTAUT2) adds 3 constructs to the UTAUT model, which are hedonic motivation, price values and habit. It has been established that the effects associated with these three constructs about behavioral intention and technology use are influenced by the age, gender and experience of the individual [24].

The model by Hassanein and Head was presented in 2005 to analyze how the manipulation of social presence perceived through the web interface impacted the attitude towards online shopping [15]. However, this model has also been employed in the use intention studies of social media frequented by Millennials and Generation Z, such as Instagram and Snapchat. This model suggests modifications to the TAM model, incorporating new variables such as trust and enjoyment, and giving special relevance to the "social presence" variable.

The proposed model for this study (see Fig. 1) is the UTAUT2 model slightly modified with two extra variables from Hassanein and Head's model, which due to its nature may affect the Behavioral Intention of Twitch users. These variables are Trust and Social Presence.

This study aims to find the factors influencing the Behavioral Intention (BI) of Twitch users, i.e., the will of individuals or users to perform a specific behavior [8].

Performance expectancy (PE) is the perception of users about the extent to which the use of a technology may improve their performance in some specific activities [23]. A higher performance expectancy is expected from users if they perceive that using a specific technology may help them achieve their objectives more effectively or efficiently, and therefore they may be more willing to adopt this technology.

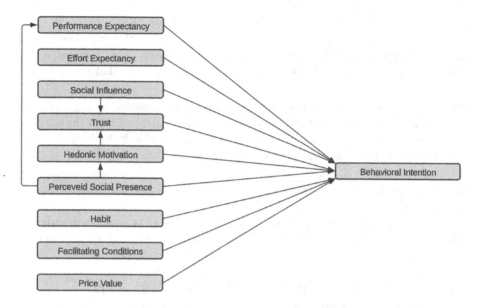

Fig. 1. Model proposed. *Source: Created by the authors.*

H1. *The Performance Expectancy (PE) variable influences the Behavioral Intention to use Twitch.*

Effort Expectancy refers to the degree of ease users associate with the use of the technology [23]. If users perceive that the use of technology is simple and they need not to make a great effort, this can influence their willingness to adopt this technology [9]. The fact that users have low effort expectations often favors the intention to use such a technology.

H2. *The variable Effort Expectancy (EE) influences the behavioral intention to use Twitch.*

Social influence is defined as the degree to which an individual perceives that other people who he considers important believe he should use the technology [23].

H3. *The variable Social Influence (SI) influences the behavioral intention to use Twitch.*

Some studies demonstrate that if people close to the user have a good experience with a technology, the user is more likely to use that technology [4]. If a user observes that people who he considers important are in favor and support the use of the technology, this is an indicator that suggests that the technology is reliable and useful, and therefore it is likely that they develop a positive attitude and that the trust of the user in employing it increases.

H3'. *The variable Social Influence (SI) influences Trust (T).*

Trust is defined as a psychological expectation from the individual that another trusted party will not behave opportunistically [2,19]. It represents the willingness from one party to be vulnerable to the actions of other parties [18].

H4. *The variable Trust (T) influences the behavioral intention to use Twitch.*

Hedonic motivation is defined as the fun or pleasure derived from the use of a technology [24]. There are multiple studies that establish that hedonic motivation is an important factor in the acceptance and use of a technology [3,6].

H5. *The variable Hedonic Motivation (HM) influences the behavioral intention to use Twitch.*

Some studies demonstrate that "compulsive shopping" is associated with the enjoyment felt by users, who continue using online shopping systems due to this "continuous entertainment" that generates trust in them [12].

H5'. *The variable Hedonic Motivation (HM) influences Trust (T).*

Social presence is defined as the extent to which a medium allows users to experience the psychological idea that people are present [11]. It is also understood as the feeling of human warmth and sociability given by the medium or technology to users [15].

H6. *The variable Social Presence (SP) influences the use behavioral intention to use Twitch.*

According to research with adaptations of the TAM model, social presence affects perceived usefulness. This last variable has performance expectancy as its equivalent in the UTAUT2 model [7,15].

H6'. *The variable Social Presence (SP) influences Performance Expectancy (PE).*

Lastly, these same studies of TAM model adaptations above [7,15], establish that the variable social presence influences perceived enjoyment, whose equivalent variable in the UTAUT2 model is hedonic motivation.

H6''. *The variable Social Presence (SP) influences Hedonic Motivation (HM).*

Habit is defined as the extent to which consumers tend to perform behaviors automatically due to learning [17]. It can be measured as the degree to which individuals believe that a behavior is automatic [24].

H7. *The variable Habit (H) influences the use behavioral intention to use Twitch.*

Facilitating conditions correspond to the degree to which individuals believe that there is both an organizational and a technical infrastructure to support the use of a technology [23].

H8. *The variable Facilitating Conditions (FC) influences the use behavioral intention to use Twitch.*

The value price is defined as the cognitive compensation of consumers between the perceived benefits of the use of a technology and the real monetary cost of using them [24].

H9. *The variable Price Value (PV) influences the use behavioral intention to use Twitch.*

3   Methodology

At the beginning of the study, a comprehensive information search was conducted focusing on the theoretical dimension, with special emphasis on the live streaming industry and more specifically delving into the history and evolution of the Twitch platform. Having an overview of the context, a literature review is conducted, which was centered on the modeling to explain the use intention of consumers of Information Technologies so these models could be later applied to the more specific case of Twitch.

The proposed model is a modification of the UTAUT2 model [24], complemented with the model proposed by Hassanein and Head [15]. Then, a 49-question questionnaire is applied. The first part of the questionnaire comprises some demographic questions, and a filter question about whether users have interacted with the platform under study and, if affirmative, how often. The second part of the questionnaire consists of questions about the model variables, which are rated on a 5-point Likert scale in which 1 corresponds to 'totally disagree' and 5 to 'totally agree'. Sampling is conducted by convenience and the survey, created on SurveyMonkey, is shared through diverse social networks such as Instagram, WhatsApp, and Facebook, reaching different people along the country. A total of 317 responses are obtained, of which 196 correspond to people who currently use the platform.

With this data, scale reliability is assessed through the IBM SPSS Statistics 29 software, and the corresponding structural equation model (SEM) is calculated using the SPSS AMOS 29 software. Subsequently, the model fit and its regression estimators are analyzed, and lastly, conclusions are drawn based on the results.

4   Results

The profile of the sample is analyzed based on the answers obtained in the survey. The results show that 92% of respondents report having used a live streaming platform at some point during their lives, of which 84% establish that their experience with them has been positive, while 16% define it as neutral. In addition, 72.3% of respondents that have used a live streaming platform like to watch video game transmissions, followed by Just Chatting with 64.2%. In turn, less popular but still with good percentages are IRL and sports content, which are liked by 30.7% and 32.8% of users, respectively. Finally, music accounts for 20.1% and arts and creation for 10.6%.

Of the 297 responses, 196 people or 66% of respondents use Twitch. Regarding the age of respondents who use Twitch, responses cover all the brackets, with a predominance of people from 19 to 25 years of age, corresponding to 69% of responses, followed by the 18 or under age bracket with 15% and the 26-to-30 years of age group with 13%. Regarding gender, there is a clear tendency towards the masculine gender, with 74% of users of Twitch responding the survey being men. Twenty-five percent of the sample reported being female and only 1% did not want to report gender and marked the option "other".

With respect to the frequency that users employ Twitch, respondents often use this platform. Thirty-five percent report using it 2 to 3 times per week, followed by 24% with 4 to 6 times per week; therefore, more than 50% of the sample use Twitch more than 2 days per week. In addition, 17% use it once per week and 16% consume content from this platform every day. The lowest percentage, at 8%, represents respondents who only use the platform once or twice per month, for more specific events that are transmitted on this medium; however, since these events have a long duration, these responses cannot be overlooked.

Subsequently, a reliability analysis is conducted to verify the consistency of the constructs of the model. Table 1 shows the Cronbach's alpha values of each construct. For this type of study, 0.6 is established as acceptable value.

According to the theory, most values are acceptable. Two variables have values just below the 0.6 limit, namely Performance Expectancy (PE) and Facilitating Conditions (FC) with a 0.579 and 0.558 index, respectively.

Performance Expectancy would increase its Cronbach's alpha over the 0.6 limit if the observable variable PE3 were removed from the proposed model; this would also be true for the variable Facilitating Conditions if the variable FC4 were removed. If the item "Twitch allows me to access content in a fast way" (PE3) and "If I have difficulties or problems using Twitch, I have the possibility to get help from others" (FC4), indexes improve considerably, which is the recommendation, and thus the analysis continues without these two observable variables.

After drawing the demographic profile of respondents and the scale reliability analysis of the variables, the analysis of the Structural Equation Model is performed to verify whether the relationships proposed at the beginning agree with the data obtained in the survey. Table 2 shows the fit indexes of the proposed model.

The CMIN/DF relationship is within the ideal value range, and therefore model fit is acceptable. Regarding the NFI and CFI indexes values, they are below the acceptable value and consequently the incremental goodness-of-fit is not as adequate in this case. Lastly, the parsimony fit measures are analyzed; PNFI specifically reaches a value of .611 and is within the desired range, which indicates that the relationship between the constructs and the proposed model is

Table 1. Cronbach's Alpha *Source: Created by the authors.*

Construct	Cronbach's Alpha	Item	Cronbach's Alpha if item deleted
PE	0.579	PE1	0.387
		PE2	0.356
		PE3	0.646
		PE4	0.564
EE	0.856	EE1	0.683
		EE2	0.714
		EE3	0.768
		EE4	0.708
SI	0.869	SI1	0.665
		SI2	0.812
		SI3	0.779
T	0.718	T1	0.583
		T2	0.665
		T3	0.713
		T4	0.658
HM	0.863	HM1	0.811
		HM2	0.803
		HM3	0.808
		HM4	0.899
SP	0.615	SP1	0.576
		SP2	0.324
		SP3	0.750
		SP4	0.464
H	0.806	H1	0.642
		H2	0.653
		H3	0.813
		H4	0.846
FC	0.558	FC1	0.446
		FC2	0.446
		FC3	0.382
		FC4	0.704
PV	0.781	PV1	0.769
		PV2	0.783
		PV3	0.677
		PV4	0.664
BI	0.847	BI1	0.813
		BI2	0.731
		BI3	0.816

Table 2. Fit indexes of the model proposed. *Source: Created by the authors.*

Index	Value
CMIN/DF	2.6
RMSEA	0.092
NFI	0.663
CFI	0.757
PNFI	0.611
PCFI	0.698

adequate. In turn, the value of PCFI indicates a good adjustment when comparing the proposed model to another model with the same number of coefficients. According to these measures that seek to relate the quality of model fit to the number of estimated coefficients required to achieve the adjustment, the model has a good fit. Considering the general results, the fit is not perfect but within acceptable parameters. The goodness-of-fit of the model is good despite some index values being out of range as this difference is also not significant.

According to the p-values of Table 3, a significant relationship is considered when p has values below 0.05. As a result, the variable Trust (T) significantly influences Social Influence (SI) and Hedonic Motivation, while the variable Social Presence (SP) influences Hedonic Motivation (HM) and Performance Expectancy (PE). However, the main variable of study is the Behavioral Intention of Use Continuance (UC). Based on the p-values obtained, behavioral intention is significantly influenced by the variables Habit (H), Social Presence (SP), Price Value and Effort Expectancy (EE). In this case, the relationships that turned out to be significant and that do not contain the variable Behavioral Intention do not provide much information after their analysis, since Hedonic Motivation, Trust and Performance Expectancy do not directly influence the main endogenous variable.

Observing the standardized coefficients, the variables Habit (H), Social Presence (SP), Price Value (PV) and Effort Expectancy (EE) explain 72.8%, 40.9%, 12.4% and 10.8% of Behavioral Intention, respectively.

Regarding the determination coefficient (R^2) of the model, a value of 0.825 is obtained for Behavioral Intention. In this case, the dependent variable Behavioral Intention of use continuance is explained 82.5% in terms of variance by the variables Habit (H) and Social Presence (SP), which is quite a high value considering the randomness of respondents. In this type of study, a value over 0.5 is already considered optimal, and therefore these results allow for establishing that it is significant and that the latent variables above successfully explain the Behavioral Intention of Twitch users.

The relationships proposed in hypotheses H2, H3', H5', H6, H6', H6", H7 and H9 are confirmed. However, the most relevant hypotheses are H2, H6, H7 and H9. Effort Expectancy influences BI, i.e., the perceived ease of use of Twitch influences the intention to continue using this platform.

Table 3. Standardized coefficients. *Source: Created by the authors.*

	Estimate	P-value
HM <— SP	0.685	***
T <— SI	0.178	0.019
T <— HM	0.608	***
PE <— SP	0.409	***
BI <— PV	0.124	0.022
BI <— SI	-0.090	0.090
BI <— FC	-0.012	0.831
BI <— H	0.728	***
BI <— EE	0.108	0.040
BI <— T	0.065	0.418
BI <— HM	0.119	0.225
BI <— SP	0.331	***
BI <— PE	0.111	0.106

Social Presence influences BI, i.e., the proximity and closeness felt by users with respect to other users of the platform or with streamers who broadcast content, influences the intention of people to continue using Twitch. Habit influences BI, i.e., the adaptation to use the platform naturally and automatically at the moment of wanting to consume live streaming content, influences the intention of users to continue using Twitch. Price Value influences BI, i.e., the benefits obtained from using money on the platform, are considered relevant by the user, influencing its use continuance intention.

5   Conclusions

This study aimed to model the behavior of Twitch users by specifically identifying the factors influencing the Behavioral Intention of the use continuance of this platform.

To understand the behavior of Twitch consumers, it was first necessary to create a model based on the UTAUT 2 and Hassanein and Head's models. The results obtained from the sample lead to the following conclusions:

Habit is the most influential variable, explaining 72.8% of the Behavioral Intention of use continuance for Twitch. This variable refers to the degree to which individuals hold the belief that the behavior and use of this platform is automatic. On some occasions, Twitch is seen by audiences as an alternative or substitute of television [5, 10]. Consumers tend to use the platform naturally and automatically when they want to access live content and many times streamers have defined times for their transmissions, which generates routines in their spectators, who faithfully watch their streams This suggests that live streaming platforms should promote this automatic behavior in users. To foster this habit, platforms should focus on making the access to the platform as instantaneous as turning on the TV and live transmissions smooth, without problems from the platform. In the events organized by Twitch, in which several streamers participate, there is often problems with the servers and therefore it is fundamental that companies have excellent servers that allow for a problem-free transmission. In addition, the notifications of streamers starting a live stream are not always sent in a timely manner and sometimes they simply do not reach users, for which the creation of a better algorithm that consistently notifies users about the start of live streams from the streamers they follow would be necessary. Furthermore, the transmission of advertisement during live streaming directed to users that formed a habit in the platform generates a subconscious familiarization with brands. Users watch these ads constantly so that sooner or later they recognize them, in a way very similar to television ads; however, in this case they do not change channels because interruptions are quite short and then they can continue watching the live streaming, being this a great opportunity for brands seeking to announce their products briefly and massively.

The Social Presence variable explains 33.1% of the Behavioral Intention of use continuance. This variable is the measure of how the platform allows users to experience the psychological idea that other people are present [11]; it is the feeling of human warmth and sociability that Twitch gives users [15]. Platforms must continue to generate opportunities for users to be able to interact with streamers and other users. Until now, Twitch has done a great job by means of the chat implemented in each channel, where users send their messages to talk with one another or with the streamer and comment on the transmission together; in addition, bit donation is a good option to highlight messages for some money and have a higher chance of the streamer responding directly. Each streamer creates his own community, generating a feeling of increased warmth in all his followers. The more streaming platforms make an effort to produce interaction opportunities, the more spectators it will have and they will have an incentive to continue using the platform, even for longer than they currently employ it, because humans are social beings and this type of platform is a great opportunity to socialize.

Price Value explains 12.4% of the behavioral intention of the use continuance of Twitch. This variable is the cognitive compensation of consumers among the perceived benefits from the use of the platform and the monetary cost for using it [24]. Twitch is a free platform through which the live streams of any streamer can be accessed. Currently, Twitch has diverse paid services such as channel subscriptions, which have the specific associated benefits of each streamer, and bit donation for the streamer to read the messages or simply to support content creators. These benefits have been well received by users, for whom the cost is suitable. Therefore, the platform should continue adding more paid benefits that may be of interest to users, such that their use intention grows and, at the same time, both the platform and streamer can benefit economically. However, it should be clarified that new paid services should be added instead of monetizing elements that now are free to access, since the platform could lose a large part of its active users and streamers could even stop live streaming due to the decrease in their visualizations.

Lastly, the variable Effort Expectancy explains 10.8% of Behavioral Intention or the degree of ease perceived by users about the use of the technology. Currently, Twitch is a quite intuitive platform, which is essential for platforms, as the clearer and easier the interaction is of users with them, the more predisposition they will have to continue using them. Therefore, it is suggested that the interface of the platform be the most efficient and intuitive possible so streamers" content and channels can be accessed rapidly and easily. Business strategic decisions that involve updates or aesthetic changes, among others, cannot overlook the original simplicity offered by this platform.

Due to the constant increase in the number of users and the success this platform has had since its creation, further research related to the topic is expected, because live streaming is an industry that seems to acquire more relevance year by year, and thus is a good opportunity for companies that wish to advertise their products or services.

References

1. Antolín Prieto, R., Reyes Menendez, A., Ruiz Lacaci, N.: Explorando los factores que afectan al comportamiento de los consumidores en plataformas de live streaming. Revista Espacios **42**(15), 29–44 (2021)
2. Bradach, J.L., Eccles, R.G.: Price, authority, and trust: From ideal types to plural forms. Ann. Rev. Sociol. **15**(1), 97–118 (1989)
3. Brown, S.A., Venkatesh, V.: Model of adoption of technology in the household: A baseline model test and extension incorporating household life cycle. MIS Q. **29:4**(4), 399–426 (2005)
4. Carvajal, C., Neira, J., Perez, J., Villamil, N.: Diseño de comercio móvil con base en el modelo UTAUT 2 PhD thesis, Pontificia Universidad Javeriana
5. Casells, C.: witch. tv, un nuevo paradigma en la comunicación y el entretenimiento en Internet. PhD thesis, Universitat Politècnica de València (2021)
6. Childers, T.L., Carr, C.L., Peck, J., Carson, S.: Hedonic and utilitarian motivations for online retail shopping behavior. J. Retail. **77**(4), 511–535 (2001)
7. Coa, V.V., Setiawan, J.: Analyzing factors influencing behavior intention to use snapchat and Instagram stories. IJNMT (International Journal of New Media Technology) **4**(2), 75–81 (2017)
8. Davis, F.: Perceived usefulness, perceived ease of use and user acceptance of information technology. MIS Q. **13**(3), 319–339 (1989)
9. Davis, F.D., Bagozzi, R.P., Warshaw, P.R.: User acceptance of computer technology: a comparison of two theoretical models. Manag. Sci. **35**(8), 982–1003 (1989)
10. Escorial, A.: Un nuevo modelo en el consumo de entretenimiento. Internet y las nuevas vías de comunicación: Twitch y Youtube. PhD thesis, Universidad Complutense (2022)
11. Fulk, J., Steinfield, C.W., Schmitz, J., Power, J.: A social information processing model of media use in organizations. Commun. Res. **14**(5), 529–552 (1987)
12. Gefen, D.: Tam or just plain habit: a look at experienced online shoppers. J. Organ. End User Comput. (JOEUC) **15**(3), 1–13 (2003)

13. Gutiérrez Lozano, J.F., Cuartero, A.: El auge de twitch: nuevas ofertas audiovisuales y cambios del consumo televisivo entre la audiencia juvenil. Ámbitos. Revista internacional de comunicación **50**, 159–175 (2020)
14. Hamilton, W.A., Kerne, A.: Streaming on twitch: fostering participatory communities of play within live mixed media. In: Proceedings of the SIGCHI Conference on Human Factors in Computing Systems, pp. 1315–1324 (2014)
15. Hassanein, K., Head, M.: Manipulating perceived social presence through the web interface and its impact on attitude towards online shopping. Int. J. Hum. Comput. Stud. **65**(8), 689–708 (2007)
16. IAB Spain. https://iabspain.es/estudio/estudio-de-redes-sociales-2023/. Accessed 17 Dec 2023
17. Limayem, M., Hirt, S.G., Cheung, M.K.: How habit limits the predictive power of intention: the case of information systems continuance. MIS Q. **31**(4), 705–737 (2007)
18. Mayer, R.C., Davis, J.H., Shoorman, F.D.: An integrative model of organization trust. Acad. Manag. Rev. **20**, 709–734 (1989)
19. Rousseau, D.M., Sitkin, S.B., Burt, R.S., Camerer, C.: Not so different after all: a cross-discipline view of trust. Acad. Manag. Rev. **23**(3), 393–404 (1998)
20. Rugg, A., Burroughs, B.: Periscope, live-streaming and mobile video culture. Geoblocking and global video culture **18**, 64–73 (2016)
21. Stewart, D.R., Littau, J.: Up, periscope: mobile streaming video technologies, privacy in public, and the right to record. Journalism Mass Commun. Q. **93**(2), 312–331 (2016)
22. Twitch statistics & charts. https://twitchtracker.com/statistics. Accessed 30 Oct 2023
23. Venkatesh, V., Morris, M.G., Davis, G.B., Davis, F.D.: User acceptance of information technology: toward a unified view. MIS Q. **27**(3), 425–478 (2003)
24. Venkatesh, V., Thong, J.Y., Xu, X.: Consumer acceptance and use of information technology: extending the unified theory of acceptance and use of technology. MIS Q. **36**(1), 157–178 (2012)
25. Video Streaming (SVOD) - Global | Statista Market forecast. https://www.statista.com/outlook/dmo/digital-media/video-on-demand/video-streaming-svod/worldwide. Accessed 29 Oct 2023

Prediction of Consumer Purchases in a Session on an EC Site Considering the Variety of Past Browsing

Yuto Fukui$^{(\boxtimes)}$ and Tomoaki Tabata

Tokai University, Minatoku, Takanawa 108-0074, Japan
3CTAD018@cc.u-tokai.ac.jp, tabata@tokai-u.jp

Abstract. Data obtained from online shops include not only consumer purchase information but also data on non-purchase behaviors. This enables the construction of models to predict consumer purchases during a session. Behaviors such as focusing on a single product or repeatedly visiting the site for product consideration are thought to influence in-session purchases. Specifically, it is believed that consumers who show a keen interest in a particular product and spend time examining it are more likely to make a purchase compared to those who evaluate and compare various attributes of products in a specific category. Additionally, even if consumers spend a significant amount of time viewing a particular product, they might do so solely for information gathering. Furthermore, consumers who have repeatedly visited the site or have made multiple purchases in the past are likely to be more familiar with purchasing on the site compared to first-time visitors, making them more inclined to make a purchase. In summary, such factors can be crucial in accurately predicting consumer purchase intentions. However, these aspects of consumer purchasing behavior have not been reflected in traditional models. Therefore, this research aims to construct a model that accounts for the diversity of consumer purchasing behaviors and visit histories, improving the accuracy of predicting purchases during a session beyond what traditional models provide. The results are intended to assist in decision-making for marketing strategies.

Keywords: Consumer behavior · Customer purchase behavior prediction · Marketing · E-commerce · Artificial intelligence

1 Introduction

In the current retail landscape, merchants are now able to construct models that represent consumer purchasing behaviors by leveraging the behavioral logs of consumers in stores or on websites (hereafter, simply referred to as "sites"). For retailers, utilizing such models to predict consumer purchases, and to identify and analyze the factors influencing these purchases, has become a critical issue in marketing.

A. Coman and S. Vasilache (Eds.): HCII 2024, LNCS 14704, pp. 247–261, 2024.
https://doi.org/10.1007/978-3-031-61305-0_17

A traditional model representing consumer purchasing behavior was proposed by McFadden (1973) [1], which introduced the multinomial logit model.

$$p(x|s, B) = \frac{e^{V(s,x)}}{\sum_{y \in B} e^{V(s,x)}}$$ (1)

$$U = V(s, x) + \varepsilon(s, x)$$ (2)

In this model, s represents the measured individual attributes, x denotes the product chosen by the consumer, and B signifies the set of products available for consumer selection. The customer's utility function U is divided into a non-stochastic component V and a stochastic component ε. The multinomial logit model, a discrete choice model, assumes that each individual selects one alternative from a set of choices.

Although the multinomial logit model has been widely adopted due to its compatibility with Point of Sale (POS) data, it is important to note that POS data focuses only on the outcomes of consumer purchases, such as what products were sold, at what prices, and in what quantities. Therefore, this model, which utilizes such data, does not reflect the consumer's purchasing process (Fig. 1).

Fig. 1. Conventional Data Acquisition (physical store)

In contrast, in the realm of online shops, a wealth of data accumulates detailing consumer activities such as the products browsed, and time spent on the site, especially when consumers visit but do not make a purchase. This data enables the prediction of whether a purchase will be made during a consumer's session. (Fig. 2) Here, the term "Session" lacks a uniform definition, being described as a series of interactions conducted by a user to fulfill a single information need [2], or as an uninterrupted sequence of activities within an e-commerce system [3]. Therefore, this study defines a session as the duration from when a consumer accesses the site until they leave.

Companies operating websites implement various approaches to encourage purchases by consumers visiting their sites daily. However, strategies such as indiscriminately implementing marketing measures for all visitors (e.g., mechanical distribution of coupons) can reduce opportunity losses but may not yield high results. This is because companies, while adhering to KPIs (e.g., CPA) on a monthly or quarterly basis, prefer to generate more profit even at the same cost. Given these circumstances, companies are required to make strategic marketing

Fig. 2. Present Data Acquisition (online store)

interventions based on consumer purchasing behavior during sessions. Nonetheless, discerning the purchasing intent of consumers, given their wide-ranging and complex behaviors, is exceedingly challenging.

A solution to this problem is the use of models representing consumer purchasing behavior during sessions. These models can capture the purchasing intent of a consumer at specific moments in terms of purchase probability. Consequently, it becomes possible to execute marketing interventions for consumers with either high or low purchase probabilities at the appropriate times. In practice, such models use data from a consumer's purchasing behavior up to the start of the current session to predict their purchasing probability at specific moments during the session. This differs from models that predict consumer purchase intentions in real-time for sequential data, as it has advantages such as lower computational requirements, making operations more straightforward.

Existing research predicting consumer purchases during sessions includes Vieira (2016) [4], who built a model using factors such as the duration of stay on a site and the prices of products viewed by the consumer. However, his model does not reflect the breadth of time spent viewing each product during a session or the consumer's past site visit experiences. It can be hypothesized that consumers focusing intensively on a single product or those who have frequently visited or made purchases on the site are more likely to make a purchase compared to first-time visitors. Overall, variables that can represent such consumer purchasing behaviors during sessions are crucial for accurately estimating purchasing intent.

Therefore, this study aims to incorporate the variance in viewing time for each product and site visit experience as new explanatory variables in the model. By doing so, we aim to construct a model with higher predictive accuracy than existing models, contributing to decision-making in marketing.

2 Previous Studies

2.1 Previous Studies

In traditional research, Vieira (2016) [4] set sessions ending in a purchase and those not ending in a purchase as dependent variables, constructing models to predict them using logistic regression, random forest, and deep learning. Deep learning yielded the highest AUC, thus affirming the model's utility. The explanatory variables used to represent consumer purchasing behavior and characteristics in the model are as follows:

1. D_s: Time duration from the start to the end of a session (session duration); represents deliberate purchasing behavior for longer durations and impulsive or planned purchasing behavior for shorter durations.
2. C/B: The value obtained by dividing the Conversion Rate (CVR) of each product during a specific period (such as weekly) by the number of times a consumer viewed those products in a session; indicates whether a consumer frequently views and purchases products that other consumers buy or focuses on less-purchased, niche products.
3. S_B: The median number of non-purchasing sessions for each consumer; represents the extent of product consideration in purchasing behavior.
4. $Desc$: Product descriptions represented in 50 dimensions (using word2vec); signifies whether a consumer focused on a specific type of product or browsed a wide variety of product types.
5. $Duration$: The duration of product viewing in a session; represents purchasing behavior similar to item 1.
6. $Hour$: The time when the session started (occurred); characterizes the consumer's purchasing behavior in terms of viewing and purchasing products during different times of the day, such as morning, afternoon, or night.
7. N_c: Number of clicks (page views) in a session; indicates how actively a consumer engages in purchasing behavior on the target site.
8. $Price$: Average price of products viewed and purchased in each session; shows consumer preference for higher (or lower) priced items.
9. $Views_{24h}$: Number of page views by all consumers in the past 24 h; demonstrates whether consumers view and purchase products during peak times with other consumers or during off-peak times like outside sales periods.
10. $Views_{week}$: Number of page views by all consumers in the previous week; represents purchasing behavior similar to item 9.

2.2 Limitations of Vieira's Model

Vieira's model reflects the purchasing behavior and characteristics of consumers visiting the site as mentioned in items 1–10 previous subsection. However, it has limitations in not reflecting the following three aspects of consumer purchasing behavior:

1. The distribution of viewing time each consumer allocates to products during a session (whether they browse a wide range of products or focus intensively on a single product).
2. The overall distribution of viewing time each consumer allocates to various products during the entire session.
3. The history of each consumer's past visits to the site.

Firstly, a limitation identified in Vieira's model (2016) [4] relates to its inability to differentiate between consumers who, for instance, spend a total of 15 min

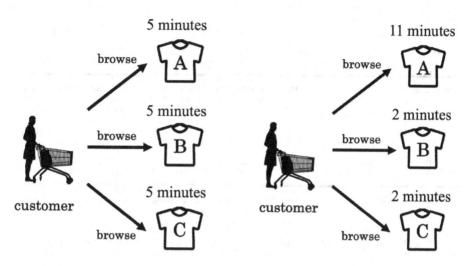

Fig. 3. Consumer purchasing behavior not captured by Vieira's model.(1)

viewing products A, B, and C collectively (Fig. 3, left) and those who spend 11 min viewing product A and 2 min each on products B and C (Fig. 3, right). It is presumed that a consumer focusing intensively on one product is engaged in a deliberate evaluation of detailed information, thus more likely to make a purchase than a consumer browsing various products. In other words, the breadth of viewing time a consumer allocates to each product may indicate the depth of their interest in making a purchase, potentially influencing their purchasing decision. For example, a consumer who equally allocates viewing time to various aspects such as fabric and color when purchasing clothing might be considered indecisive, hence less likely to make a purchase compared to a consumer focused on a single item.

Next, point 2 emphasizes the limitation of Vieira's model in distinguishing consumer purchasing behaviors solely based on the time allocated to each product during a session, as illustrated in Fig. 4. Both consumers in Fig. 4 (top and bottom) allocate most of their viewing time to specific products in each session. However, looking at the sessions in totality, the consumer in Fig. 4 (top) views ten different products (A to J), whereas the consumer in Fig. 4 (bottom) views only two products (A and B). It is anticipated that the latter, who focuses more on specific products, is more likely to proceed to purchase. The consumer in Fig. 4 (top) may exhibit lower decisiveness or engage in 'hedonic browsing,' as mentioned by Moe (2003) [5], characterized by non-specific category browsing with no clear purchasing goal, resulting in lower conversion rates but not precluding impulsive purchases. Therefore, the consumer in Fig. 4 (bottom) is considered more likely to make a purchase. From this perspective, it is essential to evaluate not only individual session behavior but also the overall session behavior when assessing the likelihood of a consumer's purchase.

252   Y. Fukui and T. Tabata

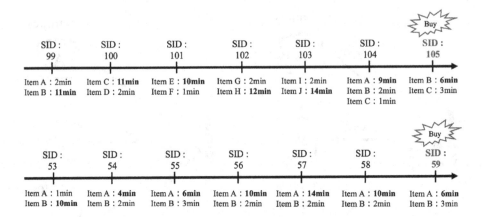

Fig. 4. Consumer purchasing behavior not captured by Vieira's model.(2)

Lastly, point 3 addresses the limitation of Vieira's model in not reflecting factors demonstrated by Weisberg et al. (2011) [6] to contribute to purchasing. Specifically, Weisberg et al. stated that past purchases positively influence future purchasing intentions, suggesting that a consumer's site visit history signifies their propensity to purchase. In contrast, Vieira's model, for instance, would only consider information from the day of purchase (e.g., February 4th) in predicting a consumer's purchase on that day, ignoring all prior interactions such as visits on January 4th, 21st, 28th, and February 1st (as shown in Fig. 5).

However, it is anticipated that consumers repeatedly visit a site for product comparison before making a purchase, and those who have previously made purchases on a site, especially if incentivized by loyalty points, are likely to return for subsequent purchases. An example could be busy professionals who browse products during their commute and engage in more thorough evaluations on their days off before making a purchase.

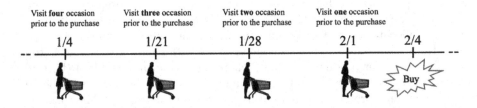

Fig. 5. Consumer purchasing behavior not captured by Vieira's model.(3)

3   Proposed Model

In this study, we address the limitations outlined in Sect. 2.2 by creating new variables that capture consumer purchasing behaviors previously unaccounted for in the existing models. Subsequently, we will compare the accuracy of a model incorporating these new variables with Vieira's model. This comparison aims to evaluate the utility of the newly created variables in enhancing the model's ability to predict consumer purchasing behaviors.

3.1   The Variety of During Session

Firstly, to address the limitation of Vieira's model regarding the breadth of viewing time consumers allocate to each product, this study introduces the concept of "diversity," as discussed in Niimi and Hoshino's research (2017) [7]. "Variety" is defined as a quantified variable representing the diversity of a consumer's actions, serving as an indicator of the breadth of product categories viewed by the consumer and their dependency on specific product categories. In their research, Niimi and Hoshino employed the Herfindahl-Hirschman Index (HHI), an economic indicator that quantifies the degree of market concentration. This index, ranging from 0 to 1, is expressed by the following Eq. (3), where s_i denotes the proportion of each of the n_k product categories purchased by a customer k in relation to their total purchases, with values closer to 1 indicating a concentration on specific product categories.

$$HHI_k = \sum_{i=1}^{n_k} s_i^2 \qquad (3)$$

While Niimi et al. used this indicator to represent the "diversity" of consumer actions within a certain period to predict future purchase frequencies, this study adapts it to predict consumer purchases during a session, thus creating a new variable named "Variety of Session."

Specifically, by creating a variable representing the"variation in viewing time across each product category viewed during a session," this study aims to model consumer purchasing behavior as illustrated in Fig. 3. The consumer in Fig. 3, left, who evenly distributes viewing time across product categories A, B, and C, is presumed to be indecisive, thus less likely to make a purchase during that session. Conversely, the consumer in Fig. 3, right, who focuses predominantly on category A, is considered more likely to proceed to purchase. To represent such consumer purchasing behaviors, this study defines the following Eq. (4) based on Niimi et al.'s HHI as "SHHI (Session-HHI)," where n_{kj} indicates the number of product categories viewed by consumer k during session j, and s_{ij} represents the proportion of viewing time for each product category i relative to the total viewing time in that session.

$$SHHI_{kj} = \sum_{i=1}^{n_{kj}} s_{ij}^2 \qquad (4)$$

Equation (4) assigns a lower value to purchasing behaviors with less variation in viewing time, as in Fig. 3, left, and a higher value to behaviors with greater variation, as in Fig. 3, right. If a consumer views only one product during a session, the SHHI becomes 1.

3.2   The Variety of Past Browsing

Next, to address the second limitation of Vieira's model regarding the distribution of viewing time consumers allocate to each product over the entire session, we directly employ the Herfindahl-Hirschman Index (HHI) used by Niimi and Hoshino in Sect. 3.1 to represent "Variety." However, since the meanings of the symbols are altered, in this study, the following Eq. (5) is defined as CHHI (Cumulative HHI). This variable functions as a measure of consumer attributes, where n_k represents the number of product categories viewed or purchased by consumer k, and s_i indicates the proportion of viewing time for each product category relative to the total viewing time of that consumer.

$$CHHI_k = \sum_{i=1}^{n_k} s_i^2 \qquad (5)$$

Equation (4) assigns higher values to consumers like those in Fig. 4 (top), who view a wide variety of products over the entire session, and lower values to the opposite scenario as in Fig. 4 (bottom). By examining Eqs. (4) and (5) concurrently, it is possible to grasp consumer purchasing behavior from two perspectives: the diversity of momentary consumer actions (session diversity in Eq. (4)) and the cumulative diversity of consumer actions over the entire session (overall session diversity in Eq. (5)).

3.3   Site Visit Experience

Lastly, to address the third limitation of Vieira's model, which concerns the consumers' site visit experience, this study represents it with two variables: "average number of visits before purchase" and "cumulative number of purchases." The first variable, "average number of visits before purchase," indicates how many site visits on average lead to a purchase. For example, as shown in Fig. 6, if the first purchase is preceded by two site visits, the value for that interval is 2, and if the second purchase follows seven cumulative site visits, the value is 3.5. The second variable, "cumulative number of purchases," represents the number of purchases a consumer has made up to a specific site visit. This approach, inspired by Weisberg et al., is exemplified in Fig. 6. Vieira's model captures past consumer purchasing behavior with variables such as past 24-hour and previous week activities, these variables are not updated as consumers accumulate experiences, marking a key distinction from our study's approach.

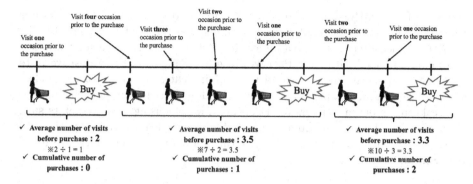

Fig. 6. An example of consumer purchasing behavior as indicated by the variables created in this study.

4   Validation

4.1   Details of Data and Method

In this section, we detail the data used for this study, its preprocessing, the variables employed, and the specifics of the model utilized.

The data utilized in this research originates from EC site A, specializing in luxury goods, covering the period from July 1, 2010, to June 28, 2011. The data is organized by session ID. As part of preprocessing, we removed all data where the browsing time per session was less than one second. This step was taken to exclude site visits due to erroneous clicks or pages opened merely as waypoints to navigate to specific pages. Consequently, the sample size was reduced to 44,299 sessions, including 2,296 purchasing sessions and 42,003 non-purchasing sessions. To address the issue of data imbalance, we employed SMOTENC (Synthetic Minority Over-sampling Technique for Nominal and Continuous) as detailed by Chawla [8], resulting in an adjusted sample size of 84,006.

The dependent variable is set as binary, where a session resulting in a purchase is denoted as 1, and a non-purchase session as 0. The independent variables include those replicated from Vieira's model, as mentioned in Sect. 2.1, and the new variables introduced in Sects. 3.1, 3.2, and 3.3. One of Vieira's variables, "(4) Desc," was replaced with Item_Genre due to the unavailability of product descriptions in the dataset. This variable, which assigns a 1 to products viewed during a session and a 0 otherwise, can adequately represent the type of products a consumer views, thus serving as a suitable substitute for "(4) Desc."

For data input into the model, we used sklearn.model_selection.train_test_split to shuffle the data before splitting it into training and test sets at a 7:3 ratio. Following Vieira's approach, we employed Deep Learning for the model and used Precision, Recall, F-Measure, Accuracy, and AUC (Area under the curve) for comparing prediction accuracy. Hyperparameter tuning was conducted using Random Search [9]. To ensure the reproducibility of the model results, we fixed the seeds for NumPy, TensorFlow, and Python, and set TensorFlow operations to be deterministic using enable_op_determinism() (TensorFlow version 2.13.0).

AUC is measured as the area under the ROC (Receiver operating characteristic) curve, plotted with True Positive Rate (TPR) against False Positive Rate (FPR) at various thresholds. An AUC of 0.5 indicates a random (useless) classifier, while 1 signifies a perfect classifier. Random Search is an efficient method for exploring hyperparameters for Deep Learning, focusing on parameters such as the number of layers and nodes in the hidden layers, learning rate, epochs, and batch size, aiming to maximize AUC. Other model-related elements are listed below in bullet points:

- Activation function: Relu (hidden layers)
- Activation function: Sigmoid (output layer)
- Loss function: Binary cross entropy
- Gradient descent method: Adam
- Network optimization: Batch Normalization

This study builds upon Vieira's model by incorporating the diversity variables (SHHI and CHHI) discussed in Sects. 3.1 and 3.2, and the variables for average number of visits before purchase (Avg_session) and cumulative number of purchases (Total_buy) mentioned in Sect. 3.3. The structure of the models subjected to accuracy verification is summarized in Fig. 7.

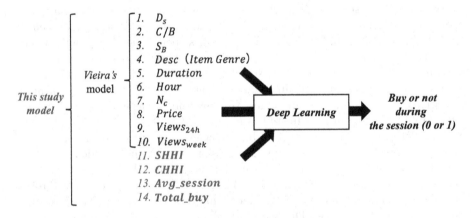

Fig. 7. Structure of the three models subject to accuracy validation

4.2   Result

The results of each model's AUC and ROC curves are presented in Fig. 8. Additionally, other performance metrics such as Precision, Recall, F-Measure, and Accuracy for each model are displayed in Table 1. The Confusion matrices are

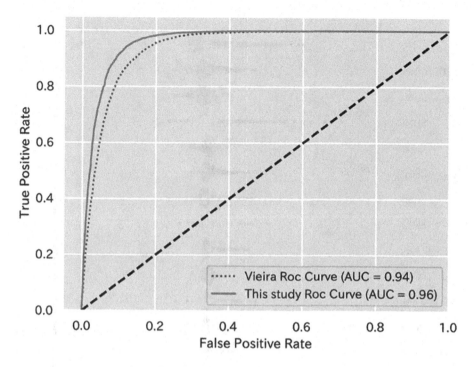

Fig. 8. AUC and ROC curves of the model

shown in Table 2 and Table 3, considering a predicted value of 1 for purchase probabilities greater than 0.5. The results indicate that while there was no significant difference in AUC, improvements in Precision, F-measure, and Accuracy over Vieira's model were observed. This confirms the utility of the model developed in this study over the traditional model.

To quantify the contribution and importance of each feature used in the model in influencing the dependent variable, we applied SHAP (SHapley Additive exPlanations) values, an approach that adapts the concept of Shapley values from game theory to machine learning, as detailed by Lundberg [10]. The results of this application are shown in Fig. 9. It should be noted that the feature of product genre (Item_Genre), due to its site-specific nature and high dimensionality, was excluded when assessing feature importance. Furthermore, in interpreting Fig. 9, white indicates larger values of the feature itself, while black denotes smaller values. The SHAP value (impact on model output) on the horizontal axis shows that features extending in the positive direction have a strong influence on purchase, whereas those extending in the negative direction have a strong influence on non-purchase.

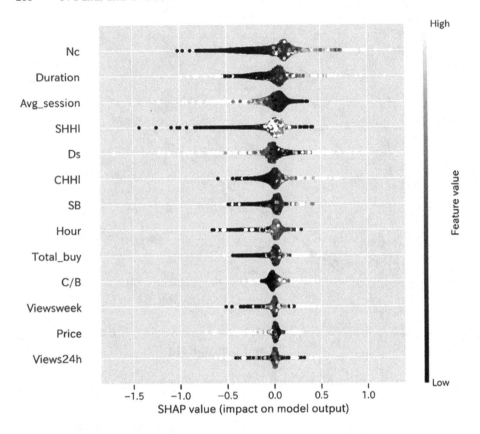

Fig. 9. Calculation of feature importance by SHAP

5   Discussions

Initially, the improvement in accuracy of the model developed in this study, which incorporated three new variables, confirmed that these variables significantly influence whether a consumer makes a purchase during a session. This finding indicates that on the site targeted in this study, there are a significant number of consumers who either browse a wide range of products evenly or spend considerable time viewing specific products, as well as those who frequently visit the site to view products and make purchases after careful consideration. The higher Precision in comparison to the traditional model suggests that our model was more effective in reducing false positives, i.e., sessions predicted to result in purchases that did not actually do so. This improvement implies that using our model could lead to a reduction in misdirected marketing efforts towards consumers less likely to make a purchase.

The SHAP results indicate that "average number of visits before purchase (Avg_session)" extending negatively in white implies that consumers are less likely to make a purchase with an increasing number of non-purchasing

Table 1. Precision, Recall, F-Measure, Accuracy for each model.

	Vieira	This study
Precision	0.84	0.9
Recall	0.94	0.95
F-Measure	0.89	0.92
Accuracy	0.88	0.92

Table 2. Confusion matrix for Vieira model

Vieira [4]		Predicted	
		Negative	Positive
Actual	Negative	10,150	2,273
	Positive	698	11,724

Table 3. Confusion matrix for This study model

Vieira [4]		Predicted	
		Negative	Positive
Actual	Negative	11,119	1,304
	Positive	654	11,768

visits. This could be because consumers find more attractive products on other sites during their consideration phase. Furthermore, "session diversity (SHHI)" extending negatively in black suggests that consumers who browse a wide range of products evenly are less likely to purchase, possibly due to indecision. Conversely, "overall session diversity (CHHI)" extending negatively in black and positively in white indicates that consumers spending time browsing a wide range of products over the entire session are less likely to purchase, whereas those focusing on specific products are more inclined to buy. These insights suggest that marketing strategies, such as distributing coupons, should prioritize consumers who focus on specific products during their sessions and have a comparatively lower number of visits.

6   Conclusion and Future Challenges

In this study, we addressed the issue that traditional models in existing research do not adequately reflect the influence of consumer purchasing behavior diversity and past site visit experience on purchasing decisions during a session. To address this, we proposed representing behavioral diversity with "variation in viewing time for each product category during a session (SHHI)" and "variation in viewing time across all products over the entire session (CHHI)." We captured past experience through "average number of visits before purchase" and "cumulative number of purchases." These variables were incorporated into a model, and its accuracy was compared with models that did not include these variables to validate our approach.

The results led to the construction of a model with higher accuracy than traditional models, confirming that the variables developed in this study are relevant factors in consumer purchasing decisions. Furthermore, the findings highlighted the existence of consumers who either browse a wide range of products or focus intensively on a single product, as well as those who repeatedly view products on the site before making a considered purchase. Particularly, the SHAP results for SHHI and CHHI aligned with real-world factors influencing consumer purchasing behavior and purchases on the site. The use of our model could reduce the misallocation of marketing efforts towards consumers with low purchasing intent and assist in decision-making regarding which consumers to prioritize for marketing strategies.

A future challenge identified is to develop a model capable of predicting consumer purchases during a session that captures consumer purchasing behaviors not considered at the time of writing this paper. Specifically, the path that consumers take within the site is thought to influence purchasing decisions, and so this aspect of consumer site navigation should be considered. Additionally, even though past experiences are significant, more recent experiences are believed to have a greater impact on purchases. Therefore, we plan to assign weights to each site visit and the volume of activity at each point in time.

Disclosure of Interests. The authors have no competing interests.

References

1. McFadden, D.: Conditional logit analysis of qualitative choice behavior. In: Zerembka, P. (ed.) Front. Econ. Academic Press, New York (1973)
2. Jansen, B.J., Spink, A., Blakely, C. Koshman, S.: Defining a session on Web search engines, J. Am. Soc. Inform. Sci. Technol. (2007). https://doi.org/10.1002/asi.20564
3. Wu, C., Yan, M., Si, L.: Session-aware Information Embedding for E-commerce Product Recommendation. In: Proceedings of the ACM on Conference on Information and Knowledge Management, pp. 2379–2382 (2017). https://doi.org/10.1145/3132847.3133163
4. Vieira, A.: Predicting online user behaviour using deep learning algorithms (2016). arXiv:1511.06247v3, https://doi.org/10.48550/arXiv.1511.06247
5. Wendy, W.M.: Buying, searching, or browsing: differentiating between online shoppers using in-store navigational clickstream. J. Consum. Psychol. **13**(1–2), 29–39 (2003). https://doi.org/10.1207/s15327663jcp13-12_03

6. Weisberg, J., Te'eni, D., Arman, L.: Past purchase and intention to purchase in e-commerce: the mediation of social presence and trust. Internet Res. **21**(1), 82–96 (2011). https://doi.org/10.1108/10662241111104893

7. Junichiro, N., Takahiro, H.: Predicting purchases with using the variety of customer behaviors: analysis of purchase history and the browsing history by deep learning. Jpn. Soc. Artif. Intell. **32**(2), B-G63_1-9 (2017). https://doi.org/10.1527/tjsai.B-G63

8. Chawla, N.V., Bowyer, K.W., Hall, L.O., Kegelmeyer, W.P.: SMOTE: synthetic minority over-sampling technique. J. Artif. Intell. Res. **16**, 321–357 (2002). https://doi.org/10.1613/jair.953

9. Bergstra, J., Bengio, Y.: Random search for hyper-parameter optimization. J. Mach. Learn. Res. **13**, 281–305 (2012). https://doi.org/10.5555/2503308.2188395

10. Lundberg, S.M., Lee, Su-In.: A unified approach to interpreting model predictions. In: Proceedings of the 31st International Conference on Neural Information Processing SystemsDecember, pp. 4768–4777 (2017). https://doi.org/10.48550/arXiv.1705.07874

Agile Assessment of Information Consumer Experience: A Case Analysis

María Paz Godoy[1]([⊠]) [iD], Cristian Rusu[2] [iD], Isidora Azócar[1], and Noor Yaser[1]

[1] Carrera de Información y Control de Gestión, Facultad de Ciencias Económicas y Administrativas, Universidad de Valparaíso, Valparaíso, Chile
`mariapaz.godoy@uv.cl`

[2] Escuela de Ingeniería en Informática, Pontificia Universidad Católica de Valparaíso, 2340000 Valparaíso, Chile
`cristian.rusu@pucv.cl`

Abstract. In the context of a private organization, this study focuses on the implementation of an agile methodology for assessing Information Consumer Experience (ICX). The objective of this research is to diagnose and apply a simplified version of the methodology within the organizational setting. The proposed agile methodology offers a rapid approach to evaluate ICX in smaller organizations or departments within the organization, intending to enhance it through the generation of recommendations based on information consumer perceptions. This approach centers on Customer Experience (CX). The methodology is divided into three sequential stages: Characterization, Experimentation, and Analysis. In the Characterization stage, information consumers, providers, and the products, systems, or services delivering information are identified. The Experimentation stage focuses on data collection, employing various information collection instruments, as well as both qualitative and quantitative approaches to gather insights into consumer expectations and perceptions. The third stage, Analysis, involves the processing and analysis of the collected data, using both quantitative and qualitative methods to integrate the findings. This study introduces an innovative methodology for evaluating and enhancing the Information Consumer Experience in any organization that manages data and information. The results obtained in this research provide guidance for improving ICX within the organization under study and serve as a resource for future research in the fields of information management and customer experience.

Keywords: Information Consumer Experience (ICX) · Agile Methodology · Information Management · Customer Experience (CX)

1 Introduction

The landscape of business competition has undergone a significant transformation in recent decades, compelling companies to continually devise innovative strategies for acquiring and retaining customers [14]. This evolution has paved the way for an in-depth exploration of Consumer Experience (CX) by scholars in recent years. CX is a multifaceted concept encapsulating the expectations, satisfactions, and challenges encountered by customers during their interactions with a brand or company, encompassing the acquisition of products and services [16]. Enhancing CX represents a mutually beneficial endeavor, where companies can bolster their profits through heightened customer engagement, while customers receive improved experiences and product/service quality, fostering a virtuous cycle. Achieving this symbiosis necessitates a meticulous focus on refining each interaction point, commonly referred to as touchpoints, throughout the customer journey. Proficiency in CX management can thereby differentiate companies from their competitors, positioning them advantageously [14].

Similarly, analogous to customers engaging with a brand or company, employees interfacing with organizational data interact with a spectrum of information products, systems, or services provided by a company or organization. Organizations typically house one or more information administration departments facilitating access to these information products, systems, and services for employees across various departments. Within organizations, employees from diverse departments such as executive management [4], people management [3,13], data analytics [5–7], finance, operations, among others, rely on information products, systems, and services for their daily tasks and decision-making processes. Generally, these information assets are administered by informatics or analytics departments. The consumption of information by employees within an organization encompasses various elements, such as reporting systems, data management systems, data analytics tools, data extraction tools, data visualization services, and communication services, among others. Each of these information products, systems, and services represents an interaction point between information consumers and the organization. In this sense, employee experience [19], information systems success [20] and user experience [1,2,8,12,17] related topics have been explored in the literature.

In this context, employees can be viewed as customers or information consumers provided by the organization through its information administration departments. Consequently, the concept of Information Consumer eXperience (ICX) emerges, encompassing the expectations, satisfactions, and challenges encountered by information consumers within the organization. ICX can be examined as an analysis of the interaction between employees or departments (in the role of information consumers) and the organization or information providers departments (fulfilling the role of a company), mediated by information products, systems, and services offered.

In order to asses information consumer analysis with an integral manner, including customer experience, user experience and information system success approaches, an agile adaptation for ICX evaluation is presented in this study based on the full version of the ICX evaluation methodology proposed in previous work [10]. The main goal of this study, is to describe our simplified methodology for ICX evaluation, focused in small and medium companies that doesn't have the time or resources available to perform a full evaluation of ICX. Despite this proposal has a small amount of analysis instruments, it focus on crucial evaluation stages of the full version ensuring a comprehensive evaluation of ICX into a company and the interaction between information consumers and the products, systems, and services they utilize in their organization.

The rest of this work is structured as follows: Sect. 2 present key concepts necessary to understand how the proposed ICX evaluation methodology works. In Sect. 3, the structure of the methodology and the instructions for every stage are described. Section 4 shows the results of the application of our proposed methodology into an engineer service company. Finally, conclusions and future works are discussed in Sect. 5.

2 Background

This section elucidates the foundational concepts subsequently employed in the proposed Methodology for Evaluating Information Consumer Experience (ICX). These concepts are intricately linked to various stages of the methodology.

In this section, we present a series of foundational concepts subsequently employed in the proposed Methodology for Evaluating Information Consumer Experience (ICX). These concepts are intricately linked to the various stages of the methodology.

2.1 Customer Experience (CX)

Despite the prevalence of the Customer Experience (CX) approach in the literature, a standardized definition is yet to emerge. CX pertains to the customer's perception, stemming from interactions with a brand's products, systems, and services [15]. This perception is delineated into six dimensions [9]: Emotional, Sensory, Cognitive, Pragmatic, Lifestyle, and Relational. These interactions, termed Touchpoints, describe the customer's journey based on interactions before, during, and after the consumption of a product or service. In this work, we define the concept of Information Consumer Experience (ICX) as an extension of CX, wherein information consumers differ from customers based on the scope of products or services with which they can interact. Information consumers solely engage with information products, systems, or services, while customers can interact with a broad range of products, systems, and services.

2.2 Information Consumer Experience (ICX)

Information Consumer Experience (ICX) explores interactions wherein, in an organizational context, workers consuming information provided by the organization engage with various information products, systems, and services [11]. These interactions encompass activities such as information utilization in specific tasks (reports, decision-making, among others), data generation, information exchange between departments, team collaboration, and decision-making.

This diverse array of interactions thus represents touchpoints between workers and all information products, systems, and services provided by the organization. Consequently, ICX can be regarded as an extension of CX applied to a specific organizational context, wherein CX evaluation instruments and methods can be adapted to the distinctive context of ICX.

2.3 Information Management

Information management strategically enhances organizational effectiveness by fortifying adaptive capacity in the face of dynamic or stable internal and external demands. This comprehensive discipline involves formulating organization-wide information policies, establishing interconnected systems, maintaining services, refining information circulation processes for timeliness and relevance, and deploying advanced technologies to meet diverse end-user needs [18]. The dual dimensions of information management [18] encompass the management of the information process and data resources. The former involves activities related to information creation, dissemination, and utilization, incorporating policies, workflows, and technologies for efficient information flow. The latter focuses on data storage, organization, quality assurance, and security, encompassing databases, repositories, and governance practices to ensure reliability and regulatory compliance. These dimensions, interrelated yet distinct, are vital for effective information management, contributing to organizational goal attainment and adaptability to evolving environments.

3 Agile ICX Evaluation Methodology

As a proposal, we introduce a methodology to formalize the process of Information Consumer Experience (ICX) assessment within the organizational context. This methodology represents an agile adaptation of the ICX evaluation methodology outlined in prior works [10]. To address ICX assessment comprehensively, we delineate three sequential stages, each comprised of sub-sequential phases interlinked with various evaluation process stages. The entirety of evaluation tasks encompassed in each stage is delineated in Fig. 3.

3.1 Characterization Stage

The aim of the Characterization Stage is an exploratory diagnosis of the organization, its information consumers, and providers. It is divided into three sub-stages. The first sub-stage, "Planning," involves tasks to select information from four fundamental elements for subsequent stages: information-consuming departments, providers, participants, and information products. The second sub-stage, "Preliminary Data Collection," uses an instrument with a Likert scale survey and open-ended questions to gather preliminary information. The third sub-stage, "Exploration of Consumer Behavior," diagnoses consumer needs, profiles, and generates a preliminary customer journey map (Fig. 1).

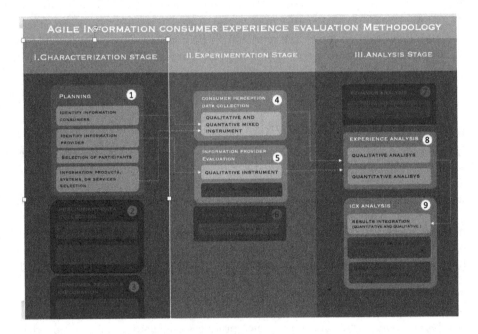

Fig. 1. Agile ICX evaluation methodology proposal

Sub-stage: Planning

- **Identify Consumers:** Identify information consumers within the organization.
- **Identify Information Providers:** Identify information-providing departments, levels, or individuals.
- **Select Participants:** Define and select information consumers and providers for planned experiments, ensuring diverse representation.
- **Selection of Information Products, Systems, or Services:** Select information products for comprehensive organizational analysis.

3.2   Experimentation Stage

The goal of the second stage, the Experimentation Stage, is to generate information through different data collection instruments applied in various experiments. This stage is divided into three sub-stages, aiming to address perceptions of information consumers, providers, data quality in the organization, and the perception of an expert panel. This stage begins with the sub-stage called "Perception Data Collection," intending to use a mixed qualitative and quantitative instrument to extract information about consumer expectations and perceptions. Subsequently, in the sub-stage named "Information Provider Evaluation," a qualitative instrument is applied to extract information from information providers, along with an assessment of the quality of data held by the organization. Finally, in the "Expert Evaluation" stage, a simulation of the processes that an information consumer would undertake when interacting with a system, product, or services in the organization is conducted.

Sub-stage: Perception Data Collection of the Consumer

- **Mixed Qualitative and Quantitative Instrument:** Building upon the two instruments applied in the "Preliminary Data Collection" sub-stage, an adaptation of ICX instruments from literature is explored. It aims to collect data on expectations and perceptions across different dimensions of information consumer measurement related to the "Exploration of Consumer Behavior" sub-stage.

Sub-stage: Information Provider Evaluation

- **Qualitative Instrument:** Regarding the identification of information providers, a qualitative instrument is proposed to gain a detailed understanding of the information extraction process and the perception of providers about it. This qualitative approach aims to delve into specific aspects related to information extraction, exploring the perspectives, experiences, and opinions of information providers regarding this process.

3.3 Analysis Stage

The purpose of the third phase, termed the "Analysis" phase, is to conduct a series of analyses regarding the behavior and perception of information consumers. Subsequently, a qualitative and quantitative analysis will be conducted based on instruments employed during the "Experimentation" phase. Finally, conclusions and recommendations for enhance ICX into the organization are given.

Sub-stage: Experience Analysis

- **Qualitative Analysis:** In this task, a qualitative analysis of data obtained through the mixed data collection instrument and the qualitative instrument applied to providers is conducted.
- **Quantitative Analysis:** In this task, a quantitative analysis of data collected from the mixed data collection instrument applied during the "Perception Data Collection" sub-stage of the "Experimentation" phase will be conducted.

This Agile ICX Evaluation Methodology aims to provide a structured approach to comprehensively assess and enhance the Information Consumer Experience within an organization. The proposed stages and sub-stages offer a systematic framework for conducting evaluations, extracting valuable insights, and formulating targeted improvements to elevate the overall information consumption experience. The utilization of mixed qualitative and quantitative instruments enhances the depth and breadth of the evaluation, ensuring a holistic understanding of the intricate dynamics of information consumption within the organization. Moreover, our methodology provides flexibility in terms of data collection and analysis instruments, which can be modified or replaced by instruments that best suit the needs of each organization. For instance, in the current case study, the instruments employed were constructed based on an adaptation of previous works [11].

4   Experimental Results

The proposed methodology was implemented in the data analytics department of an engineering services company. This department comprises 24 analysts fulfilling various roles and positions, addressing specific information needs from other departments. Serving as information providers, the data analytics department collaborates with the IT department, responsible for managing databases, tools, and information services utilized by the analysts in their tasks. Specifically, this case study considered an information repository system and the company's proprietary ERP system. With this delineation, the first stage of the methodology is satisfied, identifying participants as members of the data analytics department. The IT department serves as the information provider, and the information services under analysis encompass an information repository system and an ERP system.

4.1   Information Consumer Data Collection

To gather information regarding the perception of information consumers participating in the experiment, a mixed Qualitative and quantitative instrument was employed. This instrument consists of a two-stage survey. The first stage comprises questions with quantitative responses on a 5-level Likert scale. The second stage involves open-ended questions aimed at eliciting more in-depth insights into aspects previously addressed in the initial section. Both instruments have a set of questions distributed into 4 sections, which are presented in Tables 1 and 2 respectively.

The first section of the quantitative instrument aimed to collect general information and work experience. In a second section, consumers are asked for their perception of their work environment and information data usage. The third section aims to meet consumer's experience working with information in an organizational scope. Finally, in the fourth section, consumers are consulted for their perception and evaluation about the information products, systems and services they used in the organization. The quantitative instrument's structure is presented in Table 1

The qualitative instrument follows the same structure that the quantitative instrument. The first section includes general information and work experience

Table 1. Quantitative section of the data collection instrument

No.	Section	Question	Type
QS01	General Data	How old are you?	Optional by Age Range
QS02	General Data	What is your academic degree?	Optional Category
QS04	General Data	How many years of work experience do you have?	Optional Range
QS05	General Data	How many years have you been in the organization?	Optional Range
QS06	General Data	How would you evaluate your work experience in the organization?	Likert scale 5 levels
QS07	General Data	How would you evaluate the labor efficiency in your department?	Likert scale 5 levels
QS08	Individual Usage	What is the importance of the data in your daily tasks?	Likert scale 5 levels
QS09	Individual Usage	What kind of data do you use most often?	Optional Category
QS10	Individual Usage	What are you based on to make decisions in your work?	Optional: in experience, in data, or both
QS11	Individual Usage	Do you collect your own data collections?	Likert scale 3 levels
QS12	Organizational Usage	Does the company provide all the necessary data to fulfill its daily tasks?	Likert scale 3 levels
QS13	Organizational Usage	What external data manipulation tools do you use?	Optional Category
QS14	Organizational Usage	Do you have access to sensitive or confidential data?	Likert scale 3 levels
QS15	Organizational Usage	Do you use external tools to manipulate sensitive data?	Likert scale 3 levels
QS16	Organizational Usage	What is the scope of dissemination of sensitive data?	Optional Category
QS17	Organizational Usage	How would you evaluate the collaborative work with other departments of your organization?	Likert scale 5 levels
QS18	Products, systems and Services	Do you know the technological tools and information systems offered by the organization for work?	Likert scale 3 levels
QS19	Products, systems and Services	Do you use organizational information systems?	Likert scale 5 levels
QS20	Products, systems and Services	How do you perceive the role of information systems in your company?	Likert scale 5 levels
QS21	Products, systems and Services	How would you evaluate the services offered by the information systems available to you in your organization?	Likert scale 5 levels
QS22	Products, systems and Services	How would you evaluate the integration of institutional information systems?	Likert scale 5 levels

questions. In the second stage, consumers are asked for individual data usage. The third stage aims to meet consumer's experience working with information in an organizational scope. Finally, in the fourth stage, consumers are consulted for their perception and evaluation about the information products, systems and services they used in the organization. The quantitative instrument's structure is presented in Table 1

Table 2. Qualitative section of the data collection instrument

No.	Section	Question
IS01	General Data	What is your position? What are your main functions in the organization?
IS02	General Data	What is your career or area of profession?
IS03	General Data	What has been your professional experience inside or outside your organization?
IS04	Individual Usage	What is your perception or opinion about the efficiency of your organization's work? How would you rate it?
IS05	Individual Usage	Do you think that data to support decision-making should be provided by the organization? or should they be compiled by the professionals themselves?
IS06	Individual Usage	What is the basis for making decisions in your work? In experience, intuition, data, or a mixture of the above?
IS07	Individual Usage	How important is data in your daily work?
IS08	Individual Usage	In your experience, what types of data do you use the most, quantitative data or qualitative data? Why is that?
IS09	Individual Usage	In your organization or in your daily work, is sensitive or confidential data handled? Why are they considered sensitive or confidential?
IS10	Organizational Usage	What protocols or practices are considered when working on this type of data?
IS11	Organizational Usage	Do you share data or information with the other units or areas of your organization? How is collaborative work in this sense?
IS12	Organizational Usage	In your opinion, what would be the ideal way for an organization to work with its data and information systems?
IS13	Products, systems and Services	Do you use tools or systems not provided by your organization for your daily tasks? (Example: Reports, etc.)
IS14	Products, systems and Services	How do you perceive the role of the repository and ERP systems in your organization?
IS15	Products, systems and Services	In your opinion, how would you evaluate the repository and ERP systems provided in your organization?
IS16	Products, systems and Services	In your experience, do the information systems provided by your organization need improvement? What are the functionalities or features that you like or dislike the most?

The obtained responses from both instruments facilitated the acquisition of valuable insights pertaining to the utilization of information within the organizational framework. Additionally, it provided an in-depth understanding of the information consumers' perceptions regarding various systems, products, and information systems. The subsequent analysis, detailed in Sect. 4.3, further elaborates on this information. Simultaneously, as part of the sample characterization representing information consumers from the data analytics department involved

in the data collection process, Fig. 2 illustrates general participant demographics. This includes information on academic background, age distribution, and
work experience, both within and outside the organization.

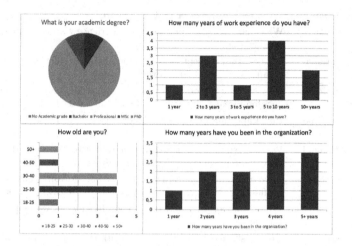

Fig. 2. Information Consumers Characterization

In general, information consumers within the data analytics department
exhibit characteristics of young adult professionals with a college background,
falling within the age range of 25 to 40 years. Their collective professional experience ranges from 2 to 10 years, with a predominant majority possessing 3 or
more years of tenure specifically within the organization.

4.2 Data Provider Evaluation

Table 3 delineates the qualitative data collection instrument designed for the
evaluation of data providers within the organizational context. The table comprises various sections, each encapsulating pertinent questions aimed at comprehensively gauging the perspectives and experiences of the participants.

The "General Data" section (IS01 to IS03) seeks information about participants' positions, main functions in the organization, career or professional areas,
and their cumulative professional experiences within or outside the organization.

Transitioning to the "Organizational Work" section (IS04 to IS08), participants express opinions on the efficiency of their organization's work, the necessity
of organizational data provision for decision-making, the perceived importance
of information within the organization, and expectations regarding the role and
function of a data provider department. Additionally, participants share insights
into the handling of sensitive or confidential data and the associated protocols.

The "Information Usage" section (IS09 to IS12) delves into the practices
and protocols considered when working with sensitive data, collaborative data

Table 3. Qualitative data collection instrument for data provider evaluation

No.	Section	Question
IS01	General Data	What is your position? What are your main functions in the organization?
IS02	General Data	What is your career or professional area?
IS03	General Data	What has been your professional experience within or outside your organization?
IS04	Organizational work	What is your perception or opinion about the efficiency of your organization's work? How would you rate it?
IS05	Organizational work	Do you think the organization should provide data to support decision-making, or should professionals collect it themselves?
IS06	Organizational work	How important do you think information is in the organization?
IS07	Organizational work	What do you believe should be the role or function of a data provider department within an organization?
IS08	Organizational work	In your organization or in your daily work, do you handle sensitive or confidential data? Why are they considered sensitive or confidential?
IS09	Information Usage	What protocols or practices are considered when working with this type of data?
IS10	Information Usage	Do you share data or information with other units or areas of your organization? How is collaborative work in this regard?
IS11	Information Usage	In your opinion, what would be the ideal way for an organization to work with its data and information systems?
IS12	Information Usage	Is there business expertise in the organization's team providing information? Are there specialized systems for the business?
IS13	Products, Systems, and Services	Do you think the information systems provided by the organization are used for daily work?
IS14	Products, Systems, and Services	In your experience, does the information found in the organization's information systems follow data quality standards? For example, clean, opportunity, real-time information, etc.
IS15	Products, Systems, and Services	What is your opinion on the use of systems, products, or services that are not provided by your department in daily tasks? (Example: reports, etc.)
IS16	Products, Systems, and Services	In your experience, do the information systems, products, or services provided by your department have shortcomings or areas for improvement to meet the needs of their users? What is your perspective on this assessment?

sharing practices, ideal approaches for an organization to work with its data and information systems, and the presence of business expertise and specialized systems within the information-providing team.

Concluding with the "Products, Systems, and Services" section (IS13 to IS16), participants offer perspectives on the daily utilization of information systems, the adherence of information systems to data quality standards, opinions on non-departmental systems, and insights into potential shortcomings or areas for improvement in the information systems, products, or services provided by their department.

The responses gathered from the data provider team, exemplifying the IT department, underscore their unwavering commitment to maintaining elevated standards for data quality, software quality, and ensuring that the functionalities of information systems align precisely with the specific needs of the data analytics department. One response highlighted, "In our experience, the information systems, products, or services provided by our department follow data quality standards, such as clean, timely, and real-time information." This assertion exemplifies the IT department's dedication to delivering information that is not only accurate but also timely and aligned with the real-time demands of the data analytics workflow.

Despite the commendable success of the IT department in meeting these stringent standards, a noteworthy observation emerges from the responses - the apparent underutilization of certain functions within the information systems by information consumers. A respondent stated, "The information systems provided by the organization are used for daily work, but there might be functionalities that are not fully explored." This acknowledgment points to a potential gap in awareness or understanding among information consumers regarding the full spectrum of functionalities available to them. It suggests a disconnect between the capabilities offered by the IT department and the comprehensive utilization of these capabilities in the daily tasks of information consumers.

This discrepancy prompts the need for a thorough analysis, considering factors such as user behavior and potential barriers to the optimal use of information systems. A response mentioning, "There might be a lack of awareness or training among information consumers regarding the full functionality of the systems," highlights the significance of addressing potential knowledge gaps. This implies that efforts should be directed not only towards technical excellence but also towards cultivating a user-centric approach. Collaborative initiatives and targeted training, as suggested by another response, could serve to bridge the gap and enhance the effective utilization of information system functionalities for organizational benefit.

4.3   Experience Analysis

The responses of the information consumers to the quantitative instrument offer response to the situation described by the data providers department. In the "Individual Usage" section, the responses for the importance of data in daily tasks (QS08) reveal a majority attributing high importance to data, emphasizing its crucial role in their work. The data-driven decision-making approach (QS10) is prevalent among participants, indicating a reliance on both expertise and data, fostering a balanced decision-making culture within the organization. The responses to QS10 also indicate that while some information consumers rely on both expertise and data, there may be a lack of awareness or understanding of the full range of functionalities offered by the organizational systems. This suggests a potential knowledge gap or communication breakdown between the

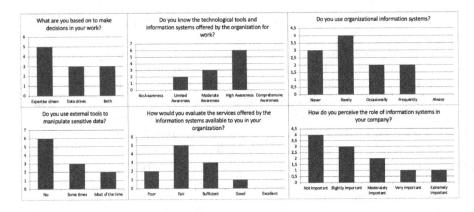

Fig. 3. Results of more

IT department and information consumers, limiting the optimal use of available tools.

Similarly, responses to QS15 reveal that a significant number of information consumers use external tools for manipulating sensitive data. This points towards a preference or reliance on tools not provided by the organization, signaling a potential gap in functionality or awareness of existing internal systems. There might be a need for improved communication to inform users about the capabilities of in-house tools.

Finally, in the "Products, Systems, and Services" section, the responses for awareness of technological tools (QS18) reveal a need for increased awareness, emphasizing the importance of effective communication and training programs. This lack of awareness could be a barrier preventing users from fully embracing and utilizing the available systems and services. Improved training programs or informational campaigns may be necessary to bridge this awareness gap.

In the "Organizational Usage" section, the responses for whether the company provides necessary data (QS12) show a positive trend, with a majority indicating partial or complete provision. However, the count for external tools usage (QS13) suggests a significant reliance on tools like data visualization and processing beyond the organization's offerings, indicating potential areas for improvement or integration of such functionalities within internal systems. While most respondents use organizational information systems (QS19), the evaluation of these services (QS21) suggests room for enhancement, emphasizing the importance of optimizing existing systems to meet user expectations.

Furthermore, the responses to QS19 and QS21 suggest that while information consumers use organizational information systems, their evaluations of these services indicate room for improvement. This misalignment could be attributed to a lack of awareness of the full range of functionalities or a mismatch between user expectations and the actual capabilities of the provided systems.

5   Conclusions

In this study, an agile version was introduced for the comprehensive version of the ICX evaluation methodology. This agile version was implemented in an engineering company, specifically within a data analytics department, with the IT department serving as the data provider. Findings derived from this case study underscore the importance of addressing awareness gaps, enhancing communication, and optimizing the usability of information systems to improve overall user satisfaction and effectiveness.

Firstly, it is evident from the responses that there exists a considerable lack of awareness among information consumers regarding the full range of functionalities offered by the organizational information systems. This necessitates targeted efforts to improve communication channels between the IT department and end-users, ensuring that comprehensive information about available tools and services reaches all relevant stakeholders.

The reliance on external tools, as indicated by responses to questions such as QS15, suggests that there may be acceptance barriers to the internal information systems. To address this, the organization should focus on showcasing the advantages and capabilities of in-house tools, coupled with user training programs to facilitate a smoother transition and encourage information consumers to utilize the provided systems more effectively.

Furthermore, the lukewarm evaluations of the services offered by information systems, as reflected in responses to questions QS19 and QS21, signal the need for enhancements. The organization should conduct user-centric design reviews to align system functionalities with user expectations, ultimately leading to an improved user experience. Regular feedback loops and iterative improvements will be crucial to ensuring that the systems evolve in tandem with user needs.

Additionally, the low awareness levels highlighted in question QS18 regarding technological tools emphasize the necessity for comprehensive training programs. These initiatives should not only focus on introducing users to available tools but also on imparting in-depth knowledge on how to leverage these tools for optimal productivity.

As future work, we expect to apply our agile methodology on other organizations or departments, and to subject the application of our agile methodology to evaluation by experts in the fields of Customer Experience and Information Success.

References

1. Alhendawi, K.M., Baharudin, A.S.: The impact of interaction quality factors on the effectiveness of web-based information system: the mediating role of user satisfaction. Cognition Technol. Work **16**(4), 451–465 (2013). https://doi.org/10.1007/s10111-013-0272-9
2. Ali, B.M., Younes, B., et al.: The impact of information systems on user performance: an exploratory study. J. Knowl. Manage. Econ. Inf. Technol. **3**(2), 128–154 (2013)

3. Cumberland, D.M., Alagaraja, M., Shuck, B., Kerrick, S.A.: Organizational social capital: ties between HRD, employee voice, and CEOs. Hum. Resour. Dev. Rev. **17**(2), 199–221 (2018). https://doi.org/10.1177/1534484318772488

4. Dixon, S.M., Searcy, C., Neumann, W.P.: Reporting within the corridor of conformance: managerial perspectives on work environment disclosures in corporate social responsibility reporting. Sustainability **11**(14), 3825 (2019). https://doi.org/10.3390/su11143825

5. Domaszewicz, J., Parzych, D.: Intra-company crowdsensing: datafication with human-in-the-loop. Sensors **22**(3), 943 (2022). https://doi.org/10.3390/s22030943

6. Fischer, H., Engler, M., Sauer, S.: A human-centered perspective on software quality: acceptance criteria for work 4.0. In: Marcus, A., Wang, W. (eds.) DUXU 2017. LNCS, vol. 10288, pp. 570–583. Springer, Cham (2017). https://doi.org/10.1007/978-3-319-58634-2_42

7. Fréour, L., Pohl, S., Battistelli, A.: How digital technologies modify the work characteristics: a preliminary study. Span. J. Psychol. **24**, e14 (2021). https://doi.org/10.1017/sjp.2021.12

8. Ganeshan, M.K., Vethirajan, C.: Electronic human resource management practices and employees perception towards information technology industry. Int. J. Sci. Technol. Res. **9**, 86–90 (2020)

9. Gentile, C., Spiller, N., Noci, G.: How to sustain the customer experience: an overview of experience components that co-create value with the customer. Eur. Manag. J. **25**(5), 395–410 (2007)

10. Godoy, M., Rusu, C., Ugalde, J.: A preliminary methodology for information consumer experience evaluation. In: Coman, A., Vasilache, S. (eds.) Social Computing and Social Media: 15th International Conference, SCSM 2023, Held as Part of the 25th HCI International Conference, HCII 2023, Copenhagen, Denmark, July 23-28, 2023, Proceedings, Part I, pp. 506-519. Springer-Verlag, Berlin, Heidelberg (2023). https://doi.org/10.1007/978-3-031-35915-6_36

11. Godoy, M.P., Rusu, C., Ugalde, J.: Information consumer experience: a chilean case study. In: Meiselwitz, G. (ed.) International Conference on Human-Computer Interaction, pp. 248–267. Springer, Cham (2022). https://doi.org/10.1007/978-3-031-05064-0_19

12. Gunadham, T., Thammakoranonta, N.: Knowledge management systems functionalities enhancement in practice. In: Proceedings of the 5th International Conference on Frontiers of Educational Technologies - ICFET 2019. ACM Press (2019). https://doi.org/10.1145/3338188.3338213

13. Hou, A.C., Chen, Y.C., Shang, R.A.: Mutual relations in ERP implementation: the impacts of work alienation and organizational support in state-owned enterprise. Procedia Comput. Sci. **100**, 1289–1296 (2016). https://doi.org/10.1016/j.procs.2016.09.244

14. Keiningham, T., et al.: Customer experience driven business model innovation. J. Bus. Res. **116**, 431–440 (2020)

15. Lemon, K.N., Verhoef, P.C.: Understanding customer experience throughout the customer journey. J. Mark. **80**(6), 69–96 (2016)

16. Meyer, C., Schwager, A., et al.: Understanding customer experience. Harv. Bus. Rev. **85**(2), 116 (2007)

17. Morales, J., Rusu, C., Botella, F., Quiñones, D.: Programmer experience: a systematic literature review. IEEE Access **7**, 71079–71094 (2019)

18. Mugejjera, E., Nakakawa, A.: Elements of an information management framework: findings from existing literature. Int. J. Innov. Digit. Econ. **14**(1), 1–8 (2023)

19. Vasilieva, E., Tochilkina, T.: Design thinking and process transformation: Synergy of these approaches. In: CEUR Workshop Proceedings (2020)
20. Watungwa, T., Pather, S.: Identification of user satisfaction dimensions for the evaluation of university administration information systems. In: ICICKM 2018 15th International Conference on Intellectual Capital Knowledge Management & Organisational Learning, p. 346. Academic Conferences and Publishing Limited (2018)

Identifying Topics in the Community Related to Women's Fashion Magazines Using the Topic Model

Emi Iwanade[1]($\boxtimes$) and Kohei Otake[2]

[1] Graduate School of Information and Telecommunication Engineering, Tokai University, 2-3-23Minato-Ku, TakanawaTokyo 108-8619, Japan
`3cjnm003@mail.u-tokai.ac.jp`
[2] Faculty of Economics, Sophia University, 7-1 Kioi-cho, Chiyoda-Ku, Tokyo 102-8554, Japan
`k-otake@sophia.ac.jp`

Abstract. In recent years, with the increase in the use of SNS to gather fashion-related information, a fashion-related consumer community has formed on SNS. On the other hand, the demand for women's fashion magazines is on the decline, print content that integrates with SNS is required. In this study, we aim to propose a framework that supports the planning of a fashion magazine that takes into account the consumer community. Specifically, we used data on official accounts of women's fashion magazines collected from X (formerly Twitter) to identify communities through social network analysis. In addition, we attempted to clarify the topics related to each community by performing natural language processing analysis on the post contents which are text data.

Keywords: Social Networking Service · Social Network Analysis · Natural Language Processing · Fashion Magazine

1 Introduction

With the increase in Internet use in recent years, e-commerce sites have been increasing. Among these, demand for fashion e-commerce sites has been increasing further after the COVID-19 pandemic. According to a survey on e-commerce by the Ministry of Economy, Trade and Industry [1], the market size in Japan in 2022 is on an increasing trend compared to the previous year, amounting to 2,549.9 billion yen.

These fashion e-commerce sites transmit information on sales and new products through SNS (Social Networking Service). SNS is a place where users can easily interact with each other. Recently, consumers are using SNS to gather fashion information. In addition, consumers are also becoming more active in two-way communication with each other. As a result, there are consumer communities related to fashion on SNS with trends.

In the fashion industry, it is necessary for social media marketing to consumers information. Angella et al. [2] conducted a study to identify the impact of social media marketing on customer relationships and purchase intentions for a luxury fashion brand. The

© The Author(s), under exclusive license to Springer Nature Switzerland AG 2024
A. Coman and S. Vasilache (Eds.): HCII 2024, LNCS 14704, pp. 278–291, 2024.
https://doi.org/10.1007/978-3-031-61305-0_19

results revealed that social media information dissemination was significantly effective in promoting purchase intention. They also indicated that social media content should emphasize entertainment value. Nawaz et al. [3] identified social media as a significant predictor in the fashion industry. Therefore, social media marketing activities are important for customer acquisition in the fashion industry.

On the other hand, the use of fashion magazines to gather information is on the decline with the development of information dissemination through SNS. According to a survey by Institute of Publication Science [4], the share of sales of both electronic and paper magazines in publications is expected to decrease by approximately 17% between 2014 and 2022. However, fashion magazines have their own attractions, such as being coordinated from a professional perspective and having an established concept for each magazine. Altuna et al. [5] conducted a survey of readers regarding factors that influence their purchase of fashion magazines. Consequently, they showed that the factor of "Brand Recommendation" was the most important reason for purchasing fashion magazines. Therefore, it is thought that the easy-to-understand attractiveness of each brand's products in women's fashion magazines is consider important by consumers.

However, there has been little research activity to understand the latent needs of fashion magazine readers on SNS. It is necessary to understand the consumer communities of women's fashion magazines with the increase in SNS use and the formation of numerous consumer communities in various domains. We believe that it lead to the provision of pages that are appropriate for the readers of each magazine to identify the consumer communities of women's fashion magazines. In addition, we consider that it will be possible to propose plans that incorporate the immediacy of information from social networking services. We believe that this will once again increase the demand for fashion magazines.

2 Purpose

In this study, we propose a framework to support the planning of fashion magazine pages that take into account the contemporary consumer community. We believe that this lead to the provision of value in the pages of fashion magazines that is more in line with the needs of today's consumers. In this study, we use data collected from X (formerly Twitter). We will identify the structure of the consumer community and the topics within the community, which are the readers of fashion magazines.

3 Dataset

In this study, among fashion magazines for women in their 20s, who are frequent accounts of SNS, three popular fashion magazines (Magazine I, II, III) with a long history, which were first published in the 1980s, and two magazines (Magazine IV, V) that have been attracting attention since 2022 are the subjects of analysis.

3.1 Data Collected From X

In this study, we attempt to understand the reader community at the present time. For this purpose, we collected data from the official accounts on X of the target women's fashion magazine for 1,000 accounts that had recently followed the official account, and used them as primary followers. To collect the data on X, we created X API and performed scraping. We collected account names, account introductions, and account-posted text data used. According to a study by Kitajima et al. [6], it has been identified that there are a certain number of accounts on X for the purpose of entering sweepstakes. In this study, we exclude these accounts from the analysis because our goal is to understand the network structure formed by accounts for the purpose of general communication. For the same reason, accounts with a very large number of followers, such as celebrities and influencers, are also excluded from the analysis. Accordingly, we collected accounts that met the following conditions.

- Accounts with more than 100 but less than 10,000 followers
- Unlocked account
- Account name and introduction do not include "bot," "懸賞(sweepstakes)," or "当選(winning)"

Table 1 shows the magazines concept and the number of data collected for each magazine.

Table 1. Summary of Data from Each Women's Fashion Magazine Collected

Magazine Name	Concept	Number of Primary Followers	Number of Secondary Followers
Magazine I	Flashy	1,000	519,895
Magazine II	Feminine	1,000	563,947
Magazine III	Feminine	1,000	655,285
Magazine IV	Casual	1,000	649,669
Magazine V	Girly	1,000	643,672

4 Understanding the Community in Each Magazine

In this study, we initially use social network analysis to visualize the network and detect communities to identify the communities that are the consumers present in each magazine. Furthermore, we attempt to identify the topics of each reader community using text data, which is the text data posted by primary followers. Figure 1 shows the analysis flow in this study.

Step 1 Identifying Communities	1-1. Visualization of Network Structure Through Social Network Analysis
	1-2. Community Division Using Modularity
Step 2 Identifying Topics	2-1. Vector Calculation of Documents Posted
	2-2. Topic Extraction Using Cluster Analysis on Calculated Vector
	2-3. Extraction of Feature Words in Topics

Fig. 1. Analysis Flow of Content Estimation

4.1 Identifying the Structure of the Community for Each Magazine

At first, we created several adjacency matrices based on the acquired data and performed a social network analysis. Network analysis is an analytical method based on graph theory and is used to explore relationships among components. Among its analyses, social network analysis is used to identify human relationships such as kinship and friendship. Nodes and edges are used to visualize the network. In social network analysis, nodes represent individuals and edges represent some kind of relationship. In this study, we defined a node as a primary follower and a relationship as the existence of a common secondary follower among primary followers, creating an edge between primary followers. We used a common quadratic follower count for the edge weights. In addition, since we compare among magazines, we normalized the data. We only included edges with weights greater than 0.01 to identify relationships between first-order followers with stronger connections. We further reduced the number of nodes according to the degree that each node had. In this study, we included in our analysis nodes with a total node number of degree greater than or equal to 12. These were nodes with a degree of 100 or more and an overall network degree of 0.1 or more.

We also performed community detection using modularity, which groups nodes based on network structure. Equation 1 shows the formula for modularity.

$$\frac{1}{2m} \sum_{ij} \left[A_{ij} - \frac{k_i k_j}{2m} \right] \delta \left(c_i, c_j \right) \tag{1}$$

In this equation m represents the sum of the weights of all edges in the network, A_{ij} represents the weights of the edges of node i and node j, k_i represents the sum of the weights of the edges bound to node i and k_j represents the sum of the weights of the edges bound to node j. δ is the Kronecker delta, c_i represents the community to which node i belongs and c_j represents the community to which node j belongs. In this study, we performed community detection using the Louvain method [7] with modularity.

We named all the communities in each magazine using the self-introductions of the primary followers who were the nodes of each community. Table 2 shows the names of the communities and the number of primary followers belonging to each magazine.

As a results, we revealed that there are differences in the communities that exist in each magazine. Magazine I has several communities of fans of male popular idol groups. We suggest that this is largely due to the fact that Magazine I regularly introduces a ranking of the most popular good-looking celebrities. On the other hand, we identified

Table 2. Name of the Community and the Number of Primary Followers to Which It Belongs

Magazine	Name of Community	Number of Total Nodes
Magazine I	&TEAM Fans (Male Popular Idol Group)	42
	MAZZEL Fans (Male Popular Idol Group)	36
	Cosmetics Records	31
	Cosmetics Information Collection	34
	YouTuber Fans	45
	Mothers of a Child	35
Magazine II	Interested in Beauty and Dieting	59
	NiziU Fans: individual (Female Popular Idol Group)	69
	NiziU Fans: all members (Female Popular Idol Group)	94
	Nogizaka 46 Fans (Female Popular Idol Group)	84
Magazine III	Nogizaka 46 Fans (Female Popular Idol Group)	90
	Personal Merchandise Sellers	4
	NMB 48 Fans (Female Popular Idol Group)	25
	College Student Influencers	46
	Japanese Actresses Fans	18
	Fan of STARTO ENTERTAINMENT's idols	12
	Health Conscious	3
	SKE 48 Fans (Female Popular Idol Group)	15
Magazine IV	Fashion Conscious	57
	Interested in Beauty and Cosmetics	15
	Bookstores	22
	Working on a Lifelog	15
Magazine V	MAG	23
	Distributors	20
	=LOVE Fans (Female Popular Idol Group)	105
	Fan of Japanese Indie Idols	46
	Japanese Indie Idols	47

that Magazine II has several communities of fans of female popular idol groups. We therefore focused on the models for Magazine II. We found that members of a group in the community were used as the models for Magazine II. Also, we found the same thing for the community in Magazine III. Therefore, we suggest that a certain segment of fans of the models for these magazines is the readership. Magazine IV has a fashion-related community. In other words, we consider that there are more readers who share the fashion concept of the magazine in Magazine IV than in Magazine I, Magazine II, and Magazine III. We identified that Magazine V has a fan base of celebrities who are used as the models for Magazine V in the community. In addition, MAG Community that exists in this magazine is a generic term for the manga, anime and game genres. We believe that the readers interested in these genres are unique to this magazine, since we did not detect such a community in the communities of other magazines. In other words, Magazine V has a community that does not compete with other magazines.

4.2 Topic Identification of Each Community

Next, we attempted to identify topics within each community by performing natural language processing analysis on the posted contents of primary followers belonging to each detected community. Specifically, we calculated a vector for each post document, performed cluster analysis on the calculated vector values, and extracted topics. Furthermore, we named each topic by extracting the words that characterize the documents for each extracted topic.

Preprocessing of Text Data. We performed preprocessing of the data for natural language processing analysis. We removed spaces and the following text from the documents in this study because they are related to topics discussed in the community. We have also standardized the use of all lower-case letters in the English language.

- URL beginning with https
- Post addresses beginning with @
- Symbols
- Numbers

Calculation of Document Vectors and Extraction of Topics by Cluster Analysis. First, we used the BERT (Bidirectional Encoder Representations from Transformers) [8] model to compute document vectors for the topic-based partitioning of all text data posted by each community. In recent years, BERT model has been used in text analysis in various fields. In this study, we used the trained Japanese version of the BERT model [9] provided by a laboratory in Tohoku University. To calculate the document vectors, we used the average of the word vectors, which is consider to provide better accuracy by Nils et al. [10]. We used MeCab [11] for morphological analysis to split sentences into words.

Furthermore, we attempted to extract topics from all the post contents in the community by performing cluster analysis on the obtained 762-dimensional document vector. Cluster analysis is an analysis method that groups similar data. In this study, we attempted to divide all the documents in the community into topics by cluster analysis using the value of each document vector. We used K-means++ method [12], which is a non-hierarchical type of cluster analysis. We used Elbow method to determine the number of clusters, which is the number of topics. As a result, the number of topics in each community was 3.

Extraction of Feature Words for Each Topic.

We attempted to estimate the topic content. First, we combined the documents classified by topic into one. Then, we extracted the feature words in each document. To extract feature words, we used the Okapi BM25 [13] computation method. Okapi BM25 is a natural language processing method used in search algorithms. In general, the TF-IDF method is frequently used. However, this method has a problem that its value varies greatly depending on the number of words in a document. In this study, Okapi BM25 was used to extract words that are more characteristic of the topics in the community. Equation 2 shows the formula of Okapi BM25 for feature word extraction.

$$score(t_k) = idf(t_k) \cdot \frac{tf(t_k,d_j)\cdot(k_1+1)}{tf(t_k,d_j)+k_1\cdot\left(1-b+b\frac{dl(d_j)}{avgdl}\right)} \qquad (2)$$

In this equation t_k represents a target word, d_j represents a target document. *idf* Represents inverse document frequency, *dl* represents total number of words, *avgdl* represents average number of words in the whole document. Also, k_1 and b are arbitrary parameters, and we set $k_1 = 2.0$ and $b = 0.75$, which are more frequently used. To use this formula, we attempted to extract feature words from a single document that belongs to a segmented topic in the community. In this study, we identified each topic by extracting the top 10 words of nouns that are consider to represent the characteristics of the topic. Among the extracted words, we removed those that could not be understood in a single word. We added proper nouns such as celebrity names that were not registered in MeCab. We deleted topics that did not contain more than 10 feature words because we consider them to be unimportant topics in the community.

Table 3 shows the names of topics and the top 10 feature words for each topic in communities of fans of male popular idol groups that were listed as features of Magazine I.

In &TEAM Fans Community, we extracted the topics K-Pop Popularity Ranking Site, &TEAM Collaboration Products, and &TEAM Live Tour. In K-POP Popularity Ranking Site Topic, we extracted the word "音韓(NEHAN)" in addition to the words related to &TEAM's new songs. This is a site that compiles the latest popularity rankings of Korean entertainers and K-POP groups. The rankings are determined by the votes of fans on the site. The rankings are determined by the votes of fans on the site. When X and this site are linked, the name of the celebrity to vote for is posted along with a message. Therefore, we consider that words related to "人気(popularity)" and new songs were extracted together with "音韓(NEHAN)". In &TEAM Collaboration Products Topic, we extracted the words "めざましどようび(MEZAMASHI SATURDAY)" which are the names of morning information programs and "エンプッチョ (Enpuccho)". We consider that this is because of the collaboration between &TEAM and Puccho, a Japanese snack, and the program introduced them. In the third topic, we named it &TEAM Fan Tour Topic, because we extracted the word "月波 (LUNE MARE)". This word is the tour title of the fan tour they held.

Table 3. Name of Topics in the Magazine I Communities

&TEAM Fans			MAZZEL Fans		
K-POP Popularity Ranking Site	&TEAM Collaboration Products	&TEAM Fan Tour	BE:FIRST	MAZZEL RADIO STATION	MAZZEL Events
人気 (Popularity)	めざましどようび (MEZAMASHI SATURDAY)	昨日 (Yesterday)	レオ (LEO)	DA PUMP	古家蘭 (Ran Furuie)
現在 (The Present)	エンプッチョ (Enpuccho)	ライブ (Live)	三山凌輝 (Ryoki Miyama)	Ano	Shazam
音韓 (NEHAN)	ケイタキハグ (KEI and TAKI Hug)	成長 (Growth)	友達 (Friend)	かくし芸 (Hidden talents)	得票 (Votes Obtained)
Under The Skin	ケミ (Kemi)	番組 (Program)	アキテク (Akiteku)	やり取り (Interaction)	票 (Vote)
優勝 (Victory)	ダンスグル (Dance Group)	CD	スタイル (Style)	ウィダーコーヒー (Widder Coffee)	Takuto
投稿 (Posting)	チェウォン (Chae Won)	参加 (Participation)	ツアー (Tour)	ウインナーゼリー (Vienna Jelly)	Debut Show Case
Dunk	チョロオタ (Chorota)	アップ (Up)	ビジュ (Visual)	ソウタ (SOTA)	GENERATIONS
Spotify	ナムジャ (Youth)	名古屋 (Nagoya)	公演 (Performance)	リクエストエムオン (Request M-ON)	Line Music
めざましテレビ (MEZAMASHI TV)	ハイタッチ (High Five)	月波 (LUNE MARE)	沼 (Numa)	慶太 (KEITA)	Live
ENHYPEN	フラワー (Flower)	東京ドーム (Tokyo Dome)	蘭 (RAN)	ツッコミ (Tsukkomi)	FC

Next, we explain the three topics extracted from MAZZEL Fans Community. In the first topic, we obtained words with the names "レオ (LEO)" and "三山凌輝 (Ryoki Miyama)". We searched for these names. We found out that it is a Japanese boy group called BE:FIRST. We also named it the BE:FIRST Topic, because it was a word related to the group's fan club, "アキテク (Akiteku)". In the second topic, we extracted many words related to topics talked about in a radio program called MAZZEL RADIO STATION in July, the time when the data was collected. Therefore, we named it MAZZEL RADIO STATION Topic. In the third topic, we extracted words that belonged to members of the

MAZZEL group in the community name. We also found the words "Debut Show Case" and "Live," so we labeled it MAZZEL Events Topic.

Table 4 shows the names of the topics in the community related to fashion and cosmetics and the top 10 characteristic words for each topic, which were listed as the characteristics of Magazine IV.

Table 4. Name of Topics in the Magazine IV Communities

Fashion Conscious			Interested in Beauty and Cosmetics		
Neil	Fortune	Offering Daily Information	Fashion, Fragrance	Physical Condition	Posting Information about the Restaurant
新月 (New Moon)	牡 (Male)	CM (Commercial Message)	掲載 (Listed)	筋肉 (Muscle)	札幌 (Sapporo)
ネイルポリッシュ (Nail Polish)	Osakana	会社 (Company)	コート (Coat)	太陽 (The Sun)	めし (Food)
月齢 (Age of the Moon)	ひつじ (Sheep)	コメント (Comment)	プリント (Print)	改善 (Improvement)	純 (Pure)
満月 (Full Moon)	コブダイ (Kobudai)	学校 (School)	プリンセス (Princess)	注意 (Attention)	個室 (Private Room)
上限 (Upper Limit)	ヤギ (Goat)	国 (Country)	Princess Limited Edition	パン (Bread)	居酒屋 (Izakaya)
Kate	中野 (Nakano)	客 (Guest)	Scotch	冷え (Cold)	海鮮 (Seafood)
抽選 (lottery)	水瓶座 (Aquarius)	年齢 (Age)	ニット (Knit)	血流 (Blood Flow)	酒 (Sake)
Moon Phase Collection	永遠 (Eternity)	手入れ (Care)	ホワイトムスク (White Musk)	不足 (Lack)	皆様 (Everyone)
鎌倉 (Kamakura)	泊 (Overnight)	経験 (Experience)	雑誌 (Magazine)	人間 (Human)	直送 (Direct Delivery)
New Moon	Happy	結論 (Conclusion)	ジャケット (Jacket)	今朝 (This Morning)	うに (Sea Urchin)

We extracted Neil Topic, Fortune Topic, and Offering Daily Information Topic in Fashion Conscious Community. The words related to the moon in Neil Topic are the names of products sold under the &ante. Brand, which sells nail products. In Fortune Topic, we found that many words related to the zodiac signs were extracted. We consider that this was due to a special feature on astrology in Magazine IV. However, we did not extract similar topics from the other communities in Magazine IV. Therefore, we consider that astrology is of great interest to the Fashion Conscious Community. We named the third topic "Offering Daily Information Topic" because it contains many words used in posts about daily events such as "学校(School)" and "会社(Company)".

Next, we explain the topics we extracted from Interested in Beauty and Cosmetics Community. In the first topic, we found words related to winter fashion items such as "コート (Coat)" and "ニット (Knit)". In addition, we surveyed princesses and "Princess Limited Edition," and found that the brand johns-blend offers a fragrance in collaboration with Disney princess characters. The word "ホワイトムスク(White Musk)" was one of the fragrance collaboration product. We named the second topic the "Physical Condition Topic" because we extracted not only words related to body parts but also words describing the state of those parts. For the third topic, we extracted words related to "めし(food)" and place names such as "札幌(Sapporo)" and "海鮮(seafood)".We identified the documents categorized under this topic and found that official accounts of restaurants were posting information to attract customers. Therefore, we labeled the topic Posting Information about the Restaurant Topic.

5   Result and Suggestion

In this study, we attempted to identify the interests of readers on X for women's fashion magazines. First, we divided each magazine into communities using a framework for social network analysis. In addition, we have divided the topics and identified their contents using natural language processing analysis on the text data posted by users belonging to the community. Table 5 shows the topics of the communities in each magazine.

In Magazine I, we detected communities related to male idol groups. In these communities, we extracted topics related to the group's live performances and media appearances. In the MAZZEL Fans Community, we also extracted topics related to the group BE:FIRST, which belongs to the same agency. Therefore, we can assume that in this community, there are people who are interested in not only the first group they support, but also other groups in the same vein.

We detected a community of fans in Magazine II who are not the models for this magazine. We consider that this is due to the fact that these girls appeared on the cover of this magazine during the period when the data was collected. In this community we also extracted topics related to them. On the other hand, we also extracted topics related to baseball. Similarly, we extracted topics related to soccer in the Nogizaka 46 Fans Community. These results suggest that a certain number of fans of the women's group have an interest in sports.

Table 5. Topics of the Communities in Each Magazine

Magazine	Community	Topic	Magazine	Community	Topic
Magazine I	&TEAM Fans	K-POP Popularity Ranking Site	**Magazine III**	Japanese Actresses Fans	Supporting Comments
		&TEAM Collaboration Products			Radio
		&TEAM Fan Tour		Fan of STARTO ENTERTAINMENT's idols	Official Blog
	MAZZEL Fans	BE:FIRST			TV Programs
		MAZZEL RADIO STATION		Health Conscious	Basic Cosmetics
		MAZZEL Events			Health
	Cosmetics Records	Cosmetics for the Eyes			Weather
		Medical Experience		SKE 48 Fans	Daily Log
		Cosmetics for the Masses			SKE 48 Member Information
	Cosmetics Information Collection	Gift Planning			SKE 48 Fan Project
		Official Campaigns	**Magazine IV**	Fashion Conscious	Neil
		Food			Fortune
	YouTuber Fans				Offering Daily Information
	Mothers of a Child	Athletes		Interested in Beauty and Cosmetics	Fashion, Fragrance
		Troubles in Love			Physical Condition
		Official Campaign			Posting Information about the Restaurant
Magazine II	Interested in Beauty and Dieting	Weather		Bookstores	World Situation
		Official Campaign			Japan Information
	NiziU Fans(individual)	NiziU Album Information			Bookstore Information

(continued)

Table 5. (*continued*)

Magazine	Community	Topic	Magazine	Community	Topic
		NiziU Event Lottery		Working on a Lifelog	Parenting Information
		Food			Fashion
	NiziU Fans (all members)	Baseball			Holiday Shopping
		NiziU Program Cooperation	**Magazine V**	MAG	Morning TV Show
		NiziU Original Content			Japanese Host Club
	Nogizaka 46 Fans	Soccer			Daily Log
		Daily Log		Distributors	Love Reality Show
		Nogizaka 46 TV Program			Distribution Events
Magazine III	Nogizaka 46 Fans	Birthday Celebrations			Advertising for Distribution
		Nogizaka 46 Message Application		=LOVE Fans	=LOVE Live Items
		Nogizaka 46 Handshake Review			Japanese Host Club
	Personal Merchandise Sellers	Daily Log			=LOVE Live Review
		Subscription Information		Fans of Japanese Indie Idols	Distribution Review
		news			Account Management
	NMB 48 Fans	NMB 48 Theater Performances			Distribution Information
		NMB 48Concerts		Japanese Indie Idols	Event Review
		NMB 48 Event Announcements			Live Review
	College Student Influencers	Auditions			
		Sports			
		Daily Log			

In Magazine III, we detected a community of fans of the group to which the members of the exclusive model belonged, as in Magazine II. In addition, we detected Health Conscious Community, which was not found in other magazines. We extracted Basic

Cosmetics Topic and Health Topic from this community. We consider that a certain segment of the magazine's readership is more interested in improving themselves than in improving cosmetics and fashion externally.

We detected communities related to cosmetics and fashion in Magazine IV. These are generally the main contents in women's fashion magazines. Since we extracted information on specific products in these communities. We consider that there are people who are sensitive to the topic of the products.

We detected Distributor Community in Magazine V as well as a community about women's groups. In this community, we extracted topics of information about distribution. We believe that it is possible to understand what kind of distribution events are of interest. In addition, we consider that prospective female entertainers exist as readers of this magazine. Because we extracted the names of events attended by aspiring female idols from the extracted words related to the distribution events.

We believe that the results obtained from this study will enable us to propose a magazine plan that is in line with the interests of the readers at that time. As an example, we explain Magazine I. We extracted topics related to another group in the community of fans of the group detected in this community. We consider that by using this separate group in this magazine, and expanding our new readership. In addition, we found that the community that exists in Magazine II has a sports-related topic. Therefore, we consider that the fusion of this women's group and sports will lead to the expansion of a new readership as in Magazine I. In Magazine IV, we extracted topics related to products that are considered to be in vogue. We therefore consider that featuring a product that is highly relevant to this product may attract new interest from readers.

6 Conclusion

In this study, we attempted to identify the interests of readers on X for women's fashion magazines. Specifically, we constructed social network analysis and partitioned communities using a modularity. In this way, we detected communities with different characteristics for each magazine. There were many communities that supported entertainers. On the other hand, we also identified communities that are unique to a particular magazine, such as Health Conscious Community. Next, we performed natural language processing analysis on the text data posted by users belonging to the community in order to segment the topics and identify their contents. Specifically, we calculated document vectors using the Japanese version of the BERT model. We attempted to divide topics by performing a cluster analysis on these values. Finally, we extracted feature words using Okapi BM25 from the documents of the segmented topics. We then identified the content of each topic.

Through this study, we have identified different communities that exist in different magazines. It also identified connections between different genres that could not be identified before. Using data on X, it is possible to understand the interests of readers at a particular time, where information is exchanged immediately. On the other hand, we also extracted topics that have little to do with the magazine, such as Posting Informations about the Restaurant Topic. We consider that this was largely due to the fact that the content of many posts by a single user was largely due to the topic. Therefore, it is necessary to remove official accounts that have not been authenticated by X in the future. In addition, we used Okapi BM25 to extract feature words. We believe that this method needs to be integrated with TF-IDF, because it has a large negative bias for words that also appear in other topics. In this study, we analyzed only the most recent data. However, we believe that in the future, it will be possible to compare topics by period by using a time-series framework up to topic estimation.

Acknowledgment. This work was supported by JSPS KAKENHI Grant Number 21K13385.

References

1. Ministry of Economy, Trade and Industry, "2022 Market Research Report on E-Commerce". https://www.meti.go.jp/ (2024/1/29 author checked)
2. Kim, A.J., Ko, E.: Impacts of luxury fashion brand's social media marketing on customer relationship and purchase intention. J. Glob. Fashion Mark. **1**, 164–171 (2010)
3. Ahmad, N., Salman, A., Ashiq, R.: The Impact of Social Media on Fashion Industry: empirical Investigation from Karachiites. J. Resour. Dev. Manage. **7**, 2422–8397 (2015)
4. Institute of Publication Science, "Publication Sales in Japan," https://shuppankagaku.com/statistics/japan/ (2024/1/29 author checked)
5. Altuna, O.K., Siğirci, Ö., Arslan, F.M.: Segmenting women fashion magazine readers based on reasons of buying, fashion involvement and age: a study in the Turkish market. J. Glob. Fashion Mark. **4**(3), 175–192 (2013)
6. Kitajima, Y., Otake, K., Namatame, T.: Evaluation of consumer network structure for cosmetic brands on Twitter. Int. J. Adv. Comput. Sci. Appl. **13**(2), 46–55 (2022)
7. Traag, V.A., Waltman, L., Van Eck, N.J.: From Louvain to Leiden: guaranteeing well-connected communities. Sci. Rep. **9**, 5233 (2019)
8. J., Devlin, Chang, M.-W., Lee, K., Toutanova, K.: BERT: pre-training of deep bidirectional transformers for language understanding. arXiv:1810.04805 (2018)
9. Pretrained Japanese BERT models released | Tohoku NLP Lab https://www.nlp.ecei.tohoku.ac.jp/news-release/3284/ (2024/1/29 author checked)
10. Reimers, N., Gurevych, I.: Sentence-BERT: sentence embeddings using siamese BERT-networks. arXiv:1908.10084 (2019)
11. Kudo, T., Yamamoto, K., Matsumoto, Y.: Applying conditional random fields to Japanese morphological analysis. In: Proceedings of the 2004 Conference on Empirical Methods in Natural Language Processing, pp.230–237(2004)
12. Arthur, D., Vassilvitskii, S.: "k-means++: the advantages of careful seeding," Society for Industrial and Applied Mathematics Philadelphia, PA, USA, pp.1027–1035 (2007)
13. Robertson, S.E., Walker, S., Jones, S., Hancock-Beaulieu, M.M., Gatford, M.: Okapi at TREC-3. In: Proceedings of the Third Text REtrieval Conference (1994)

Identification of Key Factors to Improve Click-Through Rates Related to Email

Akito Kumazawa[1]($\boxtimes$), Takashi Namatame[2], and Kohei Otake[3]

[1] Graduate School of Information and Telecommunication Engineering, Tokai University, 2-3-23, Takanawa, Minato-Ku, Tokyo 108-8619, Japan
3cjnm009@mail.u-tokai.ac.jp
[2] School of Science and Engineering, Chuo University, 1-13-27, Kasuga, Bunkyo-Ku, Tokyo 112-8551, Japan
nama@kc.chuo-u.ac.jp
[3] Faculty of Economics, Sophia University, 7-1 Kioi-cho, Chiyoda-Ku, Tokyo 102-8554, Japan
k-otake@sophia.ac.jp

Abstract. Email promotion is known to be an effective marketing measurement to customers, it must be appropriately targeted and configured. In this study, we identify the key factors for improving the click-through rate for emails in consumer electronics retailers. First, we identify customer loyalty through RFM analysis. Next, we construct a binomial logistic regression model and a random forest model to identify the key factors for clicking on the emails. Our analysis reveals that customer loyalty tends to be higher who have registered for email compared to those who have not. Furthermore, our findings suggest that factors contributing to increased click-through rates include past purchase history of products related to the email content, as well as consumer behaviors such as recent purchase dates and cumulative purchase frequency Building on these findings, a strategic approach to improve click-through rates involves narrowing down targets individually based on past purchase patterns and recent buying behavior.

Keywords: Email promotion · Logistic Regression Model · Random Forest

1 Introduction

Competition has intensified in Japan's consumer electronics industry in recent years. According to a survey by Japan's Ministry of Economy, Trade and Industry [1], sales in the home appliance industry increased by 468,114 million yen from FY 2016 to FY 2022. Based on this high growth, the sales value of home appliance stores is expected to continue to increase. In addition, the market size of BtoC-EC (Business to Customer Electronic Commerce) in the field of goods sales is expanding year by year [2], increasing approximately 6 trillion yen from FY2016 to FY2022, with the EC conversion rate increasing by 3.7%. Then, competition is intensifying in the consumer electronics retail industry, where sales are growing. According to Suzuki's research [3], the COVID-19 disaster will further revitalize the EC market, while the superiority of brick-and-mortar stores will be reevaluated, and omni-channel development that links EC and brick-and-mortar stores is expected.

A. Coman and S. Vasilache (Eds.): HCII 2024, LNCS 14704, pp. 292–303, 2024.
https://doi.org/10.1007/978-3-031-61305-0_20

Under these circumstances, marketing promotions to acquire customers are becoming increasingly important. One such promotion is email promotion. Email promotions are mainly used as a marketing tool to provide information, distribute content, and strengthen relationships with users. Moreover, it can increase users' interest in products by approaching prospective customers directly. On the other hand, according to Orange Spiritists [4], frequent delivery frequency and useless information are suggested as reasons why email advertisements are no longer read. According to an email delivery system developed by Benchmark [5], the average open rate in Japan is 37.42%, and the average click rate is 4.84%, suggesting that about 40% of people open emails, but only about 5% click on them. Based on the above background, we believe that there is room for further study to improve the click rate of email advertisements.

2 Purpose of This Study

In this study, we analyze historical data of outgoing emails, ID-POS data, and demographic data in order to identify factors that increase email click-through rates. Specifically, we use RFM analysis to determine whether there is a relationship between customer loyalty among email subscribers and no email subscribers. Next, we create a logistic regression model and a random forest model to predict a click using the results of the RFM analysis. In the model creation, we use demographic data such as gender and age as well as consumer behavior data such as the date of the most recent RFM purchase, the cumulative number of purchases, the cumulative frequency of purchases, and the existence of product categories that have been purchased in the past as w explanatory variables. Ultimately, we find variables that have a high influence on the presence or absence of clicks, and clarify the relationship between them, leading to the acquisition of good customers and the purchase of products.

3 Previous Studies

In this section, we summarize previous studies related to email advertising, which is the objective of this study.

As for email advertising, Yoshii et al. [6] used a large number of distribution logs from an email advertising distribution service and analyzed them for the purpose of research to explore the statistical impact of email titles on open, and based on the results, proposed a method that can produce effective creative without relying on demographic information proposed. Then, using the title score and the amount of mutual information, a detailed analysis was conducted to determine which specific phrases had an impact on open for which demographics. The analysis results showed that the model with the title information was more accurate than the model with only demographic information, confirming that the title has an impact on the open rate. It was shown that the title score can give a prior hit on the open rate. We also evaluated the impact of each phrase on openings by gender and age using the mutual information content. For example, it was suggested that job/career change mail related phrases influenced young men, while beauty-related phrases influenced women from a broad range of demographics.

Based on past mailings, Kitajima [7] clarified what kind of text to use for what kind of users leads to an increase in click and purchase rates. Specifically, they measured the effectiveness of direct mailings to companies that basically distribute segmented mailings and companies that basically distribute mailings to all users. For effect estimation, Company A, which uses segment delivery, conducted its own segment classification, and parameter estimation of a direct mail effect measurement model using MCMC with segments added as random effects was conducted. The results suggest that click behavior can be modeled using a model that takes individual differences into account. In addition, by comparing the results for each cluster, we clarified the response to the type of direct mail, which cannot be seen only by the quality of the mail.

The aforementioned studies have provided valuable insights into email advertising. However, the landscape has changed with increased challenges in utilizing personally identifiable information, and the research on email advertising remains limited with few case studies, indicating a lack of substantial progress in the field. Given this current state, it is believed that there is further room for research in the promotion of email advertising.

4 Dataset

This study used ID-POS data, demographic data, and email distribution data provided by Japanese electronics retailers. A summary of each data set is presented in Tables 1, 2, and 3.

Table 1. ID-POS data summary

Data	ID-POS data
Period	01/01/2017-2021/08/31
Number of data	9,454,632
Column	Member number, Transaction time, Store code, Product name, Amount, etc...

Table 1 shows an overview of the ID-POS data. The columns contain data related to purchase history, such as customer IDs and transaction details.

Table 2. Demographic data summary

Data	Demographic data
Column	Membership Number, Gender, Age, Address (prefecture), EC newsletter EC email registration flag, etc...
Number of users	836,019
Number of newsletter subscribers	21,5908

Table 2 shows the demographic data. It shows user characteristics such as gender, age, and hometown.

Table 3. Emails distribution data summary

Data	Direct mail distribution data
Period	06/01/2021-10/14/2021
Columns	Columns membership number, Sent open flag, Date and time of sending, delivery title, etc…
Type of DM	1. Email related to game sales 2. Email related to video/music 3. Email related to videos

Table 3 shows an overview of the email's distribution data. In this study, we analyzed three types of emails (1–3), which are emails related to product information.

5   Analysis of the Customers Loyalty

First, to identify customer loyalty we performed an RFM analysis. We included users who made purchases in the past before 2017 to ensure that the dominance of each indicator does not depend on the date of user registration. We used September 1, 2021, the day after the end of the period, August 31, 2021, as the base date for the R indicator. We used the total number of purchases by customer ID for our F indicator and the total purchase amount by customer ID for our M indicator. The ranking of each indicator is shown in Table 4.

Table 4. RFM ranking criteria

Ranks	Each Indicator		
	R. value	F. value	M. value
1	1,451days or more	1 time	1–6,999yen
2	1,101–1,450 days	2 times	7,000–16,999yen
3	701–1,100 days	3–5 times	17,000–39,999yen
4	281–700 days	6–13 times	4,0000–99,999yen
5	1–280 days	14 times or more	100,000 yen or more

Using the ranking criteria in Table 4 we calculated the number of customers for each rank. The results are shown in Table 5.

Table 5 compares users who are registered for email with those who are not registered for email. Table 5 shows that users who are not registered for email have a large number of customers with an overall RFM score of 5–10. On the other hand, users who registered for email had more customers with an overall RFM score of 11–15. This indicates that the proportion of good customers is higher for the users who registered for email.

Table 5. Total value aggregate comparison of RFM analysis

RFM overall value	Not mail registrant		Mail registrant	
3	5,003	4%	2,935	3%
4	9,353	7%	5,632	6%
5	11,155	9%	6,735	7%
6	11,665	9%	7,234	8%
7	11,537	9%	7,052	7%
8	11,713	9%	7,270	8%
9	11,583	9%	7,503	8%
10	11,162	9%	7,859	8%
11	10,264	8%	7,552	8%
12	9,406	7%	7,496	8%
13	8,443	7%	7,261	8%
14	7,732	6%	7,729	8%
15	9,407	7%	12,462	13%

6   Construction of a Predictive Model for Email Clicks

We constructed a click forecasting model using a logistic regression model and a random forest model. We performed logistic regression analysis to extract explanatory variables that were particularly influential on the objective variable. We used random forests to further refine the relationship between the objective variable and each explanatory variable and to create a predictive model. We also used confusion matrices to evaluate and compare the accuracy of our models. This was done by using different types of models in order to compare the performance of each model and to identify the better model.

6.1   Dataset

We used as explanatory variables the number of days since last purchase, number of purchases, and cumulative purchase amount used in the RFM analysis, as well as age, gender, and product category purchased in the past. A summary of the data set is shown in Table 6.

In the model construction, we sampled with the aim of increasing the number of click-users and aligning the number of click-users and non-click-users. Here we oversampled 210 click users using SMOTE (Synthetic Minority Over-sampling TEchnique) [8], and aligned the number of data with 12,974 coupon non-users. We then randomly sampled 2,500 clickers and 2,500 non-clickers, for a total of 5,000. Oversampling is a technique in machine learning to improve the learning accuracy by increasing the number of data in a few classes when the number of data belonging to a particular class is smaller than that of other classes. Here, we use SMOTE (Synthetic Minority Over-sampling TEchnique),

Table 6. Dataset summary

Variable		Variable name	Data format
Objective variable		Click (=1), Non-click (=0)	0,1
Explanatory variable	Recency	Most recent purchase date	Numeric
	Frequency	Cumulative number of purchases	Numeric
	Monetary	Cumulative purchase amount	Numeric
	Gender	Male Yes (=1), No (=0)	0,1
		Female Yes (=1), No (=0)	0,1
	Age	20–24 years old Yes (=1), Not (=0) 5-year age increments thereafter	0,1
		Over 70 years old Yes (=1), No (=0)	0,1
	Product categories purchased in the past	PC Software Yes (=1), Not (=0)	0,1
		iPad Yes (=1), Not (=0)	0,1
		Anime goods Yes (=1), Not (=0) etc.	0,1

an over sampling technique to increase the number of minority-class data points by finding regions containing minority-class data points and randomly generating new data points from them. In order to evaluate the accuracy, we divided the data into training data and test data: the training data consisted of 5000 data points multiplied by 0.7 (3500 persons), and the test data consisted of 1500 persons multiplied by 0.3 (1500 persons).

6.2 Model Comparison

Logistic regression analysis and random forest using the data set in Table 6.

To we use the stepwise method of variable selection for logistic regression analysis. The stepwise method is one of the methods to select explanatory variables, and it is a method to find the best combination of explanatory variables through operations such as adding and deleting explanatory variables [9].

Random forests are then a type of ensemble learning that combines the basic principles of feature bagging and random selection to further increase the diversity of the decision tree model [10].

We also used Gini impurity to identify important variables. Gini impurity is a measure of how many different classifications exist in the data for each node.

Table 7 shows the results of the accuracy comparisons using each of these models.

Table 7 shows that Random Forests had higher values for Accuracy, Precision, and F1 Score than Logistic Regression Analysis. On the other hand, logistic regression analysis showed a higher value for Recall. Overall, Random Forests showed slightly higher accuracy.

Table 7. Model accuracy comparison

	Logistic Regression Model	Random Forest
Metric	Value	Value
Accuracy	0.935	0.948
Precision	0.901	0.967
Recall	0.970	0.935
F1 Score	0.935	0.951

Therefore, in the following sections, we will use a click prediction model with a random forest and discuss it.

6.3 Random Forest

In this section, we present the results of the random forest.

Table 8 shows the top 10 explanatory variables for the random forest results with Gini impurity.

Table 8. Top 10 Feature Importance by Random Forest

	Mean Decrease Gini
Video Software	136.78
Cumulative purchase amount	109.09
Most recent purchase date	93.41
Cumulative number of purchases	84.40
Gaming Software	80.05
Delivery Charge	68.22
45–49-year-olds	63.82
In-house Games	60.80
Used games	52.35
Music software	46.51

Table 8 shows that the above explanatory variables are likely to have a significant impact on clicks. The variables related to the cumulative purchase amount, the most recent purchase, the cumulative purchase frequency, and customer loyalty showed high values. In addition, video, game, and music related to email showed high values.

6.4   Partially Dependent Plots

Using the results in Table 8 we perform a partial dependent plot. A partial dependent plot is a visualization of how the predictions of a model change when a explanatory variable changes from minimum to maximum [11].

Figures 1, 2, and 3 show the continuous variables with the highest variable importance such as most recent purchase date, cumulative factory count, and cumulative purchase amount. The vertical axis represents the objective variable, and the horizontal axis represents the value of each explanatory variable.

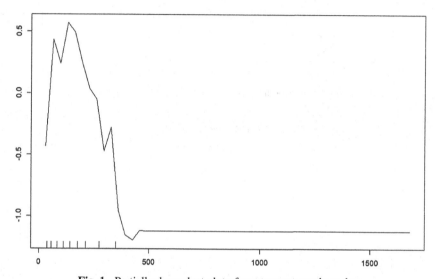

Fig. 1. Partially dependent plot of most recent purchase date

Figure 1 shows a partial dependent plot of the most recent purchase date. The probability of being clicked changes in a negative direction when the most recent purchase date is as small as about 30. This suggests that when there was a recent purchase, the tendency to click is low. For medium values of about 100, the probability of clicks changes in a positive direction. This may indicate that the tendency to click increases as a little time passes since the most recent purchase. On the other hand, after about 300, the probability of being clicked on changes again in a negative direction. This suggests that the tendency to click may decrease as a period of time passes without a purchase.

Figure 2 shows a partial dependent plot of the cumulative number of purchases. When the cumulative number of purchases is as small as 1, the probability of being clicked changes in a positive direction. From this, it is possible that the tendency to be clicked increases with the first purchase. However, the probability of being clicked changes in a negative direction up to about 100. After the first purchase, the tendency to be clicked may decrease. After that, the probability of being clicked changes in a positive direction again until about 200 times.

Figure 3 shows a partial dependent plot of cumulative purchase amounts. Until the cumulative purchase amount is about 1.6 million, the probability of being clicked acts

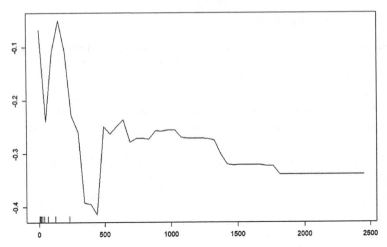

Fig. 2. Partial dependent plot of cumulative number of purchases

Partial Dependence on m

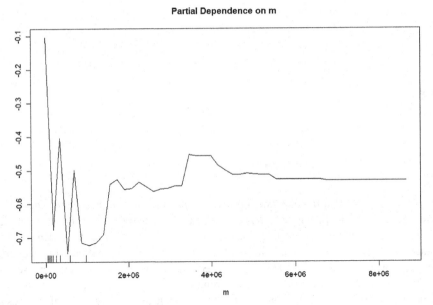

Fig. 3. Partial dependent plot of cumulative purchase amount

alternately in the negative and positive directions. Thereafter, it changes in a positive direction and converges after about 2 million yen. This indicates that the probability of clicks increases when the total amount of purchases reaches a certain level, and that the probability of clicks does not change after that.

In addition, we presented the binary variables, i.e., the product category purchased in the past and age, in Table 9.

Table 9. Value of partial dependent plot with binary variables

Explanatory variable	0	1
Video Software	−0.960	1.560
Gaming Software	−0.798	1.341
Delivery Charge	−0.539	0.969
45–49-year-olds	−0.065	1.045
In-house Games	−0.490	1.280
Used games	−0.294	1.161
Music software	−0.516	1.360

Table 9 show that purchasing the product categories indicated in the table positively affects clicks. Also, being 45–49 years old positively affects clicks.

7 Discussion

In this section, we discuss the results of our previous analyses.

First, we discuss the results of the RFM analysis. This suggests that customers who subscribe to email have higher customer loyalty. Therefore, we considered that it is important to induce customers to subscribe to email because subscribing to email increases the likelihood of becoming a good customer.

Next, the random forest model showed that the variables (video software), (total purchase amount), (date of most recent purchase), (number of purchases), (game software), (shipping cost), (age 45–49), (in-house games), and (music software) were highly important. The results indicate that users who have purchased product categories related to the content of the email, such as game-related products, music-related products, and video products, in the past are more likely to click on the email. The partial dependent plot also showed that users who had purchased the above product categories in the past increased their click probability. And we considered that the 45–49-year-olds were the generation accustomed to email as the reason for the clicks. Currently, the number of people who use email on a regular basis is decreasing due to the development of SNS and chat-type applications other than email. Therefore, we believe that promote advertisements on SNS and chat-type applications through media other than email in order to increase the number of people who click on emails in the future. Next, we found that the cumulative purchase amount had alternating positive and negative effects on clicks up to about 1.6 million yen but had an effect on clicks after that. This suggests that the advertisers did not establish themselves as good customers until approximately 1.6 million yen, and that they established themselves as good customers after that time, which had an effect on clicks. The most recent purchase had a positive effect up to about 300 days, but a negative effect after that. This may be due to the fact that the customers were interested in the products at the electronics retail store immediately after the purchase. On the other hand, the negative effect after about 300 days was due to the decrease in interest in the product as time passed after the purchase, which may have resulted in a decrease in clicks.

And in the cumulative number of purchases, the probability of clicks decreased after the initial purchase and changed in a negative direction up to about 100. This may indicate that interest and interest in the initial purchase gradually waned, resulting in a decrease in the probability of clicks. After that, the click probability changed in a positive direction again until about 200 times. This may indicate that the customer's interest increased again after a certain number of times. After that, it changed in a negative direction, and then converged in a positive direction from about 500 times. This may indicate that the customer became established as a good customer.

Based on these results, it can be inferred that consumer behavior significantly influences the presence or absence of clicks. Consequently, to enhance the click-through rate of email advertising, a strategy involving the individual targeting based on past purchasing patterns and recent buying behaviors is suggested.

8 Conclusion

In this paper, we examine the identification of factors that increase click-through rates.

First, we conducted an RFM analysis to identify customer loyalty. We found that the percentage of good customers was higher among email subscribers. Next, we created a logistic regression model and a random forest model using the results of the RFM analysis. The models were then compared, and it was shown that Random Forest was a superior model compared to Logistic Regression Analysis. The results were then interpreted for the random forest model. The results of the analysis indicated that (video software), (total purchase amount), (date of most recent purchase), (number of purchases), (game software), (shipping costs), (age 45–49), (in-house games), and (music software) had high values.

These results suggest that consumer behavior influences email clicks. Therefore, in order to improve the click, rate of email advertisements, a strategy to individually target consumers based on their past purchase patterns and recent purchase behavior is considered.

These results suggest that consumer behavior influences email clicks. As a future issue, we will examine the effect of the subject line of the email on the clicks on the delivery target. Specifically, we will create a topic model using text data contained in email subject lines, propose email subject lines that are likely to be opened and clicked on, and conduct empirical experiments such as A/B testing to verify whether there is a difference and to infer whether there is actually an effect.

Acknowledgment. We thank the appliance retailers for providing us with the data. This work was supported by JSPS KAKENHI Grant Numbers 21K13385, 21H04600.

References

1. Ministry of Economy, Trade and Industry, Survey of Current Survey of Commerce in FY2022 (2023)

2. Ministry of Economy, Trade and Industry, Survey of Electronic Commerce Transactions in FY2022 (2023)
3. Suzuki, M.: The direction of retailing in the with corona era, toward rebuilding the relationship between online shopping and real stores. Logist. Rev. **71**, 194–206 (2021). (in Japanese)
4. Orange Spirits, Independent Survey Email will still be effective in 2020! Social Media Awareness Survey 2020 (2020). https://note.com/os070601/n/n189fa1c286f5
5. Benchmark, Average Email Open Rate and Click Rate Report (2022 Edition) by Industry and Region (Country) (2023). https://www.benchmarkemail.com/jp/email-marketing-benchmarks/
6. Yoshii, T., Shirota, K., Ichikawa, T., Sano, Y., Mochihashi, D.: Impact of titles on opens in mail-based advertising. In: IPSJ Technical Report, IFAT-148, vol. 2022-IFAT-148, no. 44, pp. 1–11 (2022). (in Japanese)
7. Kitajima, Y.: A study on the effectiveness of direct mail delivery and customer behavior. In: Graduate School of Science and Engineering Annual Report, vol. 52 (2022). (in Japanese)
8. Chawla, V., Bowyer, W., Hall, O., Philip Kegelmeye, W.: SMOTE: synthetic minority over-sampling technique. J. Artif. Intell. Res. **16**, 321–357 (2002)
9. Kin, M.: Data Science in R 13 Marketing Models. Kyoritsu Publishing (2016)
10. Lants, B.: Machine Learning with R, 3rd edn. ShoeiSha (2021)
11. Ariga, Y., Ohasi, S.: Practical Data Science & Machine Learning with R and Python. Gijutsuhyoronsha (2021)

Detection of Branded Posts in User-Generated Content

Clement Levallois[(✉)] [iD]

Emlyon Business School, 15 Boulevard Diderot, 75012 Paris, France
levallois@em-lyon.com

Abstract. User-generated content (UGC) is a fundamental source of information for the study of consumer behavior, product development, and to assess the quality of service. The expansion of branded content, published and mixed with "ordinary" UGC on the same online platforms, blurs the notions of which content should be considered for these studies. This contribution draws on the notion of "authenticity" to offer a taxonomy distinguishing "branded" from "organic" content and presents a computational method to detect branded content in UGC.

Keywords: user-generated content · branded content · text mining · Organic content

1 Introduction: Defining UGC and "Authenticity"

"User - generated content" (UGC) is a broad denomination covering the textual and visual elements produced by individuals and published online, typically on social media in the form of private and public conversations, posts, comments and on e-commerce platforms in the form of reviews, ratings and comments. UGC is often perceived to be a distinctively "authentic" form of content when compared to alternative sources of information, which explains its strong appeal to consumers to inform their purchase decisions and to researchers investigating consumer sentiment. In this contribution, we take a second look at the authenticity of UGC, by offering a matrix crossing six components of authenticity with different types of UGC – including branded content posted by influencers. Based on this taxonomy, we then present a method to improve the detection and removal of branded UGC from a corpus.

UGC has been deemed valuable as a source for text analysis in market research [3, 10] as it can provide near real-time, high volume customer sentiment and customer feedback on their experiences at reduced cost, which classic sources for market research such as focus group, poll or surveys struggle to achieve. Product reviews have served identifying customer needs [30] and the product features which can meet these needs [5, 6]. Reviews can help assess the quality of service, for instance in the hospitality industry [4, 19, 23].

A (sometimes implicit) assumption made when performing analysis on UGC is that, besides the convenience to collect it, it derives a special value from a series of qualities, which can be summed up as "authenticity". "Authenticity" of UGC would stem from

A. Coman and S. Vasilache (Eds.): HCII 2024, LNCS 14704, pp. 304–312, 2024.
https://doi.org/10.1007/978-3-031-61305-0_21

the fact that it is contributed in an unsolicited manner (as opposed to opinions shared in response to polls or surveys), in natural settings (when contrasted with the experimental environment of a focus group), and independently from editorial supervision and professional hierarchies (contrary to the content produced by traditional news media). As such, UGC is considered a trustworthy reflection of consumer knowledge and sentiment [13, 29, 31]. When UGC is analyzed in market research with text mining, which "can reveal patterns of attention or focus of which the speaker may not be conscious" [10], the assumption is reinforced that UGC would grant an unmediated access to the candid, "authentic" state of mind of the content producer.

The assumption of the unqualified authenticity of UGC can however be easily questioned. Is the post by an influencer promoting a product as "authentic" as the post by an ordinary, amateur individual discussing their recent experience of the same product? Disentangling the issue requires first to unpack the multifaceted notion of "authenticity". The concept is usefully decomposed from the perspective of the consumer's experience by Nunes et al. [21], through their qualitative fieldwork examining data collected directly from consumers. Their study validates a definition of authenticity as a "holistic consumer assessment determined by six component judgments (accuracy, connectedness, integrity, legitimacy, originality, and proficiency)" (see Table 1).

Table 1. Components of authenticity, from Nunes et al. [21]. Used with permission.

Table 2. Components of Authenticity.

Component	Definition
1. Accuracy	The extent to which a provider is perceived as transparent in how it represents itself and its products and/or services and, thus, reliable in terms of what it conveys to customers.
2. Connectedness	The extent to which a customer feels engaged, familiar with, and sometimes even transformed by a source and/or its offering.
3. Integrity	The extent to which a provider is perceived as being intrinsically motivated, not acting out of its own financial interest, while acting autonomously and consistently over time.
4. Legitimacy	The extent to which a product or service adheres to shared norms, standards, rules, or traditions present in the market.
5. Originality	The extent to which a product or service stands out from mainstream offerings present in the market and does so without unnecessary embellishments.
6. Proficiency	The extent to which a provider is perceived as properly skilled, exhibiting craftsmanship and/or expertise.

A second step to comprehend better how UGC relates to the notion of authenticity requires to trace a clear and meaningful delineation between the different types of motivations driving the creation of otherwise similar content. In the following, we will designate the content created by authors who post without an ulterior motive as "organic UGC": authors are intrinsically motivated, and the content is not created for (typically) monetary gain.

In contrast, "influencers" will be defined as authors who publish content for extrinsic motives, deriving typically from a contractual commercial partnership with a brand [26] or from the participation to a referral program [18]. A common extrinsic motive is monetary or material gain, which rejoins established definitions of "branded content" in the industry: content which is at least partially funded and created for marketing purposes [2, 8]. Hence, we will define influencers as producers of branded content.

2 A Taxonomy of UGC and Their Authenticity

With these conceptual and terminological clarifications at hand, we can draw a taxonomy of different types of UGC according to the six components of authenticity identified by Nunes et al. [21]. The taxonomy includes "organic UGC" and "branded content" as defined above with three other types of content (user generated or not) which are typically also posted and mixed with UGC on the same online platforms: advertisements, spam and fake reviews [11, 14, 22] (Table 2).

Table 2. Taxonomy of different types of UGC (plus advertising) and their relative strengths on the components constituting "authenticity" (as defined by Nunes et al. [21]), from the point of the view of the consumer's experience.

	licit types of content			illicit or illegitimate types of content	
	"organic UGC"	Branded content	Advertisement	Spam	Fake reviews
Accuracy	Medium to strong	Weak to medium	Medium	Weak	Weak
Connectedness	Medium to strong	Medium to strong	Highly dependent on the campaign	Weak	Weak
Integrity	Strong	Weak to medium	Weak to medium	Weak	Weak
Legitimacy	Weak to medium	Medium	Strong	Weak	Weak
Originality	Highly dependent on the individual	Highly dependent on the influencer	Highly dependent on the campaign	Weak	Weak
Proficiency	Highly dependent on the individual	Medium to strong	Strong	Weak	Weak

Table 3. Evaluation of the method.

	n	True positives	False positives	False negatives	F1
MongoDB	218	13	1	55	**0.32**
Club Med	132	12	0	12	**0.67**
Veuve Cliquot	181	5	2	31	**0.23**
HP printer	205	4	0	51	**0.14**

The table illustrates the contrasted scoring of different kinds of UGC on the six components forming authenticity. Spam and fake reviews stand out as uniformly weak on all components. The remaining types follow different logics. Organic UGC scores the highest on integrity and accuracy, but the lowest on legitimacy. Advertisements score the highest on legitimacy and proficiency, but the lowest on integrity.

A perspective per type of UGC provides an interesting view on a possible reason why the market for branded content and influencers is growing exponentially [8]: branded content scores high on connectedness and proficiency, all while remaining relatively legitimate (more than an advertisement) as they produce content in a more established, standard style than the ordinary, amateur user posting on the same topic.

3 The Case for Isolating Branded Content from UGC for the Study of Authentic Consumer Sentiment

Are all types of UGC to be considered for all types of inquiries? Studies concerned with the magnitude and spread of (dis)information typically include all forms of UGC – including spam and fake reviews - to feed into their analysis [7, 20, 31]. In contrast, studies investigating consumer sentiment would be tainted by the inclusion of spam and fake reviews. Marketers and researchers are reminded that they "should vigorously identify and isolate these predatory comments from the analysis" [24]. A large research stream has developed methods for the removal of spam and fake reviews [11, 12, 22, 27][1].

For the purpose of investigating the *formation* of consumer sentiment, branded content and advertisements must naturally be included in the investigations mapping the information flowing along the ties connecting taste makers and susceptible members in online social networks [1], contributing to identifying the dynamics of information sharing and the determinants of virality [26, 28].

The characterization of *the state* of consumer sentiment would presumably require a different approach. While consumer sentiment is indeed shaped by the variety of online contents it coexists with – branded content, ads, spams and fake reviews – it arguably relates to a distinct subset of UGC, which we named "organic content": the content posted by ordinary, intrinsically motivated individuals sharing their thoughts transparently. This subset matches most of the components of the definition of authenticity offered by Nunes et al. [21], which is coherent with the notion that consumer sentiment would reflect the "authentic" expression of consumers.

Detecting branded content would allow for more accurate consumer sentiment analysis, centered on organic UGC, reflecting consumer's thoughts with higher fidelity. This would benefit market research tasks performed on UGC which hinge on the premise that UGC is the "authentic" reflection of consumer expression. In the following section, we offer a preliminary version of a method for the identification of organic and branded content.

---

[1] In practice, the step of spam removal is unfrequently performed (and if so, not documented in detail) in marketing research papers on online consumer sentiment.

4 Detection of Branded Posts

We design a method for detection which follows a rule-based approach derived from Umigon, which is a model for sentiment analysis developed by the author [15, 16]. The model can be decomposed in:

1. Pre-processing of the UGC: tokenization, detection of phrases, ngrams, removal of stopwords.
2. for each phrase, each n-gram is compared with entries from a lexicon.
3. in case of a match, zero or several Boolean conditions attached to the lexicon entry are evaluated and return a result: branded content or not.

4.1 Pre-Processing

Tokenization. Tokenization is performed with a custom parser[2]. The parser splits the text at white spaces and identifies a series of categories of tokens: words, emojis, emoticons, punctuation signs, "non words" (onomatopes, abbreviations) and white spaces. Indices of Each Token in the Text Are Recorded.

Phrases. A phrase is defined as a relatively independent proposition in a text. Periods, commas, exclamation and question marks all delineate phrases within a text. Parentheses and quotes also play this role in a more elaborated way (with a logic of opening and closing characters). Identifying phrases can be useful to ignore irrelevant fragments (such as content in parentheses), and to identify tokens at positions with special significance in the text – such as a word at the beginning of a phrase, or a punctuation sign at the end of it.

Ngrams. Ngrams are consecutive sequence of terms. We use a custom implementation which leverages the tokenization and sentence fragment detection presented above: Ngrams are detected within sentence fragments and are guaranteed not to include punctuation signs, emojis, emoticons or non words. Ngrams are also filtered to remove less frequent ones already included in lengthier ngrams (the trigram "United States of" will be removed if the quadrigram "United States of America" appears more frequently).

Stopword Removal. Stopwords are removed, only after processing ngrams so that stopwords embedded in ngrams will not be removed: the stopword "of" is removed but not when embedded in "United States of America".

4.2 Matching with Lexicon Entries

Each ngram of the text is compared with entries of a lexicon. The lexicon is a list of ngrams which are frequently found in branded content. This list is curated by the author and expands steadily (with 104 entries as of February 2024)[3]. Entries are selected by culling "manually" social media posts. UGC which appears to be a form of branded content is scrutinized for typical semantic features of branded content:

---

[2] The source code of all steps of the method is available under an Creative Commons Attribution 4.0 International Public License at https://github.com/seinecle/umigon-family.

[3] https://github.com/seinecle/umigon-static-files/blob/main/src/main/resources/net/clementle vallois/umigon/lexicons/en/9_commercial%20tone.txt.

- calls to action. Organic UGC rarely includes calls to action while branded content often does.
- addresses to an audience, from the perspective of an unspecified "we" ("we offer...", "you will appreciate").
- use of vocabulary typical of a corporate voice. Organic UGC rarely uses phrases like "complimentary", "for a chance to", "stoked to", "boasts" and similar expressions, which are characteristic of an intent to promote or embellish a product or service.

4.3 Evaluating Boolean Conditions

Lexicon entries alone are frequently insufficiently specific to afford a precise characterization of the content. Each entry can be supplemented by several Boolean conditions which help capture the context of use of the lexicon entry. For instance, the expression "find out" is not a specific marker of branded content in itself, however when used as an imperative at the beginning of a phrase it evokes a clear call to action. The condition `isStartOfSegment` attached to the lexicon entry allows to assess this element of context. 40 Boolean conditions have been designed to assist in qualifying lexicon entries[4].

5 Evaluation

Four brands have been selected to cover a variety of products and services from a hedonist, utilitarian, B2B and B2C contexts: MongoDB (database), Club Med (French travel and tourism operator), Veuve Cliquot (Champagne house) and HP printers. A search for 200 tweets has been performed in February 2024 for each of them, using the twscrape library[5]. A number of tweets were removed as the search term was included in the twitter handle, not in the content of the post. The dataset was annotated by the author for organic vs branded tone. The coding procedure followed these heuristics:

- a post with a call to action, or promoting a product or an event, or addressing an impersonal audience ("you...") from an impersonal standpoint ("we..."), will tend to be annotated as "branded".
- other posts will tend to be annotated as "organic"

The tweets were analyzed with the method presented in this paper and implemented in the platform Nocode Functions (https://nocodefunctions.com).

F1 scores are noticeably low (Table 3). The method offers however promising perspectives, for three reasons.

The method is inherently interpretable, as the internals of rule-based systems can in principle be decomposed to reveal the chain of causal processed which led to the classification outcome [25]. The system presented here can effectively be used to share

---

[4] https://github.com/seinecle/umigon-lexicons/tree/main/src/main/java/net/clementlevallois/umigon/heuristics/booleanconditions.

[5] https://github.com/vladkens/twscrape. The search on MongoDB returned 218 tweets and the search on HP printer returned 206 results, despite the parameter set.

with the analyst a full report of the rules which were followed to arrive at the classification of each piece of text[6].

The rate of false positive is close to zero: the method is very precise. One of the strengths of lexicon-based methods, compared to models based on statistical learning, is that expert-crafted rules can be designed with great precision, avoiding the inherent element of randomness introduced by a supervised learning approach. The adjunction of Boolean conditions to further characterize lexicon entries limits even further the rate of false positives, as confounding elements of context can be evaluated and considered.

Finally, the recall is very low, due to the very weak coverage of the lexicons. A low number of lexicon entries implies that a large number of expressions typically characterizing "branded content" are not currently captured by the lexicon. This is sometimes described as a limiting factor of all lexicon-based methods [9]. However, such methods have proven to be able to achieve high levels of recall in a similar categorization task (sentiment analysis), leading to F1 scores competitive with large language models [17][7]. The resource needed to achieve such levels of recall, and overall precision, is a continuous expansion of the lexicons to gradually expand their coverage. This traces an encouraging roadmap for future work.

References

1. Aral, S., Walker, D.: Identifying influential and susceptible members of social networks. Science **337**(6092), 337–341 (2012). https://doi.org/10.1126/science.1215842
2. Asmussen, B., Wider, S., Williams, R., Stevenson, N., Whitehead, E.: Defining Branded Content for the Digital Age: The Industry Experts' Views on Branded Content as a New Marketing Communications Concept (A Collaborative Research Project Commissioned by the Branded Content Marketing Association (BCMA), p. 42). Branded Content Marketing Association. https://research.cbs.dk/en/publications/defining-branded-content-for-the-digital-age-the-industry-experts
3. Berger, J., Humphreys, A., Ludwig, S., Moe, W.W., Netzer, O., Schweidel, D.A.: Uniting the tribes: using text for marketing insight. J. Mark. **84**(1), 1–25 (2020). https://doi.org/10.1177/0022242919873106
4. Calheiros, A.C., Moro, S., Rita, P.: Sentiment classification of consumer-generated online reviews using topic modeling. J. Hosp. Market. Manag. **26**(7), 675–693 (2017). https://doi.org/10.1080/19368623.2017.1310075
5. Decker, R., Trusov, M.: Estimating aggregate consumer preferences from online product reviews. Int. J. Res. Mark. **27**(4), 293–307 (2010). https://doi.org/10.1016/j.ijresmar.2010.09.001
6. Haddara, M., Hsieh, J., Fagerstrøm, A., Eriksson, N., Sigurðsson, V.: Exploring customer online reviews for new product development: the case of identifying reinforcers in the cosmetic industry. Manag. Decis. Econ. **41**(2), 250–273 (2020). https://doi.org/10.1002/mde.3078
7. Hajli, N., Saeed, U., Tajvidi, M., Shirazi, F.: Social bots and the spread of disinformation in social media: the challenges of artificial intelligence. Br. J. Manag. **33**(3), 1238–1253 (2022). https://doi.org/10.1111/1467-8551.12554

---

[6] Single tests can be performed on the homepage of https://nocodefunctions.com. Text files can be analyzed on the same platform, returning explanations for each of the results in a spreadsheet format. An API access is also available.

[7] See also the public benchmark: https://github.com/seinecle/umibench.

8. Hardy, J., Karagiorgou, I., Keddo, N., Moise, R., Sujon, Z., Yesiloglu, S.: The UK Branded Content Industry: Report and Survey (p. 97). Branded Content Research Hub (2023)
9. Hartmann, J., Huppertz, J., Schamp, C., Heitmann, M.: Comparing automated text classification methods. Int. J. Res. Mark. **36**(1), 20–38 (2019). https://doi.org/10.1016/j.ijresmar.2018.09.009
10. Humphreys, A., Wang, R.J.-H.: Automated text analysis for consumer research. J. Consum. Res. **44**(6), 1274–1306 (2018). https://doi.org/10.1093/jcr/ucx104
11. Jindal, N., Liu, B.: Analyzing and detecting review spam. In: Seventh IEEE International Conference on Data Mining (ICDM 2007), pp. 547–552 (2007). https://doi.org/10.1109/ICDM.2007.68
12. Kaddoura, S., Chandrasekaran, G., Elena Popescu, D., Duraisamy, J.H.: A systematic literature review on spam content detection and classification. PeerJ Comput. Sci. **8**, e830 (2022). https://doi.org/10.7717/peerj-cs.830
13. Kannan, P.K., Li, H.: Digital marketing: a framework, review and research agenda. Int. J. Res. Mark. **34**(1), 22–45 (2017). https://doi.org/10.1016/j.ijresmar.2016.11.006
14. Lappas, T., Sabnis, G., Valkanas, G.: The impact of fake reviews on online visibility: a vulnerability assessment of the hotel industry. Inf. Syst. Res. **27**(4), 940–961 (2016). https://doi.org/10.1287/isre.2016.0674
15. Levallois, C.: Umigon: sentiment analysis for tweets based on terms lists and heuristics. Second Joint Conference on Lexical and Computational Semantics (*SEM), Volume 2: Proceedings of the Seventh International Workshop on Semantic Evaluation (SemEval 2013), pp. 414–417 (2013). https://aclanthology.org/S13-2068
16. Levallois, C.: Reintroducing qualitative insights in big data: the case of "sentiment" in textual analysis. Under Rev. (2023)
17. Levallois, C.: Umigon-lexicon: a contribution to inherently interpretable sentiment analysis. Lang. Resources and Evalution (forthcoming) (n.d.)
18. Lobel, I., Sadler, E., Varshney, L.R.: Customer referral incentives and social media. Manage. Sci. **63**(10), 3514–3529 (2017). https://doi.org/10.1287/mnsc.2016.2476
19. Luo, J., Huang, S., Wang, R.: A fine-grained sentiment analysis of online guest reviews of economy hotels in China. J. Hospitality Market. Manage. **30**(1), 71–95 (2021).https://doi.org/10.1080/19368623.2020.1772163
20. Mayzlin, D., Dover, Y., Chevalier, J.: Promotional reviews: an empirical investigation of online review manipulation. Am. Econ. Rev. **104**(8), 2421–2455 (2014). https://doi.org/10.1257/aer.104.8.2421
21. Nunes, J.C., Ordanini, A., Giambastiani, G.: The concept of authenticity: what it means to consumers. J. Mark. **85**(4), 1–20 (2021). https://doi.org/10.1177/0022242921997081
22. Paul, H., Nikolaev, A.: Fake review detection on online E-commerce platforms: a systematic literature review. Data Min. Knowl. Disc. **35**(5), 1830–1881 (2021). https://doi.org/10.1007/s10618-021-00772-6
23. Pizam, A., Shapoval, V., Ellis, T.: Customer satisfaction and its measurement in hospitality enterprises: a revisit and update. Int. J. Contemp. Hosp. Manag. **28**(1), 2–35 (2016). https://doi.org/10.1108/IJCHM-04-2015-0167
24. Rambocas, M., Pacheco, B.G.: Online sentiment analysis in marketing research: a review. J. Res. Interact. Mark. **12**(2), 146–163 (2018). https://doi.org/10.1108/JRIM-05-2017-0030
25. Rudin, C.: Stop explaining black box machine learning models for high stakes decisions and use interpretable models instead. Nature Mach. Intell. **1**(5), 5 (2019). https://doi.org/10.1038/s42256-019-0048-x
26. Schulze, C., Schöler, L., Skiera, B.: Not all fun and games: viral marketing for utilitarian products. J. Mark. **78**(1), 1–19 (2014). https://doi.org/10.1509/jm.11.0528
27. Spirin, N., Han, J.: Survey on web spam detection: principles and algorithms. ACM SIGKDD Explor. Newsl **13**(2), 50–64 (2012). https://doi.org/10.1145/2207243.2207252

28. Subramani, M.R., Rajagopalan, B.: Knowledge-sharing and influence in online social networks via viral marketing. Commun. ACM **46**(12), 300–307 (2003). https://doi.org/10.1145/953460.953514
29. Timoshenko, A., Hauser, J.R.: Identifying customer needs from user-generated content. Mark. Sci. **38**(1), 1–20 (2019). https://doi.org/10.1287/mksc.2018.1123
30. van Dieijen, M., Borah, A., Tellis, G.J., Franses, P.H.: Big data analysis of volatility spillovers of brands across social media and stock markets. Ind. Mark. Manage. **88**, 465–484 (2020). https://doi.org/10.1016/j.indmarman.2018.12.006
31. Wu, Y., Ngai, E.W.T., Wu, P., Wu, C.: Fake online reviews: literature review, synthesis, and directions for future research. Decis. Support Syst. **132**, 113280 (2020). https://doi.org/10.1016/j.dss.2020.113280

Identification of Important Products in Electronics Retail Stores Using a Product-To-Product Network

Jin Nakashima[1(✉)], Takashi Namatame[2], and Kohei Otake[3]

[1] Graduate School of Information and Telecommunication Engineering, Tokai University, 2-3-23, Takanawa, Minato-Ku 108-8619, Tokyo, Japan
3cjnm017@mail.u-tokai.ac.jp
[2] School of Science and Engineering, Chuo University, 1-13-27, Kasuga, Bunkyo-Ku 112-8551, Tokyo, Japan
nama@kc.chuo-u.ac.jp
[3] Faculty of Economics, Sophia University, 7-1 Kioi-cho, Chiyoda-Ku, Tokyo 102-8554, Japan
k-otake@sophia.ac.jp

Abstract. In recent years, the rise of electronic commerce and direct-to-consumer (D2C) has significantly "showroomed" retail stores, and there is a need to maximize the consumer experience through actual products in stores. Therefore, this study aims to identify important products by quantitatively analyzing and discussing retailers' purchase history data, and to propose marketing measures focusing on value communication in stores. Specifically, we defined the degree of similarity between products based on consumer preferences from ID-POS data and constructed a network model between products using social network analysis techniques. In addition, we used community detection and centrality indices to extract similar product groups and identify important products.

Keywords: Electronics Retail Stores · Inter-Product Similarity · Social Network Analysis

1 Introduction

In recent years, the environment surrounding the retail industry has changed dramatically, requiring a reconsideration of its role. The rate of Electronic Commerce (EC) in the field of goods sales continues to rise, and the market size is expanding year by year [1]. In addition, there is a growing trend toward direct-to-consumer (D2C), which achieves higher profitability by eliminating intermediate margins and more efficient data collection and utilization through in-house production of sales [2]. This has led to the "showrooming" of retail stores, where customers visit stores to collect information to make purchasing decisions on EC sites. This "showrooming" is particularly significant in electronics mass retailers, where the number of customers who visit stores for purposes other than purchasing products is on the rise. In order to maximize the customer experience through the actual sales floor and products at the store, it is necessary to capture such a showrooming trend.

This research aims to identify important products by quantitatively analyzing and to propose marketing measures focusing on value communication in stores. Specifically, we define the product similarity based on customer preferences using ID-POS data from electronics retail stores and construct a product-to-product network model using social network analysis techniques. Furthermore, we conduct community detection and calculate centrality indices to extract similar product groups, we identify important products. We attempt to propose in-store marketing measures based on the results of these analyses.

In general, data with a graph or network structure clearly shows the relationships among objects represented as nodes. Typical examples include the hyperlink structure between web pages, followers in a social networking service (SNS), and connections between people and positions within an organization. By graphically representing the relationship structure between objects based on the presence or absence of links between nodes and applying graph mining methods such as community detection and centrality index calculation to search for closely connected groups, it is possible to measure clustering and the influence of each node [3][4]. On the other hand, Goto [5] points out that purchasing and browsing relationships among products, such as those frequently encountered in the marketing domain, "can be regarded as data representing connections among objects and can be analyzed as graph structure data. He applied network analysis to the "problem of not being able to simply define whether or not there is a relationship between nodes" by defining relationships between Web pages based on users' browsing history data. He also showed that, in contrast to network graphs constructed from high-dimensional and sparse similarity between nodes, when network graphs are constructed in conjunction with dimensionality compression methods, nodes that are more closely related may be connected and effective clustering results may be obtained. In a related study, Ito et al. [6] applied network analysis by defining the degree of similarity between products based on the number of customers who purchased common products. In addition, they extract similar product groups by community detection and identify important products using the PageRank index.

These studies show that network analysis can be applied to data with no clearly defined relationships between objects, and that useful results can be obtained by defining appropriate similarity levels. In this study, we follow the framework of Ito et al. and define similarity between products. In addition to this, assuming the implementation of practical marketing measures in the creation of a sales space in a retail store, we identify products that serve as relay points between products by using betweenness centrality. In this study, we analyze the purchase history data of three general stores that handle a wide variety of products and attempt to propose marketing measures with high reproducibility by comparing their characteristics.

2   Dataset

This study analyzes purchase history data collected at an electronics retail store. This electronics mass retailer mainly sells personal computers and peripherals, music, video, and game software, and other products. The period of data to be analyzed is one year, from January 1 to December 31, 2022. Table 1 shows an overview of the data used.

In order to construct a network among products, a node list representing each product category and an edge list representing the degree of similarity among products were created.

Table 1. Data Set Overview

Store Name	Number of Purchaser	Number of Categories
Store A	12,704	521
Store B	24,474	681
Store C	18,226	706

2.1 Node List—Product Categories

Products purchased by customers are represented as a node list consisting of product IDs and product category names (Table 2).

Table 2. Example of Node List

Category ID	Category Name
001	Category A
002	Category B
003	Category C

2.2 Edge List—Similarity Between Each Product

The similarity between each product is represented as an edge list with From-To combinations representing the similarity between each product (Table 3). For each combination of products, the similarity is given as a weight.

Table 3. Example of Edge List

From	To	Weight
001	002	0.1
001	003	0.2
001	004	0.3

In this study, these node and edge lists are used to construct an inter-product network.

3 Analysis Method

In this study, we used several methods to construct and analyze the inter-product network. We provide an overview of our analytical methodology below.

3.1 Social Network Analysis

Social network analysis is an analytical method based on graph theory that explores the relationship structure (network) among components in various objects, such as human relationships, distribution networks, and links on Web pages. In this study, we constructed a network among products by considering nodes as product categories and edges as similarities among products.

Community Detection. We performed community detection using modularity on the constructed product networks to extract groups of similar products. Community detection is a method of clustering nodes into closely connected groups for a given network structure. Modularity is often used as a quantitative measure to determine which partition is a desirable representation of community structure (1) [7].

$$Q = \frac{1}{2m} \sum_{ij} \left(A_{ij} - \frac{k_i k_j}{2m} \right) \delta\left(C_i, C_j \right) \# \tag{1}$$

In the above equation, m is the total number of edges in the network, A_{ij} is the weight of edges between nodes i and j, k_i and k_j are the orders of nodes i and j, respectively, and $\delta\left(C_i, C_j \right)$ is a function that is 1 if nodes i and j are the same community and 0 otherwise. In this study, we performed community detection based on edge-betweenness centrality using modularity.

Centrality Indicator. In this study, we used PageRank and Betweenness Centrality to identify important products in the network.

PageRank is an indicator that nodes connected from a node of high importance are important. In addition, connections from nodes of the same importance but with a lower degree of order are rated higher as "carefully selected links." Assuming that the adjacency matrix of a graph is $A = (a_{ij})$, the PageRank $C_p(i)$ of node i can be formulated as follows (2) [8]. The presence or absence of an edge between node i and node j is represented by a binary variable, PageRank $C_p(i)$, which indicates that the PageRank $C_p(j)$ of the other node j directly connected to that node has been summed. It is then normalized by dividing by the total number of nodes in the network, N.

$$C_p(i) = \sum_j \frac{a_{ij}}{N} C_p(j) \tag{2}$$

Betweenness centrality is an index of the degree to which a node is the shortest path for another node. The standardize betweenness centrality of a node v in a graph is formulated as follows (3) [9]. Where g_{ij} is the total number of shortest paths between node i and node j, and $g_{ij}(v)$ is the number of shortest paths that node v takes on the shortest path between nodes i and j. In addition, the Betweenness Centrality is calculated by summing over all nodes i, j except node v. n is the total number of nodes in the network and is normalized by $1/(n-1)(n-2)$. The $n-1$ is for considering the shortest path with all other nodes, and $n-2$ is for excluding the node itself and other nodes on the shortest path.

$$C_d(v) = \frac{1}{(n-1)(n-2)} \sum_{v \neq i \neq j} \frac{g_{ij}(v)}{g_{ij}} \tag{3}$$

3.2 PLSA

In this study, we apply the latent class model PLSA (Probabilistic Latent Semantic Analysis) [10] as a method to define the similarity between products based on customer preferences. PLSA is a method to perform dimensional compression of data by explaining large high-dimensional data with a small number of latent variables. For the target ID-POS data, soft clustering is performed based on the co-occurrence relationship between purchased products (columns) and customers (rows). This makes it possible to model customers' propensity to purchase products while taking into account the similarity and diversity of customer preferences. Figure 1 shows a graphical model of PLSA.

Latent Class

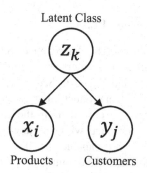

Products   Customers

Fig. 1. Graphical model of PLSA

Let $X = \{x_1, x_2, \cdots x_I\}$ be a set of I products, $Y = \{y_1, y_2, \cdots y_J\}$ be a set of J customers, and $Z = \{z_1, z_2, \cdots z_K\}$ be a set of K potential classes. In this case, the probability of the event $P(x_i, y_j)$ that customer y_j purchases product x_i is formulated as follows (4).

$$P(x_i, y_j) = \sum_{k=1}^{K} P(z_k)P(x_i|z_k)(y_j|z_k)\# \tag{4}$$

Here, the parameters $P(z_k), P(x_i|z_k), (y_j|z_k)$ that maximize the following log-likelihood function are estimated using the EM algorithm [11], an exploratory method. $\delta(x_i, y_j)$ is determined by whether customer y_j is purchasing product x_i indicator function (5).

$$LL = \sum_{i=1}^{I} \sum_{j=1}^{J} \delta(x_i, y_j) logP(x_i, y_j) \tag{5}$$

4 Proposed Method

In this study, we follow the method proposed by Ito et al. [6] to calculate the degree of similarity between products. First, we calculate the degree of similarity between products based on co-occurrence based on customers who purchased common products. Then, we multiply this by the weights of customer preferences based on PLSA and weights based on the probability of transitions between products. The similarity between products obtained by this method is used to construct an inter-product network.

4.1 Calculation of Weights by Simple Co-Occurrence

For each analyzed store, the total number of customers who purchased both product a and product b for a certain combination of two products is calculated as s_{ab}, and this is done for all combinations of two products. The similarity between product a and product b in the edge list created by s_{ab} is the symmetric relationship $s_{ab} = s_{ab}$. The reason for this is that the number of people who purchased both product a and product b is calculated to show the connection between products that are likely to be purchased by a larger number of customers.

4.2 Calculating Weights Based on PLSA

In this section, we calculate the weights based on PLSA in order to bring products that are likely to be purchased by customers with similar tastes closer together. s_{ab} The similarity between products calculated in Sect. 4.1, has difficulty expressing the connection between products based on product categories and features. In order to reflect the diverse purchasing tendencies of customers in the network, we consider strongly expressing connections between products with similar customer preferences.

Therefore, we use PLSA, which is capable of soft clustering of co-occurrence relationships between products, customers, and multiply the weights by the customers' purchasing tendencies. This is thought to allow us to take into account customer preferences and product characteristics. In this case, when the probability that product i belongs to latent class k is θ_{ik} (8), the probability that product i belongs to each latent class, or latent class distribution, is expressed as $\theta_i = (\theta_{i1}, \theta_{i2} \cdots, \theta_{iK})$. Therefore, the distance between the probability distribution θ_a of product a to the probability distribution θ_b of product b can be formulated using the Jensen-Shannon Divergence [12] (JS Divergence) in Eq. (6). Where m (9) represents the mean distribution of θ_a and θ_b, and $D_{KL}(\theta_a||m)$ and $D_{KL}(\theta_b||m)$ are the Kullback-Leibler Divergence[12] (KL Divergence) from θ_a and θ_b to m. The KL Divergence is formulated as in Eq. (7) and calculates how much the distribution θ_a differs from θ_b, with θ_b as the reference distribution JS Divergence uses KL Divergence to introduce a distribution m between the two and averages their relative entropies, thus contrasting the similarities between the distributions and treating them as distances. The similarities between the distributions can be contrasted and treated as distances.

$$D_{JS}(\theta_a||\theta_b) = \tfrac{1}{2}(D_{KL}(\theta_a||m) + D_{KL}(\theta_b||m)) \tag{6}$$

$$D_{KL}(\theta_a||\theta_b) = \sum_{k=1}^{K} \theta_{ak} log \frac{\theta_{ak}}{\theta_{bk}} \qquad (7)$$

$$\theta_{ik} = P(z_k|x_i) \qquad (8)$$

$$m = \frac{1}{2}(\theta_a + \theta_b) \qquad (9)$$

$$w_{ab} = 1 - D_{JS}(\theta_a||\theta_b) \qquad (10)$$

The smaller the value of JS Divergence, the more similar the distribution is. Since a dynamic model is used to visualize the network between products, the larger the weight of the similarity (edges) between products, the closer the products (nodes) are located to each other. Therefore, the weight w_{ab}, which represents a stronger connection between products with similar product affiliation distributions, is calculated using Eq. (10). By multiplying this by s_{ab}, a simple co-occurrence relationship between products, the similarity between products with similar product characteristics based on customer preferences is highly evaluated, and products with high similarity are attracted to each other in the inter-product network.

4.3 Calculation of Weights Based on Inter-Product Transition Probabilities

Although the similarity w_{ab} between products can express the connection between products in terms of customer preferences, s_{ab} and w_{ab} are undirected graphs because the weights of the mutual edges between products are equal and symmetric. Therefore, these weights alone cannot take into account the transition of customers' purchasing tendencies.

Therefore, by setting the transition probabilities between products as weights, we construct a network between products as a directed graph. Specifically, t_{ab} is calculated as the percentage of customers who have purchased product b among those who have purchased product a. By using the transition probabilities between products as weights, the difference between the transition probabilities t_{ab} from product a to product b and t_{ab} from product b to product a can be expressed.

The similarity h_{ab} between products calculated from the weights obtained in Sects. 4.1 and 4.2 can be expressed as follows.

$$h_{ab} = s_{ab} \times w_{ab} \times t_{ab} \qquad (11)$$

In the analysis, a product-to-product network is constructed using the product-to-customer similarity h_{ab} calculated by Eq. (11), and by adding weights based on the co-occurrence relationship between products and customers using PLSA and the product-to-product transition probability, the network structure provides insight into customer preferences and purchasing trends.

5   Result and Discussion

For each of the three store datasets shown in Sect. 2, we constructed an inter-product net-work, extracted similar product groups by community detection, and identified important products and products that serve as relay points by using centrality indices. By comparing the inter-product networks of these three stores, we attempt to propose effective measures for in-store marketing.

5.1   Extraction of Similar Product Groups and Identification of Important Products Using an Inter-Product Network

We visualize the connection between products by constructing an inter-product network using the similarity h_{ab} calculated based on the data of the three stores under analysis. In addition, we attempt to identify important products using PageRank by extracting similar product groups through community detection. The graphopt layout algorithm [13], which is a dynamical model, was used to draw the network graph. I In addition, from the perspective of readability, we set the similarity h_ab as a threshold so that the total number of nodes in the network is less than 200, and only the main connected components with a large number of nodes were extracted. Figures 1, 2 and 3 show the results of the analysis of the networks among products for which community detection was performed at each store. The top three products in terms of PageRank in each community are shown in Tables 4, 5 and 6.

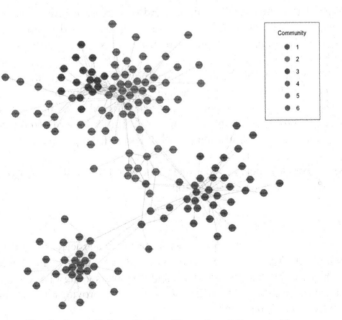

Fig. 2.   Store A's Inter-Product Network and Communities

Table 4. Similar Products in Store A's Communities and PageRank

Community 1		Community 2		Community 3	
Products	PageRank	Products	PageRank	Products	PageRank
mouse G	0.00834	game SA	0.04624	BD A	0.01266
keyboard G	0.00525	game DA	0.04408	DVD A	0.01169
mouse pad	0.00450	third A	0.04056	CD A	0.00535

Community 4		Community 5		Community 6	
Products	PageRank	Products	PageRank	Products	PageRank
mouse A	0.03200	figure R	0.00488	device C	0.01986
laptop	0.02301	kit PG	0.00245	cable	0.01295
soft V	0.01047	kit P	0.00208	RAM	0.01238

The inter-product network of Store A consists of six community. The size of Communities 2, 4, and 6 is particularly large, and the PageRank of the products belonging to these communities is relatively high. In addition, the product group in Community 1 (Gaming Devices) seems to be a bridge between these communities.

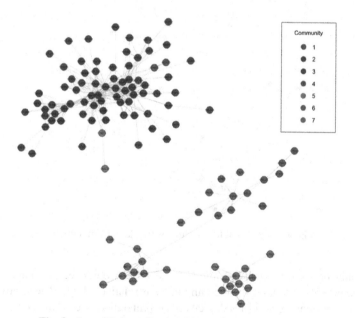

Fig. 3. Store B's Inter-Product Network and Communities

The inter-product network in Store B consists of two connected components, and seven communities. The size of Community 3 is particularly large, and the PageRank of the products belonging to this community is high. The upper connected component contains subcultural products related to games, animation, and figures, while the lower component contains PC-related products, indicating customer preferences.

Table 5. Similar Products in Store B's Communities and PageRank

Community 1		Community 2		Community 3	
Products	PageRank	Products	PageRank	Products	PageRank
RAM	0.00881	figure R	0.012039	game SB	0.03406
PC PS	0.00675	figure A	0.009442	BD A	0.02335
HDD	0.00517	figure C	0.007904	DVD A	0.01772

Community 6		Community 7	
Products	PageRank	Products	PageRank
mouse A	0.01546	mouse G	0.01278
USB	0.00760	keyboard G	0.00835
laptop	0.00451	mouse pad	0.00793

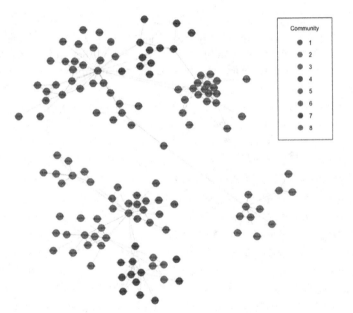

Fig. 4. Store B's Inter-Product Network and Communities

The inter-product network in Store C consists of two connected components, and eight communities. The number of communities is relatively large. The relatively large number of communities indicates that customer preferences are segmented.

By comparing the product networks among these three stores and the important products in each community, we can infer the following.

- All three stores have communities subcultural products such as home video games, anime, and figurines, and these communities are connected to each other.
- All three stores have communities for PC-related products such as notebook PCs, desktop PCs, and gaming devices, and these communities are connected to each other.

Table 6. Similar products in Store C's Communities and PageRank

Community 1		Community 2		Community 3	
Products	PageRank	Products	PageRank	Products	PageRank
figure R	0.00421	ink A	0.03236	cable	0.00638
figure A	0.00215	ink B	0.00905	device C	0.00592
figure C	0.00144	printer	0.00873	video card	0.00446

Community 4		Community 5		Community 6	
Products	PageRank	Products	PageRank	Products	PageRank
display A	0.00505	mouse A	0.04007	game SA	0.04664
display G	0.00347	laptop	0.01686	third A	0.0344
mouse G	0.00335	USB	0.01387	game DA	0.02768

Community 7		Community 8	
Products	PageRank	Products	PageRank
goods A	0.01275	game SB	0.0201
books	0.00553	game RB	0.0107
toy	0.00417	BD A	0.0091

- In Store B and Store C, the subculture product community and the PC-related product community have separate and unconnected components.

These points indicate that similar communities are formed as a common feature of the product networks of the three stores. In Store A, the structure of the gaming device bridges each community, while in Stores B and C, the structure of the connected components shows a clear division of customer preferences, which is characteristic of each store.

5.2 Identification of Relayed Products Based on Betweenness Centrality

In order to identify products that serve as relay points, bridging between products (relay products), we calculated the betweenness centrality of products in the inter-product network of the three stores. The top five products in terms of betweenness centrality at each store are shown in Table 7.

Table 7 shows that the common features of the products in each store are that mice, cables, and game software have particularly high betweenness centrality and play an important role as relay products. In addition, the high betweenness centrality of gaming headsets (head set G) in Store A supports the fact that gaming devices bridge each community in the inter-product network of Store A described in Sect. 5.1. These results indicate that it is possible to identify the relay products that connect each community based on the products with high betweenness centrality.

5.3 Proposed Sales Policies Based on Inter-Product Networks

Based on the results and discussions in Sects. 5.1 and 5.2, we propose specific sales measures. In this study, we refer in particular to specific sales measures for important

Table 7. Betweenness Centrality of Products in Each Store

Store A		Store B		Store C	
Products	Bettweenness Centrality	Products	Bettweenness Centrality	Products	Bettweenness Centrality
headset G	0.01306	mouse A	0.00819	mouse A	0.03013
third B	0.01274	game SA	0.00756	game SA	0.01263
cable	0.01109	display A	0.00579	cable	0.01218
game RB	0.01102	RAM	0.00456	ink A	0.01146
mouse A	0.01047	device PS	0.0042	game SB	0.01071

products and relay products identified based on PageRank and betweenness centrality. The following sales measures can be proposed.

- Important products are sold with emphasis (Point Presentation) as the core products of the store.
- Set up product shelves with a group of products corresponding to each community.
- The important products are concentrated at the end of the shelves to attract customers' attention.
- The relayed products are displayed and sold (Item Presentation) as products that approach a wide range of customers.
- Enhance sorting, organization, and display to make it easier for customers to select and pick up the products.
- Use to design a sales flow to attract customers to the sales floor of important products.

From the viewpoint of In-Store Merchandising (ISM), which is a guideline for in-store sales floor development based on consumer behavior, the overlap of the product set that customer evoke (evoked set) and the product set that they see on the sales floor (visible set) can be the product set that customer consider purchasing (choice set) [14]. Therefore, it is important to reduce the gap between the evoked set and the visible set, and to create a sales floor that makes it easier for customers to pick up the product.

6 Conclusion

In this study, we quantitatively analyzed ID-POS data from electronics retail stores to propose marketing measures that focus on communicating value at the point-of-sale. Specifically, we defined the degree of similarity between products based on customer preferences and constructed a network between products using social network analysis techniques. In addition, we used community detection and centrality indices to extract similar product groups and to identify important products and relay products. The results of the analysis and discussion provide useful suggestions for in-store marketing measures based on ISM.

This study evaluated three general stores, but this was only an evaluation of the inter-product network based on ID-POS data, and the specific store structure of the target stores was not taken into account. Therefore, a detailed analysis based on a comparison of the product-to-product network with the actual store structure and sales floor layout is necessary. In addition, in order to verify the sales measures obtained in this study, we plan to collect and analyze biometric data such as customers' line of sight and motion lines through experiments in actual stores in the future, in order to study a more sophisticated consumer behavior model.

Acknowledgment. This work was supported by JSPS KAKENHI Grant Numbers 21K13385, 21H04600.

References

1. Ministry of Economy, Trade and Industry, "2022 Market Research Report on E-Commerce," https://www.meti.go.jp/press/2022/08/20220812005/20220812005.html. Accessed 20 Jan 2024
2. W2 Co. Ltd., "What is D2C," https://www.w2solution.co.jp/useful_info_ec/d2c/. Accessed 20 Jan 2024
3. Onizuka, M.: Application of big data with graph mining technology and high-speed technology initiatives. Prod. Technol. **67**(2), 4–10 (2015). (in Japanese)
4. Girvan, M., Newman, M.E.J.: Community structure in social and biological networks. Proc. Nat. Acad. Sci. **99**, 7821–7826 (2002)
5. Goto, M.: Utilizing user behavior history data network analysis. Oper. Res. Soc. Japan, Official Organ **64**(11), 671–677 (2019). (in Japanese)
6. Ito, H., Goto, M.: A study on extraction of important items focused on customer growth based on network analysis. In: Proceedings of the 18th Asia Pacific Industrial Engineering and Management System Conference, ID164 (2017). (in Japanese)
7. Murata, T.: Community extraction from the network. Intell. Inf. **21**(4), 500–508 (2009). (in Japanese)
8. Suzuki, T.: Data Science in R, 8 Network Analysis, 2nd (edn.) Kyoritsu Syuppan, pp. 2–71 (2017). (in Japanese)
9. Brandes, U.: On variants of shortest-path betweenness centrality and their generic computation. Soc. Netw. **30**(2), 136–145 (2008)
10. hofmann, T.: Probabilistic latent semantic indexing. In: Proceedings of the 22nd Annual ACM Conference on Research and Development in Information Retrieval, pp. 50–57 (1999)
11. Dempster, A.P., Laird, N.M., Rubin, D.B.: Maximum likelihood from incomplete data via the EM algorithm. J. Royal Stat. Soc. Ser. B **39**(1), 1–38 (1977)
12. Fuglede, B., Topsoe, F.: Jensen-Shannon divergence and Hilbert space embedding. In: Proceedings of the Internationals Symposium on Information Theory, pp. 31–39 (2004)
13. The igraph core team. "The graphopt layout algorithm". https://igraph.org/r/doc/layout_with_graphopt.html. Accessed 20 Jan 2024
14. Distribution Economics Institute of Japan. "In-Store Merchandising, 2nd (edn.)". Nihon Keizai Shimbun Syuppansya, pp. 96–100 (2016). (in Japanese)

Opinion Patterns in Cumulative Crises of Brands on Social Media

Alena Rodicheva$^{(\boxtimes)}$ [iD], Svetlana S. Bodrunova[iD], Ivan S. Blekanov[iD], and Nikita Tarasov[iD]

St. Petersburg State University, 7–9 Universitetskaya nab., St. Petersburg 199004, Russia
st061901@student.spbu.ru, s.bodrunova@spbu.ru

Abstract. This paper analyzes opinion patterns in cumulative crises of brands on social media, taking the crisis of a Russian brand named VkusVill as a case. In our previous research, we found out that the nature of online crises is cumulative, as deliberative patterns in discussions around them are absent, and user opinions quickly rocket and get shaped, which may lead to negative actions toward the brand. Thus, there is a need to see how deliberative and cumulative features of the dialogue around the brand crisis combine, as well as how they relate to user traits, including their values-based positions on a given issue. As our analysis shows, the 'epicenter' segments of the discussion in the VkusVill account of structurally comprise polarized micro-dialogues and cumulative commenting directed *urbi et orbi*. A low enough number of comments is directed to the brand itself, but user polarization leads to mutual 'canceling' of social groups, as well as to 'canceling' the brand from both sides. This calls for rethinking of strategies of brands' participation in cumulative discussions, as brands need to engage in values-related talk, rather than use rebuttal strategies. The conversation dynamics moves from completely cumulative to micro-deliberative patterns in short dialogical sequences (<10 comments). This gives brands an opportunity to promote micro-deliberation to reduce hostility. We find that the cumulative/deliberative intention of users is not gender-dependent as it was expected, but shows dependencies on values and the addressees. Our study adds to understanding the nature of brand crises on social media and may help businesses in developing their crisis communication strategies.

Keywords: public opinion · opinion patterns · cumulative crisis · crisis communication · social media · cumulative deliberation · online discussion · social media management

1 Introduction

Many brands from time to time find themselves in rapidly developing crisis situations that are accompanied by mounting user commenting on social networks. Common sense would suggest that such comments would be predominantly negative and highly non-deliberative. However, our previous research [1] shows that brands who run into crises on social media experience rapid accumulation of commenting on their accounts, but the proportion of positive and negative sentiment remains similar to the pre-crisis periods, especially in the cases when a crisis trigger polarizes the online community around the brand.

Thus, in such polarizing cases when social values are at the heart of the trigger event and the sentiment is not completely negative, there remains room for meaningful public discussion that reveals current social values. This room, though, might be critically limited due to other features of online discussions, more than by the negative sentiment itself.

The conceptual framework of cumulative deliberation [2] implies that user speech is predominantly non-deliberative. In particular, it might be irrational, emotional, poorly grounded in argument, conflictual, polarized, opinionated, non-dialogical, fragmented and, most importantly, not seeking any meaningful consensus or even temporary agreement. This may hamper both the public dialogue on social values that the brand has triggered and the efforts on the part of the brand to diminish the harm caused by the crisis. The concept also implies that public opinion online forms in a cumulative way, via dynamic amounting of positions of users in their written utterances. The resulting opinions may either take dominant positions or fall into polarization of (nearly) equally influential user clusters. However, there is also evidence that micro-deliberative patterns, like tony discussions in small threads, diminish negativity in user talk and may foster consensual intentions, calm down the heatedness and hatred in user speech, and help raise constructive conversations [3]. The intentions of being constructive and get involved into meaningful discussing may depend on user traits, such as gender, age, or other demographic features, political and values-based positioning, or brand loyalty.

Thus, there is a need to see how deliberative and non-deliberative (that is, cumulative) features of the dialogue around the brand crisis combine and create patterns of discussion, and whether these patterns are related to user traits within a given crisis case. This is why *research questions* are the following:

RQ1. Is the nature of the discussion around a brand crisis more deliberative or more cumulative, and what discursive features tell of that?
RQ2. Are there patterns that would link user features to the discursive features?
RQ3. Do these patterns change with the course of the discussion, thus revealing the growing deliberative/cumulative nature of the crisis discussion?

To tackle the abovelisted RQs, we develop on our previous study on brand crisis communication strategies [1]. We use the case of a brand crisis of one Russian brand VkusVill. On June 30, 2021, the company published an LGBT-related post on their website and social media, aimed at promoting the brand as inclusive. A two-wave crisis followed: First, in the Russian context, by July 4, 2021, the official social media accounts of the brand were full of negative comments from supporters of 'traditional family values.' After VkusVill removed the post and published their apologies for inappropriate behavior of some unprofessional public relations team employees, the company was hit from the other side (LGBT supporters).

To conduct this case study, we have created a semi-automated method of a brand crisis communication strategy assessment that includes automated data collection, social network analysis, sentiment analysis, and manual coding with Kappa testing, as suggested by Krippendorff [4]. For this case, we limit ourselves to VK.com, the largest Russian-speaking social network.

For RQ1 and RQ2, we reveal the cumulative nature of online crisis experienced by VkusVill via combined social-network and sentiment analysis. Our mapping of the user talk aims at finding micro-patterns of dialogue; their absence is considered the cumulative pattern when individual and unrelated user comments amount. For RQ3, we select the 'temporal epicenter' of the crisis, with the overall number of 161 user posts and 989 user comments from the VkusVill's official account on VK.com. We conduct Krippendorff Kappa pre-testing (k ≥ 0.7) and code these posts and comments for nine variables: user traits (gender), discursive features (addressee, (dis)agreement, aggression), and attitudinal (towards the trigger value, the interlocutor, the brand, supporters of the trigger value, and its opponents). After that, we use descriptive statistics, such as Spearman's rho that helped us trace the correlations between user traits, discursive features, and cumulative/deliberative discussion patterns.

The paper is further organized as follows. In Sect. 2, we provide theory about the phenomenon of the cumulative crisis and polarization of online discussions. In Sect. 3, we describe our methods. Section 4 presents our results. In Sect. 5, we make conclusions and develop on them.

2 Cumulative Crises and Polarized Online Discussions

2.1 Cumulative Crisis' as a Term

We believe that the nature of the reputational crisis on social media has not yet been properly described. We offer our theoretical vision of the nature of online communication, which can help to understand the dynamics of the crisis and offer independent markers for evaluating the effectiveness of brand strategies.

As stated above, we see the nature of the reputational crisis as *cumulative*, as its two main elements are two types of accumulation of opinion – formal and substantive. The formal accumulation of opinion is expressed in a sharp (often explosive) increase in the volume of comments and its decline in overcoming the crisis. The substantive side of the crisis is the dynamics of users' moods and their opinions on the trigger event that can go down a destructive path for the brand image, e.g. the path of values-based polarization and/or partial 'cancellation' of the brand; in any case, within the formal accumulation of comments, there is a change in the semantic content of the brand and the attitude towards it from the audience.

On this basis, the concept of a cumulative crisis in a social network can be formulated. Cumulative crisis is a sharp increase in the volume of comments on a given entity provoked by a trigger event, accompanied by negative changes of the attitudes expressed by the public. Negativity may manifest as dominance of negative opinions, opinion polarization, 'canceling' of the brand, or other forms with implications for the brand's longer-standing reputation.

2.2 Applying the Cumulative Deliberation Theory to Online Brand Crises

Due to hybridization of public spheres [5] and the growing number of user-generated content, the quality of public discussions is being rethought today; some researchers note a decrease in their quality. It is the process of communication between people taking place in the public space, during which 'through dialogue, discussions, negotiations, the search for acceptable solutions to collective problems is underway, and an understanding of the common good shared by all is constructed' [6: 91] that researchers call deliberation. Its basic principles, they are publicity, inclusiveness, dialogicity, a high level of rationality, and formal and *de facto* equality of citizens [6].

The classical theory of deliberation by Juergen Habermas [7] implies that participants of a discussion seek to reach consensus as a result of discursive exchange. However, we believe that the current theory of the public sphere imposes too high regulatory requirements on participants in online discussions, while communication by ordinary users does not meet such expectations, as their speech may be meaningless, biased, and emotional. Moreover, the users who speak out on the Internet may not have any deliberative purpose [2]. At the same time, the composition of the participants in the discussion is constantly changing [8], so many researchers consider discussions on social networks as chaotic, poorly predictable, and devoid of internal integrity [9], as well as not lasting in time.

The concept of cumulative deliberation [2] is fully applicable to cumulative crises; moreover, the cumulative crisis highlights its most important features. Thus, at the moment of crisis, the real communication of users does not meet the deliberative standards; simultaneous commenting destroys the idea of a 'round table'; users allow themselves not to stand on ceremony in their statements; participants in the 'discussion' (or, rather, comment pouring) change quickly; users do not aim at dialogicity and are nonrational; leaving comments can be chaotic, unpredictable, and devoid of internal integrity. At the same time, in the total volume of statements, it is possible to trace the lines of polarization of opinions, identify the causes of the negative reaction to the brand behavior, and define the structural roles of particular users in opinion formation.

The structure of the discussion during the cumulative crisis has not yet been studied. Based on the results of past research [1, 3], we can say, though, that users in their commenting usually aim at three possible addressees: Fellow users, the author of the publication, or *urbi et orbi*, 'into the void'; in their texts, phatic communication, manifestations of aggression, and white noise (links, emoticons, code snippets, etc.) are not uncommon.

The 'spiral of silence' [10] as a pattern of cumulative deliberation suggests that, in an open discussion, people are more likely to speak out when their opinion coincides with that of the majority. Otherwise, they are less likely to comment, fearing social isolation and rejection. Gradually, the majority opinion begins to be mistakenly perceived as the only one in the discussion. We need to ask ourselves whether this dynamic is also true for the development of online brand crises. Another pattern is, obviously, the polarization one [11], when none of the positions takes over, and opinion clusters detached from each other (known as echo chambers) form; however, one may argue that, within echo chambers, 'spirals of silence' work, thus uniting the two patterns of opinion cumulation. Other, more complicated options of user clustering are also possible [12], but brand crises seem to mostly provoke one-dimensional 'pro/contra' divisions, though this needs further investigation.

To understand what a discussion looks like in a cumulative crisis, we can visualize both the structure and dynamics of the discussion and try to 'freeze' the discussion as a crystallization of majority and minority opinions, or 'yes/no' positions [13]. But it is also necessary to analyse the behavior of the brand at the time of crisis, as overcoming the crisis dynamics directly depends on it.

We believe that, in the future, methods for analyzing online discussions, including those related to system theories (for example, the theory of dissipative systems [14] or the affective publics [15]). They can be used to study the crisis communications of brands in social networks. As part of our pilot study, we will reconstruct the dynamics of opinions and try to assess how efficiently companies respond to it.

2.3 Opinion Polarization in Online Discussions

Just as cumulative deliberation suggests, online discussions are often based on a laten existing conflict, mostly a clash of opposing values and/or political preferences, which are manifested in the discourse features and network connections. Some studies have noted that the mediatized nature of online discourse and partial anonymity on the Internet contribute to non-conform speech behavior, open verbal conflicts, and confrontational communication [16]. In addition, the focus of conflicts shifts from the substantive issue to interpersonal confrontation, and, after its cessation, issues remain unresolved.

'The act of separating people into two groups with completely opposite opinions on a topic' is called opinion polarization [17]; however, binary polarization is only one option, while multi-polar discussions are a more frequent case [11]. This is an important feature of online discussions on any controversial topics, which might also include debates about a 'misbehaving' brand on social media. Some researchers emphasize that modern society is characterized by growing social polarization [18].

The content of social media is widely used for predicting consumer and/or electoral choices [19], and the popularity of studies on political polarization on social media is growing [20]. However, audience polarization is mostly studied by examining political cases, while social conflicts of race, gender or religious origins with both evident and idiosyncratic polarization [21] are rarely studied.

At the same time, polarization is often perceived by scholars as an exclusively negative phenomenon, while it can play constructive roles in delineating value thresholds, contextualization of crises, or spurring discussion pace [3]. Research on the nature and features of discursive confrontation in online discussions, confrontational speech strategies, language markers and typical roles of communicators in conflict interactions, and the 'indignation industry' in general often overlooks the constructive functions of both polarization and verbal aggression. Thus, aggressive speech can be one of the language markers and at the same time a speech strategy. This can play a lot of constructive roles in the discussion: it not only divides users into opposing camps, but also contextualizes their differences, shows their historical parallels, and spurs the general course of the discussion [3].

An important aspect of online discussions is the patterns of user agreement and disagreement [22]. It is on them that the accumulation of opinion generally depends:

A certain configuration of comments forms a collective opinion about the original discussion posts and authors [23], but, more importantly, the pattern may determine how the accumulation of opinions affects the degree of polarization and the ability to reach consensus. Thus, there are such models of disagreement as 'conflicting disagreement', 'coordinated disagreement', 'public disagreement' [24], which correlates with models of the agonistic and antagonistic public sphere [10].

Different user tactics lead to different cumulative results, and not always expected. At the same time, despite the agonistic ('recognition of the interlocutor's right to his position') ideal for online discussions, antagonistic behavior – flaming, cyberbullying, 'crowd censorship' [25], trolling, aggressive speech and open disagreement – can lead to the development of discussion, which from the point of view of normative deliberative theory it is evaluated positively. This is better than the absence of discussion or the development of a 'spiral of silence' [10] when the minority opinion remains outside the decision.

The 'spiral of silence' theory suggests that in a situation of open discussion of a problem, people are more likely to speak out when their opinion coincides with the majority of the participants in the discussion. Consequently, if their opinion is in the minority, they are less likely to speak out, as they are afraid of social isolation and rejection due to the expression of an unpopular point of view, which is supported by few people. According to the theory, this leads to a 'spiral of silence' in which the majority opinion becomes more and more dominant, and the minority point of view becomes less and less noticeable. In the end, this leads to a false perception of the majority opinion as the only existing opinion in the discussion.

Thus, we need to see how opinion polarization shapes the patterns of the discussion around the brand crisis on social media.

3   Method

3.1   The Case Under Scrutiny

We decided to conduct the case study of a crisis situation that occurred with one Russian brand, analyzing the company's communication to the audience of their VKontakte official account. VKontakte is the most popular Russian social media platform where users can exchange messages, create profiles and communities, use a variety of services, such as music subscription, money transfer, online games and so on. We analyze the crisis situation which happened to VkusVill, a Russian chain of supermarkets that positions itself as selling alimentation for healthier diets.

On June 30, 2021, the brand's PR team published an article about their customers' families, including one lesbian family that consists of four women, both on the company's official website and social media accounts. Within days, the brand's social media accounts were full of negative comments from people who do not support LGBT. On July 4, VkusVill deleted the post and published another one with apologies for posting an inappropriate story. The company claimed the problem occurred due to unprofessionalism of individual employees. This caused dissatisfaction among LGBT representatives and people who supported this agenda.

3.2 Data Collection and Analysis

In our study, we build upon our previous research on brand crises. There, we have demonstrated the cumulative nature of online crisis experienced by VkusVill. The dataset for the research was collected both manually and automatically; for the current paper, we use the manually collected dataset of the 'temporal epicenter' of the crisis, with the overall number of 161 user posts and 989 user comments from the VkusVill's official account on VK.com.

We conduct Krippendorff kappa pre-testing ($k \geq 0.7$) and code the posts and comments for nine variables, one of them is user-trait (gender), three of them are discursive (addressee (dis)agreement, and aggression), and five variables are attitudinal (towards the trigger value itself, the interlocutor, the brand, supporters of the trigger value, and its opponents). Then, we employ descriptive statistics (Spearman's rho), comparing means, in order to trace the deliberative/cumulative dynamics of the discussion.

4 Results

To identify the salient features of the discussion and their relationship to the value divide we identified, we first assessed them separately and then their correlation was assessed. Thus, in Fig. 1 we describe the nature of the debate. Overall, it appears to be more deliberative than expected. In the discussion, users most often addressed each other (almost 54% of comments), which indicates a willingness to discuss.

Almost a third more contacted the author of the post directly. This was rarely 'VkusVill', so these comments can also be attributed to attempts at deliberation. And only about 17.5% went nowhere, expressing opinion in a cumulative spirit. At the same time, the discussion was also more than 40% filled with active agreement and disagreement, which could be confirmed by markers in the text.

In our opinion, this is a significant indicator; however, almost 60% could not be classified as such. But the most surprising result is that there was negativity in the discussion, but there was no aggression at all, which indicates the readiness of the community on the social network VKontakte to discuss LGBTQ + topics without outbursts of aggression expected in a society of 'traditional values'.

In the comments, one could also find the commentators' expressed attitude towards five different actors in the conflict, namely VkusVill itself, the LGBT community, LGBT supporters, opponents of LGBT, and immediate interlocutors. Figure 2 shows that attitudes were expressed infrequently in the text, but they were quite enough to create a noticeable value gap.

Thus, the discourse cannot be called completely antagonistic; but about a third of the speakers directly expressed hostility towards their interlocutors, and only occasionally (less than 5% of comments) expressed positive attitude. In other cases the relationship was indeterminate; It is worth asking in the future to what extent such an absence can be considered expressing an attitude towards an interlocutor with a sign of agonism or antagonism in discussion.

Circa 22% of interlocutors expressed a negative attitude towards the company and the LGBT community, which was practically not compensated by a positive attitude. But

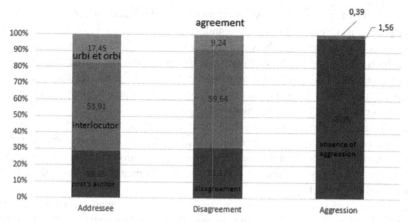

Fig. 1. Characteristics of discourse in the VkusVill case, in %

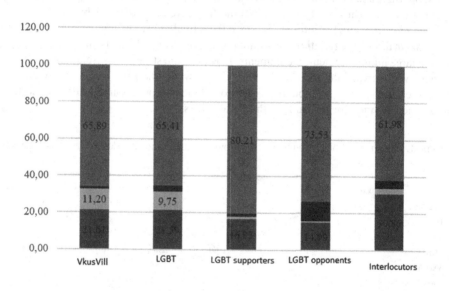

■ Negative   ▨ Neutral   ■ Positive   ■ Indeterminate

Fig. 2. Attitude towards conflict actors in the discourse of the VkusVill case

when it came to those who support or do not support LGBT people, the divide between their supporters and opponents was highlighted quite clearly.

These results confirm our earlier findings about the nature of polarizing discussions online, where a polarizing issue contributes to the consolidation of opposing groups, identification along the 'friend/foe' principle, and delineation of the boundaries of each of the communities [15]. In cumulative crises, however, polarization does not contribute to the growth of popularity or positive reputation of the brand: It can alienate both its supporters and its opponents from the brand.

Analysis of the connection between discourse features and attitudes reveals several more important aspects of the cumulative crisis (see Table 1). Some attitudes (more precisely, their expression) depend to a small extent on the gender of the speaker; yes, women are more likely to express no attitude or to express positive attitude towards the LGBT community and their supporters.

Let us pay attention to two more important features of discourse. So, the more the speaker prone to disagreement, the more he is also prone to negativity attitude towards the interlocutor and trigger actors of the conflict. Correlations are quite weak and can be explained by the large number of nonaggressive and phatic comments; this, though, requires further research.

But the second feature undoubtedly suggests that those who are inclined to treat negatively towards the LGBT community, also tend to have a negative attitude towards his supporters, and those who have a bad attitude towards LGBT supporters also talk bad about VkusVill. Thus, we can talk about the 'negative core' of the debaters. However, this also requires more careful study, since the attitude towards opponents of LGBT is also shown through correlations of a similar sign (positive), which also may be explained by the large number of neutral comments. However, the strongest correlation (0.619**) is observed between the ratio of the negativity towards the LGBT community and its supporters, which tells us about the expansion of the interpretation of LGBT supporters as an alien community, probably with liberal values.

Table 1. Spearman's correlation between discourse features and attitudes in the VkusVill case

	Gender	Addressee	Disagreement	Aggression	LGBT	VkusVill	Interlocutor	Supporters	Opponents
Gender	1,000				,139**			,132**	
Addressee		1,000	,167**				,257**		
Disagreement			1,000		,124**	,121**	**,318****	,161**	,096**
Aggression				1,000			-,137**		
LGBT					1,000	,298**		**,619****	,279**
VkusVill			▼			1,000	-,169**	**,282****	
Interlocutor							1,000	,103**	,152**
Supporters								1,000	,275**
Opponents									1,000

We have also found that, structurally, deliberative and cumulative patterns of the discussion combine. On the macro-level, the pattern is clearly cumulative, as the discussion grows within hours, and user connection is looser than the surrounding networked discussion. On the micro-level, though, the 'epicenter' segments of the discussion comprise polarized micro-dialogues and cumulative commenting directed *urbi et orbi*.

Some users supported LGBT families and entered into disputes by asking questions that provoked people to reflect on family values (*'Where* did you see propaganda? The post shows a happy wonderful family. Yes, this family is not like yours. So what? All people are different'vs. 'Don't call the abomination 'family', family is the people to whom God gave children, but homosexuals do not and will not have children. Come up with another word for your sin, don't denigrate normal human words like 'love' and 'family'.

Surprisingly, a low number of comments was directed to the brand itself. This should make the companies rethink the strategies of brands' participation in cumulative discussions, especially pre-emptive and counter-commenting, as brands may gain public recognition via engaging their audiences in values-related talks, rather than employing rebuttal strategies. Interestingly, commenting was predominantly non-aggressive, though full of actively shown disagreement. This might mean that VkusVill cleaned out uncivil comments from its account (which is an inappropriate public practice).

5 Discussion and Conclusion

Analyzing opinion patterns on the example of VkusVill's cumulative crisis, we came to the following conclusions.

RQ1. As our analysis shows, the 'epicenter' segments of the discussion in the account of Vkusvill structurally comprise polarized micro-dialogues and cumulative commenting directed *urbi et orbi*. A low number of comments is directed to the brand itself, which calls for rethinking of strategies of brands' participation in cumulative discussions, pre-emptive and counter-commenting, as brands need to engage in values-related talk, rather than use rebuttal strategies. As to the other features of discourse, we have seen non-aggressive commenting (which creates suspicions that the brands clean out uncivil comments from their accounts), though full of actively expressed disagreement. This, again, creates space for brands to step in as 'value bridges' and suggesters of agreement.
RQ2. The conversation dynamics moves from completely cumulative to micro-deliberative patterns in short dialogical sequences (<10 comments). Brands can promote micro-deliberation to reduce hostility among users towards the brand and each other. Instead of closing comments or using quick rebuttal strategy, developing dialogues assists in faster resolution of the crisis.
RQ3. There is no evidence of a correlation between gender and discursive features. Even if men in the crisis audience showed a slightly higher propensity toward traditional values, gender was not a factor linking discursive and attitudinal variables. This finding goes against the stereotype of widespread male hostility towards LGBT practices in Russia. Opposition to LGBT-inclusive messaging positively correlates with the presence of active disagreement in user speech, whereas speech in support of it does not. This may be a sign of LGBT critics, not supporters, feeling publicly attacked and needing to defend themselves. Thus, during brand crises, the discussion may reveal closer-to-reality issue-based social cleavages that companies may utilize in their brand development.

Our study helps modern businesses better understand the nature of brand crises on social media and provides advice on how to adjust corporate communication strategies to prevent them.

Acknowledgments. This research has been conducted on behalf of the Center for International Media Research of St. Petersburg State University, Russia.

Disclosure of Interests. The authors have no competing interests to declare that are relevant to the content of this article.

References

1. Rodicheva, A., Bodrunova, S.S., Blekanov, I.S., Tarasov, N., Belyakova, N.: Crisis communication and reputation management of Russian brands on social media. In: Digital Geography – Proceedings of the International Conference on Internet and Modern Society (IMS 2023). Springer (accepted for publication in 2024)
2. Bodrunova, S. S.: The concept of cumulative deliberation: linking systemic approaches to healthier normativity in assessing opinion formation in online discussions. J. Assoc. Inf. Sci. Technol., 1–13 (2023)
3. Bodrunova, S.S., Litvinenko, A., Blekanov, I., Nepiyushchikh, D.: Constructive aggression? Multiple roles of aggressive content in political discourse on Russian YouTube. Media Commun. **9**, 181–194 (2021)
4. Krippendorff, K.: Content Analysis: An Introduction to its Methodology. Sage Publications, London (2018)
5. Chadwick, A.: The Hybrid Media System: Politics and Power. Oxford University Press, Oxford (2013)
6. Pavlova, T.V.: Deliberation as a constitution factor of modern politics field. Politicheskaya nauka [Politic. Sci.] **2**, 73–94 (2018)
7. Habermas, J.: Political communication in media society: Does democracy still enjoy an epistemic dimension? The impact of normative theory on empirical research. Commun. Theory **16**(4), 411–426 (2006)
8. Smoliarova, A.S., Bodrunova, S.S., Blekanov, I.S., Maksimov, A.: Discontinued public spheres? Reproducibility of user structure in Twitter discussions on inter-ethnic conflicts. In: Stephanidis, C., Antona, M., Ntoa, S. (eds.) HCI International 2020 – Late Breaking Posters. Communications in Computer and Information Science, vol. 1293, pp. 262–269. Springer, Cham (2020). https://doi.org/10.1007/978-3-030-60700-5_34
9. Pfetsch, B.: Dissonant and disconnected public spheres as challenge for political communication research. Javnost – The Public **25**(1–2), 59–65 (2018)
10. Noelle-Neumann, E.: The spiral of silence a theory of public opinion. J. Commun. **24**(2), 43–51 (1974)
11. Bodrunova, S.S., Blekanov, I., Smoliarova, A., Litvinenko, A.: Beyond left and right: real-world political polarization in Twitter discussions on inter-ethnic conflicts. Media Commun. **7**, 119–132 (2019)
12. Bodrunova, S.S., Blekanov, I.S., Kukarkin, M.: Multi-dimensional echo chambers: language and sentiment structure of Twitter discussions on the Charlie Hebdo Case. In: Stephanidis, C. (ed.) HCI 2018. CCIS, vol. 850, pp. 393–400. Springer, Cham (2018). https://doi.org/10.1007/978-3-319-92270-6_56
13. Mouffe, C.: The democratic paradox. Verso, London (2000)
14. Prigogine, I.: Dissipative structures, dynamics and entropy. Int. J. Quantum Chem. **9**(S9), 443–456 (1975)
15. Papacharissi, Z.: Affective Publics: Sentiment, Technology, and Politics. Oxford University Press, Oxford (2015)
16. Salimovsky, V.A., Ermakova, L.M.: Extremist discourse in Runet mass communication. Rossiyskaya i zarubezhnaya filologia [Russ. Foreign Philology] **3**(15), 71–80 (2011)
17. Oxford Advanced Learner's Dictionary (10th Edn.) (2020)
18. Duca, J.V., Saving, J.L.: Income inequality, media fragmentation, and increased political polarization. Contemp. Econ. Policy **35**(2), 392–413 (2017)

19. Colleoni, E., Rozza, A., Arvidsson, A.: Echo chamber or public sphere? Predicting political orientation and measuring political homophily in Twitter using big data. J. Commun. **64**(2), 317–332 (2014)
20. Barberá, P.: How social media reduces mass political polarization. Evidence from Germany, Spain, and the US. In: 2015 APSA Conference, San Francisco, CA, USA (2014)
21. McCright, A.M., Dunlap, R.E.: The politicization of climate change and polarization in the American public's views of global warming, 2001–2010. Sociol. Q. **52**(2), 155–194 (2011)
22. Baym, N.K.: Agreements and disagreements in a computer-mediated group. Res. Lang. Soc. Interact. **29**, 315–346 (1996)
23. Koit, M.: Debate formed by internet comments – towards the automatic analysis. In: Proceedings of the 7th International Joint Conference on Knowledge Discovery, Knowledge Engineering and Knowledge Management. SciTePress, pp. 328–333 (2015)
24. Bolander, B., Locher, M.: Conflictual and consensual disagreement. In: Hoffmann, C., Bublitz, W. (eds.) Pragmatics of Social Media, pp. 607–632. De Gruyter Mouton, Berlin – Boston (2017)
25. Waisbord, S.: Mob censorship: online harassment of US journalists in times of digital hate and populism. Digit. Journal. **8**(8), 1030–1046 (2020)

Use of Artificial Intelligence as a Mechanism to Evaluate Costumer Experience. Literature Review

Fabián Silva-Aravena[1]([✉]) [ID], Jenny Morales[1] [ID], Paula Sáez[1] [ID], José Jorquera[2] [ID], and Héctor Cornide-Reyes[2] [ID]

[1] Facultad de Ciencias Sociales y Económicas, Departamento de Economía y Administración, Universidad Católica del Maule, Talca, Chile
{fasilva,jmoralesb,pfsaez}@ucm.cl
[2] Facultad de Ingeniería, Departamento de Ingeniería Informática y Ciencias de la Computación, Universidad de Atacama, Copiapó, Chile
{jose.jorquera,hector.cornide}@uda.cl

Abstract. In the contemporary era marked by the explosion of data, the widespread adoption of Artificial Intelligence (AI) technologies has become essential for companies and researchers exploring various phenomena across industries. An important focus lies on evaluating and improving customer experience (CX) through technologies such as chatbots powered by AI strategies, such as natural language processing (NLP), through the use of chatbots, voice assistants, among others. This not only optimizes CX efficiency but also contributes to improving organizations' processes. The convergence of AI and CX is evident in several sectors; highlighting smart retail, CX in the hospitality sector, and service customization in the banking sector. Additionally, the COVID-19 pandemic has further highlighted the importance of these technologies, catalyzing their accelerated integration. We propose a literature review, employing a five-stage protocol to explore key questions: How can the use of AI improve the CX? Which fields of AI are most frequently used to evaluate CX? What are the aspects of CX in which AI is most frequently used? Five databases were surveyed, yielding insights into AI strategies (e.g., NLP, Decision Trees, Naïve Bayes), and evaluation methods, such as user tests and ethical considerations. Despite progress, gaps still remain that require more research, empirical studies, and success stories to solidify the effectiveness of AI in CX. For responsible development, we suggest organizations develop implementation guides when putting into practice commercial strategies for the use of AI, which ensure ethical standards and regulate machine-client interaction.

Keywords: Customer Experience · AI Strategies · Ethical Principles · Literature Review

A. Coman and S. Vasilache (Eds.): HCII 2024, LNCS 14704, pp. 338–354, 2024.
https://doi.org/10.1007/978-3-031-61305-0_24

1 Introduction

The term artificial intelligence (AI) was often associated with futuristic scenarios, often sparsely realistic [1]. However, the current landscape has undergone significant changes [2, 3]. Thanks to technological advancements and discoveries, AI has acquired a new meaning, integrating into the daily lives of the global population [4, 5].

AI positions itself as a discipline within computer science with the purpose of developing technologies that emulate human intelligence [5]. This implies that, through the creation of algorithms and specialized systems, machines can perform processes characteristic of humans, such as learning, reasoning, or self-correction [6]. Within the objectives of AI is to enhance the performance of processes and the efficiency of businesses, as well as to improve the customer experience (CX) [7].

CX, in turn, encompasses all the perceptions that a customer experiences throughout their interaction with a company. That is, it refers to all the emotions that the consumer undergoes before, during, and after acquiring any product or service [8].

Concerning our research, the integration of AI in evaluating CX represents a fundamental advance towards a deeper and more dynamic understanding of customers' interactions with products and services [9, 10]. In the contemporary business environment, harnessing the power of AI as a mechanism for evaluating CX has become increasingly prevalent [11]. This literature review delves into the use of AI applications in evaluating the CX and the usefulness perceived by customers in the process [12], exploring the multiple methodologies developed in various industries (e.g., life and health insurance [13, 14], tobacco [15], fashion [16], among others). This has been possible thanks to the availability of data [9–13, 15, 17–30], technological advancement, and fundamental ideas that contribute to a comprehensive understanding of this constantly evolving field [9, 11, 14–16, 18, 21–28, 31–41].

In particular, it will focus on consumer behavior as an essential component of the evaluation, examining how AI not only captures but also analyzes and predicts customers' behavioral patterns [26, 35]. The intersection between AI and consumer behavior offers unique perspectives on preferences [16, 23, 26], customization of products and services that customers demand and that are essential in purchasing decisions [9–11, 16, 18, 23, 29, 30, 32, 38, 40], and also, factors that influence customer satisfaction [13, 14, 22, 23, 25–28, 30, 36, 40–42].

However, it is crucial to address the ethical component in this context [11–13]. The review will also explore the need for responsible use of AI and its interaction with humans. Ethical aspects, such as data privacy [11–13, 22, 23, 35, 37], transparency in algorithms, and fairness in automated decisions, will be considered to ensure that the implementation of AI in the evaluation of the CX is carried out ethically and responsibly. Through the synthesis of existing research, this review aims to clarify the current state of AI-driven CX evaluation, specifically considering its impact on consumer behavior and promoting ethical reflection on its implementation.

This paper is organized as follows: Sect. 2 describes related work. Section 3 shows the methodology carried out. Then, in Sect. 4, we present the results by answering the formulated research questions, and finally, in Sect. 5, the conclusions and future work are presented.

2 Related Work

In this section, we addressed concepts used during the development of this work, which cover the topics of the information searches carried out in this literature review.

2.1 Impact of Artificial Intelligence on Customer Experience

The interaction between AI and CX has generated increasing interest in the literature [9, 10]. Numerous studies have examined the impact of this interaction, highlighting the significant transformation that AI has brought to organizations and customer satisfaction [23–28, 30, 31, 37]. Companies have been adapting their processes to incorporate AI techniques with the aim of enhancing CX [9, 10, 12–16, 32]. A particular emphasis has been observed in customization, where AI offers more contextual interactions tailored to individual customer preferences [11]. Techniques such as machine learning (ML), data mining, and natural language processing (NLP) algorithms are commonly employed to achieve this level of customization [9–11].

Authors such as [43] and others have explored the practical benefits of AI in optimizing business processes, operational efficiency, decision-making, and customer relationship management. In this context, predictive analysis techniques and deep learning algorithms have been employed to anticipate customer needs and provide proactive responses to purchasing behavior patterns [26, 35, 44].

However, significant challenges are underscored, such as the need to address ethical concerns related to data privacy and fairness in algorithmic use [11–13]. Authors such as [13–16] emphasize the importance of how AI, through specific techniques, is shaping CX in various sectors and industries. Although its transformative potential is acknowledged, the relevance of addressing ethical aspects to ensure a sustainable impact on the business-customer interaction is emphasized [22, 23].

2.2 Consumer Experience Evaluation

The assessment of CX through the use of AI has been the subject of various research endeavors and comprehensive analyses at all stages [15]. Usability stands out as a central aspect, exploring how AI solutions facilitate customer interaction with services and products [9, 30]. Furthermore, customization, driven by advanced algorithms, stands out as a determining factor to improve customer experience, improving customer satisfaction [9–11].

In the evaluation process, metrics such as customer trust in AI [13, 21], the quality of provided information [15], system quality in terms of efficiency and reliability, and confirmation of customer expectations [16, 42] are explored. These elements are considered essential for a holistic assessment of CX with AI, where the reliability and transparency of algorithms are also outlined as critical aspects [10, 13].

Authors such as [14, 32, 42] and others addressed the intrinsic relationship between AI-driven service quality and customer satisfaction, acknowledging that a positive experience with the technology leads to greater customer loyalty. Additionally, challenges and ethical concerns, such as data privacy, are identified, and must be addressed to ensure a sustainable implementation that enhances the assessment of CX [22].

2.3 Artificial Intelligence Method to Evaluate the Consumer Experience

The AI techniques employed for assessing CX have witnessed substantial growth [10, 11]. These techniques are applied across various industries to analyze and enhance the interaction between consumers and products or services.

Authors such as [10, 17, 39] and others have noted that NLP techniques enable companies to assess consumer feedback on social media, online reviews, and comments by identifying sentiment patterns, thus comprehending the overall consumer perception. Similarly, [19] and others utilize facial recognition algorithms to evaluate consumers' emotional expressions during real-time interactions. This yields valuable insights into products, services, or experiences [28].

The customization of products or services offered to clients has been particularly relevant for companies, as it influences brand experience, preferences, and purchase intent [9]. To achieve this, authors like [11] employ AI and ML algorithms, such DT, NB, KNN, ANN, among others [16, 26]. The objective is to analyze consumer behavioral data to predict individual preferences and personalize products or services, thereby enhancing CX [39].

Various authors, such as [10, 21, 23, 31, 32, 42], have emphasized the implementation of AI-based conversational agents, such as chatbots and virtual assistants, noting that they have enhanced real-time interaction with consumers. These systems leverage NLP and other techniques to comprehend and respond to user queries more efficiently.

It is crucial to highlight that the continuous evolution of AI technologies gives rise to new applications for evaluating and enhancing CX.

3 Methodology

Carrying out the literature review involved a structured process of five stages: first, we formulated the research questions; next, we identified relevant data sources; then, we carefully selected the relevant articles; followed by categorizing the collected articles; and ultimately, we analyzed the results obtained.

3.1 Research Questions

Given our interest in gathering information about evaluation methods for assessing the CX in interactions with AI tools, the following research questions were formulated:

1. How can the use of artificial intelligence improve the customer experience?
2. Which fields of artificial intelligence are most frequently used to evaluate customer experience?
3. What are the aspects of customer experience in which artificial intelligence is most frequently used?

3.2 Data Sources

The search strategy for scientific articles and the formulation of research questions were guided by the following key concepts: customer experience, consumer experience, CX, artificial intelligence (AI). Finally, the search string obtained was:

((“customer experience” OR “consumer experience” OR “CX”) AND (“artificial intelligence” OR “AI”) AND (technique OR field OR method OR strategy)). With this search string, we can recognize the methods used to evaluate CX using AI tools.

To ensure a thorough compilation of scientific articles for a detailed analysis, we selected five prominent databases pertinent to the subject. The search spanned across Web of Science (WoS), Scopus, IEEE Xplore, ACM Digital Library, and Science Direct. The investigation was initiated in November and received its most recent update in mid-December 2023.

3.3 Selection Articles

The initial exploration of the specified databases employed a broad search strategy across all fields, yielding a total of 77 scientific articles. Subsequently, to enhance search efficiency, we conducted a refined search focusing on abstracts within an 11-year timeframe (2013 to 2024). This targeted search was uniformly applied across all databases included in the review; we identified a total of 35 relevant articles. The outcomes are presented in Table 1.

Table 1. Papers found in data source.

Data source	Abstract selection and limited to 11 years
WoS	2
Scopus	28
IEEE Xplore	3
ACM Digital Library	0
Science Direct	2
Total	35

Figure 1 shows the results of the process selection articles. First, articles were integrated into a unified document, and redundant entries (14 articles) were removed. Subsequently, literature reviews were excluded, making a refined selection based on the type of document, retaining only presentations and conference articles (which resulted in the elimination of 4 articles). In addition, we have carried out an exhaustive selection process focused on articles aligned with the specific scope of our work. This involved excluding those that, despite containing the searched keywords in their abstracts, simply presented disparate works on AI or CX, lacked a cohesive connection between the two components, and used alternative definitions of CX, without delving into evaluations to the consumer. Which is one of the main concerns of this study. Consequently, 23 articles were excluded. Additionally, one article required payment and was consequently not chosen, leaving a final count of 35 for review by the research team.

Fig. 1. Results of articles selection process.

3.4 Articles Classification

Out of the 35 articles chosen based on criteria specified in our work and criteria during the last eleven years of research, the majority are recent, dating back to 2019. This suggests a significant surge in the prominence of AI techniques, particularly in the 6 years marked by the pandemic. Table 2 provides a breakdown of the number of articles per year.

Table 2. Selected articles per year.

Year	Paper selected
2019	2
2020	5
2021	13
2022	2
2023	12
2024	1
Total	35

Concerning the subject under study, various pieces of literature have delved into assessing user experience employing AI. As illustrated in Fig. 2, the distribution of studies reveals compelling insights. Notably, 71.4% of the cases (25 articles) demonstrate discernible enhancements in CX when incorporating AI. Conversely, 17.1% of the examined studies (6 articles) are not of improvement, while 11.4% (4 articles) indicate a lack of clarity on the matter.

In the context of the 25 studies positing enhancement in CX facilitated by AI tools, a discernible pattern has surfaced, underscoring the significance of interactions between customers and machines. This interaction is evident both in physical settings, employing image recognition, and virtually, through NLP strategies, as elaborated in 17 articles. This encompasses the deployment of chatbots, social bots, intelligent voice assistants, among other modalities (see Table 3). While some conventional machine learning (ML) tools contribute to this evaluation, they are comparatively less prevalent. These include Decision Trees (discussed in 2 articles), Naïve Bayes (covered in 1 article), K-Nearest Neighbors (explored in 1 article), Neural Networks (delved into in 1 article), Deep Learning (addressed in 2 article), Sentiment Analysis (analyzed in 2 articles), Regression

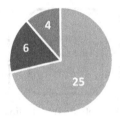

▪ Yes ▪ No ▪ No clarity

Fig. 2. Quantifying the Impact: Proportion of Articles Assessing AI's Influence on Enhancing CX.

Analysis (tackled in 1 article), and Explainability Algorithms (considered in 1 articles). It is noteworthy that certain studies within this domain do not specifically deeper into AI techniques.

Regarding the facets of the CX evaluation process, several components are analyzed. Numerous studies delve into diverse elements, with a predominant focus of 29.3% on customer satisfaction/experience/service. Additionally, 19.0% pertains to the customization of customer products or services, quality of service/information/system represents 15.5%, while loyalty/trust is addressed in 13.8% of the articles. On the other hand, convenience/intuitive and easy-to-use products represent 8.6%, transparency/communication a 3.4%, and others, such as enjoyment, perceived usefulness, etc.) are discussed at 10.3%. Figure 3 provides a summary of the evaluated aspects.

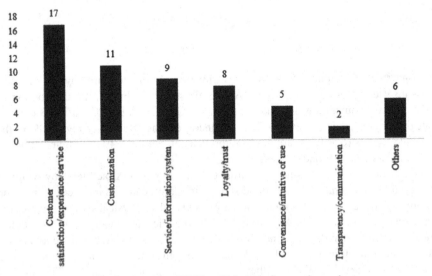

Fig. 3. Aspects of CX in which AI is frequently used.

Table 3. Papers classification.

Cite	Field of AI	Improve CX	Methods used	Ethical considerations	Aspects evaluated / analyzed
[9]	Different types of AI techniques	Yes	Questionnaire (quantitative)	No	Convenience of use, customization, and quality of information
[10]	NLP	Yes	Questionnaire (mixed)	No	Trust, intuitive and easy-to-use products, and customization
[11]	Chatbots (NLP)	Yes	Focus groups and a scenario technique approach (qualitative)	Yes, concerns about the use of personal data and privacy	Customization, efficiency, and system quality
[12]	Conversational assistants (NLP)	Yes	Descriptive research, using surveys to collect data (quantitative)	Yes, concerns raised about privacy and handling of personal information	Ease of use, enjoyment, trust, and perceived risk
[13]	Predictive models	Yes	Predictive modeling approach based on historical and current data to develop your mortality model (quantitative)	Yes, transparency in the use of data and algorithms, especially about privacy and consumer trust	Precision and transparency of the process and how they influence customer trust and satisfaction
[14]	None	No	Group discussions and interviews with consumers and healthcare professionals (qualitative)	No	Customer satisfaction, accessibility to information, and quality of service
[15]	Image recognition	Yes	Combination with image decomposition for sample processing and identification (quantitative)	No	Provide brand information and improve interaction between consumers and brands

(continued)

Table 3. (*continued*)

Cite	Field of AI	Improve CX	Methods used	Ethical considerations	Aspects evaluated / analyzed
[16]	Image processing, neural networks, and deep learning	Yes	Data analysis models (quantitative)	No	Customization, system and information quality, and customer expectations
[17]	NLP, sentiment analysis, and opinion mining	No	Bibliometric analysis using databases such as the Web of Science (qualitative)	No	Sentiment analysis and understanding of emotions from digital advertising and social networks
[18]	Automation and data analysis for personalized marketing	Yes	Analysis of current trends in digital marketing and their impact on strategy formation (mixed)	No	Customization, and efficiency in communication with customers
[19]	NLP and facial/emotional recognition	Yes	Analysis using Instagram data, NLP for sentiment analysis, and AI facial recognition (quantitative)	No	Emotions expressed by robots affect users' perception and reaction
[20]	NLP and Deep Learning	No	User data analysis (quantitative)	No	Automated classification of themes in e-vehicle
[21]	Chatbots (NLP) and voice/facial recognition systems, and analytics	No	Analysis using a questionnaire applied by social platforms such as WeChat, Weibo, and Facebook (quantitative)	No	Customer trust, commitment, and loyalty toward sharing platforms

(*continued*)

Table 3. (*continued*)

Cite	Field of AI	Improve CX	Methods used	Ethical considerations	Aspects evaluated / analyzed
[22]	iRCXM technical model and decision tree classification algorithm	Yes	Semi-structured interview (qualitative)	Yes, obtain customer consent with privacy protection of data collected by robots	Customer satisfaction
[23]	AI voice chatbots (NLP)	Yes	Open online questionnaires, interviews, and document reviews (qualitative)	Yes, it refers to privacy	Customer satisfaction and preferences
[24]	None	No	Founded and systematized analysis of the ethical principles recommended for implementing AI in companies (qualitative)	Yes, transparency of information, fairness in prices, confidentiality of personal data	None
[25]	Social bots of AI (NLP)	Yes	Interviews were conducted, and customer journey maps incorporated social robots as a point of contact throughout the service (mixed)	No	Customer satisfaction
[26]	Decision tree, naive bayes, k-nearest neighbors	Yes	Data analysis methodology that integrated 3 ML algorithms (qualitative)	No	Provide insight into customer behavior and preferences by customizing content
[27]	ML algorithms and robotics	Yes	Data analysis (quantitative)	No	Optimizing operations and improving customer service

(*continued*)

Table 3. (*continued*)

Cite	Field of AI	Improve CX	Methods used	Ethical considerations	Aspects evaluated / analyzed
[28]	NLP (Watson System)	Yes	Use and experimentation of technology, an app, based on an AI model (mixed)	No	Customer satisfaction
[29]	Various ML algorithms and a LIME explainability model	Yes	Data analysis methodology (quantitative)	No	Customer experience
[30]	Regression model	Yes	Statistical and econometric analysis (quantitative)	Yes, ethical training is suggested for AI professionals, consistent with laws, and social norms	Convenience of use, Customization, trust, customer loyalty and customer satisfaction (evaluation survey)
[31]	None	No clarity	Online opinion survey and a covariance-based structural equation model (quantitative)	No	Perceived ease of use, perceived usefulness, and behavioral intention when using chatbots
[32]	Conceptual and qualitative analysis based on the use of bots, virtual assistants, based on AI	Yes	Analysis model (qualitative)	No	Customization and quality of service through artificial intelligence tools lead to a better customer experience
[33]	NLP and computer vision	Yes	A method based on a structured survey (quantitative)	No	Customization experiences

(*continued*)

Table 3. (*continued*)

Cite	Field of AI	Improve CX	Methods used	Ethical considerations	Aspects evaluated / analyzed
[34]	None	No clarity	Qualitative method	Yes	Service interactions, special customer offers, targeted promotion, and demarketing
[35]	AI-based voice assistants (NLP)	Yes	Voice-to-buyer survey (quantitative)	No	Customer experience (Customized voice shopping)
[36]	NLP (chatbots and virtual assistant)	No clarity	A method to analyze marketing intelligence (qualitative)	Yes, it mentions zombie marketing as an element that negatively influences the client	Customer satisfaction
[37]	Analysis of structural parameters and sociotechnical systems for the design of eXplainable AI	No	Analysis model (qualitative)	Yes, dignity in people and their privacy	Not mentioned
[38]	Chatbots (NLP), digital voice assistants, smart homes, and clusters	Yes	Analysis, and image processing to personalize products. Additionally, cluster analysis is used (quantitative)	Yes, according to the study, machines should support humans, never replace them	Product customization and recommendations

(*continued*)

Table 3. (*continued*)

Cite	Field of AI	Improve CX	Methods used	Ethical considerations	Aspects evaluated / analyzed
[39]	NLP (voice assistants)	Yes	A method-based approach; which includes interviews with experts and consumers. And a cross-sectional survey with active voice assistant users (mixed)	No	Social identity, desires, customization, usefulness, and perceived joy
[40]	Using AI Chatbots (NLP)	Yes	Semi-structured interviews and the UX curve method (a method used to study User Experience) (qualitative)	No	Customer satisfaction and service customization
[41]	No special technique is specified, it only generically talks about AI	Yes	Study of cases (qualitative)	No	Better service and customer experience
[42]	Using AI Chatbots (NLP) and a structural equation model	Yes	Survey and analysis (quantitative)	Yes, emphasis is placed on data protection	Customer satisfaction, trust, perceived usefulness, and retention intention in chatbot use. The quality of information, system, and service was also analyzed
[43]	AI applied to strategic CRM processes	No clarity	Qualitative method	No	AI is addressed as a tool to improve customer relationship management processes

Regarding the types of evaluations identified, the majority consist of quantitative studies, with 16 articles. Subsequently, qualitative studies were also prevalent, with

14 articles. Mixed studies, blending both quantitative and qualitative approaches, were comparatively less common, appearing in 5 articles.

Table 3 illustrates the categorization of articles based on the study objective, specifically, the utilization of AI as a mechanism for assessing the CX.

4   Results

We present the results regarding the articles found and analyzed, considering the classification shown in Table 2 and the research questions defined in Sect. 3.1.

4.1   Answer Research Questions

1. *How can the use of artificial intelligence improve the CX?* From the analysis conducted in this study, certain elements have been identified that contribute to understanding the posed question. Firstly, companies are leveraging information on customer behavior derived from opinions, surveys, and purchases to train AI algorithms. These techniques enable the recognition of consumer preferences, driving the design of new products and services to contribute to improving CX, with a particular emphasis on the presence of chatbots, social bots, conversational assistants, and similar applications, as evidenced in 17 articles. Secondly, the intensive use of technology in conjunction with AI translates into providing customers with more comprehensive system and precise information and service, as reflected in 9 articles from this study. This is manifested in the ability to deliver real-time responses to customer inquiries, in addition to providing experiences that ensure greater well-being, as discussed in 7 articles. Finally, the application of AI contributes to optimizing business processes, thereby fostering improvements in CX.
2. *Which fields of artificial intelligence are most frequently used to evaluate customer experience?* In the conducted analysis, various AI techniques and methodologies are employed to evaluate CX. Particularly, NLP plays a central role, highlighted in 17 articles. Additionally, albeit less frequently, some conventional ML tools are utilized, including DT (discussed in 2 articles), NB (covered in 1 article), KNN (explored in 1 article), ANN (delved into in 1 article), and Deep Learning (addressed in 2 article), Sentiment Analysis (analyzed in 2 articles), Regression Analysis (tackled in 1 article), Explainability Algorithms (considered in 1 article), among others.
3. *What are the aspects of customer experience in which artificial intelligence is most frequently used?* Regarding the aspects of the CX evaluation process analyzed in the study using AI, efforts to enhance are noteworthy: (1) customer satisfaction/experience/service, addressed in 17 articles; (2) customization of products and services, discussed in 11 articles; (3) service/information/system quality, examined in 9 articles; (4) loyalty and trust, highlighted in 8 articles; (5) convenience/intuitive o use, mentioned in 5 articles; (6) transparency/communication, referred to in 2 articles; and (7) among others, discussed in 6 articles.

5   Conclusion and Future Work

We conducted a literature review focused on evaluating the CX in interactions with AI tools. Several studies indicated that companies actively utilize these techniques to enhance their processes, increase competitiveness, and respond to customer needs, ultimately improving the overall CX.

Through our analysis, it became evident that AI techniques indeed contribute to enhancing the CX. Notably, NLP techniques within the AI domain are predominantly employed, with a particular emphasis on the utilization of chatbots, social bots, and conversational assistants. This approach aims to recognize customer needs in real-time, engage with them, and deliver timely and reliable responses.

Continued refinement of these practices, encompassing their design, implementation, and interaction with clients, is imperative. The choice of technique depends on the specific sector or industry of implementation, due to privacy concerns and information security. Ethical considerations must be paramount in guiding these practices. To facilitate this, we recommend establishing comprehensive policies and implementation guidelines that ensure harmonious interaction between machines and humans.

Looking ahead, future endeavors should focus on leveraging these tools to enhance CX and satisfaction throughout the entire process of acquiring products and services. However, the cautious use of AI tools is paramount; they should serve to support organizations in achieving their objectives while safeguarding the privacy of clients.

References

1. Teigens, V., Skalfist, P., Mikelsten, D.: Inteligencia artificial: la cuarta revolución industrial. Cambridge Stanford Books, Cambridge (2020)
2. Ruibal-Tavares, E., Calleja-López, J.R., Rivera-Rosas, C.N., Aguilera-Duarte, L.J.: Inteligencia artificial en medicina: panorama actual. REMUS-Revista Estudiantil de Medicina de la Universidad de Sonora (2023)
3. Bendre, S., Shinde, K., Kale, N., Gilda, S.: Artificial intelligence in food industry: a current panorama. Asian J. Pharm. Technol. 12(3), 242–250 (2022). D
4. Yudkowsky, E.: Artificial intelligence as a positive and negative factor in global risk. Global catastrophic risks 1(303), 184 (2008)
5. Dwivedi, Y.K., et al.: Artificial Intelligence (AI): multidisciplinary perspectives on emerging challenges, opportunities, and agenda for research, practice and policy. Int. J. Inf. Manag. 57, 101994 (2021)
6. Reddy, C.D., Van den Eynde, J., Kutty, S.: Artificial intelligence in perinatal diagnosis and management of congenital heart disease. In: Seminars in Perinatology, vol. 46, no. 4, p. 151588. WB Saunders, June 2022
7. Wamba-Taguimdje, S.L., Fosso Wamba, S., Kala Kamdjoug, J.R., Tchatchouang Wanko, C.E.: Influence of artificial intelligence (AI) on firm performance: the business value of AI-based transformation projects. Bus. Process. Manag. J. 26(7), 1893–1924 (2020)
8. Manthiou, A., Hickman, E., Klaus, P.: Beyond good and bad: challenging the suggested role of emotions in customer experience (CX) research. J. Retail. Consum. Serv. 57, 102218 (2020)
9. Ho, S.P.S., Chow, M.Y.C.: The role of artificial intelligence in consumers' brand preference for retail banks in Hong Kong. J. Financ. Serv. Mark. 1–14 (2023)
10. Wang, P., Li, K., Du, Q., Wang, J.: Customer experience in AI-enabled products: Scale development and validation. J. Retail. Consum. Serv. 76, 103578 (2024)

11. Neuhofer, B., Magnus, B., Celuch, K.: The impact of artificial intelligence on event experiences: a scenario technique approach. Electron. Mark. **31**, 601–617 (2021)
12. Hasan, S., Godhuli, E.R., Rahman, M.S., Al Mamun, M.A.: The adoption of conversational assistants in the banking industry: is the perceived risk a moderator? Heliyon **9**(9) (2023)
13. Maier, M., Carlotto, H., Saperstein, S., Sanchez, F., Balogun, S., Merritt, S.: Improving the accuracy and transparency of underwriting with AI to transform the life insurance industry. AI Mag. **41**(3), 78–93 (2020)
14. Chatterjee, S., Kulkarni, P.: Healthcare consumer behaviour: the impact of digital transformation of healthcare on consumer. Cardiometry **20**, 134–143 (2021)
15. Liu, Y., Lyu, P., Gao, W.: Consumer marketing brand cultivation path based on image recognition technology. IEEE Access (2020)
16. Guo, Z., Zhu, Z., Li, Y., Cao, S., Chen, H., Wang, G.: AI assisted fashion design: a review. IEEE Access (2023)
17. Sánchez-Núñez, P., Cobo, M.J., De las Heras-Pedrosa, C., Pelaez, J.I., Herrera-Viedma, E.: Opinion mining, sentiment analysis and emotion understanding in advertising: a bibliometric analysis. IEEE Access **8**, 134563–134576 (2020)
18. Hnoievyi, V.H., Koren, O.M.: Modern digital marketing trends and their influence on the marketing strategy formation
19. Chuah, S.H.W., Yu, J.: The future of service: the power of emotion in human-robot interaction. J. Retail. Consum. Serv. **61**, 102551 (2021)
20. Ha, S., Marchetto, D.J., Dharur, S., Asensio, O.I.: Topic classification of electric vehicle consumer experiences with transformer-based deep learning. Patterns **2**(2) (2021)
21. Chen, Y., Prentice, C., Weaven, S., Hisao, A.: The influence of customer trust and artificial intelligence on customer engagement and loyalty–the case of the home-sharing industry. Front. Psychol. **13**, 912339 (2022)
22. Yang, J., Chew, E.: The design model for robotic waitress. Int. J. Soc. Robot. **13**(7), 1541–1551 (2021)
23. Abdo, A., Yusof, S.M.: Exploring the impacts of using the artificial intelligence voice-enabled chatbots on customers interactions in the United Arab Emirates. IAES Int. J. Artif. Intell. **12**(4), 1920 (2023)
24. Dolganova, O.I.: Improving customer experience with artificial intelligence by adhering to ethical principles. Бизнес-информатика **15**(2(eng)), 34–46 (2021)
25. Wilson-Nash, C., Goode, A., Currie, A.: Introducing the socialbot: a novel touchpoint along the young adult customer journey. Eur. J. Mark. **54**(10), 2621–2643 (2020)
26. Yaiprasert, C., Hidayanto, A.N.: AI-driven ensemble three machine learning to enhance digital marketing strategies in the food delivery business. Intell. Syst. Appl. **18**, 200235 (2023)
27. Tad, M.S., Mohamed, M.S., Samuel, S.F., Deepa, M.J.: Artificial intelligence and robotics and their impact on the performance of the workforce in the banking sector. Revista de Gestão Social e Ambiental **17**(6), e03410–e03410 (2023)
28. Ferràs, X., Hitchen, E.L., Tarrats-Pons, E., Arimany-Serrat, N.: Smart tourism empowered by artificial intelligence: the case of Lanzarote. J. Cases Inf. Technol. (JCIT) **22**(1), 1–13 (2020)
29. Sharma, R., Kumar, A., Chuah, C.: Turning the blackbox into a glassbox: an explainable machine learning approach for understanding hospitality customer. Int. J. Inf. Manag. Data Insights **1**(2), 100050 (2021)
30. Tulcanaza-Prieto, A.B., Cortez-Ordoñez, A., Lee, C.W.: Influence of customer perception factors on AI-enabled customer experience in the Ecuadorian banking environment. Sustainability **15**(16), 12441 (2023)
31. Iancu, I., Iancu, B.: Interacting with chatbots later in life: a technology acceptance perspective in COVID-19 pandemic situation. Front. Psychol. **13**, 1111003 (2023)
32. Sujata, J., Aniket, D., Mahasingh, M.: Artificial intelligence tools for enhancing customer experience. Int. J. Recent Technol. Eng. **8**(2), 700–706 (2019)

33. Almustafa, E., Assaf, A., Allahham, M.: Implementation of artificial intelligence for financial process innovation of commercial banks. Revista de Gestão Social e Ambiental **17**(9), e04119–e04119 (2023)
34. Lu, F.C., Sinha, J.: Understanding retail exclusion and promoting an inclusive customer experience at transforming service encounters. J. Consum. Aff. (2022)
35. Bawack, R.E., Wamba, S.F., Carillo, K.D.A.: Exploring the role of personality, trust, and privacy in customer experience performance during voice shopping: evidence from SEM and fuzzy set qualitative comparative analysis. Int. J. Inf. Manag. **58**, 102309 (2021)
36. Lies, J.: Marketing Intelligence: Boom or Bust of Service Marketing? (2022)
37. Wulff, K., Finnestrand, H.: Creating meaningful work in the age of AI: explainable AI, explainability, and why it matters to organizational designers. AI & Soc.1–14 (2023)
38. Loureiro, S.M.C., Jiménez-Barreto, J., Bilro, R.G., Romero, J.: Me and my AI: exploring the effects of consumer self-construal and AI-based experience on avoiding similarity and willingness to pay. Psychol. Mark. (2024)
39. Malodia, S., Islam, N., Kaur, P., Dhir, A.: Why do people use artificial intelligence (AI)-enabled voice assistants? IEEE Trans. Eng. Manag. (2021)
40. Flandrin, P., Hellemans, C., Van der Linden, J., Van de Leemput, C.: Smart technologies in hospitality: effects on activity, work design and employment. A case study about chatbot usage. In: Proceedings of the 17th "Ergonomie et Informatique Avancée" Conference (pp. 1–11, October 2021
41. Sujata, J., Mukul, P., Hasandeep, K.: Role of smart communication technologies for smart retailing. Int. J. Innov. Technol. Explor. Eng. **8**, 213–218 (2019)
42. Nguyen, D.M., Chiu, Y.T.H., Le, H.D.: Determinants of continuance intention towards banks' chatbot services in Vietnam: a necessity for sustainable development. Sustainability **13**(14), 7625 (2021)
43. Ledro, C.: Artificial intelligence applied to customer relationship management: an empirical research. In: European Conference on Innovation and Entrepreneurship, pp. 1153-R23. Academic Conferences International Limited, September 2021
44. Gupta, K., et al.: Harnessing AI for strategic decision-making and business performance optimization. Int. J. Intell. Syst. Appl. Eng. **11**(10s), 893–912 (2023)

Factors Influencing the Selection and Review of Social Media Platforms in the South African SMME Hospitality Industry

Taboka Velempini and Salah Kabanda$^{(\boxtimes)}$ ⓘ

Department of Information Systems, University of Cape Town, Cape Town, South Africa
Taboka.velempini@alumni.uct.ac.za, salah.kabanda@uct.ac.za

Abstract. The adoption and use of social media by Small, Medium and Micro-Sized Enterprises (SMMEs) is an area that has received attention from scholars. Yet, there remains a limited understanding of what informs an SMME's decision to adopt a specific social media platform and how SMMEs review the performance of adopted platforms. The study sought to address this gap and primarily examined SMMEs in the hospitality sector in South Africa.

The study followed a qualitative enquiry with data collection using semi-structured interviews from 15 Small, Medium and Micro-Sized Enterprises (SMMEs).

The findings identified four key factors that influenced the selection of social media platforms within the trade and accommodation industry. Additional findings elicited the various techniques utilised by SMMEs to review the performance of adopted social media platforms and the impact of analysed data in guiding strategic decision-making. Key organisational driver behind SMMEs selection of a particular social media platform was the business value they anticipated to create from its integration with business objectives. Individual factors of age and digital literacy of the manager influenced the selection of a particular social media platform. The findings provide practical implications to practice and a better explanation of how SMMEs make strategic decisions when adopting and use social medial.

Keywords: Social media · Hospitality sector · Digital business transformation · E-Business

1 Introduction

Social media can afford businesses many opportunities including electronic communication, user-generated content, and cost-effective marketing strategies (Jones, Borgman, and Ulusoy, 2015). Ndekwa and Katunzi (2016) state that through the adoption of digital technologies Small, Medium and Micro-Sized Enterprises (SMMEs) are provided with the opportunity to not only obtain access to the global market but also compete with larger (and market-leading) enterprises. However, for SMMEs to survive in an African market, and operate in a global market, they need to use their inherently flexible structure to adapt to digital and market developments (Gümüs & Kütahyali, 2017). Oji, Iwu and

A. Coman and S. Vasilache (Eds.): HCII 2024, LNCS 14704, pp. 355–369, 2024.
https://doi.org/10.1007/978-3-031-61305-0_25

Haydam (2017) state that special attention should be paid to social networking tools and microblogs. This is due to many SMMEs appreciating features such as built-in analytical tools as well as similarities in the identified tools with traditional communication tools (McCann & Barlow, 2015). Through the use of those tools, SMMEs can potentially derive functional business value–which focuses on financial improvements afforded through the adoption of IT systems–and symbolic business value–which focuses on monitoring and improving brand reputation and recognition (Grover et al, 2018). Prior studies such as those of Fan and Gordon (2014), have shown that business value can be best achieved when organisations can make sense of their data. Seddon et al (2017) propose business analytics as one avenue through which organisations can understand their data and subsequently gain a competitive advantage that can assist in increasing their profit margins. In the context of social media, the concept of social media analytics is more relevant and imperative due to the amount of data generated from social media platforms. Social media platforms afford users the ability to generate content online, where the data from the content collected can provide businesses with potential innovation ideas once analysed (Dong & Wu, 2015). Although there have been several studies that seek to understand the influence of social media analytics on an organisation's ability to generate business value, these have been few (Stockdale, Ahmed, & Scheepers, 2012). In addition, there remains limited number of studies focusing on the factors that influence SMMEs' selection of social media in developing economies; and how these SMMEs go about evaluating the success of their social media platforms (Tiago & Veríssimo, 2014). This is problematic, given that most SMMEs–particularly those in developing economies–fail to succeed within the first few years of establishment (Bushe, 2019).

This study sought to understand what informs an SMME's decision to adopt a specific social media platform and how SMMEs review the performance of their social media platform. The study examined SMMEs in the hospitality sector in South Africa. The selection of the sector was due to the Small-Enterprise-Development-Agency (2019) categorising the hospitality sector as the largest sector within the service industry contributing towards economic development and job creation. The study categorised SMMEs based on the criteria shown in Table 1. There were two categories used to segregate the types of SMMEs, these are namely the number of employees and the annual turnover range–with the upper and lower bounds representing the minimum and maximum annual turnovers across all sectors (Zulu, 2019).

Table 1. SMME Criteria (Zulu, 2019)

Size	Total full-time Equivalent of paid Employees	Total Annual Turnover (Million)
Micro-sized Enterprises	0–10	R5–20
Small-sized Enterprises	11–50	R15–80
Medium-sized Enterprises	51–250	R35–220

2   Literature Review

This study adopted a combination of the Normative Decision-Making Model, the Social Media Analytics Model, and the E-Business Value Model–as shown in Fig. 1–to understand the factors influencing SMMEs selection of social media tools and how SMMEs engage in evaluating the success of these tools. The Normative Decision-Making Model has been used to understand how organisations select information technology applications with the focus on the organisation's business goals and objectives prior to making recommendations (Nagle & Pope, 2013). The model has four phases: Intelligence, Design, Choice and Review. In the Intelligence phase, the organisation takes into consideration the prerequisites required of the selected social media tools during the pre-planning phase (DiMicco et al. 2008). The organisation identifies key value drivers and metrics that they would like to achieve through the introduction of specific social media tools into their business strategy. Then, the process of identifying unique features of various social media tools as well as the uses of those social media tools is undertaken during the design phase. Such uses include gaining a competitive advantage, creating stronger relationships with consumers, creating cost-effective marketing strategies, and promoting new partnerships (Nagle & Pope, 2013). In the choice phase, a shortlist of possible social media tools is made, and the tools are ranked based on the most favorable features and affordances. Nagle and Pope (2013), state that at this stage, tools that can offer "value for more focused activities" will be considered. In the final phase, management reviews the deployed social media tools to determine whether the implementation was a success or failure.

To derive business value from social media, organisations are encouraged to deploy a Social Media Analytics Model that gathers and analyses social media data from various platforms to assist in making strategic decisions (Lee, 2018). Having analytical tools such as Radian6 and SAS, offers organisations services to monitor factors such as traffic and impressions (likes and comments) (McCann & Barlow, 2015). To effectively measure the data collected, organisations should have metrics, frameworks and objectives to capture, understand and present social media data taking into account the velocity, volume, variety, and variability of the data (Wamba et al, 2016). A successful model with predefined metrics will afford advancements in marketing, sales and customer service (Davis & Logan, 2019), and in so doing, contribute towards business value.

Lee (2018) argues that to better understand consumers, one needs to have a model that captures, understands, and presents social media data. By paying attention to choosing, monitoring and listening to social media platforms, "businesses can better target their product offerings" and ultimately "find new participants" (Ketelaars 2011, 28). Duong-Van (2014), highlights the importance of sentiment analysis in assisting organisations to better understand consumer's opinions by site crawling and identifying data to be analysed. Through the process of cleaning the data, measuring the frequency of certain keywords and evaluating the relevance of the data to the business, a 'sentiment' will be created (Duong-Van, 2014). Organisations can use this data to "predict future outcomes and behaviours", forecast the "growth of customer[s] or sales" and ultimately create business intelligence that subsequently promotes new transactions, new customers, brand awareness, brand recognition, and brand engagement (Fan & Gordon, 2014,5).

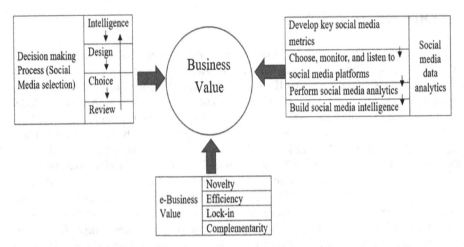

Fig. 1. Conceptual framework for business value

Finally, the conceptual model includes key E-Business Value Model drivers of Novelty, Efficiency, Lock-in and Complementarity that are perceived to contribute towards business value. Ketelaars (2011) states that the transaction efficiency increases as the transaction cost decreases and this is often prompted by social media encouraging a reduction of search costs. Through the introduction of social media, businesses can gain access to a larger demographic of their target markets, thus, decreasing search costs (Amit & Zott, 2001). In addition, social media promotes efficiency and transparency by providing consumers with symmetric information between all parties involved in the business. E-business platforms using social media promote the creation of new products, services, marketing methods, in addition to providing access to new markets in ways that traditional businesses failed to. Social media specifically encourages efficient communication mechanisms that allow businesses to find new consumers and "engage in new timely and direct end-consumer contact at relatively low cost[s] and higher levels of efficiency" (Ketelaars, 2011, 27). Nagle and Pope (2013) argue that both efficiency and novelty should be considered as the greatest factors contributing to value creation in e-business. The combination of the two value drivers promotes new transaction structures, new participants, reduced search costs and growth in the scale of economies (Amit & Zott, 2001). Although complementarities are not widely discussed in literature and are less apparent through the introduction of social media, Amit and Zott (2001) highlight that social media can offer ease of access to complementary products and services. Ketelaars (2011) states that the ability to use e-business platforms to facilitate cross-selling, direct advertising and create virtual communities are important factors in promoting value creation.

3   Methodology

This study followed an interpretive approach to document the experiences of SMMEs–in the hospitality industry–with social media. Purposive sampling was used to select SMMEs to participate in the study. To initiate the process of identifying a sample population, the researcher identified accommodation establishments in the Western Cape province and Gauteng province using the South African Tourism Grading Council's public database. These provinces were selected as they have the highest number of SMMEs in the hospitality industry in South Africa (Small-Enterprise-Development-Agency, 2019). Subsequently, SMMEs that had adopted social media were identified to participate in the study. Target respondents included (i) the SMME owner or manager–due to their overall knowledge of their SMME, its business objectives, the processes and practices; (ii) the IT manager as well as those with technical expertise to understand the technologies adopted by the SMME and how the adopted digital technologies impacted the organisation's creation of business value; (iii) and finally the marketing manager to gain an understanding of the tools adopted for marketing strategies, brand and reputation management strategies as well as how social media played a role in their marketing activities. Data was collected using semi-structured interviews and the interviews were informed by the conceptual framework in Fig. 1 as well as the key questions: what business value do SMMEs derive from the use of social media and how is business value derived through the use of social media?

The analysis process followed the phases laid out by Braun and Clarke (2006) for thematic analysis. In the first phase titled Familiarisation of Data, the researcher transcribed the data and routinely engaged with the data set to document "verbatim account of all verbal and nonverbal utterances" (Braun & Clarke, 2006, p.18). Although Otter.ai was used to assist in auto-generating transcriptions of semi-structured interviews, the researcher reviewed the audio recordings whilst reading the Otter.ai transcriptions to ensure that the correct information was presented in the transcriptions. In the next phase (Generating Initial Codes), the transcribed data was organised into groups which were subsequently categorised into initial units of analysis (codes) to identify "semantic content or latent content that appears interesting" (Braun & Clarke, 2006, 19). Subsequently, in the Searching for Themes phase, the codes were analysed to identify those that denoted similar concepts. The codes were merged or collapsed together to form a major theme and those that did not have enough data to qualify as themes were removed in the Reviewing of Themes phase. Finally, in the Naming of Themes phase, five major themes were identified to be influential in selection a social media platform: Business Value SMMEs Derive from the Use of social media, availability of in-house social media skills, financial support and decision makers demographic and digital literacy. Emergent themes regarding the techniques which organisations use to review their social media platform were social engagement, direct sales, consumer reviews, social media analytics and a combination of these identified techniques.

4 Findings

Data was collected from 15 SMMEs operating in the Hospitality Sector. Table 2 shows a summary of organisational information and respondent information pertaining to each interview. The table highlights that most respondents held positions in management (46%) or ownership (40%) within their organisation. Only two respondents held positions directly related to social media management or social media consulting. The data collection process further highlighted that that the most popular social media tools adopted by accommodation establishments were Facebook and Instagram.

Table 2. Demographic details of organizations and respondents

	Organisation	Location	Vision for Adopting social media Tool(s)	Social Media Tool(s)	Professional Position	Experience with social media
Airbnb	AirbnbINV1	Western Cape	Increase brand awareness and facilitate bookings.	Instagram	Manager	Limited
	AirbnbINV2	Western Cape	Increase brand awareness and promote ease of access to accommodation information.	Instagram, Facebook, and WhatsApp	Ad-Hoc Manager	Intermediate
	AirbnbINV4	Western Cape	Increase communication with customers.	WhatsApp	Owner	Limited
	AirbnbINV5	Western Cape	Increase brand awareness and facilitate bookings.	Instagram and Facebook	Manager	Limited
Boutique Hotel	BoutiqueHotelINV1	Gauteng	Increase brand awareness, create an online community, and promote co-creation between local brands.	Instagram, Facebook, Tik Tok, Twitter and Twitch	Owner	Advanced
	BoutiqueHotelINV2	Western Cape	Increase brand awareness, ease of access to information and encourage communication with customers.	Instagram, Facebook, Twitter, and WhatsApp	Manager	Advanced
	BoutiqueHotelINV3	Western Cape	Increase brand awareness.	Instagram, Facebook, WhatsApp	Owner	Limited
	BoutiqueHotelINV4	Gauteng and Western Cape	Increase brand awareness and create customer loyalty.	Instagram, Facebook, and Twitter	Social Media Consultant	Advanced
Guest House	Bed&BreakfastINV1	Gauteng	Increase brand awareness and access a younger target market.	Facebook	Owner	Advanced
	GuestHouseINV1	Gauteng	Increase brand awareness and promote co-creation between local brands.	Instagram and Facebook	Owner	Intermediate
	GuestHouseINV3	Western Cape	Increase brand awareness, manage customer feedback, and promote ease of access to information.	Instagram, Facebook, and Twitter	Manager	Intermediate
	GuestHouseINV4	Western Cape	Increase brand awareness and access a younger target market.	Instagram, Facebook, and Twitter	Social Media Manager	Advanced
	GuestHouseINV5	Gauteng	Access new target markets and increase brand awareness.	Facebook and WhatsApp	Manager	Intermediate
	GuestHouseINV6	Western Cape	Increase brand awareness and facilitate communication with customers.	Instagram, Facebook, and Twitter	Owner	Limited
	GuestHouseINV7	Western Cape	Increase brand awareness and facilitate bookings.	Instagram, Facebook, and Twitter	Owner	Intermediate

Factors Influencing the Selection of a Social Media Platform. Business Value.

Promote Website Traffic. There was a consensus amongst organisations that their websites were static and lacked traction from consumers. As highlighted by BoutiqueHotelINV2, the introduction of social media assisted in increasing and promoting click-throughs to organisations' websites. According to respondent GuestHouseINV4, *"with social media, it's just enough to really get people onto the websites and try and get them hooked in other ways if that makes sense"*. This sentiment was agreed upon by several respondents such as BedandBreakfastINV1 who saw social media as not presenting the *"whole story"* but could be used as a tool that enabled or channelled customers to their website in stating: *"In my personal experience if I wanted to Google a company and they only have a Facebook page, I don't like it. I want to see a proper website, and see if I can click on many things, with proper details. It seems to me that the Facebook site does not give enough information, you know. You just see posts. We have a website, with an address, with proper pictures, you know, like a whole story. I like it that way"*.

Communication, Transparency and Effective Marketing. Respondents stated that social media had the potential to provide consumers with access to more information regarding their organisation and thereby facilitate direct bookings. AirbnbINV1 stated that "we wanted consumers to see pictures [view previous customer's experiences of our services] and book straight away". Respondent GuestHouseINV1 implied that their organisation adopted social media as a tool to facilitate communication and provide a platform to respond to queries efficiently and in a formal yet personal manner. This was an important affordance of social media, given that prior websites were static. The need to communicate and be transparent was important because "guests do not want surprises. For example, my dogs, they are on our websites because I don't want anybody pitching up and saying they didn't know we had dogs. So that is for me complete transparency" [GuestHouseINV6]. The cost-effective marketing approach of social media was also noted. GuestHouseINV4 highlighted this factor stating "we post more frequently, it's mostly like sharing if we have specials or sales. We do the Facebook advertising and Instagram. So, if I am running a campaign then, I run the same campaign on both platforms". This ability to run the same post on multiple platforms at a low cost was seen as advantageous as it allowed them to increase access to new target markets.

Brand Awareness. 12 SMMEs stated that their adoption of a social media tool was strongly influenced by its ability to increase brand recognition and brand awareness. The ability for social media to create awareness for a business—through boosted posts, advertisements, and general content sharing—was perceived as an important factor and was identified as a key criterion influencing the adoption of social media for strategic purposes. Social media was seen as a *"good marketing tool for brand awareness not only from just a purely visual perspective, but also from doing live talks and things like that. It has brought a new audience in, so half of our followers are from America and half of them are from South Africa"*. [BoutiqueHotelINV1].

Promotion of Services and Direct Bookings. Respondents identified the Paid Promotions feature on Instagram (GuestHouseINV7) as well as the Boosted Posts feature on Facebook (AirbnbINV2) as the most frequently utilised features to promote their products and services. According to respondent BoutiqueHotelINV2, social media "allowed us to post something that's happening now. You know, a beautiful fireplace, snow in the mountains; whereas the website has a bigger, better overall description". According to BoutiqueHotelINV2 the combination of promoted posts coupled with Call-To-Action features such as 'Book', 'Reserve', and 'Contact Us' encouraged direct bookings. This new manner of making bookings was desirable as it ensured that establishments could easily monitor bookings, have control over-bookings and reduce commission expenses. Respondent BoutiqueHotelINV4 explained that "We have a book now button on Facebook which allows prospective customers to book their order. Generally, it links directly to the website.... we want to entice more direct bookings". Respondent GuestHouse-INV7 shared their experience of securing bookings through social media: "If we have a special or a competition, then those are ones that I track, and I can see when people share, and we've had bookings from that and even further enquirers which would not have been booked if it was not for the sharing feature of social media". These benefits of social media were perceived to be cost-effective for the organisations because "there isn't any commission requested from a middleman" (BoutiqueHotelINV4) thereby increasing financial gains from bookings.

Provide Complementary Products and Services.   To acquire more traffic on their websites, respondents indicated that their organisations used complementary products and services when "promoting products to provide prospective clients with a holistic view or information of their trip" (GuestHouseINV7) thus assisting in encouraging prospective clients to make a booking. Most organisations indicated that they used social media platforms to provide information on various activities consumers could take part in if they stayed at their accommodation establishment. According to respondent GuestHouseINV4: "We try to create that theme of a united a stay. You know, it's not just this where you're going to sleep at night, it's: this is where you could eat on the weekends, and this is what you could do. So yeah, we do a lot of that sort of thing".

Develop and Facilitate Partnerships with Industry Partners.   Most respondents indicated that social media allowed them to create new business partnerships with other organisations and influential members of society. Five SMMEs stated that they partnered up with community influencers or organisations that could provide digital content that could contribute to making their organisation more desirable to consumers. Respondent AirbnbINV2 highlighted the positive influence that these partnerships had on creating exposure for their organisation in stating: "We were approached by a woman who is a travel blogger and two other Instagrammers to stay here and advertised our place. They had quite a wide following. we got so much more exposure than we would have got from probably nine months of promoting posts like this. But it's hard to say what the financial payoff will be". Respondent GuestHouseINV5 indicated that when a "very influential somebody" agrees to partner, they give "credibility to the place and for us, we actually noticed how we immediately got something like close to 297,000 likes on our page". Furthermore, GuestHouseINV1 identified that in most cases, this partnership goes hand in hand with the provision of "complementary products that we offer".

Availability of In-House Skills.   Several SMMEs highlighted that acquiring and retaining employees who had the necessary skills to adopt, implement and maintain their social media platforms was a challenge and costly. These challenges according to respondent BoutiqueHotelINV3 encouraged their negative attitude towards social media because: *"we are small, it doesn't warrant me having someone do it for me because I can't afford that person. It is quite difficult unless, you know, you yourself become clued up with technology.".*

Eleven SMMEs highlighted that they independently managed their platforms even though they did not have the necessary IT and marketing skills to do so. Respondent AirbnbINV1 indicated the need for skilled personnel who understood "*social media and my website. I am just busy so I might hire someone for that because I cannot keep up with Instagram and websites you know there are all kinds of tricks and trades to keep your website alive and going. I do not know all these things and I do not think I got time for it*". The lack of in-house technical and social media management expertise resulted in most managers assuming several roles within their organisation including that of a social media manager.

Financial Support Acquiring financial resources for marketing on social media was identified as a challenge. Respondents highlighted their concerns with having limited funds to compete with the tourism industry's pressure for establishments to engage in aggressive targeted marketing on social media. SMMEs' lack of funds was emphasised by GuestHouseINV4 stating that many SMMEs did not have a dedicated budget for social media activities, whether it be for hiring an expert or marketing purposes. According to respondent AirbnbINV2: "*It's a tough market because now everybody is promoting themselves strongly on these platforms, like Instagram especially. I think it's quite hard for us, compared to some other or larger guest houses*".

Eight SMMEs were facing financial constraints to employ skilled professionals, upskilling, and increasing their marketing budgets. Furthermore, the financial constrain became exacerbate by COVID-19 which made some organisations to downsize or lost income. Respondent BedandBreakfastINV1 explained the financial challenges related to maintaining an SMME by stating: "*In the beginning, the overheads were covered by about 40% occupation. But as we continued, we needed more than 40% to break even and everything thing started getting more expensive. I got another company to do our social media. From the page, they gave me statistics every month or so. So, I only stopped using them because I could not afford their cost - because of COVID, the economy has been bad*".

Age and Digital Literacy of Decision-Makers. It was made apparent that SMMEs with older owners initially adopted social media platforms that owners were familiar with and believed to be easier to use. Most older owners preferred the use of Facebook as it "*was the easiest one to use*" (BedandBreakfastINV1). Respondent BoutiqueHotelNV1 explained how the owner's age influences the platform adopted: "*we have Twitter and Facebook. We tried Tik Tok, I am a little older for that. So, I got somebody to run that for me*".

Eight SMMEs identified that a critical factor influencing their choice of a social media tool was its ability to increase their direct marketing capabilities by increasing their access to their current and new target markets. In most cases, Instagram was adopted to target a younger demographic whereas Facebook was adopted to target an older demographic profile. Respondent GuestHouseINV6 confirmed that "*Instagram is more for the younger people. For the older people, my age–sixty-year-olds–would not read those, so I would do Facebook for older people to target them and Instagram for younger people*". The sentiment was affirmed by respondents GuestHouseINV4: "*we chose Instagram to reach a bit of a younger market, I think Facebook tends to be getting like an older market*".

Review of Social Media

Social Media Engagement. Respondents stated that they reviewed the performance of their social media tools based on content and viewer engagement rates. Organisations set metrics to monitor the number of followers, views, shares, and likes they received on their social media platforms because this assisted in maintaining and building customer relationships (BoutiqueHotelINV2). Respondent GuestHouseINV5 explained that: *"we look at the number of likes. A couple of days after we post something, we monitor the amount of people directly calling and emailing to inquire or make bookings and all of that".* The most frequent types of conversations monitored were those related to inquiries and feedback. Respondents identified that platforms that did not encourage engagement or promote brand awareness were often neglected. In many instances Twitter was neglected by GuestHouseINV4: *"because I don't think it was beneficial. It wasn't really reaching many people and it was time-consuming. So, to sit and do a tweet or blog post for few people to read it, is a waste of time rather than putting your time and energy into face-to-face marketing".*

Reviews as part of engagement, were perceived to be an important criterion in determining the success of an establishment, particularly in the business's early stages. Respondents noted that reviews, both positive and negative assisted in providing constructive feedback that can be used to improve the establishment (GuestHouseINV3). Furthermore, it was made apparent that social media was beneficial in allowing organisations to promptly respond to reviews and feedback. For example, *"If someone has a bad experience, or they mentioned something that I don't necessarily want anyone to share, then I would acknowledge that and try to mediate the situation."* [GuestHouseINV7].

Direct Sales. When the adopted social media platform did not promote bookings, some organisations reverted to traditional means of marketing as indicated by respondent GuestHouseINV6 in stating: *"I paid some money in lockdown to promote the guesthouse on Instagram. I got a lot of views but obviously no bookings. So, it's hard to measure that. For me it is a very personal business, so emails and telephones are best the way of dealing with customers".* Feedback from respondents highlighted that although social media created brand awareness and resulted in increased views, in most cases, the brand awareness generated failed to translate into direct sales. Most sales according to GuestHouseINV1 were derived from a customer *"referral, relationship, and trust in my experience".* Thus, taking into consideration that social media can facilitate bookings, this response emphasises the importance of monitoring social media platforms to determine if engagement rates are translating into consumer conversions.

Limited use of Social Media Analytics. A minimal number of SMMEs stated that they performed social media analytics due to various factors including limited knowledge on how to perform social media analytics and having limited knowledge on its significance. Respondents, such as BoutiqueHotelINV2 had minimal interest in the information collated from performing analytics: "We do, but I would say in limited capacity. I do sometimes read the data, probably not as often as I should". Similar sentiments were echoed by respondent GuestHouseINV7: "I look at the insights on Instagram, but I have not used them as much". Nevertheless, four SMMEs stressed their interest in engaging in social media analysis, particularly in trend analysis, sentiment analysis and conversation analysis to monitor engagement rates and subsequently implement strategies to address negative feedback (if required). Respondent BoutiqueHotelINV4 noted the importance of performing sentiment analysis to understand customer behaviour: "You look at all kinds of things like the behaviour of your followers. Basically, the interaction that you have, and the engagement and the reach as well that you have with your client base or your followers". Respondent AirbnbINV5 stated that trend analysis helped to ensure maximum occupancy, particularly during seasons where tourism levels were lower. The respondent further explained that "We look at more specific data. We do have Google business, that one we track a bit more to see, when are people looking at our pages and when the views are down, to sort of pick up the trends of when the markets busy and what can we do for the downtime".

Airbnb used a combination of metrics. These included but were not limited to social media interactions, Airbnb views, income, Airbnb ratings, and bookings. Respondent AirbnbINV1 would *"check how many views I get, average income and my average of my star rating. You know a lot of times when I get a two-star, it will bring my five stars right down, so I got to check that"*. The importance of consumer reviews was also perceived to be significant. Other respondents used data collated from analysis to ensure that they were posting according to their followers' interests and actively engaging with followers during the times where the level of engagement was predicted to be higher (BoutiqueHotelINV1, GuestHouseINV3 and GuestHouseINV4). Findings also show that to effectively build business intelligence from the analysed data it was important to identify metrics linked to consumer demographic information, specifically information linked to customers' *"geolocation, age group, gender base, and who is engaging with the brand the most"* [BoutiqueHotelINV1]. This demographic information was particularly important for organisations that had a customer base that was both local and international, as it would allow them to better cater for their respective customers' needs.

5 Discussion

This study had two objectives. Firstly, to identify the factors influencing how an SMME in developing countries selects a social media platform. Four key themes were identified to be influential. One of them is the business value SMMEs derive from the use of social media. Social media was able to provide four notable business values: *increase in traffic to static websites; promotion of communication and transparency of the establishment's products and services; increase in brand recognition and awareness through complementary products and services; as well as an increase in bookings encouraged by online campaigns and promotions.* There was a strong perception that social media had minimal influence in promoting brand loyalty. Participants identified that traditional communication methods such as word of mouth, emails and newsletters were more successful in remaining in contact and solidify relationships with previous customers. Respondent BoutiqueHotelINV2 explained that the use of traditional communication methods was the *"biggest communication strategy of keeping up with clientele"*. Traditional means of communication allowed organisations to maintain loyal customers or those who were not exposed to social media. Organisations in this study found websites and traditional means of communication as being more valuable than the use of social media in establishing trust and communicating with their existing–especially older–customers. This is significant because as much as social media is being hailed as a tool for attracting new customers, cultivating relationships with existing ones and improving collaborations with customers (Shaltoni, 2017), organisations in this study did not perceive it as a tool that encouraged trust to ensure the survival of their establishment.

The business value derived from social media was constrained by the organisation's internal resources, specifically, financial resources, technical and marketing expertise related to social media. Factors such as limited financial resources and the impact of COVID-19 played a critical role in their inability to adopt and maintain their social media platforms. The results echo Mosweunyane's (2016) findings that identified that a lack of financial support–particularly from governmental organisations–prevents the advancement of SMMEs, particularly those in the tourism sector. This is due to the lack of financial assistance often limiting the ability for SMMEs to introduce technologies that require organisations to dedicate a substantial amount of capital to implement and manage technologies (Tiago & Veríssimo, 2014). In addition, Kalidas et al (2020) highlighted that SMMEs are less likely to manage the burden imposed by COVID-19 due to their limited access to cash, operating with a smaller client base and having a limited capacity to manage commercial pressures in comparison to larger organisations. Findings show that external support from family members, acquittances and influential community members/celebrities were deemed to be an important factor in assisting to distribute social media content–particularly through features such as *post sharing*.

SMMEs perceived social media as an effective marketing tool that led to transaction efficiency (Ketelaars, 2011), *"because of some of the engagements that led to direct bookings was because there was no middle-man involvement"* [BoutiqueHotelINV4]. For some SMMEs, their adoption of a social media platform was influenced by its ability to facilitate or offer online booking options. SMMEs in this study saw Call-to-Action features such as Book, Reserve and Contact as a novelty of social media that created new and efficient ways in which transactions such as direct bookings could occur. These perceptions echo Zubia's (2018), who argues that Call-to-Action features are desirable as they ensure that the purchasing journey is simplified to encompass fewer steps between the time in which the consumer is influenced, and the reservation is confirmed. In addition to the Call-to-Action features, social media features found to be important include the *Paid Promotions* feature, the *Boosted Posts* feature as well as features that enabled SMMEs to evaluate their social media performance.

Individual factors of age and digital literacy of the manager and or the owner influenced the selection of a social media platform. Similar findings are reported by He et al. (2017). These factors together with organisational constraints such as lack of in-house expertise, unfortunately, resulted in organisations not being able to fulfil [all] the phases of the normative decision-making model due to the lack of know-how and awareness of, for example, value drivers and metrics that are necessary to achieve when introducing social media tools into their business strategy (DiMicco et al., 2008). To remedy the challenges posed by individual factors, it is advised that SMMEs be provided with social media and related technology training to create not only "awareness but also to improve their ability to increase the usage of these platforms" (Žufan et al, 2020, 109).

The second goal of the study was to explore how SMMEs reviewed their social media platforms. The criterion used to review and measure the success of a particular social media tool rested on monitoring customer engagement rates, direct sales made, consumer reviews and feedback, and to some extent basic data analytics. However, a limited number of SMMEs identified that they used social media analytics for trend analysis, sentiment analysis and conversation analysis. It was made apparent that their rationale for performing social media analytics was mainly to monitor customer conversations as these allowed organisations to acquire information related to consumers' perceptions towards their brand which could be used to improve customer services (Lee, 2018) However, some organisations stated that they faced challenges with performing social media analysis as they often relied upon the built-in social media listening features offered by social media platforms which have limited capabilities thus making it difficult to monitor, listen to and analyse data. These challenges negatively influenced SMMEs' ability to engage in building social media intelligence as the social media platforms only provided participants with aggregate-level data. These findings support the view of Moe and Schweidel (2017) who state that social media listening platforms are not effective when used in isolation as they provide a high-level view of data collated from automated sentiment analysis, limited conversation analysis and volume breakdowns. Those that did not regularly engage in social media analytics cited minimal interest in the information collated from performing analysis. This was due to the information being analysed in isolation; the lack of in-house analytical expertise to do the analysis and make sense of the results; and the lack of awareness of what data analytics can do for the organisation. These findings were in alignment with Oji et al.'s (2017) results that highlight that a lack of in-house skills–particularly those related to marketing, management and IT–often contribute to a business's failure especially in countries such as South Africa where entrepreneurs lack training and education.

6 Conclusion

This study sought to understand what informs an SMME's decision to adopt a specific social media platform and how SMMEs review the performance of their social media platforms. The findings show that the selection of social media platforms was influenced by both organisational and individual factors. The key organisational driver behind SMMEs selection of a particular social media platform was the business value they anticipated to create from its integration with business objectives. This was then followed by the availability of in-house technical and marketing expertise, financial support. It was observed that SMMEs put trust at the forefront of their operations and were cognizant of the fact that although social media presented its benefits; as a tool, it did very little to facilitate trust, build brand loyalty and establish communication with existing loyal customers. With these findings, this study recommends that rather than forcing SMMEs to institutionalise social media, they should adopt a moderate use of social media whilst engaging in their traditional methods of communicating with their customers. In addition, SMMEs use of social media should be seen as a complementary tool to their websites where extensive information on the establishment is presented. Individual factors influencing the selection of a particular social media platform were related to demographic factors such as the age and digital literacy of the manager or owner of the organisation. This study recommends that SMMEs are provided with social media and related technology training, information literacy and the relevant digital resources to create not only awareness of the influence of social media on an organisation's success but to also improve adoptee's ability to effectively maximise the potential of adopted platforms.

References

Amit, R., Zott, C.: Value creation in E-business. Strateg. Manag. J. **22**(6–7), 493–520 (2001)

Braun, V., Clarke, V.: Using thematic analysis in psychology. Qual. Res. Psychol. **3**(2), 77–101 (2006)

Bushe, B.: The causes and impact of business failure among small to micro and medium enterprises in South Africa. Africa's Public Serv. Deliv. Perform. Rev. **7**(1), 1–26 (2019)

Davis, M., Logan, D.: Market guide for social analytics applications. Gartner (2019)

DiMicco, J., Millen, D. R., Geyer, W., Dugan, C., Brownholtz, B., & Muller, M.: Motivations for social networking at work. In: Proceedings of the ACM Conference on Computer Supported Cooperative Work, CSCW, pp. 711–720 (2008)

Dong, J.Q., Wu, W.: Business value of social media technologies: evidence from online user innovation communities. J. Strateg. Inf. Syst. **24**(2), 113–127 (2015)

Duong-Van, M.: United States Patent. Metavana Inc. US 8,849,826 B2 (2014)

Fan, W., Gordon, M.D.: The power of social media analytics. Commun. ACM **57**(6), 74–81 (2014)

Grover, V., Chiang, R.H.L., Liang, T.P., Zhang, D.: Creating strategic business value from big data analytics: a research framework. J. Manag. Inf. Syst. **35**(2), 388–423 (2018)

Gümüs, N., Kütahyali, D.N.: Perceptions of social media by small and medium enterprises (SMEs) in Turkey. Int. J. Bus. Inf. **12**(2), 123–148 (2017)

Hajli, M.N.: A study of the impact of social media on consumers. Int. J. Mark. Res. **56**(3) (2014)

He, W., Wang, F.-K., Chen, Y., Zha, S.: An exploratory investigation of social media adoption by small businesses. Inf. Technol. Manag. **18**(2), 149–160 (2017)

Jones, N., Borgman, R., Ulusoy, E.: Impact of social media on small businesses. J. Small Bus. Enterp. Dev. **22**(4), 611–632 (2015)

Kalidas, S., Magwentshu, N., Rajagopaul, A.: How South African SMEs can survive and thrive post-COVID-19. McKinsey Insights (2020). http://search.ebscohost.com/login.aspx?direct=true&db=bth&AN=144541557&site=ehost-live

Ketelaars, H.: The Perceived Impact of Social Media on Employee Performance and Effectiveness [Tilburg University] (2011). https://search.proquest.com/docview/2058039553?accountid=14169

Kiráľová, A., Pavlíčeka, A.: Development of social media strategies in tourism destination. Procedia Soc. Behav. Sci. **175**, 358–366 (2015)

Lee, I.: Social media analytics for enterprises: typology, methods, and processes. Bus. Horiz. **61**(2), 199–210 (2018)

McCann, M., Barlow, A.: Use and measurement of social media for SMEs. J. Small Bus. Enterp. Dev. **22**(2), 273–287 (2015)

M'manga, A., Faily, S., McAlaney, J., Williams, C., Kadobayashi, Y., Miyamoto, D.: A normative decision-making model for cyber security. Inf. Comput. Secur. **27**(5), 636–646 (2019)

Moe, W.W., Schweidel, D.A.: Opportunities for innovation in social media analytics. J. Prod. Innov. Manag. **34**(5), 697–702 (2017)

Mosweunyane, L.D.: Free State Tourism SMMEs' Utilisation of Social Media Technologies for Business Competitiveness: A Stakeholders' Perspective. Central University of Technology. (2016)

Nagle, T., Pope, A.: Understanding social media business value, a prerequisite for social media selection. J. Decis. Syst. **22**(4), 283–297 (2013)

Ndekwa, A.G., Katunzi, T.M.: Small and medium tourist enterprises and social media adoption: empirical evidence from Tanzanian tourism sector. Int. J. Bus. Manag. **11**(4), 71–80 (2016)

Oji, O.N.E., Iwu, C.G., Haydam, N.: The use of social media marketing strategies by SMMEs in the hospitality sector in Cape Metropole, South Africa. Afr. J. Hosp. Tour. Leis. **6**(1), 1–16 (2017)

Seddon, P.B., Constantinidis, D., Tamm, T., Dod, H.: How does business analytics contribute to business value? Inf. Syst. J. **27**(1), 237–269 (2017)

Shaltoni, A. M.: From websites to social media: exploring the adoption of internet marketing in emerging industrial markets. J. Bus. Ind. Mark. Transforming decision-making processes: a research agenda for understanding the impact of business analytics on organisations

Sharma, R., Mithas, S., Kankanhalli, A.: Transforming decision-making processes: a research agenda for understanding the impact of business analytics on organisations. Eur. J. Inf. Syst. **23**(4), 433–441 (2014)

Small-Enterprise-Development-Agency. SMME Quarterly Update 1 st Quarter 2018. In: SEDA, pp. 1–29 (2019)

Stockdale, R., Ahmed, A., Scheepers, H.: Identifying business value from the use of social media: an SME perspective. In: Pacific Asia Conference on Information Systems (2012)

Tiago, M.T.P.M.B., Veríssimo, J.M.C.: Digital marketing and social media: why bother? Bus. Horiz. **57**(6), 703–708 (2014)

Wamba, S.F., Akter, S., Kang, H., Bhattacharya, M., Upal, M.: The primer of social media analytics. J. Organ. End User Comput. **28**(2), 1–12 (2016)

Zubia, A.: The Secret to Boosting Your Appointment Bookings via Social Media (2018). https://www.liveplan.com/blog/the-secret-to-boosting-your-appointment-bookings-via-social-media/

Žufan, J., Civelek, M., Hamarneh, I., Kmeco, Ľ: Impacts of firm characteristics on social media usage of SMEs: evidence from the Czech Republic. Int. J. Entrep. Knowl. **8**(1), 102–113 (2020)

Zulu, L.D.: Revised schedule 1 of the national definition of small enterprise in South Africa. In: Government Gazette, pp. 110–111 (2019)

Theoretical Foundations of Customer Engagement in Social Media – Implications for Businesses

Malte Wattenberg[✉] [iD]

University of Applied Sciences and Arts, Bielefeld, Germany
malte.wattenberg@hsbi.de

Abstract. Customer engagement (CE) is a conceptual approach to describing the engagement and interactions of social media users with company websites. The vast majority of empirical research is dedicated to the factors influencing CE based on selected theories. A translation of the factors into recommendations for action for companies only takes place to a limited extent. With the help of a qualitative approach in the form of a focus group, prominent theories of CE were examined. The aim was to develop a set of possible recommendations for the effective design of corporate communication on social media and to name their respective theoretical basis. The article therefore follows a practical approach, connecting theoretical frameworks to actionable insights. As a result, it is recommended to use a high level of vividness and interactivity in posts, to use means of sales promotion, to be thematically diversified, to choose a personal, benefit-oriented, emotional, and entertaining message appeal, and to engage in active community building. It was also shown that recommendations for action are usually covered by several theories. The combination of elements of media richness and uses and gratifications theory proved to be particularly promising.

Keywords: Social Media · Customer Engagement · Theoretical Foundations · Practical Recommendations

1 Introduction

Social media platforms are proving to be ever more popular and the number of users is steadily increasing. The market research institute Kepios collects current figures on social media usage in an annual report [1]. At the beginning of 2024, a global user base of 5.04 billion was recorded, with an increase of 266 million in the reporting period. The largest platform by far is the social network Facebook with 3.05 billion users, followed by the video platform YouTube (2.5 billion users), WhatsApp and Instagram (2 billion users each), and TikTok (1.56 billion users). The main reasons given for using various platforms are connecting with friends (49.5%), followed by passing the time (38.5%), and reading news stories (34.2%). 90% of users follow one or more brands on social media [2]. A total of 73.9% use social media to research brands and products they are considering buying, and 48.9% use social media to learn about brands and consume their content [1]. The high number of social media users is partially offset by companies' social media presence. While 87% of Fortune 500 companies already use social media to get in touch with their customers in 2018 [3], the figure for small businesses is 77% [2].

Regarding the platform, an international survey revealed that 89% of social media marketers utilized Facebook with another 80% using Instagram. The primary reasons are to increase brand awareness (86%), as well as to generate traffic for the website (76%) and leads (64%) [4].

Customer engagement (CE) has been drawing more attention lately [5]. CE is a widely known and accepted conceptual approach to describe the engagement and interactions of social media users with company websites. Though there is a growing body of study on the subject, its substantive focus is still unclear. As a result, many unanswered questions remain about the causes, effects, and various types of CE [5, 6]. In particular, much work is conceptual [7], with a remarkably notable research gap concerning social media [8]. In contrast, however, there is a high practical relevance: 69% of all CEOs assign the highest strategic priority to digital consumer engagement [9].

In the social media literature, various theories are included in the research as the basis for CE. Based on these theories, candidates for communicative success factors for corporate presences are often derived and empirically analyzed. These also relate to the particular platform and the companies analyzed. These in turn vary in terms of orientation, sector, and regional anchoring. Overall, this approach leads to a very limited set of recommendations for action for companies depending on the respective underlying data set. There is no overview of which recommendations for action are effective regardless of the platform and company. This study attempts to fill this gap by deriving and structuring recommendations for action from the most frequently encountered theories, across all platforms.

The remainder of the paper is organized as follows. Section 2 presents the theoretical background. Section 3 is then devoted to the research question and objectives. Section 4 presents the method before the results are presented in Sect. 5. The paper ends with a discussion and conclusion in Sects. 6 and 7.

2 Customer Engagement on Social Media

2.1 Background and Definition

The foundation of customer engagement can be found in service-dominant logic (SDL) [10] and social exchange theory [11, 12]. The basic idea of SDL is that providers cannot offer customers services with material value, but rather that value is only created by integrating the customer into the value creation process [10, 13]. Social exchange theory, on the other hand, is dedicated to the voluntary actions of consumers as a type of exchange motivated by the expectation of a service in return [11].

Customer Engagement is defined as "a psychological state that occurs by virtue of interactive, cocreative customer experiences with a focal agent/object (e.g., a brand) in focal service relationships. [...] It is a multidimensional concept subject to a context- and/or stakeholder-specific expression of relevant cognitive, emotional, and/or behavioral dimensions." [14: p. 260].

According to Kuvykaitė & Tarutė [15], this multidimensional view has been accepted, mostly in the form of an affective, cognitive, and behavioral component [5]. However, some researchers emphasize the advantages of a behavior-oriented view, as it does not exclude psychological constructs such as satisfaction and cognitive or affective engagement [7].

2.2 Conceptualization

However, there is broad agreement that CE is influenced by various factors and that CE leads to different effects.

In the conceptualization of CE, the study by van Doorn et al. [13] is often referred to and supported [e.g.: 16, 17]. They characterize behavior-oriented CE based on valence, scope, form/modality, nature of its impact, and the customer goal. Other options include differentiating between the dimensions of customer- and provider-initiated engagement as well as offers and activities [18] or indirect and direct contributions [7].

Online environments based on social media such as Social Network Sites (SNS) have expanded the type and depth of interactions between companies and consumers [19].

The typology of user activities in social media by Muntinga et al. [20] has received much attention. This classification is based on the work of Shao [21] and his classification of user-generated media into the three engagement levels of consuming, participating, and producing company-related content. Muntinga et al. [20] call these three engagement levels "consumers' online brand-related activities" (COBRAs) and associate certain activities with them [22]. However, they point out that engagement should be understood as a continuum [20].

Dolan et al. [16] offer a more comprehensive breakdown and differentiate between active and passive [23, 24], as well as positive and negative engagement, in a similar way to Muntinga et al. [20].

As a result, all types of social media use can be assigned to different degrees of activation, although this is not done consistently in research.

According to Calder & Malthouse [25], factors influencing the CE can generally be divided into intrinsic and extrinsic motives [26]. Van Doorn et al. [13] distinguish between customer-specific, company-specific, and context-dependent influencing factors, which are also adopted by Esch & Köhler [27]. Customer-specific influencing factors include attitude-based variables such as customer satisfaction, customer loyalty, brand trust, brand loyalty, and perceived brand performance. In addition, emotional states, personality traits, identity, customer goals, and the resources of time, effort, and money of consumers are further influencing factors. Company-specific factors are the reputation and characteristics of the company. Context-dependent influencing factors essentially result from the political/legal, economic/ecological, social, and technological aspects of society [13]. Other influencing factors are involvement and participation [18], customer satisfaction, emotions, type of offer, supplier-customer constellation, brand value, convenience, and level of involvement [7].

In the literature, only a few authors have dealt conceptually with the factors influencing customer engagement and its effects on social media. The main focus is on company-related factors, and social and functional drivers [28–30]. Barger et al. [31]

include customer-, product-, content-related, and social media factors. Tsiotsou's framework [24], on the other hand, differentiates between intrinsic and extrinsic factors. A recent study by Deng et al. [32] is based on a systematic literature review of CE on various social media platforms. Their categorization includes the four elements communicator, stimulus, communicatee, and context together. Wattenberg [33] was able to confirm this framework to a certain extent for Facebook.

The effects of the CE can also be analyzed according to the influencing factors. Van Doorn et al. [13] again address customer-related and company-related consequences, while Pansari & Kumar [7] differentiate between tangible and intangible benefits. Vivek et al. [18] consider the consequences of CE to be the perception of greater perceived value, trust, affective commitment, loyalty, and participation in the brand community as well as word-of-mouth.

The effects of CE on social media are seen by Barger et al. [31], especially in the attitudes toward the brand, the product, and the content. In addition, there are consumer effects such as the consumer's position of power or social capital as well as market-related effects such as purchase intention, product choice, and sales [31]. Tsiotsou [24] differentiates between attitude-related effects such as trust, satisfaction, commitment, loyalty, or eWOM, as well as joint value creation and market research as effects of CE.

2.3 Underlying Theories

In the social media literature, various theories are included in research as the basis for CE. The most relevant are, but not limited to, motivation theories, personality theories, attitudinal theories, social theories, marketing theories, and media theories [33–35].

All theory groups have in common that they can explain the behavior of users on social media platforms from their perspective.

The following overview of the relevant theories is divided into classical motivation theories, personality-based approaches, attitude-based approaches, and theories of the social and media environment.

Classical Motivation Theories. Deci & Ryan's Self-Determination Theory (SDT) [36] makes a fundamental distinction between extrinsic and intrinsic motivation and explains behavior based on the degree of self-determination. The degree of autonomy of extrinsic motivation increases the closer the perceived location of the cause of action is to the person, e.g. if the action is in line with their values and goals. Intrinsic motivation has the highest degree of autonomy and is controlled by internal regulatory mechanisms such as interest, pleasure, and satisfaction. SDT, like McClelland's motive theory [37], then explains the central motives of people. The need for power focuses on the ability to control or influence other people. The need for achievement can explain why users create their content, collect information [38], and exchange knowledge [39]. Finally, the motive theory attests to the need for affiliation that a large part of human action results from the need for social relationships, acceptance, belonging, and exchange. It also correlates with the frequency of use of social media [40].

Personality-Based Approaches. Meffert et al. [41] see motives and emotions (emotional theory, ET) in close connection with each other and as active processes which, alongside cognitive processing, constitute an important sub-process of the communication impact. The relevant behaviors based on emotions relate primarily to interaction with other people [42] and customer communication in the scope of consumer behavior [43]. However, companies cannot trigger a predefined emotion in the consumer with their communicative attitude. Instead, they can only align their communication based on the expected effect of the influencing factors on the communication [44]. Positive emotions have a specific effect on CE in social media [45]. Emotions also affect loyalty [46], satisfaction [47], and thus customer retention. They can also influence word-of-mouth behavior and customer feedback, e.g. on social media [7, 48]. Emotions are evoked reliably in connection with key stimuli [43], whereby the use of images and film material promises particular success [42], as does humor and astonishment [44, 49].

In addition to emotions, personality traits (PT) also count as personality-related factors. The 5-factor model reduces personal traits to neuroticism, extraversion, openness to experience, agreeableness, and conscientiousness and thus explains individual differences in motivation [50, 51]. Extroverted people, for example, are more likely to initiate or contribute to conversations, while introverted people exhibit fundamentally more passive communication behavior [52]. For social media, Barker [53] found that people with high self-confidence are highly motivated to communicate via SNS. People with low self-esteem use SNS communication as a means of compensation [53]. Users with a high extraversion level are members of significantly more Facebook groups [54], use communicative functions more intensively [55, 56], and have more friends [57]. Introverts and neurotics spend more time on Facebook than their counterparts [57]. Self-presentation behaviors on Facebook are best predicted by low conscientiousness and high neuroticism [56]. Overall, Facebook users tend to be extroverted and open to new things [55]. Reliability, on the other hand, has a negative effect on the number of friends and does not influence the intensity of Facebook use [55], just like openness to new experiences [54, 57].

Attitude-Based Approaches. Factors influencing the CE in social media can be characterized by different attitudes towards a brand or company. The attitudinal construct of customer retention is a form of enduring customer relationship [58] with the central building blocks of customer satisfaction [59], loyalty [60], and trust [61, 62]. Customer retention shows the willingness of users to engage in long-term online interactions with companies and to commit to the brand [63]. On social media, high customer retention leads to increased engagement [45]. Satisfied customers also tend to be enthusiastic and happy [63, 64], which in turn is reflected in their engagement on the social media platform [45]. Furthermore, participants in a community create a feeling of belonging to a group, which in turn increases trust in the community [65] and the brand [66] and also increases CE [45]. There are strong connections and dependencies between the individual attitudinal factors towards a brand [45]. For example, customer trust is directly related to customer satisfaction [63], but also directly influences CE in social media, just like customer satisfaction [45].

The Theory of Planned Behavior (TPB) can be considered another attitude-based model to explain CE. Here, the attitude towards the behavior, social norms, and perceived behavioral control affect the intention to behave [67]. However, the attitude is only characterized by a positive or negative evaluation of an object. The social norm is based on the perceived social pressure to perform a certain action, while the perceived behavioral control reflects one's assessment of being able to realize a behavior. Also, the TPB is often used in science to predict behavior in social media. The attitude and subjective norm have thus been confirmed in various studies as a significant factor in predicting the intention to use SNSs [68, 69].

Theories of the Social and Media Environment. Social-Cognitive Theory (SCT) is one of the theories of the social environment. The core element is the expectation of self-efficacy concerning a goal, the expected output, and socio-structural factors [70]. Self-efficacy expectation is the self-assessment of the extent to which one's actions successfully complete a task or achieve a goal. Striving for efficacy thus means the desire to achieve a certain result in the social or physical environment. Furthermore, the theory does not assume that experiences have to be made by oneself, but that individuals also learn through observation to what degree other users experience reinforcements for their behavior [71]. Bandura [72] states that self-efficacy expectations determine the extent and purpose of media use. People with high self-efficacy expectations are therefore more likely to share their knowledge in an online community [73]. A high expectation of results influences the quality and quantity of the knowledge shared [74]. However, Schunk & DiBenedetto [75] point out the necessity of adapting SCT in the context of social media and the opportunities for communication and social comparisons that exist there.

Word-of-mouth (WOM) is a form of social influence on behavior and attitudes through company-related communication among consumers [76–79]. Central motives are social interaction, altruism, extraversion, and incentives. Above all, WOM is becoming increasingly important in the context of social media because information about companies and products is no longer only shared between known parties, but also between strangers [71]. Conversely, individuals can actively search for information, confirmation, or opinions from their reference groups on social media. As a result, online communities, for example, benefit from WOM through increased consumer engagement [80]. Furthermore, eWOM contributes to brand loyalty via social media platforms [81]. SNSs in particular satisfy the motive for social interaction and gain additional relevance through the social connections between potential customers [82]. The eWOM behavior in SNSs is facilitated by the strength of social connections [83], and expressive-ness, but also by social reinforcement, relationship management, normative and informal influence, as well as other personal factors such as altruism, narcissism, image building, and achievements [84]. Companies, for their part, can use WOM behavior to spread their messages [71].

The Uses and Gratification Theory (UGT) assumes that individuals use certain media or media messages to satisfy their needs [85–87]. The UGT follows the approach of a user-centered expectancy-by-value model, in which the gratifications sought are compared with the gratifications received respectively not received and co-determine the future of active use and interaction. As an example, a social media user could be actively looking for up-to-date information on a company profile, but not find it and consequently visit the profile less frequently or not at all. Central needs are, for example, information, entertainment, rewards, or social interaction [86]. According to Muntinga et al. [20], these can be applied to social media as well and are widely used [16, 88]. In addition, a brand appeal based on attractiveness, credibility, and expertise impacts user participation [88].

3 Research Question and Aim

This study intends to fill the resulting gap in the literature by addressing the research questions listed below:

- RQ1: "To what extent can recommendations for action be derived directly from the theories and their influencing factors on CE so that companies can optimize their social media communications design?"
- RQ2: "How can these recommendations for action be structured?"
- RQ3: "Which of the recommendations for action are covered by several theories simultaneously?"

Therefore, the study's objective is to create a comprehensive set of recommendations for the design of social media communication, including their theoretical foundations. The main target group of the article is companies that want to enhance their communication strategy on social media.

4 Method

To answer the research question and achieve the objective, a divergent approach is chosen.

First, theories relevant to the CE on social media, including antecedents, were selected based on their orientation. The selection of the theories (see above) was based on the statements of relevant authors on their significance for CE [34, 35], the frequency of their use in studies [33], and the author's assessment of their relevance.

Subsequently, colleagues in business psychology and social media communication [n = 6] were asked in a group interview in the fall of 2023 to give their assessments of possible activities by companies to promote CE based on the selected theories.

To this end, the author first provided an overview of the relevant theories to bring all participants to the same level of knowledge. It is important to emphasize that the participants were familiar with these theories and that this was a means of consolidating their knowledge. Likewise, all participants are social media users on different platforms.

The discussion was minimally structured to leave room for individual priorities and to promote a richer discussion. In parallel, the researcher reflected on the above-mentioned topic, whereby his considerations were substantially incorporated into the overall view.

Results in the form of recommendations were collected on virtual post-its. A handwritten protocol was used to record contributions to the discussion, which primarily related to the applicability of the suggestions. The results were collected completely anonymously and did not allow any conclusions to be drawn about the identity of the participants.

In total, 52 distinct recommendations for action were identified based on the theories presented.

Subsequently, the collected recommendations for action were grouped by the author in a content analysis process [89].

The resulting categories are media (vividness, interactivity), content (sales promotion, topic, communication style), and community building.

5 Results

5.1 Media

Vividness. Social media posts represent different levels of vividness or media richness. Steuer defines vividness as „the representational richness of a mediated environment as defined by its formal features; that is, the way in which an environment presents information to the senses. "[90: p. 81]. Images, for example, are more appealing than text as they convey a richer visual impression [91].

Accordingly, the recommendation for companies is to post visually appealing content. This primarily includes the use of images, graphics, and videos. Participants emphasize the relevance of high-quality material that matches the topic of the content. The content should also be quickly recognizable and convey a clear message. For videos, this also means limiting the length, as otherwise users' attention is lost. It is also recommended to add visual effects or filters to either improve the quality of the material, make content more appealing, or highlight interesting aspects. Visual material supports the communication of information, entertainment, and emotions and is therefore mainly based on UGT and ET, but also on intrinsic motivation (SDT).

Interactivity Interactivity influences participation and engagement [92] and is defined as „the degree to which two or more communication parties can act on each other, on the communication medium, and on the messages and the degree to which such influences are synchronized." [93]. It can refer to technical properties such as links [90] as well as emphasizing the extent of the reciprocity of messages [94]. Interactivity therefore stands for the entire interactive potential of a communication situation or a technical medium.

Suggested recommendations in the area of interactivity include links, @-mentions, questions, calls to action (CTAs), and quizzes.

Links are one of the ways to generate interactivity in the form of clicks. For example, other social media content can be linked or the company's website. As a rule, social media portals show a preview of the expected content in the form of a snippet. In terms of content, the entire range of different formats, orientations, and topics should be addressed. The main objective is to satisfy the user's need for information and possibly entertainment (UGT). In addition, links increase the degree of self-determination (SCT), the sense of control (TPB), and thus the intrinsic motivation and sense of autonomy of users (SDT), as users must actively decide to obtain more information on a topic.

An @-mention is usually introduced by the "@" sign, whereupon the platforms offer the option of selecting profiles to be mentioned. Corresponding profiles then receive a message that they have been featured. This increases the likelihood that these users will also interact with the company profile. Companies can use @-mentions to promote the intrinsic motivation of users, address the affiliation motive (SDT) or social motivation (WOM), increase customer retention, and address the expectation of self-efficacy (SCT).

Companies can also offer quizzes, ask users questions, or directly ask them to respond. Relevant and interesting topics for the target group, for example about products and services, the company, or the industry, are suitable for quizzes. The format can be a knowledge quiz or a personality test that results in a different range of offers depending on the user, for example. Simple and clearly formulated questions that are easy for the target group to answer are especially suitable. CTAs should also be precisely formulated and can refer to liking posts, commenting or sharing content, clicking on further links, participating in promotions, or contacting the company in various ways. Questions and CTAs represent extrinsically motivated factors, promote social connection (SDT, WOM, customer retention), appeal to the user's achievement motive (SDT), increase the perception of control (TPB), and give extroverted and open-minded people the opportunity to express themselves (PT). Quizzes also represent a strong extrinsically motivated stimulus, which appeals to both the need for achievement (SDT) and the expectation of self-efficacy (SCT).

5.2 Content

Sales Promotion. Focus group participants recommend various means of sales promotion, which are covered by the theoretical principles of customer retention.

The most prominent elements of sales promotion are incentives. These include, for example, giveaways, discount campaigns, vouchers, loyalty programs, special offers, or a shortage of products. Incentives act as strong extrinsic motivation (SDT) as well as sought-after gratification in the context of UGT and pro-mote WOM behavior. However, competitions and prize draws are also forms of incentives that are addressed in particular via the user's need for achievement. In addition, competitions affect the expectation of self-efficacy (SCT).

Other customer retention measures include cross-selling and upselling, the introduction of customer service and complaint management, consistent marketing branding, and events. Live webinars, live chats, and product demonstrations are mentioned as examples. Events with user participation are also covered by personality theories, as extroverted and open individuals in particular find the opportunity to communicate (PT).

Topic. Participants also commented on the different thematic focuses of companies' social media posts.

Possible topics include product-, company-, market- and society-related information. Users' need for information on various topics can be seen as a gratification sought, especially in the context of UGT. Information and knowledge are also mainly received by intrinsically motivated individuals and users with a high need for achievement motive (SDT). The use of advice, instructions, or courses is also conceivable, whereby open and conscientious persons (PT) as well as users with a high perceived behavioral control (TPB) or self-efficacy expectation (SCT) are also addressed. The latter also supports the recommendation to post case studies and success stories.

Communication Style. Participants also formulate recommendations for action that address the communication style and therefore how people communicate with each other.

These include a personal approach, gratitude and consent, appreciative, benefit-oriented communication, entertaining content, and up-to-date information.

In particular, it is recommended that companies address users personally and be dialog-oriented. This can be achieved, for example, by addressing users with their names or pseudonyms or by creating personalized offers. It is also advisable to listen attentively to users and to refer to their personal experiences in the dialog. In many languages, two common forms of address correspond to levels of formality: a casual, familiar "you" used among friends and peers, and a more formal "you" employed in professional or distant relationships. The choice between these two forms of address can reflect the degree of social distance or closeness between the company and the user. This means that the informal form is also more approachable and personal on social media and therefore promotes dialog. The recommendation of the personal approach is supported by a large number of the theories presented. The connection motive and intrinsic motivation (SDT) are named as the key basis, while customer retention and WOM as well as the expectation of self-efficacy (SCT) also play a decisive role.

In the context of the personality traits of agreeableness and neuroticism, the communication of companies should, according to the participants, generally be appreciative, express understanding of the concerns of the users, and be friendly and respectful (PT).

In addition, companies should thank users for their interactions and tend to agree with them when they express their opinions. This can be done by the company, for example, by posting another comment or giving likes. This recommendation is again covered by the self-efficacy expectation (SCT), the need for affiliation (SDT), and as a means of customer retention, but also by the expectation that this is in line with applicable social norms (TPB). Moreover, approval appears to be particularly beneficial for people having a strong desire for compatibility (PT).

Accurate and precise communication by companies and a high-benefit orientation of the content are based on the personality trait of conscientiousness (PT). Content with high usefulness also includes contributions with innovative and inspiring content. According to the participants, open people particularly benefit from this.

In addition, posts with a high degree of up-to-dateness are recommended, which benefit the user's need for information (UGT), promote the need for achievement (SDT), and increase customer retention.

Finally, participants recommend that companies use emotional and entertaining content (ET, UGT, customer retention). Emotional content is conveyed, for example, through the use of storytelling and is promoted through exciting content, astounding stories, and the use of humor. The use of emoticons also helps to convey emotions better and emphasize the message. The same applies to entertaining content, which, according to the participants, can also take the form of anecdotes, funny sayings, small talk, teasers, games, puzzles, or, for example, a live chat (ET, UGT).

5.3 Community Building

Community building was identified as a further category of recommendations for action based on the theories presented. This initially includes all measures taken by companies on their social media sites to offer community-promoting structures.

These are for example the establishment of community rules and netiquette. People with high levels of neuroticism and agreeableness (PT) in particular can benefit from framework conditions in the form of community rules, as these can convey a sense of security. In addition, community rules can also increase the perceived behavioral control and social norms in the context of TPB.

Companies can also offer assistance and procedures for settling disagreements, which are particularly beneficial for people with a high level of agreeableness. Furthermore, companies could use moderators from the community to ensure compliance with the rules. According to the participants, people with a pronounced need for power (SDT) and high agreeableness and extraversion (PT) appear to be particularly suitable for becoming community moderators. The opportunity to apply for the moderator position could be linked to prior conditions, e.g. co-creation.

In order to increase customer retention in particular, companies should promote co-creation, for example by enabling feedback in the form of platform-dependent types of interaction with products and services or by actively requesting and discussing suggestions for improvement. Companies can also initiate co-creation projects that involve customers in the development and design of products. In this context, companies should actively encourage and demand the creation of user-generated content, e.g. the discussion of the product or service in the form of reviews, experience reports, or images. If there is sufficient participation, companies could award certain users with reviewer badges and helpfulness scores. By involving customers through reviews or testimonials, the personality traits of openness and extraversion (PT, WOM) as well as the need for achievement (SDT) are again primarily addressed. The same applies to reviewer badges and helpfulness scores, which also address users' self-efficacy expectations (SCT) and perceived behavioral control.

Companies are also advised to allow users to interact with each other. This is mainly in response to the desire for social interaction (UGT, WOM). For instance, this can be achieved by encouraging users to help each other. In turn, the promotion of mutual assistance among users can be explained primarily by the central motivation of altruism in word-of-mouth behavior.

Alongside this and to strengthen the sense of community, it is advisable to organize community events. These include, for example, webinars, meetings, or virtual events that allow the community to get to know each other personally. Once again, the need for social interaction (UGT, WOM) and affiliation (SDT) form the theoretical basis for these events.

Finally, the promotion of diversity in the community is also mentioned. In this regard, companies can emphasize diversity in their content presentation, for example by showing people from different age groups, ethnic backgrounds, genders, cultures, and social classes. Communication should also show a variety of perspectives and alternatives, avoid stereotypical representations, and accept different opinions. The promotion of diversity, different points of view, and alternatives can be justified above all by the user's need for affiliation (SDT) and the desire for social interaction (UGT, WOM). However, the perceived social norm of inclusive content and the perceived behavioral control for pointing out alternatives can also be used as a basis.

6 Discussion and Analysis

The discussion of the results in the form of recommendations for action and theoretical foundations is based on the established categories.

The media category can be further subdivided into the areas of vividness and interactivity. While some studies find that vividness has a significant effect on CE on social media, other studies cannot confirm this [32, 33]. Similarly, some studies show inconsistent influences on different types of engagement (e.g. likes, comments, shares). Furthermore, correlations between vividness and effect are identified as partly linear, partly with an optimal degree of vividness [32].

The recommendation to use visual material can mainly be explained by the UGT and ET. Interactivity, on the other hand, can make use of a wide range of theoretical foundations. UGT supports the need for information in the form of links, while SDT, WOM, customer retention, SCT, TPB, as well as personality traits, underpin @-mentions, questions, quizzes, and CTAs. It is important to note that vividness and interactivity are typically located outside of classic behavioral CE theories. In addition to the telepresence theory [90], this is in specific the media richness theory and thus the richness of a medium in terms of channel diversity, directionality, linguistic variety, and personal reference [95].

Overall, the recommendations on vividness and interactivity not only have a broad theoretical grounding within CE but also attract substantial research interest in the literature as success factors [96].

The content category contains CE factors that are frequently addressed in research using sales promotion methods. The majority of studies attest that campaigns and incentives have a positive effect on the CE [e.g. 97].

The topic of a post and informative content also influence the CE [98]. Once again, research finds different effects depending on the type of engagement, e.g. incentives only affect comments, and informative content tends to affect likes and comments, but not shares [98]. Communicative means are only occasionally addressed in previous research and are also recognized as affecting the CE. These include personal address and appreciation as well as the use of up-to-date content and error-free communication [33]. The recommendation to agree with users was not found to affect engagement [99]. Emotional and entertaining content as an influencing factor, on the other hand, is widely accepted and confirmed in research [100].

Overall, sales promotions are primarily customer retention measures, which are also recommended in the classic marketing literature. Theoretically, incentives can be seen in the context of UGT, particularly as gratification. They are also justified by extrinsic motivation (SDT) and WOM behavior. Different thematic orientations can also be explained by the need for information and the desire for entertainment in the scope of UGT. The recommendations on communication style are generally based on addressing different personality traits.

The community-building category includes recommendations such as the establishment of community rules, the use of moderators, and the promotion of diversity. However, to the author's knowledge, the effects on CE have not yet been sufficiently investigated in research. Community-building measures are primarily based on motivation, personality, and attitudinal theories and thus have a broad theoretical foundation.

Overall, the recommendations show a broad set of possibilities. The categorization into media and content also reveals similarities with previous overview studies [32, 33].

Based on the available formats in social media, the degree of vividness and interactivity should always be taken into account. As social media mainly addresses identity and relationship management in functional terms, general motives (SDT), the motive of social interaction (WOM/UGT), and the motive of self-expression and extraversion (WOM, PT) appear to be relevant. Incentives are postulated as a success factor or relevant need in the context of both WOM and UGT. Concerning content, it can also be assumed that informative and entertaining content is helpful for CE. These can also be found in the UGT based on the need for information and entertainment. Vividness, interactivity, and the UGT therefore appear to be a particularly useful basis for recommendations for action when explaining the CE on social media.

7 Conclusion and Outlook

The study aimed to obtain a set of recommendations for action that would allow companies to make their customer communication on social media more successful. These recommendations were based on the most relevant theories cited in the literature as the foundation of CE.

Concerning the research questions, it turned out that the methodological approach allowed recommendations for action for companies' social media communication to be derived directly from the CE's behavior-oriented theories. Structuring these recommendations led to the categorization according to media, content, and community building. It also became apparent that many of the recommendations are confirmed in existing research literature as an influencing factor on CE. Furthermore, it can be seen that most recommendations for action are covered by several theories. One example of this is incentives, which are based on media theories, motive theories, and marketing theories. Overall, the UGT appears to be a good basis for explaining the CE on social media and for making recommendations for action. Future research can focus on factors of CE that have been of little research interest to date. These can be found, for example, within the communication style and linguistic factors. There also seems to be a need for further research into community-building measures such as the effect of rules, moderators, or the promotion of diversity. Finally, the question arises as to how recommendations and factors can be reasonably combined.

Limitations of the study can be found especially in its explanatory power and completeness, which is due to the unconventional methodology. Accordingly, the recommendations are based exclusively on the selected theories. A broader theoretical approach would complete the picture.

Disclosure of Interests. The author has no competing interests to declare that are relevant to the content of this article.

References

1. Kepios: Digital 2024: Global Overview Report (2024). https://datareportal.com/social-media-users

2. Bottorff, C.: Top Social Media Statistics and Trends of 2024 (2023). https://www.forbes.com/advisor/business/social-media-statistics/
3. Porteous, C.: 97% of Fortune 500 Companies Rely on Social Media. Here's How You Should Use It for Maximum Impact (2021). https://www.entrepreneur.com/science-technology/97-of-fortune-500-companies-rely-on-social-media-heres/366240
4. Stelzner, M.A.: 2023 Social Media Marketing Industry Report (2023). https://www.socialmediaexaminer.com/social-media-marketing-industry-report-2023/
5. Bruhn, M., Keller, C., Batt, V.: Formen des Customer Engagement – Entwicklung einer Typologie. In: Bruhn, M., Hadwich, K. (eds.) Interaktive Wertschöpfung durch Dienstleistungen. Strategische Ausrichtung von Kundeninteraktionen, Geschäftsmodellen und sozialen Netzwerken. Forum Dienstleistungsmanagement, pp. 83–109. Springer Gabler, Wiesbaden (2015). https://doi.org/10.1007/978-3-658-08518-6_4
6. Lim, W.M., Rasul, T., Kumar, S., Ala, M.: Past, present, and future of customer engagement. J. Bus. Res. (2022). https://doi.org/10.1016/j.jbusres.2021.11.014
7. Pansari, A., Kumar, V.: Customer engagement: the construct, antecedents, and consequences. J. Acad. Mark. Sci. (2017). https://doi.org/10.1007/s11747-016-0485-6
8. Bitter, S., Grabner-Kräuter, S.: Consequences of customer engagement behavior: when negative Facebook posts have positive effects. Electron. Mark. (2016). https://doi.org/10.1007/s12525-016-0220-7
9. McKinsey: The digital tipping point (2014). https://www.mckinsey.com/business-functions/mckinsey-digital/our-insights/the-digital-tipping-point-mckinsey-global-survey-results. Accessed 21 Jan 2021
10. Vargo, S.L., Lusch, R.F.: Evolving to a new dominant logic for marketing. J. Mark. (2004). https://doi.org/10.1509/jmkg.68.1.1.24036
11. Blau, P.M.: Exchange and Power in Social Life. Wiley, New York, NY (1964)
12. Homans, G.C.: Social behavior as exchange. Am. J. Sociol. 63, 597–606 (1958)
13. Doorn van, J., et al.: Customer engagement behavior: theoretical foundations and research directions. J. Serv. Res. (2010). https://doi.org/10.1177/1094670510375599
14. Brodie, R.J., Hollebeek, L.D., Jurić, B., Ilić, A.: Customer engagement. J. Serv. Res. (2011). https://doi.org/10.1177/1094670511411703
15. Kuvykaitė, R., Tarutė, A.: A critical analysis of consumer engagement dimensionality. Procedia Soc. Behav. Sci. (2015). https://doi.org/10.1016/j.sbspro.2015.11.468
16. Dolan, R., Conduit, J., Fahy, J., Goodman, S.: Social media engagement behaviour: a uses and gratifications perspective. J. Strateg. Mark. (2016). https://doi.org/10.1080/0965254X.2015.1095222
17. Jaakkola, E., Alexander, M.: The role of customer engagement behavior in value co-creation. J. Serv. Res. (2014). https://doi.org/10.1177/1094670514529187
18. Vivek, S.D., Beatty, S.E., Morgan, R.M.: Customer engagement: exploring customer relationships beyond purchase. J. Mark. Theory Pract. (2012). https://doi.org/10.2753/MTP1069-6679200201
19. Christodoulides, G.: Branding in the post-internet era. Mark. Theory (2009). https://doi.org/10.1177/1470593108100071
20. Muntinga, D.G., Moorman, M., Smit, E.G.: Introducing COBRAs. Int. J. Advert. (2011). https://doi.org/10.2501/IJA-30-1-013-046
21. Shao, G.: Understanding the appeal of user-generated media: a uses and gratification perspective. Internet Res. (2009). https://doi.org/10.1108/10662240910927795
22. Schivinski, B., Christodoulides, G., Dabrowski, D.: Measuring consumers' engagement with brand-related social-media content. JAR (2016). https://doi.org/10.2501/JAR-2016-004
23. Tsiotsou R. H.: The social aspects of consumption as predictors of consumer loyalty: online vs. offline services. J. Serv. Manag. (2016). https://doi.org/10.1108/JOSM-04-2015-0117

24. Tsiotsou, R.H.: Social media and customer engagement. In: Bridges, E., Fowler, K. (eds.) The Routledge Handbook of Service Research Insights and Ideas. Routledge Handbooks, pp. 373–388. Routledge Taylor & Francis Group, London, New York (2020)
25. Calder, B.J., Malthouse, E.C.: Media Engagement and Advertising Effectiveness. In: Calder, B.J. (ed.) Kellogg on Media and Advertising, pp. 1–36. John Wiley & Sons, Hoboken (2008)
26. Esch, F.-R., Manger, I.: Aufbau, Wirkung und Messung von Brand Engagement. In: Esch, F.R. (eds.) Handbuch Markenführung. Springer Reference Wirtschaft, pp. 1347–1364. Springer Gabler, Wiesbaden (2019). https://doi.org/10.1007/978-3-658-13342-9_79
27. Esch, F.-R., Köhler, I.: Brand Engagement – Wie Marken versuchen, enge Kundenbeziehungen zu generieren. transfer Werbeforschung Praxis **62**, 20–28 (2016)
28. Chahal, H., Wirtz, J., Verma, A.: Social media brand engagement: dimensions, drivers and consequences. JCM (2019). https://doi.org/10.1108/JCM-11-2018-2937
29. Dessart, L., Veloutsou, C., Morgan-Thomas, A.: Consumer engagement in online brand communities: a social media perspective. J. Prod. Brand Manag. (2015). https://doi.org/10.1108/JPBM-06-2014-0635
30. Wirtz, J., et al.: Managing brands and customer engagement in online brand communities. J. Serv. Manag. (2013). https://doi.org/10.1108/09564231311326978
31. Barger, V., Peltier, J.W., Schultz, D.E.: Social media and consumer engagement: a review and research agenda. J. Res. Interact. Mark. (2016). https://doi.org/10.1108/JRIM-06-2016-0065
32. Deng, Q., Hine, M.J., Ji, S., Wang, Y.: What makes brand social media posts engaging? An integrative framework and future research agenda. J. Internet Commer. (2021). https://doi.org/10.1080/15332861.2021.2011599
33. Wattenberg, M.: Erfolgsfaktoren des Customer Engagements von KMU auf Social Media. Dissertation (in prep. 2024)
34. Jayasingh, S.: Consumer brand engagement in social networking sites and its effect on brand loyalty. Cogent Bus. Manag. (2019). https://doi.org/10.1080/23311975.2019.1698793
35. Kaur, P., Dhir, A., Rajala, R., Dwivedi, Y.K.: Why people use online social media brand communities. Online Inf. Rev. (2018). https://doi.org/10.1108/OIR-12-2015-0383
36. Deci, E.L., Ryan, R.M.: The general causality orientations scale: self-determination in personality. J. Res. Personal. (1985). https://doi.org/10.1016/0092-6566(85)90023-6
37. McClelland, D.C.: Human Motivation. Cambridge University Press, New York, NY, US (1987)
38. Masur, P.K., Reinecke, L., Ziegele, M., Quiring, O.: The interplay of intrinsic need satisfaction and Facebook specific motives in explaining addictive behavior on Facebook. Comput. Hum. Behav. (2014). https://doi.org/10.1016/j.chb.2014.05.047
39. Wu, W.-Y., Sukoco, B.M.: Why should i share? Examining consumers' motives and trust on knowledge sharing. J. Comput. Inf. Syst. (2010). https://doi.org/10.1080/08874417.2010.11645426
40. Clark, R., Moloney, G.: Connections across the ages: facebook use and self-determination theory. In: Proceedings. Southern Cross University 14th Annual Honours Psychology Research Conference, New South Wales (2017)
41. Meffert, H., Burmann, C., Kirchgeorg, M., Eisenbeiß, M.: Marketing. Grundlagen marktorientierter Unternehmensführung Konzepte - Instrumente - Praxisbeispiele, 13th edn. Springer Gabler, Wiesbaden (2019). https://doi.org/10.1007/978-3-658-02344-7
42. Brandstätter, V., Schüler, J., Puca, R.M., Lozo, L.: Motivation und Emotion. Springer Berlin Heidelberg, Berlin, Heidelberg (2018). https://doi.org/10.1007/978-3-662-56685-5
43. Kroeber-Riel, W., Gröppel-Klein, A.: Konsumentenverhalten. Verlag Franz Vahlen GmbH (2019)

44. Scharfenberger, P., Tomczak, T., Henkel, S.: Emotionen aus Sicht der Kommunikation. In: Rüeger, B.P., Hannich, F.M. (eds.) Erfolgsfaktor Emotionalisierung. Wie Unternehmen die Herzen der Kunden gewinnen, pp. 3–16. Schäffer-Poeschel Verlag, Stuttgart (2010)
45. de Oliveira Santini, F., Ladeira, W.J., Pinto, D.C., Herter, M.M., Sampaio, C.H., Babin, B.J.: Customer engagement in social media: a framework and meta-analysis. J. Acad. Mark. Sci. 48(6), 1211–1228 (2020). https://doi.org/10.1007/s11747-020-00731-5
46. Shaw, C., Hamilton, R.: Imperative 7: Realize the only way to build customer loyalty is through customer memories. In: Shaw, C., Hamilton, R. (eds.) The Intuitive Customer. 7 Imperatives for Moving Your Customer Experience to the Next Level, pp. 141–159. Palgrave Macmillan, London, UK (2015)
47. Oliver, R.L., DeSARBO, W.S.: Processing of the satisfaction response in consumption: a suggested framework and research propositions. J. Consum. Satisfaction Dissatisfaction Complain. Behav. 2, 1–16 (1989)
48. Bagozzi, R.P., Gopinath, M., Nyer, P.U.: The role of emotions in marketing. J. Acad. Mark. Sci. (1999). https://doi.org/10.1177/0092070399272005
49. Stürmer, R., Schmidt, J.: Erfolgreiches Marketing durch Emotionsforschung. Messung, Analyse, Best Practice, 1st edn. Haufe Gruppe, Freiburg, München (2014)
50. Costa, P.T., McCrae, R.R.: Four ways five factors are basic. Personal. Individ. Differ. (1992). https://doi.org/10.1016/0191-8869(92)90236-I
51. Goldberg, L.R.: Language and individual differences: the search for universals in personality lexicons. Rev. Personal. Soc. Psychol. 2, 141–165 (1981)
52. Kleine-Kalmer, B.: Brand Page Attachment. Springer Fachmedien Wiesbaden GmbH, Wiesbaden (2016). https://doi.org/10.1007/978-3-658-12439-7
53. Barker, V.: Older adolescents' motivations for social network site use: the influence of gender, group identity, and collective self-esteem. Cyberpsychol. Behav. (2009). https://doi.org/10.1089/cpb.2008.0228
54. Ross, C., Orr, E.S., Sisic, M., Arseneault, J.M., Simmering, M.G., Orr, R.R.: Personality and motivations associated with Facebook use. Comput. Hum. Behav. (2009). https://doi.org/10.1016/j.chb.2008.12.024
55. Kneidinger, B.: Facebook und Co. Eine soziologische Analyse von Interaktionsformen in Online Social Networks. Zugl.: Wien, Univ., Diplomarbeit, 2010, 1st edn. VS Research. VS Verl. für Sozialwiss, Wiesbaden (2010)
56. Seidman, G: Self-presentation and belonging on Facebook: how personality influences social media use and motivations. Personal. Individ. Differ. (2013). https://doi.org/10.1016/j.paid.2012.10.009
57. Moore, K., McElroy, J.C.: The influence of personality on Facebook usage, wall postings, and regret. Comput. Hum. Behav. (2012). https://doi.org/10.1016/j.chb.2011.09.009
58. Homburg, C., Bruhn, M.: Kundenbindungsmanagement - Eine Einführung in die theoretischen und praktischen Problemstellungen. In: Bruhn, M. (ed.) Handbuch Kundenbindungsmanagement. Strategien und Instrumente für ein erfolgreiches CRM, 5th edn., pp. 3–40. Gabler Verlag, Wiesbaden (2005)
59. Oliver, R.L.: Satisfaction: A Behavioral Perspective on the Consumer. McGraw Hill, New York (1997)
60. Oliver, R.L.: Whence consumer loyalty? J. Mark. (1999). https://doi.org/10.2307/1252099
61. Moorman, C., Zaltman, G., Deshpande, R.: Relationships between providers and users of market research: the dynamics of trust within and between organizations. J. Mark. Res. (1992). https://doi.org/10.2307/3172742
62. Morgan, R.M., Hunt, S.D.: The commitment-trust theory of relationship marketing. J. Mark. (1994). https://doi.org/10.2307/1252308

63. Brodie, R.J., Ilić, A., Jurić, B., Hollebeek, L.D.: Consumer engagement in a virtual brand community: an exploratory analysis. J. Bus. Res. (2013). https://doi.org/10.1016/j.jbusres.2011.07.029

64. Gummerus, J., Liljander, V., Weman, E., Pihlström, M.: Customer engagement in a Facebook brand community. Manag. Res. Rev. (2012). https://doi.org/10.1108/01409171211256578

65. Hollebeek, L.D.: Exploring customer brand engagement: definition and themes. J. Strateg. Mark. (2011). https://doi.org/10.1080/0965254X.2011.599493

66. Laroche, M., Habibi, M.R., Richard, M.-O.: To be or not to be in social media: how brand loyalty is affected by social media? Int. J. Inf. Manag. (2013). https://doi.org/10.1016/j.ijinfomgt.2012.07.003

67. Ajzen, I., Fishbein, M.: Understanding Attitudes and Predicting Social Behavior. Prentice-Hall Inc., Englewood Cliffs, N.J (1980)

68. Darvell, M.J., Walsh, S.P., White, K.M.: Facebook tells me so: applying the theory of planned behavior to understand partner-monitoring behavior on Facebook. Cyber Psychol. Behav. Soc. Netw. (2011). https://doi.org/10.1089/cyber.2011.0035

69. Pelling, E.L., White, K.M.: The theory of planned behavior applied to young people's use of social networking Web sites. Cyber Psychol. Behav. (2009). https://doi.org/10.1089/cpb.2009.0109

70. Bandura, A.: Self-Efficacy. The Exercise of Control. Freeman, New York, NY (1997)

71. Hoffmann, S., Akbar, P.: Consumer Behavior. Understanding Consumers - Designing Marketing Activities. Springer Fachmedien Wiesbaden GmbH, Wiesbaden (2023). https://doi.org/10.1007/978-3-658-39476-9

72. Bandura, A.: Social cognitive theory of mass communication. In: Bryant, J., Oliver, M.B. (eds.) Media Effects: Advances in Theory and Research, pp. 94–124. Lawrence Earlbaum, Mahwah (2009)

73. Cho, H., Chen, M., Chung, S.: Testing an integrative theoretical model of knowledge-sharing behavior in the context of Wikipedia. J. Am. Soc. Inf. Sci. (2010). https://doi.org/10.1002/asi.21316

74. Chiu, C.-M., Hsu, M.-H., Wang, E.T.: Understanding knowledge sharing in virtual communities: An integration of social capital and social cognitive theories. Decis. Support Syst. (2006). https://doi.org/10.1016/j.dss.2006.04.001

75. Schunk, D.H., DiBenedetto, M.K.: Motivation and social cognitive theory. Contemp. Educ. Psychol. (2020).https://doi.org/10.1016/j.cedpsych.2019.101832

76. Arndt, J.: Word of Mouth Advertising: A Review of The Literature. Advertising Research Foundation Inc., New York (1967)

77. Berger, J.: Word of mouth and interpersonal communication: a review and directions for future research J. Consum. Psychol. (2014). https://doi.org/10.1016/j.jcps.2014.05.002

78. Hennig-Thurau, T., Gwinner, K.P., Walsh, G., Gremler, D.D.: Electronic word-of-mouth via consumer-opinion platforms: what motivates consumers to articulate themselves on the Internet? J. Interact. Mark. (2004). https://doi.org/10.1002/dir.10073

79. King, R.A., Racherla, P., Bush, V.D.: What we know and don't know about online word-of-mouth: a review and synthesis of the literature. J. Interact. Mark. (2014). https://doi.org/10.1016/j.intmar.2014.02.001

80. Algesheimer, R., Borle, S., Dholakia, U.M., Singh, S.S.: The impact of customer community participation on customer behaviors: an empirical investigation. Mark. Sci. (2010). https://doi.org/10.1287/mksc.1090.0555

81. Balakrishnan, B.K., Dahnil, M.I., Yi, W.J.: The impact of social media marketing medium toward purchase intention and brand loyalty among generation Y. Procedia Soc. Behav. Sci. (2014). https://doi.org/10.1016/j.sbspro.2014.07.032

82. Eisingerich, A.B., Chun, H.H., Liu, Y., Jia, H., Bell, S.J.: Why recommend a brand face-to-face but not on Facebook? How word-of-mouth on online social sites differs from traditional word-of-mouth. J. Consum. Psychol. (2015). https://doi.org/10.1016/j.jcps.2014.05.004

83. Chu, S.-C., Kim, Y.: Determinants of consumer engagement in electronic word-of-mouth (eWOM) in social networking sites. Int. J. Advert. (2011). https://doi.org/10.2501/IJA-30-1-047-075

84. Luarn, P., Huang, P., Chiu, Y.-P., Chen, I.-J.: Motivations to engage in word-of-mouth behavior on social network sites. Inf. Dev. (2016). https://doi.org/10.1177/0266666915596804

85. Katz, E., Haas, H., Gurevitch, M.: On the use of the mass media for important things. Am. Sociol. Rev. (1973). https://doi.org/10.2307/2094393

86. McQuail, D.: Mass Communication Theory, an Introduction. SAGE Publications Inc., London (1983)

87. Palmgreen, P.: Uses and gratifications: a theoretical perspective. Ann. Int. Commun. Assoc. (1984). https://doi.org/10.1080/23808985.1984.11678570

88. Kamboj, S.: Applying uses and gratifications theory to understand customer participation in social media brand communities. APJML (2020). https://doi.org/10.1108/APJML-11-2017-0289

89. Kuckartz, U., Rädiker, S.: Qualitative Content Analysis. Methods, Practice and Software, 2nd edn. Sage, Los Angeles, London, New Delhi, Singapore, Washington DC, Melbourne (2023)

90. Steuer, J.: Defining virtual reality: dimensions determining telepresence. J. Commun. (1992). https://doi.org/10.1111/j.1460-2466.1992.tb00812.x

91. Ji, Y.G., Chen, Z.F., Tao, W., Cathy Li, Z.: Functional and emotional traits of corporate social media message strategies: Behavioral insights from S&P 500 Facebook data. Public Relat. Rev. (2019). https://doi.org/10.1016/j.pubrev.2018.12.001

92. Bucy, E.P.: Interactivity in society: locating an elusive concept. Inf. Soc. (2004). https://doi.org/10.1080/01972240490508063

93. Liu, Y., Shrum, L.J.: What is interactivity and is it always such a good thing? Implications of definition, person, and situation for the influence of interactivity on advertising effectiveness. J. Advert. (2002). https://doi.org/10.1080/00913367.2002.10673685

94. Sundar, S.S., Kalyanaraman, S., Brown, J.: Explicating web site interactivity. Commun. Res. (2003). https://doi.org/10.1177/0093650202239025

95. Daft, R.L., Lengel, R.H.: Organizational information requirements, media richness and structural design. Manag. Sci. (1986). https://doi.org/10.1287/mnsc.32.5.554

96. Annamalai, B., Yoshida, M., Varshney, S., Pathak, A.A., Venugopal, P.: Social media content strategy for sport clubs to drive fan engagement. J. Retail. Consum. Serv. (2021). https://doi.org/10.1016/j.jretconser.2021.102648

97. Thongmak, M.: Engaging Facebook users in brand pages: different posts of marketing-mix information. In: Abramowicz, W. (eds.) Business Information Systems. BIS 2015. LNBIP, vol. 208, pp. 299–308. Springer, Cham (2015). https://doi.org/10.1007/978-3-319-19027-3_24

98. Pletikosa Cvijikj, I., Michahelles, F.: Online engagement factors on Facebook brand pages. Soc. Netw. Anal. Min. (2013). https://doi.org/10.1007/s13278-013-0098-8

99. Yousaf, A., Amin, I., Jaziri, D., Mishra, A.: Effect of message orientation/vividness on consumer engagement for travel brands on social networking sites. J. Prod. Brand Manag. (2021). https://doi.org/10.1108/JPBM-08-2019-2546

100. Pezzuti, T., Leonhardt, J.M., Warren, C.: Certainty in language increases consumer engagement on social media. J. Interact. Mark. (2021). https://doi.org/10.1016/j.intmar.2020.06.005

Author Index

Printed in the United States
by Baker & Taylor Publisher Services